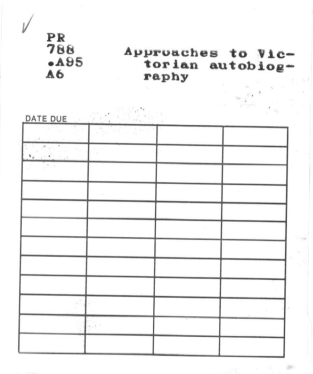

APPROACHES TO VICTORIAN AUTOBIOGRAPHY

edited by
GEORGE P. LANDOW

OHIO UNIVERSITY PRESS
Athens, Ohio

Copyright © 1979 by Ohio University Press
Printed in the United States of America by
Oberlin Printing Company

ISBN-0-8214-0400-8

Library of Congress Cataloging in Publication Data
Main entry under title:

Approaches to Victorian autobiography.

Includes bibliographical references.
1.   English prose literature—19th century—History and criticism—
Addresses, essays, lectures.   2.   Autobiography—Addresses, essays, lectures.   3.   Authors, English—19th century—Biography—Addresses, essay
lectures.   I.   Landow, George P.
PR788.A95A6   820'.9'08   77-91505

For Ruth, Shoshana, and Noah

TABLE OF CONTENTS

PART THREE

Autobiography and Autobiographicality

ACKNOWLEDGMENTS

Since the time this volume first took form, Mutlu Konuk Blasing's "The Story of the Stories: Henry James's Prefaces as Autobiography" has appeared, in slightly different form, in her book *The Art of Life: Studies in American Autobiographical Literature* and is reprinted with the permission of the University of Texas Press, Elizabeth K. Helsinger's two chapters, "Ulysses to Penelope: Victorian Experiments in Autobiography" and "The Structure of Ruskin's *Praeterita*," have also since appeared as parts of a longer essay in *Modern Philology*, whose editors have kindly allowed it to appear here. Michael Ryan's "A Grammatology of Assent: Cardinal Newman's *Apologia pro Vita Sua*"—one of the papers delivered at the MLA seminar on Victorian autobiography which was the origin of this book—has also since appeared in *The Georgia Review* in slightly different form, and his essay, (C) 1977 by the University of Georgia, is reprinted by permission of the editors. David J. DeLaura's "The Allegory of Life: the Autobiographical Impulse in Victorian Prose" has appeared previous to publication in this volume in *The Wascana Review* by arrangement with Ohio University Press and the editor.

I would like to thank William Condon, Sarah C. Frerichs, Ruth M. Landow, Shoshana M. Landow, Linda H. Peterson, Joan Pettigrew, and Sarah Webster for helping me read proof.

G.P.L.

CONTRIBUTORS

Mutlu Konuk Blasing is Assistant Professor of English at Pomona College.

George Bornstein is Professor of English at the University of Michigan.

Claudette Kemper Columbus is Assistant Professor of English at Hobart and William Smith Colleges.

David J. De Laura is Professor of English at the University of Pennsylvania.

Avrom Fleishman is Professor of English at The Johns Hopkins University.

Sarah Cutts Frerichs teaches at Bentley College.

Phyllis Grosskurth is Professor of English at University College, the University of Toronto.

Elizabeth K. Helsinger is Assistant Professor of English at the University of Chicago.

Howard Helsinger, who has taught English at Boston and Northwestern Universities, is an attorney-at-law.

Frederick Kirchhoff is Assistant Professor of English at Indiana University—Purdue University at Fort Wayne.

Robert L. Patten is Professor of English and Secretary of the Faculty at Rice University

Linda H. Peterson is Assistant Professor of English at Yale University.

Michael Ryan teaches English and comparative literature at the University of Virginia.

LuAnn Walther, who has taught in the City University of New York, is on the editorial staff of Bantam Books.

George P. Landow is Professor of English, Brown University.

GEORGE P. LANDOW

Introduction

Like all writings about the self, Victorian autobiographies
embody the question of how the individual relates to what
is outside himself; and what makes autobiography as a
literary mode so representative of its time—in a word, so
"Victorian"—is that a concern with this problematic relationship lies close to the heart of all literature, all culture,
of the age. As E.D.H. Johnson long ago taught students of
the period, its major literary figures made heroic attempts
to strike a proper balance between the demands of society
and self. In particular, Tennyson, Browning, and Arnold
strove "to define the sphere within which the modern poet
may exercise his faculty, while holding in legitimate balance
the rival claims of his private, aristocratic insights and of
the tendencies existing in a society progressively vulgarized
by the materialism of the nineteenth and twentieth centuries. Thus it came about that the double awareness, which
so generally characterized the Victorian literary mind,
grew almost into a perpetual state of consciousness in
these poets through their efforts to work out a new aesthetic
position for the artist."[1] Many components contribute to
this characteristic "double awareness," for the major writers
of the Victorian age attempted to maintain their hold upon a
series of polarized oppositions, refusing to choose between
(and thus relinquish) either private or public, subjective or
objective, feeling or fact. Like poetry, the novel, painting,
and other nonfiction in the period, autobiography sought
new forms to accommodate private experience simultaneously making it relevant to the needs of others. Like

In Memoriam, David Copperfield, The Light of the World, and *Modern Painters,* these histories of the self find public uses for private experience in forms which simultaneously open the self to others and yet seek some way to protect that fragile individuality against them.

Victorian autobiography, in other words, is characterized by many of the central concerns which also inform modern literature. Critics of the past decade have increasingly begun to recognize that Victorian literature has similarities to the work of the first third of this century, and now that modern literature, the literature, say, of Joyce, Eliot, Yeats, and Pound, is no longer contemporary—now that we have seen these once so daring, so abrasively *new* creations begin to recede into the past—we are beginning to observe that no great divide separates Victorians and moderns. The time has come, perhaps, when critics can realize that it is just as useful to see Eliot as the last great Victorian poet as the first great modern one. Indeed, when students of modern literature perceive, as some have just begun to do, that the imagery of the wasteland, use of personae, rhetorical discontinuity, and personal appropriations and recreations of myth characterize Victorian poetry, then perhaps it will be possible to evaluate the true position of tradition and the individual talent—neither overly praising Eliot for supposedly radical originality nor denigrating him for lack of it, but rather observing how well he takes his place within a major poetic continuity. Similarly, it seems that we have arrived at a point from which we can perceive that Pound's translations and exploration of poetic forms follow rather naturally from the work of Rossetti; that Stevens's late poems much resemble the landscape meditations of Swinburne; that Mailer, who seeks the heroic in a mechanical age, is the true disciple of Carlyle; and that the great narrative experiments which inform the writings of Conrad, Woolf, Joyce, and Faulkner are found much earlier in Victorian poetry. Indeed (to borrow the words of Mark Twain) it is astonishing how much the Victorians have learned since the twentieth century came of age—how much more original, how much wiser, how much more sophisticated they have become!

Therefore, a consideration of Victorian autobiography not only offers something of interest about works excellent in their own right but also promises to tell us something of value about nineteenth- and twentieth-century culture as well. Victorian autobiographers were writing the stories of their own lives at a particularly interesting moment in the history of human consciousness: romanticism had done much to change the way man thought about and experienced himself, but Freud had not yet appeared on the scene with his radical redefinitions of self, society, and discourse. This historical situation thus makes the latter half of the century simultaneously the most and least "Freudian" of ages—the most because nineteenth-century European middle-class society with its strongly paternal family structure had a genetic relation to the neuroses Freud encountered and the theories he formulated as a result; while it was the least because men could quite unselfconsciously discuss matters soon to appear in an entirely new light. It is hard to believe, for instance, that John Stuart Mill could have recounted his famous reading of Marmontel so frankly had he read Freud. As Paul Murray Kendall remarks: "Today the self is more exposed and yet more elusive, more comprehensible but less manageable, more fascinating but not so palatable. Undertaking an autobiography, under the aegis of modern psychology, is like signing a contract with the Devil: there is much to be won and everything, especially honor, to be lost. In the Age of Freud, to look no deeper than Gibbon looked in the Age of Hume is to perpetrate an anachronism; but to subject oneself to even amateur psychological scrutiny seems rather like performing an act of private therapy in public."[2] According to Kendall, the chief result is that most twentieth-century autobiography avoids these fatal depths by keeping close to the safer coasts of memoir, and one may add that the autobiographical impulse, when it does turn inward, therefore tends to appear in more explicitly fictional modes.

Victorian autobiography thus embodies a unique moment in the history of man's conception of himself, a moment which comes as the heir of two millenia of western civilization. Autobiography, as many students of the mode remind us, is a rare and very late phenomenon in the growth of the human spirit, requiring literacy, individuality, and a sense of history. Without literacy the author cannot write his own life for others and without widespread literacy there are not enough others for whom to write. Of course, one can envisage illiterate people dictating their life histories, but to conceive such an enterprise is only possible in a cultural setting which already possesses autobiography.

More basically, without a conception of individuality, without a notion of one's own selfhood, autobiography is impossible. As many philosophical anthropologists have observed, primitive, tribal man does not possess a sense of individuality, and this sense of himself is lacking precisely because he lacks a sense of history. Emphasizing that "from the point of view of anhistorical peoples or classes 'suffering' is equivalent to 'history,' " Mircea Eliade reminds us that archaic man achieves his sense of *communitas* by denying history and the individuation it creates. "Interest in the 'irreversible' and the 'new' in history is a recent discovery in the life of humanity. . . . The crucial difference between the man of the archaic civilizations and modern, historical man lies in the increasing value the latter gives to historical events, that is, to the 'novelties' that, for traditional men, represented either meaningless conjunctures or infractions of norms (hence 'faults,' 'sins,' and so on) and that, as such, required to be expelled (abolished) periodically."[3] In other words, for archaic, preliterate, tribal humanity, which conceives of the universe in terms of archetypal, ever-recurring processes and rituals, to be different—to be *individual*—is to fall. For to be different is to botch a planting ritual, violate some taboo, or otherwise fall away from the way things are and always have been. "We are therefore," says Nietzsche, "to regard the state of individuation as the origin and primal cause of all suffering, as something objectionable in itself."[4] Such is the manner in which primitive civilization regards the unique, the *individual,* man or woman, and this kind of "difference" is not something for which one strives or, having attained it, wishes to remember.

We find it difficult to bring home to ourselves how essentially our assumptions about man differ from those of tribal humanity, but we need go back no further than Homeric Greece to perceive what has been added to man's experience of himself. Homer, for example, had no word for the living personality and neither did he have a unified concept of what we term "soul" or "personality."[5] The absence of a sense of individuality goes even further, for "the early Greeks did not, either in their language or in the visual arts, grasp the body as a unit."[6] According to Georg Misch's *History of Autobiography in Antiquity,* Aristotle was the first to create a means of comprehending the individual "philosophically," something he achieved by postulating a static but "consistent self-determined character" uniting all apparently divergent and even contradictory actions. Aristotle thus "conceived development as a process through which the individual attains to his own essence or true 'nature' in the course of his life—in fact, as an eternal 'pattern imprinted in the individual and growing in the vital process' . . . instead of the outgrowth, as we conceive it historically, of the characteristics and the many possibilities of human nature." The philosopher's conception of a static human character therefore directs chief attention to the mature person.

> All that lay before this, the whole youthful career, is then an irrelevance, or at most to be stated in advance as a forecast of the traits of the character of the grown man. Thus the real task of a description of development—the demonstration of the way the unity of the personality is formed in the course of life, in the individual's dealings with the environment—remained essentially beyond the horizon of this ancient type of biography.[7]

Such a static conception of personality does much to explain the "remarkable incongruity" noted by Misch that classical Greek civilization which did so much to discover and create the human personality made of autobiography little more than exercises for the display of rhetorical ingenuity.[8] Only when classical civilization was beginning to collapse did autobiography appear, and here we can observe what appears to be an essential fact about this literary mode: societal disturbances and dislocations, the break-up of a culture, produce that sense of self necessary to write one's own life.[9] When communal bonds dissolve, when a shared sense-of-being fails, the individual finds himself cast adrift and, becoming more self-aware, he may also come to believe that he has something to say that could help others in the same difficulties. Scholars have observed that in the ancient world, the Renaissance, and seventeenth-century England such destruction of cultural assumptions and social dislocation produced a new sense of selfhood, and it seems clear that the political, economic, and spiritual crises of the nineteenth century had the same effect. Max Scheler, the German phenomenologist, holds that "creative dissociation . . . is the basic process of psychic evolution," and that therefore at any stage in the evolutionary scale from simplest microorganism to man, such dislocation is the necessary condition of achieving a higher level of complexity. In cultural terms this physiological law still holds true:

> Human evolution . . . depends upon a progressive decomposition of tradition. Conscious memory of an individual, unique event, and the constant identification of a plurality of memories as constituting one and the same past, are possible only for man. It is a process which invariably contributes to the dissolution, yes, the actual death, of a living tradition. . . . The reduction of the power of tradition is a continuous process in human history. It is an achievement of human reason which, in one and the same act, *objectifies* the content of the tradition, thus throwing it back, as it were, into the past where it belongs and, at the same time, clearing the ground for new discoveries and inventions in the present.[10]

Although major cultural upheavals in culture and society are thus historically related to the invention of individuality (which in turn provides the basis of autobiography), such disruptions alone cannot produce a modern sense of the self. As Wayne Shumaker's brilliantly suggestive analysis of the rise of autobiography points out, before one can assume that each person is inherently unique and interesting, one must first possess a complex set of assumptions about nature and the human mind. For a modern conception of individuality to come into being, the static Aristotelian view of human character must give way to one which emphasizes development. This crucial idea of development requires a notion of causality, since "development implies order, and not accidental change. One state contains within itself the seeds of the next; the second contains the seeds of the third, which were therefore also implicit in the first; and so on. In other words development implies causality."[11] Until western culture placed great importance upon causality, until it posited a mechanistic or naturalistic universe, it was impossible to explain the uniqueness of an individual human being.

Causality implies a particular conception of the human mind, and before one could account for the unique development of any one individual, new models of mind have to come into being. "So long as the will maintained a princely rank in the hierarchy of the 'faculties,' life inevitably appeared self-directed, unpredictable, arbitrary. . . . As a natural consequence, in earlier centuries life was viewed as actions performed and decisions arrived at; and written lives, in the form of *res gestae,* followed the philosophical assumption."[12] As soon as men began to postulate determinism, they began not only to describe but also to *explain* why lives had developed in one way and not another. (In passing one may remark upon the paradox that it was at the point in history when man began to accept a deterministic causation that he also began to describe human life in terms of choice and explanation.)

One may further add to Shumaker's analysis the recognition that an important effect of this severely intellectualistic philosophy was the creation of subjectivist-emotionalistic moral theories of the eighteenth-century Scottish school. After Locke convinced Englishmen that man possesses no innate ideas, not even those of goodness, philosophers sought some replacement for them. Lord Shaftesbury, Francis Hutcheson, and Adam Smith postulated that men have an innate moral sense, and, according to Smith,

whose formulation was the most influential of the eighteenth century, the human being recognizes the moral value
of his acts by vicariously experiencing their effect upon another, which he does by an instinctive process of imaginative projection or "sympathy." Such a conception of moral
processes, which for the first time gives a positive value to
the emotions, of course provided a major impetus to romanticism.[13] Furthermore, by supporting conceptions of art and
man which emphasize the importance of subjective experience, it also does much to justify autobiography.

These changing conceptions of the mind were, in turn,
part of a broader philosophical movement which radically
changed western man's notions of reality. In fact, Shumaker suggests that the single most important cause of interest in " 'truthful' life histories" appears in the Baconian
"substitution of inductive thought habits for deductive,"
behind which lay the assumption that truth can be "discovered only by the slow accumulation of particulars." As
he reminds us, individual facts did not seem as theoretically
or practically interesting in the middle ages as they do now,
since without an inductive method it served no purpose to
gather individual facts, because "details illustrated instead
of revealing."[14] Not until the West adopted the Baconian
method of working from part to the whole in the late eighteenth century did individual facts become material for a
new synthesis.

In addition to these changes in fundamental attitudes and
assumptions, several other factors combined to support developing conceptions of self. For instance, puritanism did
much to move the locus of reality within the individual.
Karl Mannheim thus argues that

at the beginnings of modern times, the Protestant movement set up in
place of revealed salvation, guaranteed by the objective institution
of the Church, the notion of the subjective certainty of salvation. It
was assumed in the light of this doctrine that each person should
decide according to his own subjective conscience whether his conduct was pleasing to God and conducive to salvation. Thus Protestan-
tism rendered subjective a criterion which had hitherto been objective, thereby paralleling what modern epistemology was doing when
it retreated from an objectively guaranteed order of existence to the

individual subject. It was not a long step from the doctrine of the subjective certainty of salvation to a psychological standpoint on which
gradually the observation of the psychic process, which developed
into a veritable curiosity, became more important than the harkening
to the criteria of salvation.[15]

Furthermore, puritanism, as R.H. Tawney has shown, also
did much to give rise to the socio-economic system which
produced the material conditions necessary for individualism, while its emphasis upon economic individualism
supported secularization of western thought which has so increased its pace since the later seventeenth century.[16]

Technological developments also played major roles in
bringing about these changes in basic attitudes towards
man, society, and the world. In *Medieval Technology and
Social Change,* Lynn White, Jr. demonstrated how the introduction of the horse-collar, stirrup, and metal plow provided the necessary conditions for the feudal society which
characterized Europe for a thousand years, and yet in general students of humanistic culture have been quite reticent
about postulating relations between technology and ideology, historical psychology, and man's conception of himself. One suspects that many fear such attempts will result
in a revival of late nineteenth-century determinist explanations of culture. Perhaps the best way to avoid such misun-
derstandings of what the history of technology has to offer
the student of the humanities is to perceive that something
which provides a necessary condition does not provide the
only or even a sufficient one.

J.C. Carothers, one of Marshall McLuhan's major
sources, points out how technology present in the everyday
environment indoctrinates the Western child to accept
those notions of causality which we have seen to be one of
the cornerstones of autobiography. Unlike the child raised
in a tribal environment which stresses the spoken word,
"the Western child is early introduced to building blocks,
keys in locks, water taps, and a multiplicity of items and
events which constrain him to think in terms of spatiotem-
poral relations and mechanical causation."[17] As McLuhan
emphasizes, anyone raised in a modern European or Amer-

ican milieu "is surrounded by an abstract explicit visual
technology of uniform time and uniform continuous space
in which 'cause' is efficient and sequential, and things move
and happen on single planes and in successive order."[18]
Of course, much of the technology which thus surrounds
us is the creation, and not the creator, of these habits of
mind.

On the other hand, certain technological developments
do appear more directly implicated in the invention of our
conceptions of the self. For example, Carlyle long ago
pointed out that gunpowder was one of the two chief causes
of the disappearance of feudalism, and Jacques Lacan has
argued that the seventeenth-century Venetian invention of
large mirrors played an important part in modern man's
self-consciousness and sense of identity.[19] But the printing press, which has had an astonishingly complex effect on
European culture for the past several centuries, is clearly
the most important technological factor here. Shumaker
suggests that by stimulating book production printing both
invited the "discovery of new literary modes" and made
men aware of an unsuspected variety in human nature, but
its effects have been more important, and far more complex, than that.[20] First of all, as Carlyle's Teufelsdröckh insists, printing, like gunpowder, created modern politics, for
"he who shortened the labour of Copyists by device of
Movable Types was disbanding hired Armies, and cash-
iering most Kings and Senates, and creating a whole new
Democratic world."[21] Similarly, mechanical book production provided a major impetus for nationalism. Since printing required a large financial investment, publishers sought
the largest possible market, and that market was to be
found in publishing vernacular books. In thus promulgating
an entire range of ideas destructive of the old order of
things, printing contributed to those many forms of cultural
disruption which gave rise to modern selfhood.

Furthermore, as William M. Ivins has demonstrated, the
capacity of mechanical printing processes to reproduce
exact visual information made possible a rapid expansion of
science and technology, and one may add that it was the

rapid diffusion of maps, diagrams, and other precise forms
of scientific information which has done much to produce
the artifacts which instill in us our notions of causation.[22]
Similarly, by stimulating private invention and discovery,
such mechanical processes of conveying verbal and visual
information prompted a kind of "technological individualism"—the notion that an individual could discover or create
a unique solution to problems which concerned him. One
of the most important effects of the printed book comes from
the fact that it is convenient, far more so than any text in
manuscript. The printed book is thus not only more accessible and more portable than most manuscripts, it also encourages much faster reading speeds. Observing that before the invention of the printed book men read aloud
rather than "to themselves," McLuhan proposes that these
changed habits of reading create a private space for the individual. In fact, Carothers and McLuhan perceive an even
more basic effect of printing, for in what is their most con-
troversial, and yet I find most compelling, claim, they hold
that the actual process of reading the mechanically reproduced word effects major changes in human perception,
psychology, and culture.[23]

Whatever the precise relations among the various factors
which have created our conceptions of the self, it is clear
that these ideas and the literary mode which embodies them
rapidly begin to develop in the second half of the seventeenth century. Paul Delany's excellent study of English
autobiography in this period points out that whereas spiritual histories of the time naturally followed the examples
of Augustine and Paul, contemporary secular autobiographers had to search for a way to go about their enterprise,
and details of their lives which would have seemed of crucial importance to later writers had not yet become significant to them. In other words, the "English were still uncertain of the meaning and value of life in the everyday
world of getting and spending, and the philosophical justification of 'life for its own sake' had not yet been clearly
formulated and defended against clerical opposition."[24]
Without twentieth-century assumptions of democratic indi-

vidualism, the seventeenth-century writer of his own life claimed significance for his personal history only on the basis of some singular quality, accomplishment, or experience. According to Delany, one of the crucial features of Renaissance individualism "lies in the emergence of men who are able to imagine themselves in more than one role; who stand outside or above their own personalities,"[25] and yet during the seventeenth century Englishmen still tended to define these roles very narrowly, usually in terms of profession or social position.

The idea which had emerged in the late seventeenth century that people would naturally be interested in the private lives of public figures became a commonplace assumption in the next century. Another movement towards modern democratic individualism occurs when autobiographers begin to assert that even the lives of humble people possess interest for the public. According to Shumaker, *The Life of Mrs. Charlotte Charke* (1755), the autobiography of Colley Cibber's daughter, makes what is probably the earliest outright "justification in English for the writing of obscure lives,"[26] while *A Short Account of the Life of James Fergueson* (1773) relies on none of the usual allusions to broad political or spiritual issues, taking as its subject how one man managed to educate himself in the face of major, almost insurmountable obstacles.[27] For Shumaker, the real "turning point" occurs in 1797 with the publication of Gibbon's *Memoirs,* for it marked "the first time the extended autobiography of a celebrated Englishman, intimate but not bearing upon religious experience, was printed and widely disseminated within a few years of his death."[28]

At the same time that such relatively public versions of autobiography were becoming socially and literarily acceptable in England, other writers of their own lives, of whom Boswell is the finest example, "were undergoing and valuing" what John N. Morris terms "a kind of extreme and private experience that the representatives of the official culture could scarcely bring themselves to admit to consciousness, let alone find any virtue in."[29] The most important, most infamous eighteenth-century exploration of such intensely private experience is of course the *Confessions* of Jean-Jacques Rousseau. But "where was Rousseau?" asks Phyllis Grosskurth in her essay in this volume, and this is a particularly significant question to ask about Victorian writings about the self, "because Rousseau's is the first great secular confession, a defiant assertion of the right of the ordinary man to command attention. . . . In terms of both form and content the *Confessions* was a breakthrough—but one which the Victorians chose to ignore." One explanation she offers for this phenomenon is that "the typical Victorian autobiographer was acutely aware of his audience. A mutual complicity shaped the genre, and language became a screen to shelter the vulnerable egos of writers and readers alike." In other words, one major difference between Rousseau and his Victorian heirs who refused their inheritance appears in changed assumptions about the autobiographer's relation to his audience.

This problematic relationship of autobiographer to audience is central to the understanding of the form, because, as Paul Delany reminds us, it is never "disinterested self-expression"—even were such a thing possible. "Rather, it is a 'performance' staged by the autobiographer for the benefit of his audience. Erving Goffman, in *The Presentation of the Self in Everyday Life* (p. 242), states the implications of the confrontation thus: 'When an individual appears before others, he knowingly and unwittingly projects a definition of the situation, of which a conception of himself is a part.' "[30] Since autobiography, unlike everyday life, does not allow direct interaction it must rely upon literary devices, such as a persona, to control the audience's reactions. Any attempt to control the reactions of the reader, however, threatens to disrupt the delicate relationship between him and the author. In "Credence and Credibility," Howard Helsinger shows how basic is this rhetorical problem of creating an appearance of honesty: "Testifying to his own character, the autobiographer is a suspect witness whom even the least skeptical auditors might doubt. . . . The more personal his testimony, the less liable to corrobora-

tion by public knowledge, and hence the paradox: the
greater the autobiographer's effort at introspective honesty,
the more subject he grows to doubt."

Rousseau himself was aware of this central difficulty
which renders the autobiographer's endeavor so problematic, and he makes several gestures at a solution. First,
after telling us on the opening pages of the *Confessions*
that he is unique, far different from other men, he later attempts to assure us that he has never bothered about "acting like other people or differently from them," a claim
which, while not logically incompatible with his first one
—and, indeed, which if true would "prove" its validity—remains   nonetheless   rhetorically   ineffective.[31]   Rousseau
makes a second attempt to achieve credibility by claiming
that he will tell all, something which Tristram Shandy demonstrates to be clearly impossible. Explaining his use of
trivial details, Rousseau informs the reader that they prove
his sincerity and thus authenticate his narrative:

> The task which I have undertaken, of showing myself completely
> without reserve to the public, requires that nothing that concerns
> myself shall remain obscure or hidden; that I shall keep myself con-
> tinually before its eyes; that it shall accompany me in all the errors of
> my heart, into all the secret corners of my life; that it shall not
> lose sight of me for a single instant, for fear that, if it finds in my nar-
> rative the least gap, the least blank, it may ask, What was he doing
> during that time? and accuse me of unwillingness to tell all.[32]

This readiness to communicate everything involves his
third try at convincing us of his essential sincerity, for he
adopts the rather naive position, one admittedly shared by
many, that to say something bad about oneself is necessarily to
say something true. Such a strategy, however, cannot convince, since we all know that some days the ears of police-
men and psychoanalysts alike are filled with false confessions.

Rousseau therefore succeeds largely because of the very
abundance and intensity of the experiences he relates, but
this is not a direction which many Victorian autobiographers are willing to take. One explanation for Rousseau's
apparent lack of influence upon them may well lie in what

Lionel Trilling takes to be differences between French and English modes of sincerity. To the French sincerity "consists in telling the truth about oneself to oneself and to others; by truth is meant a recognition of such of one's own traits or actions as are morally or socially discreditable and, in conventional course, concealed." The English, in contrast, ask of the sincere man only that "he communicate without deceiving or misleading."[33] The English conception of sincerity, in other words, makes it largely a matter of public discourse. Indeed, whereas Rousseau proposes to go ever deeper into himself to counter suspicions of insincerity, the characteristic Victorian response to the problem of autobiographical credibility suggests, as Howard Helsinger argues, that they understood the mode "not as intimate speech but as public discourse." Thus conceiving the history of one's own life as public speech, they avoid introspection, and adopt one of two characteristic solutions to the problem of authorial credibility. Either, like Hume and Darwin, they adopt what Helsinger terms the defence *ex morte* and write as though they were already dead, making pretensions to complete objectivity about themselves; or else, like Gibbon and Trollope, they adopt the defence *ex vita* and throw themselves, as fellow gentlemen, upon the sympathies of living men. Furthermore, as the essays in this volume by Sarah Frerichs and Linda Peterson show, the problem of audience becomes even more complicated and difficult for women, since to write at all was in some manner to question the role society had assigned them: the really proper woman was not supposed to have a public audience at all. Mrs. Oliphant's *Autobiography* points to this problematic relation to audience with particular clarity, since her intended audience changed while she was in the process of writing the story of her life, for her son to whom it had been directed died and, having no other reader, she turned towards the public.

The chief rhetorical problem in establishing the autobiographer's credibility before his audience comes to this: if he or she attempts the Rousseauean method of self-consciousness, the autobiographical act immediately be-

comes subject to all kinds of suspicions about accuracy and
intention; whereas if the writer of one's own life adopts the
supposedly unself-conscious roles of the author speaking
to equals or of the natural historian of self, the rhetorical
effect may be even less convincing. In general, the Victorians elect to forgo the self-conscious mode, and they do so
because they do not conceive Rousseau's approach to be
either necessary or proper to autobiographical discourse.
Such revelations about one's intimate self, whether distasteful or not, are not what one *says* to one's peers.

Even more importantly, Victorian autobiographers
choose not to follow Rousseau because they often suspect
that such a quest for self is fruitless. The author of the
Confessions confidently informs us that he has taken the
first step into the "dark and dirty labyrinth"[34] of his confessions, but many Victorians felt that such steps would
only get one inevitably lost. "Introspection," Elizabeth K.
Helsinger points out, does not lead for them "to a visionary
knowledge of self and the world, the prelude to action
which autobiographers from Augustine to Wordsworth
promised. The isolated quest for private identity is, in the
Victorian experience, almost always a failure. . . . The
Victorians knew what Wordsworth never quite admitted:
that self-discovery has become not the prelude to an active
life but an inadequate substitute for it." Thus disillusioned
with introspective quests for self, Victorian writers sought
different modes of self-definition and self-presentation.
As Helsinger points out, by mid-century the major poets
were already working out alternatives to traditional crisis
autobiography, and although most autobiographers were
slower to experiment, a few, like Ruskin, attempted entirely
new approaches to the mode. In "Travel as Anti-Autobiography: William Morris' *Icelandic Journals,*" Frederick
Kirchhoff further demonstrates the presence of radical
attempts to avoid the flaws of introspection. According to
him, Morris' journals provide another alternative to crisis
autobiography. "Where Morris' self-confrontation differs
is that it takes the form of an 'objective' response to the
Icelandic landscape. His introspection is contained and

thus controlled by the 'short, swallow flights' of his daily journal entries. The Journals are anti-autobiography because they provide Morris with this alternative to conventional autobiographical self-examination."

Furthermore, many Victorians, particularly in the later part of the century, were convinced of the essential fruitlessness and impropriety of the Rousseauean quest, because they had begun to suspect that the "deeper" one got into the labyrinth of self, the less one found. Oscar Wilde thus hardly finds psychological analysis worthwhile either in autobiography or fiction, since, as he explains in "The Decay of Lying," we are all essentially alike anyway. "It is a humiliating confession, but we are all of us made out of the same stuff. . . . The more one analyzes people, the more all reasons for analysis disappear. Sooner or later one comes to that dreadful universal thing called human nature."[35] But other men of the nineteenth century began to feel that although one might finally encounter this basic human nature, one could not capture that illusive individuating self. With a characteristically sublime mixture of confidence and naiveté Rousseau offers to provide us with "an accurate knowledge of my inner being. . . . What I have promised to relate, is the history of my soul. I need no other memoirs in order to write it faithfully; it is sufficient for me to enter into my inner self, as I have hitherto done."[36] During the second half of the nineteenth century European and British thinkers questioned whether anyone could enter into that "inner self," or indeed, if such a self was not merely a convenient fiction. In *Beyond Good and Evil* Nietzsche casts the projects of introspection and retrospection into doubt by forcing us to recognize how many unfounded assumptions they require:

> When I analyze the process that is expressed in the sentence, 'I think,' I find a whole series of daring assertions that would be difficult, perhaps impossible, to prove; for example, that it is *I* who think, that there must necessarily be something that thinks, that thinking is an activity and operation on the part of a being who is thought of as a cause, that there is an 'ego,' and finally, that it is already determined what is to be designated by thinking—that I *know* what thinking is.

This most mischievous of earnest men continues his attack on philosophical prejudice by emphasizing the crucial fact "that a thought comes when 'it' wishes, and not when 'I' wish, so that it is a falsification of the facts of the case to say that the subject 'I' is the condition of the predicate 'I think,' *it* thinks; but that this 'it' is precisely the famous old 'ego' is, to put it mildly, only a supposition, an assertion, and assuredly not an 'immediate certainty.' "[37] Rousseau is considered to be a sophisticate in ways of the self, while Robert Louis Stevenson, that innocent Victorian, is today valued primarily as a writer for children; and yet it was Stevenson who remarked that "we cannot even regard ourselves as a constant; in this flux of things, our identity seems in a perpetual variation; and not infrequently we find our own disguise the strangest in the masquerade."[38]

This Victorian recognition of how elusive—and perhaps illusory—the self can be appears with particular clarity in the autobiography of Herbert Spencer, the philosopher of development. Since none of the essays included in this volume discuss Spencer in detail, it will be worth our while to observe how he embodies essential problems facing the nineteenth-century self-historian. Francis R. Hart's valuable essay on modern autobiography mentions the paradox of retrospective point of view in autobiography: "Effective access to a recollected self or its 'versions' begins in a discontinuity of identity or being which permits past selves to be seen as distinct realities. Yet only a continuity of identity or being makes the autobiographical act or purpose meaningful. The paradox of continuity in discontinuity is itself a problem to be experimented with, and it is a problem both of truth and of form."[39] Spencer frequently forces his reader to encounter this basic paradox when he makes the admission, unusual for an autobiographer, that his memories fail him, thus depriving him of continuity with his past self or selves. To remedy this lack he often has recourse to letters and diaries, and while such documentation is hardly unusual, since many autobiographers, including Ruskin and Newman, employ it, Spencer is either more ingenuous or more honest than most, for he willingly brings

to the reader's attention the implications of using such
data. There is nothing, of course, unusual in his remark
that his use of "letters dating fifty odd years back enabled
me to give the last chapter a much more graphic character
than memory alone would have enabled me to give it,"[40]
since such frank admission of his procedure makes no explicit point about the relative significance of the facts he
has thus rediscovered. We do not know, for instance, if
those graphic facts of which he writes are essential to his
basic self-conception or merely furnish some interesting atmosphere. Similarly, when he tells us that "memory does
not tell me the extent of my divergence from current beliefs" (I, 171) about religion between the ages of eighteen
and twenty, we do not feel anything more than confidence
in the author's open admission of his limitations. But when
he repeats such admissions, it becomes increasingly obvious
that he realizes and is willing to admit that whole sections
of his life have been lost to him. Unlike Rousseau, Spencer
sees the clear impossibility of telling "all."

Such a conclusion appears when he relates minor matters, such as a holiday, and what is unusual is that Spencer
presses the implications of such failures of memory upon
his reader. Thus, after quoting a letter from 1844 to one of
his uncles, he draws a general conclusion about the fallibil-
ities of memory which has major implications for autobiography: "Here I am shown how dangerous it is to say that
an incident never happened because there is no recollection
of it. Had I not by this, and another passage in the letter,
been made to think about it, and had it not been that while
all the rest had faded absolutely, one solitary incident at
the hotel at Kidderminster was recalled by effort, I should
have asserted quite positively that no such expedition as
this ever took place" (I, 331). The memory itself is here
of course rather unimportant and the presence of documen-
tary evidence successfully prompted Spencer to recall this
otherwise lost event. Such stark confrontations of empty
memory and a full written text from the past occur quite
frequently in his long autobiography, and they produce a
particularly unsettling effect upon the reader. At first we are

gratified to have come upon an author who so openly and honestly confesses his shortcomings as self-historian, and we begin by assuming that once we have learned about them we can place even more confidence in what he does remember. Such placing of the author's discourse within the context of his frankly confessed limitations superficially resembles Montaigne's always effective creation of credibility in the presence of his reader; and yet there is a major difference: for all of Montaigne's major epistemological skepticism, he is yet able to convince us that, given his admitted shortcomings, he speaks as truly as he can—as truly, if not more truly, than anyone else can. Spencer's admissions, in contrast, strike deeper into the problem, undermining the validity of his whole undertaking. For example, when telling about his reading—something crucial, one would think, to the development of a philosopher—he again readily admits his memory has falsified the facts, for, if asked what he had read at one important period, he comments: "Did I trust to memory only, I should reply that I read nothing but newspapers and periodicals, not even reading novels, much less any serious books. Reference to correspondence, however, has undeceived me" (I, 401). The most disturbing instance of such freely admitted discontinuity with his past self occurs when the philosopher of development, who had partially anticipated Darwin, mentions (one cannot say "describes") his reaction to the appearance of *The Origin of Species:*

> That reading it gave me great satisfaction may be safely inferred. Whether there was any setoff to this great satisfaction, I cannot now say; for I have quite forgotten the ideas and feelings I had. . . . Whether proof that what I had supposed to be the sole cause, could be at best but a part cause, gave me any annoyance, I cannot remember; nor can I remember whether I was vexed by the thought that in 1852 I had failed to carry further the idea, then expressed, that among human beings the survival of those who are the select of their generation is a cause of development. (II, 57)

Similarly, Spencer, who placed great importance upon his origin, development, and continued work outside any academic establishment, is all but incredulous to learn that he had once been invited to apply for a professorship (II, 172). Rarely has an autobiographer been so willing to admit that his past has eluded him time and time again.

Freely admitting major discontinuities between his present self and the self who wrote these earlier texts, Spencer, a true believer in·objective fact, consciously adopts the procedure of writing about himself as if he were another person. Employing the historian's methods of evaluating written evidence, he chooses the method of fact over that of introspection. We have already observed how having forgotten his reaction to Darwin's first great work, the best Spencer could do is place himself outside himself alongside the reader, concluding "that reading it gave me great satisfaction may be safely inferred." Such treatment of himself, his past self, as wholly other occurs at crucial points in the autobiography when Spencer, looking at his past, tries to find some answer, some clue, and discovers only that he is as shut out from it as is his reader. For example, when arriving at the place when he will discuss what is for him one of the essential points in his intellectual development, that stage at which he discovered the unity of various fields of inquiry, he finds himself reduced to the vantage point of the exterior observer. "What initiated the unification?" he asks himself, and continues: "No positive answer is furnished by my memory; but there is an answer which, on reviewing the circumstances, may be considered *as almost certainly* the true one" (II, 14). The autobiographer has become a biographer, the historian of another's actions. Having freely chosen the method of an external observer, he finds some minor solace there, candidly admitting of a trip to the Isle of Wight in 1872: "I may remark in passing, that the last sentence gives me the date of an excursion which otherwise I should have been puzzled to fix" (II, 285). True scholar, not of his emotions and inner consciousness, but of dates and texts, Spencer, who often finds references to his own past life puzzling, manages to decipher his previous selves only after collating the evidence of several texts. Thus he tells us that "no memories were raised by coming upon the following sentence in a letter written on 14 April 1869:—

'Though better, I am still not well, and am leaving town today for a short ramble in the country.' But for a letter written
on June 15, I should have failed to identify the occasion as
one which I first went to Oxford" (II, 242). Indeed, Spencer
places such implicit reliance upon the written texts of the
past that for him autobiography becomes the arrangement
of texts preserved from the past. One suspects that such
gaps in memory, reliance on the written word, and application of historical method are probably not all that unusual
in autobiography, but other writers do not press them forward so insistently. Spencer may have made so many admissions of discontinuity as a conscious means of demonstrating
to us his essential honesty, but he manages only to raise
more problems than he solves. Clearly, treating oneself as
the proper topic for a dispassionate monograph does not
produce satisfactory autobiography.

To make such pretensions to objectivity is rather point-
less, because all autobiography forces the writer to make
arbitrary—subjective—choices. As Mutlu Konuk Blasing
argues, "autobiographical writing fictionalizes life by introducing order and establishing connections or relations between events. In autobiography, then, what was perhaps
arbitrary becomes necessary." Furthermore, representation
or "the telling of events" inevitably fictionalizes, because
"narratives have beginnings and ends. . . . It is in narrative
that things 'happen.' " According to Avrom Fleishman, one
of the most basic ways that the autobiographer has of ordering the experiences of that paradoxical, problematic, elusive
entity he seeks "is to choose a metaphor of the self and
develop it in a narrative or other sequence, which may be
called a conversion of metaphor into myth. . . . The completed sequence is a *personal myth.*" Choosing three different kinds of autobiographical writings, he then demonstrates
that for Mill such a mythic pattern takes the form of the concept of progress, while in Butler it appears as a sun myth
and as a seasonal one in Gissing. Spencer, one may add,
believes his entire existence embodies the principle of natural selection, and he attempts to make it the basic structure
of his narrative, while Carlyle relies upon a personal myth

which re-presents himself as the heroic survivor of shipwreck.[41] If we turn to the essays in this volume, we readily
observe the many kinds of personal myths that Victorian
autobiographers employ. Both Dickens and James employ
the myth of the artist-writing-himself, while Mrs. Oliphant
sees herself as a Victorian Andrea del Sarto—an artist whose
sacrifices for family prevented her reaching greatness.
Browning, no Andrea del Sarto, employs biblical typology
for his self-representations. Newman borrows the theological notions of justification and economy, turning himself
into the Divine Word, while John Butler Yeats, the poet's
father, sees himself as the incarnation of a far different
cosmic principle or scheme according to which the universe
is composed of a series of polar oppositions. Elizabeth Missing Sewell, the archetypal Victorian spinster, embodied her
life in a myth of Victorian Motherhood.

The evidence of Victorian autobiography suggests, moreover, that some writers of their own lives may employ a complex layering of such personal myths. Ruskin is a case in
point, for he offers a particularly complex combination of
these metaphoric structures to re-present himself. Thus,
Claudette Kemper Columbus sees him as the figure of the
man unable to speak or hear the necessary Word, and Elizabeth K. Helsinger conceives him as a spirit of place—a consciousness who exists only in phenomenological contact
with landscapes. Citing another Ruskinian personal myth, I
would also suggest that he experiences his life as a series
of contrasted Paradises Lost and Pisgah Visions. The losses
include time lost, but more importantly people lost as well,
for this gentle memory fugue contains an astonishing number of deaths and deathbed scenes, while the gains occur
almost entirely in terms of vision, in learning to see things
correctly, whatever the cost, whatever the pain. And so Ruskin comes to see himself first as Adam being driven from
Paradise and then as Moses permitted to catch sight of the
new Paradise but never to enter it. Perhaps the next stage
in considering such complex layerings of personal myth
would be to develop a semiotic method that could perceive
the relation of these various voices.

One obvious source of complexity appears in the fact that in adopting any one personal myth the autobiographer can combine it with the myths of another author or in some way join it to a culturally shared myth. Thus, as David J. DeLaura comments, "What is most notable about the famous elevated passages in Arnold is, first, that they form a more or less 'coherent myth' regarding Arnold's life, and second, and perhaps more startlingly, that they are the elaboration of, as well as the response to, the pattern established by Newman." Adopting this insight, one perceives that it has much to tell us about autobiographical elements in literature: Proust sees himself in part as Ruskin, and many religious autobiographers have seen themselves as Paul, Augustine, or Bunyan.

The single most pervasive set of autobiographical myths available to the Victorians concerns childhood—a fact of central importance because the genesis, conventions, and problems of autobiography are so intimately related to this period of human life. What complicates this subject is that, as several recent authors have shown, modern conceptions of childhood, immaturity, and the process of maturation are barely two centuries old. Earlier in human history one encounters few of our most basic assumptions about the nature of the child and his relation to the adult. The Dutch psychologist J. H. van den Berg thus points out that "pedagogic manuscripts of the past do not contain anything on the nature of the relationship between old and young. Even the greatest authors do not mention the subject," and, moreover, "before Rousseau, nobody ever mentioned maturation."[42] What surprises us about even Rousseau's discussion of the process of achieving maturity is that he conceives it as extremely brief, whereas today we assume it takes many years. Looking at the historical evidence, van den Berg concludes that "nowadays two separate states of human life can be distinguished: the state of maturity, with all the mature attributes belonging to it, like birth, death, faith, and sexuality; and the state of immaturity, which lacks all these attributes."[43]

Furthermore, the "invention" of childhood seems to have been occasioned by the same forces which produce auto-biography—the need and ability to choose between various roles. Thus, a major reason "for the child's increasing child-ishness and for the origin, the lengthening, and the deepen-ing of maturation" is in "the multivalent pluralism peculiar to modern maturity."[44] For most of the history of civiliza-tion, the child has followed closely in the footsteps of a parent, adopting the same occupation, social position, sex-ual role, and political and religious allegiance. Today, freer to choose—*condemned* to choose—among many alternatives, the adult makes a series of decisions which succeed in establishing a "small and relatively simple domain in this complex society; to the rest we are blind, we do not see it, and so we can act as if it were not there." But wandering within a confusing welter of partially comprehended and often competing sign-systems, the child has not yet learned to choose and survive. "That is exactly what being a child means—to be defenceless against this multivalency and to shrink back from it."[45]

Positing a relationship between modern conceptions of childhood and the growth of autobiography in the starkest terms, one would state that at that point in human history when choices become so abundant, autobiography, the jus-tification of one's choices, becomes increasingly important as a literary mode. This relationship does not take the form of simple cause and effect; that is, the growth of modern con-ceptions of immaturity did not produce autobiography. Rather it seems more likely that both the modern notions of immaturity and of autobiography are alike responses to a changing cultural situation in which the individual is in-creasingly required to make choices which earlier were made for him—which, in other words, did not exist before.

Although the inventions of both childhood and literary autobiography owe much to modern pluralism, the role of childhood within this literary mode is even more complex than this historical relation might suggest. As LuAnn Walther argues in her essay on "The Victorian Invention of

Childhood," part of the complexity arises in the fact that many Victorians were able to hold, simultaneously, two contradictory conceptions of childhood:

> On the one hand the child was the source of hope, of virtue, or emotion; along with the angelic wife, he was the repository of family values which seemed otherwise to be disappearing from an increasingly secular world. . . . But at the same time, and of course much less obviously, the child was a hardship, an obstacle to adult pleasure, and a reminder of one's baser self. He might be innocent, untainted by sexual knowledge, uncorrupted by the world of business, free from the agony of religious doubt; yet he was also potentially wicked and needed constant guidance and discipline.

These contradictory attitudes towards childhood create, in turn, two tendencies in the portrayal of youthful experience by Victorian autobiographers. "First, is the need to emphasize childhood adversity, to portray oneself as not having been spoiled by overindulgence, even, in some cases, to have deserved hardship. Second, and in conflict with this, is the desire to present childhood as an Edenic, blissful state, a time of past blessedness, a world completely different from the grating present." From this recognition follow several important points, the first of which is that one must be very careful about relying upon such evidence to create a history of Victorian childhood or child-rearing practices. The historian, in other words, must not only determine the accuracy of such frequently harsh pictures of childhood, many of which conform as much to the demands of a literary mode as to actual experience, but he must also determine why such stereotypes were culturally necessary. Within literary autobiography the Edenic conception of childhood also had a clear function, since, as Walther points out, "it provided the autobiographer with a workable approach to the past and it allowed him to create, in the richness of memory, a place of repose from the harsh 'fast-hurrying stream of Time' which threatened him."

A crucial aspect of this cultural myth is that it furnishes a point of departure, a way of beginning, and one should not underestimate the importance of such a moment of origin, for it is always essential and yet always hard to locate. As

Edward Said argues, "consciousness of a starting point, from the viewpoint of the continuity that succeeds it, is a consciousness of a direction in which it is humanly possible to move, as well as a trust in continuity."[46] The problem for the autobiographer, of course, is to find his beginning, to re-experience and re-present it—something which, like his ending, it is clearly impossible to do.[47] One can choose some first memory, some early experience, but such a procedure, since it does not go back to one's origin, one's *beginning*, only reminds us how arbitrary the writer's decision has been, thereby raising the spector of fictionality in what is supposed to be literally true. On the other hand, choosing to talk about one's parents or even more distant ancestry does not solve the problem either, since such a strategy not only skips over the crucial moment or fount of origin rather obviously but it also transforms a record of one's own experience into a record of another's.

Unable to discover or re-present his origin, the autobiographer has recourse to a myth, thus repeating a common pattern in human thought, and it should not surprise us at all when we discover that Victorian autobiographers cast their narratives of early life in similar molds. Speaking of revolutionary myths, Georges Sorel claims that they "are not descriptions of things, but expressions of a determination to act. . . . A Myth cannot be refuted, since it is, at bottom, identical with the convictions of a group."[48] If one accepts Hannah Arendt's claim that a true revolution must not only destroy the old order but replace it with a new one,[49] it appears that Victorian myths of childhood are very accurately described as revolutionary myths: they found a new order; they contain prescriptions about how one group (the generation which holds the myth) should act towards the new children, who occupy the position of Others; and they also instruct the autobiographer how to act toward the Other who was once himself. It is therefore almost inevitable that autobiographies will contain definite structural breaks as their authors move from a mythic to a narrative mode, from a timeless, static realm to one in which development and change rule. Shumaker has remarked upon a similar phenomenon, pointing out that autobiographies often contain abrupt divisions between adolescence and maturity: "At the moment at which the writer's personality and character, emerging from adolescence into maturity, become relatively stable, relatively fixed, the continuity may be broken. What follows will be treated differently."[50] Many autobiographies therefore contain a tripartite division in which two static periods, the first containing the mythic childhood and the second the stable present "I," surround a period of development.

Of course, autobiography shares with other forms of literature these paradoxes of origins and endings, just as it also shares its use of myth, whether personal or culturally shared. Furthermore, according to writers such as Roland Barthes, other literary modes also share the paradoxical, problematic relation between the writing self or voice and the one written (or written about).[51] Such convergences remind us that there are two basic approaches to the subject of autobiography, each with its own contributions to make, and they both appear in this volume. The first conceives of autobiography as a genre or mode, while the second accepts that all self-expression or self-representation is autobiography. The recognition that anything a person says or writes tells us something essential about the speaker or writer is a commonplace of romanticism, which extends it to all areas of discourse, so that not only literature but philosophy and science are seen as self-expression. "When the torrent sweeps the man against a boulder, you must expect him to scream, and you need not be surprised," says Stevenson, "if the scream is sometimes a theory."[52] Nietzsche, who was fascinated and appalled by the screams of moralists, theologians, and metaphysicians, urged that "every great philosophy so far has been . . . the personal confession of its author and a kind of involuntary and unconscious memoir." According to him, therefore, one can see any theory as a mask—an ambiguous self-presentation which simultaneously conceals and reveals the theorizer.

One can still always ask: what does such a claim tell us about the man who makes it? There are moralities which are meant to justify their

creator before others. Other moralities are meant to calm him and
lead him to be satisfied with himself. With yet others he wants to
crucify himself and humiliate himself. With others he wants to wreak
revenge, with others conceal himself, with others transfigure himself
and place himself way up at a distance. This morality is used by its
creator to forget, that one to have others forget him or something
about him. Some moralists want to vent their power and creative
whims on humanity; some others, perhaps including Kant, suggest
with their morality: "What deserves respect in me is that I can obey—
and you ought not be different from me."[53]

Even supposedly objective sciences bear the imprint, the
desires, of their creators. "Physics, too, is only an interpretation and exegesis of the world (to suit us, if I may say so!)
and *not* a world explanation."[54] James Olney, whose recent
Metaphors of Self takes as its point of departure this self-
expressive will to order, adds that all psychological theories
are also necessarily self-representations: "To write about
the self, as, for example, Jung does in his psychological
texts, can really only be to produce autobiography (i.e. the
writing of one's own life) of a sort."[55] And for those literary scholars who believe they can easily avoid seeing their
own face in the mirror we have Paul Murray Kendall to
remind us how difficult it is to avoid self-portraiture. "On the
trail of another man, the biographer must put up with finding himself at every turn: any biography uneasily shelters
an autobiography within it. He begins with somebody else's
papers, and ends with his own."[56]

Such recognitions have been inevitable since the advent of
romanticism, which sees the work of art as an expression of
the author's inner feelings and imagination. As soon as
readers accept that a literary text expresses, or makes exterior, something within its author, then it becomes inevitable
that they will use that text as a key to that interior. As M.H.
Abrams explains, "Furnished with the proper key, the
romantic extremist was confident he could decipher the
hieroglyph, penetrate to the reality behind the appearance,
and so come to know an author more intimately than his
own friends and family; more intimately, even, than the
author, lacking this key, could possibly have known himself."[57] Abrams credits Blake with inventing that radical
form of such criticism which holds that "the latent personal

significance of a narrative poem is found not merely to
underlie, but to contradict and cancel the surface intention."[58] Blake's radical approach has become quite common
today, and it is not difficult to perceive to what a large extent
structuralist, psychoanalytic, and phenomenological criticisms still have the goals first established in the early nineteenth-century. For example, Jeffrey Mehlman explains that
his "effort has been, in each case, to reach that level of
analysis at which a persistent textual organization is
revealed, whose coherence throws into jeopardy the apparent intentions of the author. . . . In confronting texts, the
search for repetitions, aberrant details, seeming contradictions, surprising omissions has, I believe, allowed me to
generate between texts the kind of insistent structure for
which Freud (and Mauron) used the term 'unconscious.' "[59]
In other words, Mehlman, following Blake, seeks that level
at which the author "contradicts" his explicit or conscious
discourse, and there he locates the author's essential self.

Such broad approaches to the autobiographical in literature have much to offer, for they force us to confront those
basic questions which it raises about self, language, and
society. One reason that autobiography is so fascinating, so
challenging, as a subject for criticism is that it quickly forces
us out of any narrow specialization to look at the methods
and conclusions of psychology, history, philosophy, anthropology and other disciplines. Since structuralism offers a
methodology which promises to bridge various disciplines,
it has particular value for such a study, and many of the
essays in this volume carry on dialogues with Barthes,
Lacan, Derrida, and others. The broad approaches to the
subject of autobiography, which see it present in all forms
of discourse, thus make us aware of what autobiography,
strictly conceived, shares with all other forms of literature
and similar semiotic systems, such as painting, which may
also be used for self-representation.

As valuable as are recognitions of such underlying similarities, they have the disadvantage of making it difficult to
discern if one can usefully treat autobiography as a clearly
defined literary mode, or if it possesses any strengths and
weaknesses peculiar to itself. Self-representation is not

autobiography, I would suggest. To qualify as autobiography a work must not only present a version, myth, or metaphor of the self, but it must also be retrospective and hence it must self-consciously contrast two selves, the writing "I" and the one located (or created) in the past. If a work does not meet this description, it seems more helpful to see it as an example of self-representation or autobiographicality.

One finds autobiography, even thus strictly defined, in what may seem unusual forms. For example, Mutlu Konuk Blasing demonstrates that taken together the prefaces to the New York edition of James's novels "may be seen as the autobiography of an artist—the 'story' or 'representation' of a career. Moreover, as James's revisions of his novels for the New York edition suggest, the 'continuity' of his career required him to 're-see' it. Since in James's case the life and the career were closely identified, we witness in the Prefaces the process by which James rewrote his life in writing the story of his career. . . . The Prefaces should be seen as experience taking note of itself, for in their self-consciousness as a 're-presentation' of the creative process, they make 'everything count' and thereby rescue the 'clumsy Life' that surrounds the art." Indeed, as David J. DeLaura has shown, such a procedure in which experience takes note of itself characterizes the writer of Victorian non-fiction as well: "Whole careers in Victorian prose can be legitimately read as being as intensely and continuously 'autobiographical' as the career of any novelist or poet. A number of writers—De Quincey, Carlyle, Newman, Ruskin, Arnold, and even Pater—spend their lives defining and redefining their past experiences for present purposes, while ostensibly talking about something else: society, literature, or religion."

The following attempt to map the territories of Victorian autobiography begins with broad historical and theoretical considerations, next looks at individual self-histories, and closes with the relations of this to other literary modes. My purpose has been to assemble a gathering of essays which place equal importance upon the autobiographies themselves and those methodologies most helpful in understanding them. The essays by Blasing, Columbus, Patten, and Ryan employ various structuralist approaches, while those by Grosskurth and the Helsingers raise problems that are simultaneously historical and theoretical. Blasing, Bornstein, Frerichs, Patten and Peterson examine the self-histories of artists, and Frerichs and Peterson also concern themselves with the problems of women's autobiography; taken together with Grosskurth, they can be seen to place their subjects within the context of sexual politics. In this mapping expedition, I have constantly transgressed boundaries, some proper and some not, and I have most shamelessly stretched the limits of our inquiry to include Henry James as an English Victorian (and if the purpose of categories is to make us see something in a particular way, perhaps a new one, why not?). Together we have wandered across the boundaries of autobiography into closely situated regions, so that this volume includes Elizabeth Helsinger's relation of autobiography to the situation in contemporary poetry, and Kirchhoff and DeLaura relate it to other forms of non-fiction. As one might expect from any examination of autobiographies written during the golden age of the English novel, many of the essays concern themselves with the relation of self-history to fiction: Blasing, Frerichs, Fleishman, Patten, Peterson, and others discuss this problem in a way that helps us better understand both autobiography and the novel. Here, as throughout this gathering of essays, the attempt has been to suggest the usefulness of paying attention to the literary work and the way we read it.

1. *The Alien Vision of Victorian Poetry: Sources of the Poetic Imagination in Tennyson, Browning, and Arnold* (Princeton: Princeton University Press, 1952), p. xiii.

2. *The Art of Biography* (New York: W. W. Norton, 1965), p. 125.

3. *Cosmos and History: The Myth of the Eternal Return,* trans. W. R. Trask (New York and Evanston: Harper and Row, 1959), pp. 48, 154.

4. *The Birth of Tragedy* (Section 10) in *Basic Writings,* trans. and ed. Walter Kaufman (New York: Modern Library, 1968), p. 73.

5. E. R. Dodds, *The Greeks and the Irrational* (Berkeley and Los Angeles: University of California Press, 1964), pp. 15–16.

6. Bruno Snell, *The Discovery of the Mind: The Greek Origins of European*

Thought, trans. T. G. Rosenmeyer (New York and Evanston: Harper & Row, 1960), p. 7.

7. Trans. E. W. Dickes, 2 vols (Cambridge, Mass.: Harvard University Press, 1951), I, 289, 291.

8. Misch, I, 61.

9. Misch quotes and then comments upon the following remark Dilthey made about the Renaissance: " 'Every time a culture dies out and a new one is to arise, the world of ideas that proceeded from the older cultures fades and dissolves. The individual experience is, as it were, emancipated for a time from the fetters of conceptual thought: it becomes a power in itself over men's minds.' Accordingly we may say that at such times individual life—devoid of objective support, as it is no longer merely a part of the community and is not yet developed in relation to well-established cultural influences—may attain a new importance as a single whole" (I, 72).

10. *Man's Place in Nature,* trans. Hans Meyerhoff (New York: Noonday Press, 1970), pp. 20, 26-27. For other expressions of this view, *see* José Ortega y Gasset, "In Search of Goethe from Within" and "The Self and the Other," *The Dehumanization of Art and Other Writings on Art and Culture* (Garden City, N. Y.: Doubleday Anchor, n.d.), pp. 123-87; and Morse Peckham, *Man's Rage for Chaos: Biology, Behavior and the Arts* (New York: Schocken, 1967).

11. *English Autobiography: Its Emergence, Materials, and Form* (Berkeley and Los Angeles: University of California Press, 1954), p. 89.

12. Shumaker, pp. 89-90.

13. For a detailed discussion of the development of these theories of moral sympathy, *see* my *Aesthetic and Critical Theories of John Ruskin* (Princeton: Princeton University Press, 1971), pp. 151-61.

14. Shumaker, p. 29.

15. *Ideology and Utopia: An Introduction to the Sociology of Knowledge,* trans. Louis Wirth and Edward Shils (New York: Harcourt, Brace & World, n. d.), p. 34.

16. *See* especially "The Rise of Individualism" (Chapter 3, section iii) in *Religion and the Rise of Capitalism* (Harmondsworth, Eng.: Penguin, 1966), pp. 179-96.

17. "Culture, Psychiatry and the Written Word," *Psychiatry* (November, 1959), p. 308, quoted in Marshall McLuhan, *The Gutenberg Galaxy: The Making of Typographic Man* (Toronto: University of Toronto Press, 1965), p. 18.

18. McLuhan, p. 19.

19. For Carlyle, *see* n. 21 below; Lacan, "Le stade du miroir comme formateur du fonction de Je," *Revue Française de Psychanalyse,* 13 (1949), 449-55. Valuable discussions of this seminal essay, which has influenced several contributors to this volume, are found in Maurice Merleau-Ponty, "The Child's Relations with Others," *The Primacy of Perception,* ed. James M. Edie (Evanston: Northwestern University Press, 1964), especially pp. 134ff; and Anthony Wilden's notes and commentary in his edition of Lacan's *The Language of the Self: The Function of Language in Psychoanalysis* (New York: Delta, 1975).

20. Shumaker, p. 29.

21. *Sartor Resartus,* ed. C. F. Harrold (New York: Odyssey, 1937), p. 40.

22. *Prints and Visual Communication* (Cambridge, Mass.: Harvard University Press, 1953).

23. McLuhan, pp. 18-21, 24-28, 33-35, 43.

24. *British Autobiography in the Seventeenth Century* (London: Routledge & Kegan Paul, 1969), p. 107.

25. Delany, p. 11.

26. Shumaker, p. 24.

27. *Ibid.*, p. 25.

28. *Ibid.*, p. 28.

29. *Versions of the Self: Studies in English Autobiography from John Bunyan to John Stuart Mill* (New York: Basic Books, 1966), p. 8.

30. Delany, p. 114.

31. (New York: Modern Library, n.d.), p. 57.

32. Rousseau, p. 60.

33. *Sincerity and Authenticity* (Cambridge, Mass.: Harvard University Press, 1972), p. 58.

34. Rousseau, p. 16.

35. *Aesthetes and Decadents of the 1890's,* ed. Karl Beckson (New York: Vintage, 1966), p. 175.

36. Rousseau, p. 284.

37. *Basic Writings of Nietzsche,* pp. 213–14.

38. "Crabbed Age and Youth," *Selected Poetry and Prose,* ed. Bradford A. Booth (Boston: Houghton Mifflin, 1968), p. 5.

39. "Notes for an Anatomy of Modern Autobiography," *New Literary History,* I (1970), 500.

40. *An Autobiography,* 2 vols. (New York: D. Appleton, 1904), I, 134. Hereafter cited in text.

41. *See* my " 'Swim or Drown': Carlyle's World of Shipwrecks, Castaways, and Stranded Voyagers," *Studies in English Literature* (1975), 641–55.

42. *The Changing Nature of Man: Introduction to a Historical Psychology,* trans. H. F. Cores (New York: Delta, 1975), pp. 25–26.

43. van den Berg, p. 32.

44. *Ibid.*, p. 42.

45. *Ibid.*, p. 43.

46. "A Meditation on Beginnings," *Salmagundi,* 2 (1968), 44.

47. On endings in autobiographical writings, *See* Hart, p. 506 and the essays by Blasing and Fleishman in this volume.

48. *Reflections on Violence,* trans. T. E. Hulme and J. Roth (New York: Collier, 1961), p. 50.

49. *On Revolution* (New York: Viking, 1965), pp. 140ff; she also points out that "revolutions are the only political events which confront us directly and inevitably with the problem of beginning" (p. 131).

50. Shumaker, pp. 70–71.

51. "To Write: An Intransitive Verb?" *The Structuralist Controversy: The Languages of Criticism and the Sciences of Man,* eds. Richard Macksey and Eugenio Donato (Baltimore: John Hopkins University Press, 1970), pp. 134–45.

52. *Selected Poetry and Prose,* p. 9.

53. *Beyond Good and Evil* in *Basic Writings,* pp. 203, 289–290.

54. *Basic Writings,* p. 211.

55. (Princeton: Princeton University Press, 1972), p. 35.

56. Kendall, p. x.

57. *The Mirror and the Lamp: Romantic Theory and the Critical Tradition* (New York: Oxford University Press, 1953), pp. 228–29.

58. Abrams, p. 251.

59. *A Structural Study of Autobiography: Proust, Leiris, Sartre, Levi-Straus* (Ithaca: Cornell University Press, 1974), pp. 14, 16.

PART ONE

Approaches to Victorian Autobiography

ELIZABETH K. HELSINGER

Ulysses to Penelope: Victorian Experiments in Autobiography

Between Wordsworth's *The Prelude* and Pater's "Conclusion" to *The Renaissance,* attitudes toward the self and how it should be presented in literature changed radically. Wordsworth, at the beginning of his autobiographical poem, is lifted by the "gentle breeze" of inspiration to one of the imagination's lookout points, from which he sees spread out before him both life and poem as a single path from past to present. "With a heart/Joyous, nor scared at its own liberty," he cries out "I cannot miss my way" (I.14–15, 18). Pater concludes his *Renaissance* on a note of subdued sadness, apologizing for the impressions which he has substituted for biography:

> To such a tremulous wisp constantly reforming itself on the stream, to a single sharp impression, with a sense in it, a relic more or less fleeting, of such moments gone by, what is real in our life fines itself down. It is with this movement, with the passage and dissolution of impressions, images, sensations, that analysis leaves off—that continual vanishing away, that strange, perpetual weaving and unweaving of ourselves.[1]

For Pater, the road connecting past and present is no longer an appropriate image for the self. One's life is not a stream but "a tremulous wisp constantly reforming itself on the stream." The self has no continuous existence in time which memory can retrieve, and so cannot define itself through chronological narrative. Representative experience may evoke memories of similar situations or responses ("a single sharp impression, with a sense in it . . . of such moments

3

gone by"), but to extend this atemporal sense of recognition into a consistent progressive sequence is to construct a fiction which is psychologically false and philosophically impossible. Autobiographers earlier in the century, like Tennyson's "Ulysses," "cannot rest from travel." They share his "gray spirit yearning in desire/To follow knowledge"—self-knowledge, the end of the quest which is a shaping metaphor of life itself and of the autobiography which narrates it. Tennyson's Ulysses is already strangely slow to depart. Pater gives up the voyage entirely, turning from Ulysses' mode of self-exploration to Penelope's, "that strange, perpetual weaving and unweaving of ourselves." In 1868 and 1873, when Pater's "Conclusion" was published, his Penelope was condemned for seducing young men from the Ulyssean quest. Twenty years later in 1888, when Pater reprinted the suppressed "Conclusion," an increasing number of Victorian Ulysses were dead or permanently shipwrecked. The time of the Penelopean autobiographer was at hand. Ruskin began the last volume of *Praeterita* in the same year. Proust, who was to translate him before beginning to remember his own past, had just turned seventeen. Joyce was a (nicens) little boy meeting a moocow coming down along the road.

The prose autobiographies of the high Victorian period, with the exception of Ruskin's *Praeterita,* show few radical departures from a tradition which reaches from Wordsworth back to St. Augustine. The major Victorian poets, however, expressed in the 1850s their discontent with Wordsworth's sublime egotism, and experimented with poetic structures which would allow them to explore a different concept of selfhood. These poetic alternatives to spiritual or crisis autobiography prepare the way for Pater's Penelope.

I

Tennyson, Arnold, Browning, or Ruskin were all uncomfortable with sustained self-reflection as a subject for their writing. Their common judgment of introspection, especially in public, was that it was "morbid," unhealthy both for the poet and for his readers. Arnold puts it succinctly: "the

dialogue of the mind with itself" is a characteristic subject
of modern poetry, and too often it creates a situation

> in which the suffering finds no vent in action; in which a continuous
> state of mental distress is prolonged, unrelieved by incident, hope, or
> resistance. . . . In such situations there is inevitably something mor-
> bid, in the description of them something monotonous. When they
> occur in actual life, they are painful, not tragic; the representation of
> them in poetry is painful also.[2]

Ruskin called modern poetry the poetry of pathetic fallacy:
a poetry of feeling in which the poet's concern with himself
colors all his perceptions. "The temperament which admits
the pathetic fallacy" he judged "weak," and its perceptions
not only "inaccurate" but "morbid."[3] Tennyson spoke out
against "all those morbid and introspective" modern tales,
and once advised a young man to "develop his true self
. . . by casting aside all maudlin and introspective mor-
bidities."[4] John Stuart Mill, after reading the young Browning's "Pauline," wrote that "the writer seems to me possessed with a more intense and morbid self-consciousness
than I ever knew in any sane human being."[5] Browning
never forgot Mill's acerbic comment on his first long poem.

There are several possible reasons for the Victorians'
dislike of direct exploration or exhibition of the self in literature. In the first place, they find introspection fruitless; it
does not lead to a visionary knowledge of self and world,
the prelude to action which autobiographers from Augustine
to Wordsworth promised.[6] The isolated quest for private
identity is, in the Victorian experience, almost always a
failure. Empedocles' "dialogue of the mind with itself"
leads him to despair and death; Childe Roland's quest gives
him at most a final revelation of the futility of his questing
life. The Victorians know what Wordsworth never quite
admitted: that self-discovery has become not the prelude
to an active life but an inadequate substitute for it.

Arnold is spokesman for those who see these failures as a
phenomenon peculiar to their times, to "an age wanting in
moral grandeur," "an age of spiritual discomfort."[7] Ruskin
also associates the poetry of pathetic fallacy with what he
calls the "cloudy" modern temper, a quality of mind distin-

guished by its preference for vagueness, darkness, and change (5.317,322). Poets like Dante whose perceptions were not affected by strong personal feeling saw more clearly than modern poets—they "saw life steadily and saw it whole," in Arnold's phrase. Ruskin concludes that they saw by the light of faith, which the moderns do not have. But there is something strange in these explanations. Both Arnold and Ruskin include the romantics together with themselves in their condemnation of the age. When they talk about the handicap of belonging to the modern age or temper, they do not simply mean the difficulty of being last romantics in a time of material prosperity. That is our analysis of their failure to follow romantic example. Both men did aspire to imaginative quests for identity through poetry, but they found the experience painful and fruitless. Their explanation is that solitary questing is itself a symptom of the moral atmosphere of the times. The best poets, Arnold declares, "do not talk of their mission, nor of interpreting their age, nor of the coming Poet; all this, they know, is the mere delirium of vanity."[8] Arnold's last phrase is telling. The strongest reason for the Victorian objection to self-revealing literature seems to be not that it fails to lead to identity and action, but that it is "the mere delirium of vanity," an act of selfish pride. Their objection is profoundly moral. It is an attitude which can be found throughout the literature of the period. Tennyson's Princess, for example, is a blatant egoist. "On me, me, me, the storm first breaks," she cries: "*I* dare/ All these male thunderbolts" (IV.478–79). Her precipitate fall is not just Tennyson's condemnation of her masculinity; it is a punishment for the moral sin of pride. In fact, Victorian critics and poets were right when they said that the quest for identity was usually painful and fruitless; their conviction that it was ethically wrong insured that they would find such selfhood a burden, and turn aside from internal quests.

The injunction to forget oneself to find oneself is, of course, a commonplace of Christian and romantic tradition, but the Victorians took it further. Christians must remember God, and God, according to Augustine, will "recollect" the

Christian, giving him a sense of himself he will only discover in the experience of conversion. The romantic poet seeks self-forgetfulness in imaginative experience, which will, in turn, offer the poet an identity. For many Victorians, such pursuits remained too self-involved, especially when they became subjects for literature. The way out was a deliberate shift in focus from the self to mutuality: friendship and marriage, or to community: the writer's concern for his audience and the reformer's vision of society.[9] At the very least, the escape from self-involvement led the writer to complain of isolation, to criticize his romantic predecessors, and to subvert the forms of introspective literature, even when he continued to practice them.

Tennyson's *In Memoriam* is the clearest and earliest example of an autobiographical poem which opposes the internal quest for identity. For Tennyson, an identity independent of other people and even of achievements other than the act of self-discovery is an isolating identity. It is the child's painful sense of self to which his loss of Hallam threatened to return him.

> The baby new to earth and sky,
>   What time his tender palm is prest
>   Against the circle of the breast,
> Has never thought that "this is I;"
>
> But as he grows he gathers much,
>   And learns the use of "I" and "me,"
>   And finds "I am not what I see,
> And other than the things I touch."
>
> So rounds he to a separate mind
>   From whence clear memory may begin,
>   As thro' the frame that binds him in
> His isolation grows defined. (Section 45)

At the deepest point of his despair at Hallam's death, Tennyson is further reduced to the baby's helpless inability to say that "this is I";

>   . . . but what am I?
>   An infant crying in the night;
>   An infant crying for the light,
> And with no language but a cry. (Section 54)

The loss of Hallam is the loss of the sense of himself which their friendship had given Tennyson—a mature sense of self which had replaced the baby's fears of nonexistence and the child's isolating identity. The most frightening consequence of the death is not Tennyson's loss of faith in a fatherly God and a benign Nature, but his sense of a dissolving self, the return of what he sees as the infant's terror that he and the rest of his world will cease to exist when the lights go out. The infant's cry in the night is Tennyson's cry to Hallam in the great Section 50: "Be near me when my light is low. . . . Be near me when I fade away." Without Hallam, Tennyson must, like the infant, begin again the isolating process of self-discovery. To learn that "I am not what I see,/And other than the things I touch" will protect him from the infant's night fears, but at the price of erecting a "frame that binds him in" and secures his isolation.

In Memoriam makes clear, however, that Tennyson has no desire to seize the occasion of Hallam's death to forge an independent identity for himself. The resolution of his poem is his recovery of Hallam's companionship: "A friendship as had master'd Time:/Which masters Time indeed, and is/ Eternal, separate from fears" (Section 85). The closing lyrics assert again and again that Tennyson has not recovered *from* Hallam's death; he has recovered Hallam himself: "Mine, mine, for ever, ever mine" (Section 129); "I shall not lose thee tho' I die" (Section 130). Hallam's friendship provided Tennyson with an alternative to the burdensome identity of isolation: identity through mutuality. The epithalamion which concludes the poem is Tennyson's praise of mutuality in its most firmly recognized social form: the institution of marriage. His conviction that a lasting and more satisfying identity can be achieved through a turning outward of the self in love is expressed throughout his poetry: it lies behind his early dramatizations of futile introspection ("The Two Voices," "The Supposed Confession of a Second-Rate Sensitive Mind") and his brilliant portrait of an isolated mind in "Maud." The *Idylls* envision an entire social order created through a communal sense of identity—and dependent on the commitment to mutuality of a representative marriage.

Browning maintained that he had always intended to write dramatic rather than introspective poetry.[10] After "Pauline" he made certain that his monologues did not suggest their author's public exploration of his own identity. But Browning had once been attracted by lyrical, openly autobiographical poetry. He wrote Elizabeth Barrett that "you *do* what I always wanted, hoped to do. . . . You speak out, *you,*—I only make men and women speak—give you truth broken into prismatic hues, and fear the pure white light, even if it is in me."[11] The poet of "the pure white light" was, of course, Shelley, the "sun-treader" whom he had evoked as inspiration in his "Fragment of a Confession," "Pauline," and whose spirit he deliberately banished from "Sordello" and the poetry that followed.[12] Shelley was the type of the "subjective" poet, as Browning was later to describe him, for whom song and self were the same: "what he produces will be less a work than an effluence . . . indeed the very radiance and aroma of his personality, projected from it but not separated."[13] In his own poetry self was to have no such role. "*My* poetry is far from 'the completest expression of my being.' "[14]

This deliberate suppression of self had potentially frightening consequences, as Browning hinted in an extraordinary description of himself to Elizabeth Barrett.

> To be grand in simile, for every poor speck of a Vesuvius or a Stromboli in my microcosm there are huge layers of ice and pits of cold water—and I make the most of my two or three fire-eyes, because I know by experience, alas, how these tend to extinction—and the ice grows and grows. . . . I am utterly unused, of these late years particularly, to dream of communicating anything about *that* to another person (all my writings are purely dramatic as I am always anxious to say). . . .[15]

Purging his poetry of morbid introspection, the young poet felt he risked extinguishing vital emotion in himself altogether, risked condemning himself to a kind of Dantean hell where "the ice grows and grows." Elizabeth Barrett did not require him to extinguish the "fire-eyes" he showed to her, and in the next twenty years Browning articulated his new method for exploring the "layers of ice and pits of cold water," without introspection, in his poetry.

"Fra Lippo Lippi" (1855) first described the redirection of the autobiographical impulse which Browning defended at length in his own voice at the beginning of *The Ring and the Book* (1868). Fra Lippo will paint only what he sees outside himself. He refuses to maintain artistic isolation, moving back and forth over the walls of monastery or Medici mansion. And the artistic process itself, he argues, permits him an imaginative participation in the society he paints, like that he claims when he follows pretty girls down Florentine alleys. "Lending our minds out" (I.306) we embody ourselves in what we see and paint. This desire is graphically realized at the end of the poem when Fra Lippo imagines how he will paint himself into his picture. His art becomes a means, not for direct self-exploration, but for the affirmation of an identity based on community. Returning to this conception of the artist in *The Ring and the Book,* Browning describes how "by a special gift, an art of arts. . . ./ I can detach from me, commission forth/ Half of my soul" (I.746, 749–50) and send it out to reanimate the shades of the dead. The artist or poet who

> bounded, yearning to be free,
> May so project his surplusage of soul
> In search of body, so add self to self
> By owning what lay ownerless before (I.722–5)

can not only, as Browning claims, give dramatic life to the past, he can also free himself from the restrictions of morbid introspection or of a deliberate suppression of identity in his work. Under the guise of a dramatic fiction, the poet can "add self to self," reaching out to affirm his own now-multiplied identity through his sympathy for the people for whom he speaks. He finds a route through poetry to the identity of mutuality. At the same time, of course, he permits himself and his readers to regain the distance necessary for moral judgment—a distance which the youthful author of

"Pauline" could not achieve. In the dramatic monologue, Browning finds a way for the objective poet to make his work, too, "the very radiance and aroma of his personality, projected from it but not separated."

Arnold does not share Browning's and Tennyson's radical struggle to alter the metaphors, form, and structure of the greater romantic lyric in order to praise mutuality. He does articulate more exactly and powerfully than any of his contemporaries their conviction that neither Christian remembrance of God nor romantic imaginative experience could change a painful isolation of the self. "Yes! in the sea of life enisled, . . . We mortal millions live *alone*," his "To Marguerite—Continued" begins. The perplexing word is "Yes!"; the tone of the poem is hardly affirmative. Between the first and last stanzas something happens which makes that "Yes!" impossible. Isolation, at the beginning of the poem, may even be fruitful. Through it, the islands know "their endless bounds." The phrase is marvellously ambiguous. If "endless" is temporal, the mortal millions discover that individual identity is permanent, and as such, a kind of bondage. The "Yes!" is contradicted even before the "But" of the second stanza. But "endless" is also spatial, and suggests that the individual, circular bounds of each island may potentially be extended infinitely—to include every island. The character of the sea in the preceding line strengthens this possibility. The mortal islands perceive it as "enclasping," folding each of them in a common embrace. They also feel it as "flow": the "sea of life" has suddenly become something very like a river of life. The islands perceive in it not only a shared embrace but also a shared directional movement. Individual identity then becomes the means to mutual identity, and a shared sense of purpose. We are probably not mistaken if we are reminded of "the sea of faith" in "Dover Beach," and follow the metaphor back to Donne's "No man is an island."

The desire which is kindled in the next two stanzas, however, ignores the uniting potential of the sea and regrets the absence of more solid connections ("For surely once, they feel, we were/Parts of a single continent!"). The setting (moonlit hollows, balmy spring, singing nightingales) allows us to recognize this impulse as a specific romantic one. But Arnold's poem ends very differently from Keats'. The last stanza allows neither uncertainty nor ambiguity: the romantic desire is "cool'd" and "render[ed] vain"; the "enclasping flow" is altered to "The umplumb'd, salt, estranging sea." Both romantic and Christian attempts to nullify individual isolation are declared void. Song is abandoned, verbal paradox is given up, metaphor is progressively reduced to single, separate terms. The sea of life is lifeless, the sea of faith, faithless. The link established in metaphor is destroyed, and we are left with seas and lives and a memory of faith, which the imagination cannot unite. Figurative connection becomes literal isolation, a characteristic movement in Arnold's poetry. This disintegration of metaphor can be as moving as its incredible extensions by Ruskin, but both lead, as Arnold recognized, to the end of poetry.

Ruskin shared the poets' distaste for solitary self-discovery in print, and for very similar reasons. *Praeterita,* like "The Two Voices," "Empedocles on Etna," and "Childe Roland to the Dark Tower Came," portrays introspective journeying as isolated, self-involved, and finally fruitless: incapable of yielding a confident sense of self, or an exhilarating view of a purposeful life. Ruskin began his autobiography with the sense that the solitary quest for identity had failed, and, indeed, had been mistaken from the start.

A passage from an early version of *Praeterita* is a quite candid confession of shapelessness: "I was a mere piece of potter's clay, of fine texture, and could not only be shaped into anything, but could take the stamp of anything, and that with precision." So far of his 23-year-old self, but Ruskin continues in the present tense:

> Which is the real virtue of me as respects other people. What shape of vase or cylinder I may arrive at myself is really of small consequence to them, but the impressions I take of things of them are trustworthy to the last line, and by the end of the forty years became sufficiently numerous. (618)

Ruskin's familiar arrogance is there in the assertion that his impressions are "trustworthy to the last line." There is also a note of apology or defense, perhaps for the absence (and indeed, the condemnation) of introspection: Ruskin's self is "of small consequence" to his readers. But the final admission, which Ruskin may have wished to suppress when he cancelled the passage, is telling: at the age of 65 he felt he still had no shape, no identity beyond that of passive and precise observer. He was too amorphous to impress himself upon others. Shape or shapelessness may have been "of small consequence" to his readers, but it was of great concern to Ruskin himself. Again and again in *Praeterita* he regrets lost opportunities to *be* something or someone more definite than a sensitive eye: a geologist, a skilled draftsman; or a lover, friend, or husband.

Ruskin's distaste for his protean identity is reflected in his playful epithets for his younger self. At 21, for example, he is "simply a little floppy and soppy tadpole,—little more than a stomach with a tail to it, flattening and wriggling itself up the crystal ripples and in the pure sands of the spring-head of youth" (279–80). He is as unformed and self-contained as "a squash before 'tis a peascod," a "codling or cocoon" (261); as ludicrously but pathetically inept in social situations "as a skate in an aquarium trying to get up the glass" (180). Ruskin's humor, for all its deliberate grotesqueness, allows him to convey an important perception about himself while keeping "morbid" introspection out of the autobiography. The unformed or amorphous creatures to which he compares himself are almost totally self-contained or self-involved. Their innocent, stubborn self-sufficiency is both ridiculous and sad, seen from any other perspective than their own. Though the bitterness in the observation is muted, Ruskin portrays the process through which his identity was formed as excessively isolated and self-absorbed, a chrysalid period which, however, failed in the end to yield the expected psyche.

Praeterita, like *In Memoriam,* is autobiography which opposes a self-involvement which it must nonetheless record. In Ruskin's case the persistence of the child's view of the world, shaping the memories of the older man, is itself the best evidence that he is right: he has not escaped the self-involvement of his childhood, in spite of opportunities to do so. He has, however, consciously rejected it, and he presents in *Praeterita* an alternative to introspective isolation. Each of the three major Victorian poets had preceded him in the attempt to replace a program of internal questing, identified with romanticism, with a deliberate turning outward of the self. For Tennyson this outward turn was a movement of the heart and feelings, first experienced in his friendship with Hallam, then lost and recovered in a subversive romantic lyric, *In Memoriam*. Arnold's movement outward is accomplished by giving up poetry for criticism, where the concern for self-expression is consciously replaced by a concern for the needs of his audience. Browning's turn is a change of voice, from lyric to dramatic monologue, displacing and multiplying the "self" of his poetry. For Ruskin the change is learning to see in a different way, turning the self outward through the eyes. The most important episodes in *Praeterita* are those in which Ruskin's eyes are opened—to mountains at Schaffhausen and the Col de la Faucille, to ivy or aspen structure at Norwood and Fontainebleau, to art in Italy, to Veronese in the sunlight at Turin. These views become emblems of Ruskin's peculiar sensibility—a way of describing the self while at the same time extending the self. Sharing his landscapes with thousands of readers of his prose descriptions, he makes these visual analogues of himself a means of breaking the chrysalid of his childhood. But Ruskin's escape from isolating forms of self-discovery and self-involved writing is only partly successful. The descriptions of his childhood perceptions show us that visual study of everything outside the self tended to become a form of self-regarding vision after all. The "secluded years" (132) in the "self-engrossed quiet of the Herne Hill life" (138) appear in *Praeterita* as one long process of morbid introspection because everything the young Ruskin sees *becomes* himself. The book suggests that his redirected visual appetite did not entirely relieve him of the burden of an unsatisfying identity, conceived in an isolation which the hungry eye could not alter.

II

Discontent with solitary self-discovery appears also as direct criticism of the romantic programme, especially of the private quest, in the poetry of the 1850s. It was almost always a critique from within: poems whose nominal form and kind were introspective, like *In Memoriam* (1850), or in which quests were major metaphors ("The Scholar-Gypsy" in 1853, "Childe Roland" in 1855), yet which questioned the validity of this pursuit of self-knowledge and fulfillment. In their quarrel with romantic models for discovering the self, the poets turned the forms and metaphors of the introspective romantic lyric inside out.

Perhaps the most influential of these models was Wordsworth. *The Prelude,* published posthumously in 1850, invites comparison with the Victorian alterations of introspective poetry in the decade that followed.[16] There are two points of particular importance to be noted from *The Prelude:* first, Wordsworth is as confident at the beginning of his poem as he is at its end that he can perceive his life as a movement in a single direction. Second, his confidence is confirmed in the famous spots of time, moments of private vision which give him what is really self-revelation. This is the pattern which both Ruskin and the poets attempt to follow and finally reject.

Book I of *The Prelude* closes with Wordsworth's anticipation of shape in the life he is about to recount:

> forthwith shall be brought down
> Through later years the story of my life.
> The road lies plain before me;—'tis a theme
> Single and of determined bounds. . . . (638–41)

At the end of Book XIV he again describes a view of his life attained before the beginning of his song:

> I said unto the life which I had lived,
> Where art thou? . . .
> . . . Anon I rose

> As if on wings, and saw beneath me stretched
> Vast prospect of the world which I had been
> And was; and hence this Song. . . . (377–82)

To the road and the prospect he adds a third metaphor for his sense of an inner life forming a continuous, clearly visible whole, the stream:

> We have traced the stream
> From the blind cavern whence is faintly heard
> Its natal murmur; followed it to light
> And open day: accompanied its course
> Among the ways of Nature, for a time
> Lost sight of it bewildered and engulphed;
> Then given it greeting as it rose once more
> In strength, reflecting from its placid breast
> The works of man and face of human life;
> And lastly, from its progress have we drawn
> Faith in life endless, the sustaining thought
> Of human Being, Eternity, and God. (XIV.194–205)

The tracing of the stream makes explicit what the image of the road already promised: that Wordsworth's life is not only continuous movement but purposive movement in one direction: it is progress towards a goal, "The Growth of a Poet's Mind" to maturity, a journey to a now-achieved identity which is profoundly satisfying to the poet.

The prospect of his life as road or stream is attained in the ascent to vision. Wordsworth revisits "spots of time" which "retain/A renovating virtue . . . which enables us to mount/When high, more high, and lifts us up when fallen" (XII.210; 217–18). The remembered spots of time reveal to reflection what the vision on Mt. Snowden—the classic moment of revelation—immediately illuminated: the imagination or "Power of mind" which both shapes the poet's life and gives it its purpose, to celebrate the "mind of Man" in poetry. The mind reveals itself to itself, both in Wordsworth's visions and, for the reader, in the experience of the poem.

Tennyson's subtitle for *In Memoriam,* "The Way of a Soul," suggests that he will, like Wordsworth, trace a single movement or progress in time. Some structural features of the poem confirm this, notably the periodic measurement of passing time in the Christmas sections. Tennyson also makes an ascent to visionary experience (Section 95) following a major depression, and after that vision accepts his present life. The poem ends with the celebration of a marriage. All these elements link his poem not only with Wordsworth's but with the long tradition of spiritual autobiography descending from Augustine.[17] But external structure and subtitle—imposed, in fact, after much of the poem was written—do not entirely correspond either to what the poem says or how it is said. More accurately, the poem subverts the form which it nominally resembles. The effect of Hallam's death on Tennyson is to make him reject the idea of life as a way, road, path, or track, and to try to replace it with a different sense of life's shape.

The speaker's attitude toward the traditional autobiographer's view of his life changes only gradually in the course of the poem. In Section 22 he recalls "the path by which we twain did go" in their four years of friendship. This view of their entwined lives is quite adequate; in fact, he remembers, "we with singing cheer'd the way." In Section 23, abandoned by Hallam, Tennyson is left to "wander, often falling lame." In this and the next three sections, he looks "back to whence I came,/Or on to where the pathway leads" (23), but the prospect is in both cases painful. Looking back, he cries "How changed" (23); looking forward, he finds "Still onward winds the dreary way; I with it" (26). "I know that this was Life,—the track/Whereon with equal feet we fared" (25), he reflects, but his perception of life as a track is strongest when it has become least appealing, when he is left to walk it alone. By Section 38, Tennyson's progress along the track has slowed almost to a halt, and his views, both forward and backward, have disappeared.

> With weary steps I loiter on,
>   Tho' always under alter'd skies
>   The purple from the distance dies,
> My prospect and horizon gone.

Once Tennyson's and Hallam's paths diverge (40), the single motion and prospect of which Wordsworth was so

confident become, for Tennyson, first a burden and finally
an impossibility. Section 46 confirms the viewlessness as a
general human phenomenon. Memory, especially, fails to
provide us with a sense of continuous life, "The path we
came by, thorn and flower,/Is shadow'd by the growing
hour/Lest life should fail in looking back." Autobiography,
in the usual sense of the word, is under such conditions
impossible. There is, for Tennyson, only one perspective
from which a view is possible:

> . . . there no shade can last
>   In that deep dawn behind the tomb,
>   But clear from marge to marge shall bloom
> The eternal landscape of the past. (46)

From that perspective, however, life does not appear as a
track or path or way at all. It is fully occupied space, not
time stretched like a road from point to point. It is a flower-
ing "eternal landscape," "a lifelong tract of time" with rich
fields and "fruitful hours of still increase"—where "still"
is a wonderful paradox of silent, stopped motion which
nonetheless suggests continued fruitfulness. This view of
life as a fruitful landscape, in which loitering will be a
pleasure, is already Hallam's, and it resembles the view
which Tennyson and Hallam took of their lives when they
were together and still unconscious of passing time.
Tennyson does not want to ascend to Wordsworth's clear
view of his life as road or stream progressing to a goal. He
wants to see it as a landscape, preferably fruitful, of course:
a whole in which progress or purposive action do not exist.
Hallam holds the memory of Tennyson's past, and thus his
identity; he also holds the secret of a way of viewing that
identity which Tennyson finds far more satisfactory.

There are only two ways for Tennyson to attain this
vision: to die, or somehow to regain Hallam's companionship. This is what he achieves in Section 95, after he has
at last relaxed his conscious will (Section 70) which clings,
like the yew tree, to the memory of the dead Hallam. Gradually and involuntarily, in dream, daydream, memory, and
trance, Tennyson moves outward from himself to his friend,

until he has recaptured the experience of mutuality which had once given him a different sense of his identity. Section 95 is not, like Wordsworth's Snowden experience or Augustine's vision in the garden, the revelation to Tennyson of who he is, or where he is going. It is a reunion ("The living soul was flashed on mine,/And mine in this was wound") accompanied by a new, musical harmony in what Tennyson, treading the weary path, had heard as "The steps of Time the shocks of Chance—/The blows of Death." The reunion makes possible the marriage at the poem's end, a "happy hour" which recalls the "fruitful hours" of Hallam's view of life, or of Tennyson's and Hallam's mutual experience. The marriage itself may exemplify the harmonization of temporal steps which Tennyson, united with Hallam, could hear, for he says "In that it is thy marriage day/Is music more than any song." His own poem is not that music; "the songs I made" sound to him, after his reunion with Hallam, "As echoes out of weaker times,/As half but idle brawling rhymes." This is harsh, but we should recognize that Tennyson's poem is a mixed vision and a mixed music. Its external structure is that of the spiritual autobiography. But as we follow the poem, we, like Tennyson, lose our way, and find ourselves loitering and viewless, turned back on ourselves in beautiful lyrics of enclosing rhymes—by a poet who is curiously indirect about what is happening to him. The poem means to question, I think, the essential elements of the pilgrimage autobiography, both Christian and romantic: the view that one's self can be discovered by tracing the temporal path of one's life, that the self must be a solitary figure, and that that figure can or should pursue an introspective journey toward a self-revealing vision.

Yet, paradoxically, Tennyson recovers the identity of mutuality when he is most alone. Hallam touches him, in Section 95, after his friends leave him. His final vision of Hallam as the type of a perfected humanity comes when he retires from the marriage feast to watch the moon rise. And in that vision Tennyson finds a perspective from which life *can* be seen as temporal path. The way of the soul which cannot be traced by the isolated traveler reappears as a collective destiny. Tennyson finally has it both ways: for the individual, identity is conferred through mutuality, and life assumes the aspect of the fruitful field. But through friendship and marriage the individual also affirms his membership in a larger community. The evolution of the human race possesses that linear shape which the isolated individual cannot see in his own life. *In Memoriam* does not dispense with solitary vision or linear progress, but it does deliberately frustrate our expectations of an introspective journey towards that vision, and alter the content of that vision as well. If Tennyson succeeds, he will finally convince us that his strangely atemporal wanderings among regretful and happy memories, daydreams, and dreams, constitute a different approach to exploring and presenting the self.

The "river of our life" ("The Buried Life," 1.39) proves as unsatisfactory a metaphor for Arnold as "Life's track" for Tennyson. Arnold's stream cannot be traced as Wordsworth's could and was. It is buried permanently, not just "for a time/Lost sight of." "Unregarded" (39) and indeed "indiscernible" (40), the stream cannot fulfill its major function, to assure a perception of purposive movement in a single direction. Even if one's life really does have such a shape (and Arnold, unlike Tennyson, does not deny that it does), the knowledge is useless to the individual in search of himself, who can only perceive that we "seem to be/ Eddying at large in blind uncertainty" (42-3). The ascent to vision is as impossible as the preliminary view. The most one can hope for is a momentary awareness "of his life's flow" (88), which comes, significantly, not through introspection but through the hand, the eyes, the voice of someone else. Mutual recognition *may* lead to self-cognition, but the moment is hardly visionary. At best, "he thinks he knows/The hills where his life rose,/And the sea where it goes" (96–8).

The speaker in "The Scholar-Gypsy," like the modern man of "The Buried Life," is a latter-day romantic quester, but the man he seeks and finds is not himself. The speaker

follows the scholar-gypsy, who is looking for a lost art. It
is the art of questing which the speaker has lost, however.
His quest provides him with a kind of identity, but only by
contrast with the quester of old:

> O life unlike to ours!
> Who fluctuate idly without term or scope,
> Of whom each strives, nor knows for what he strives,
> And each half lives a hundred different lives;
> Who wait like thee, but not, like thee, in hope. (166-70)

Arnold's scholar-gypsy, Tennyson's Ulysses and Galahad,
and Browning's Childe Roland, are sadly out of date. Their
solitary journeys are possibly glorious but almost certainly
suicidal. They bring back no visions and no gospel. The
would-be modern quester, like Arnold's speaker, does not
even attain the prospects afforded to his ill-fated models. In
place of the single life, he is likely to perceive "a half a
hundred"—loose threads attached to no ends, which only
later autobiographers will discover are perpetually woven
and unwoven, Penelope-fashion, into the fabric of a differently conceived self.

Childe Roland, last of the late questers of the 1850s, out-
lives his companions but not his quest. He has no emula-
tors. His quest has none of the appeal to which someone
like Arnold's speaker can respond. The scholar-gypsy is im-
mortally young; the "childe" is a perpetual adolescent,
still seeking his adult identity. The scholar-gypsy wanders
through an anachronistically pastoral landscape; the childe
tries vainly to see symbolic significance in what might well
be an industrial wasteland. The childe's path behaves very
much like Tennyson's track: it disappears behind him and
darkens in front of him. The reasons for the shadowing
may be the same: "Better this present than a past like that"
(103), the childe says. The fading path is not replaced by
any vision of fruitful space like that Tennyson can imagine,
however. The childe remains committed to his path and his
goal; he sees everything else as "gray plain all round:/
Nothing but plain to the horizon's bound" (52-3). The
childe's goal is quite dark, too, and what is more, it remains

so when he finally reaches it—not only dark, but viewless: "blind as the fool's heart" (182). The signs of the long-expected revelation are all there: recognition ("This was the place!" 176), light ("why, day/Came back again for that!" 187-8), and annunciatory sound ("it tolled/Increasing like a bell" 193-4). But the tolling bells are doubly ominous; they announce his death, he assumes, but to us they may also echo a forlorn return "to my sole self." The childe's arrival at a tower "blind as the fool's heart" supports that possibility, but it doesn't promise much in the way of self-revelation. Sight and sound do tell the childe something, but he does not directly apply it to himself. "Names in my ears/ Of all the lost adventurers my peers,— . . . /Lost, lost! one moment knelled the woe of years" (194-5, 198). "In a sheet of flame/I saw them and I knew them all," he continues, "And yet . . ." (201-2). The childe blows his horn to proclaim an arrival already stated in the past tense.

The poem ends, but the "sheet of flame" has not illuminated either the Dark Tower or the disappearing path along which he has come. His consciousness of his past, of his present identity, and of his apparently achieved goal is no different than it has ever been. The ascent to vision, if that is what it was, was a hoax: it gave him no new prospect. His life is what he experienced while he lived it, not to be transformed by a single moment of action or vision, no matter how faithfully pursued. We don't know whether the childe sees even this much before he blows his horn. It is a wonderful gesture, but just how blindly heroic we can't tell. Is he still looking for his moment of truth, in a final confrontation with the unknown? Or does he realize he has had it, that the end of his quest is only to be able to announce, "Childe Roland to the Dark Tower came"?

Browning's poem is a radical critique of the romantic programme, yet it acknowledges the attraction as well as the dangers of the solitary quest to a Victorian. It is in some ways the most personal of Browning's poems, to be read together with the essay in praise of Shelley which he finished only two years later. Yet the personal material—the same that he used in the "intense and morbid" "Pauline" seventeen years earlier—is brilliantly controlled in "Childe Roland." The means by which this poetic control is achieved, lending the mind out to realize itself in dramatic fictions, is Browning's alternative to Childe Roland's suicidal heroism.

Sixty-seven years later Pound recognized in Browning's dramatic experiment "Sordello" the redirected autobiographical impulse I have suggested. "You had your business," he tells Browning in an early draft of Canto I:

> To set out so much thought, so much emotion;
> To paint, more real than any dead Sordello,
> The half or third of your intensest life
> And call that third *Sordello;*
> And you'll say, "No, not your life,
> He never showed himself."
> Is't worth the evasion, what were the use
> Of setting figures up and breathing life upon them,
> Were't not *our* life, your life, my life, extended?[18]

But fragmented, fictional autobiography was not, finally, what Pound wanted in his *Cantos*. His rejection of the romantic quest for identity was still more drastic than Browning's. The monologues were too taken up with the narrative, "prose part" of a character's life; Pound wanted only "to catch the character I happen to be interested in at the moment he interests me."[19] And in the final version of his argument with Browning, Pound rejected an autobiographical interest in multiple Pounds to concern himself with multiple Sordellos.

> Hang it all, Robert Browning, there can be but one "Sordello."
> But Sordello, and my Sordello?
> *Lo Sordels si fo di Mantovana.*

Pound's lines record the shift from autobiography to history which Browning himself began.

"The Way of a Soul," when Browning, Arnold, and Tennyson explore it in the 1850s, turns out to be far more devious than the open road which beckoned Wordsworth. To follow a single, temporal path seems difficult, perhaps impossible. Worse than that, to pursue it is to be misled, and for the poet, to be misleading as well. A growing concern with consciousness rather than simple action points to a new view of individual life not as a pilgrimage but as an intricate, unfinished web of memory and human connection, "that strange, perpetual weaving and unweaving of ourselves." Explicit concern with consciousness isolated from moral action is not acceptable to the Victorians any more than the old view of self-discovery as a form of moral action, a quest for individual truth. The deliberate pursuit of patterns of consciousness, Pater discovers, seems as morbid, self-involved, and probably fruitless as romantic questing. But those patterns can be suggested indirectly, by using literary forms and structures new to autobiographical writing. Tennyson and Browning are the great Victorian pioneers, using fictional more often than actual autobiography for their experiments. These experiments lead in two directions. Tennyson, Ruskin, and finally Proust replace the isolated traveler on the single track with views of fruitful landscapes or remembered experiences, to suggest the texture of a sensibility. Browning, the Tennyson of the monologues, Carlyle, and Butler divide the self into multiple characters—protagonists, editors, narrators—and by this imaginative displacement of the self reach out toward more complex and less introspective identities. Joyce and Pound inherit their strategies. The new *Ulysses* will be irrevocably wedded to a Victorian-born Penelope.

1. (London: Macmillan, 1910), p. 236.

2. *The Poetical Works of Matthew Arnold,* ed. C. B. Tinker and H. F. Lowry. London: Oxford University Press, 1950, p.xviii (1853 Preface).

3. *The Works of John Ruskin, Library Edition,* ed. E. T. Cook and Alexander Wedderburn 39 vols. London, (1903-1912). Vol. 5, 206, 208. Further references to Ruskin's works will be given in the text by volume and page (5.206) or by page alone in the case of *Praeterita,* volume 35 of the *Works.*

4. *Alfred Lord Tennyson. A Memoir by His Son.* (New York: Macmillan, 1897), II, 372 and I, 317.

5. Note in Mill's copy of the poem, quoted by W. Hall Griffin and Harry C. Minchin, *The Life of Robert Browning.* (Hamden, Conn.: Archon Books, 1966 [reprint of the 3rd ed., 1938]), pp. 59-60.

6. As Byron's Manfred had discovered, "The Tree of Knowledge is not that of Life" (I, 1, line 12).

7. 1853 Preface, p. xxix.

8. *Ibid.*

9. This shift had already begun, however, with Shelley and Byron.

10. *See* Browning's note in his own copy of "Pauline," and also his response to Mill in Mill's copy, quoted by William Clyde DeVane, *A Browning Handbook*. (New York: Appleton-Century-Crofts, 1955), p. 41.

11. *The Letters of Robert Browning and Elizabeth Barrett Browning,* 1845-1846, ed. Elvan Kintner. (Cambridge, Mass.: Harvard University Press, 1969), p. 7.

12. . . . stay—thou, spirit, come not near
Now—not this time desert thy cloudy place
To scare me, thus employed, with that pure face! ("Sordello" I.60-2)

13. "Introductory Essay" (for *Letters of Shelley,* 1851), in *The Complete Works of Robert Browning.* (New York: Thomas Crowell, 1898), XII, 286.

14 Quoted by Betty Miller, *Robert Browning: A Portrait.* (London: John Murray, 1952), p. 12.

15. *Letters,* p. 74.

16. Wordsworth's attitudes were known to those who had not seen *The Prelude* through the shorter autobiographical poems like "Tintern Abbey" and "Ode: Intimations of Immortality."

17. *See* M. H. Abrams, *Natural Supernaturalism.* (New York: Norton, 1971).

18. *Poetry. A Magazine of Verse* 10 (1917), 114-5.

19. *The Letters of Ezra Pound. 1907-1914,* ed. D. D. Paige. (New York: Harcourt Brace, 1950), pp. 3-4.

Where Was Rousseau?

One of the most puzzling aspects of Victorian autobiographies is the absence of evidence that they were influenced in any way by Jean-Jacques Rousseau's *Confessions*. This is a point to ponder because Rousseau's is the first great secular confession, a defiant assertion of the right of the ordinary man to command attention. Its novelistic structure was unique in its time for careful attention to the separate periods of childhood, adolescence, maturity and lonely old age. The raw material of a lifetime is skillfully crafted so that the episodes build up cumulatively to "spots of time," epiphanies, or decisive turning-points. In terms of both form and content the *Confessions* was a breakthrough—but one which the Victorians chose to ignore.

There are, of course, some obvious reasons why Rousseau could not serve as a model for the Victorians. The insularity of the English and their special suspicion of the French may be a commonplace, but it cannot be dismissed. In many minds, moreover, Rousseau was a particularly dangerous Frenchman, an instigator of the Revolution; one must remember the lamentable image Rousseau had presented on his visit to England. Then, too, many influential English figures anticipated Irving Babbitt's view that everything deplorable in Romanticism was epitomized in Rousseau; the abortive nature of the Romantic movement in Britain is an historical fact, attested to by (*inter alia*) Matthew Arnold's denigrating remarks about the Romantic tendency to self-pity and self-revelation. (Wordsworth was accepted for his practical cheerfulness and because, so far as anyone

26

knew, he led an exemplary life.) Most serious of all was Rousseau's unabashed admission of reprehensible conduct. Here was a man who had abandoned his children to a foundling home, who unhesitatingly and unequivocally described his sexual life, who displayed a paranoid obsession about his enemies and named them publicly, and who espoused an antinomianism which threatened the established social order. And it must be added that even in France many readers considered him both self-deceiving and self-serving.

How could the *épanchement de coeur* of such a monster be acceptable to the prudish and reticent world of the Victorians? A remark in Anthony Trollope's *Autobiography* (1883) is representative of the typical Victorian autobiographer, considering himself a spokesman not only for himself but also for his society: "That I or any man should tell everything of himself I hold to be impossible. Who could endure to own the doing of a mean thing? Who is there who has done none?"

Nonetheless, there is incontrovertible evidence that many Victorians venerated Rousseau. George Eliot, for example, wrote to Sara Hennell on February 9, 1849:

> It would signify nothing to me if a very wise person were to stun me with proofs that Rousseau's views of life, religion, and government are miserably erroneous—that he was guilty of some of the worst basenesses that have degraded civilized man. I might admit all this— and it would be not the less true that Rousseau's genius has sent that electric thrill through my intellectual and moral frame which has awakened me to fresh perceptions, which has made man and nature a fresh world of thought and feeling to me—and this not by teaching me any new belief. It is simply that the rushing mighty wind of his inspiration has so quickened my faculties that I have been able to shape more definitely for myself ideas which had previously dwelt as dim 'ahnungen' in my soul—the fire of his genius has so fused together old thoughts and prejudices, that I have been ready to make new combinations.[1]

John Ruskin also willingly admitted the importance of Rousseau's genius to his own life and career, and he several times compares himself to his great predecessor, telling his father, for example, "I know of no man whom I more entirely resemble than Rousseau. If I were asked whom of all men

of any name in past time I thought myself to be grouped
with, I should answer unhesitatingly, Rousseau, I judge by
The *Nouvelle Héloïse*, the *Confessions*, the writings on
politics, and the life in the Ile St. Pierre."[2] He similarly
wrote to his mother that "the intense resemblance between
me and Rousseau, in mind, and even in many of the chances
of life, increases upon my mind more and more; and as I
look this morning through the bright sunshine to the lake of
Bienne, or rather to the woods above it, I cannot help won-
dering if the end of my life is to be in seclusion or in ill-
temper like his."[3] Rousseau, in fact, left a heavy impress
upon Ruskin's thought, for, as E. T. Cook pointed out long
ago, "Ruskin—romanticist and reformer—may well be classed
among the intellectual descendants of Rousseau. Without
Rousseau, would there have been Ruskin? In describing his
visit to Switzerland, he notes the blessedness of such
entrance into life for a child of such a temperament as his.
And then he adds: 'True, the temperament belonged to his
age: a very few years—within the hundred—before that, no
child could have been born to care for mountains in that
way. Till Rousseau's time there had been no 'sentimental
love of nature.' "[4]

What George Eliot and John Ruskin are talking about is
a sensibility. Neither of them, quite clearly, felt the com-
pulsion to unburden their hearts publicly, although in both
cases there had been sufficient scandal and misrepresentation
to justify an autobiography to set the record straight. One
could argue, of course, that George Eliot's use of the novel
as a vehicle for her ethical ideas was in some measure a
form of self-justification; and in a certain sense Ruskin's
Praeterita is the rambling (if expurgated) self-indulgence
of old age. But neither sought, as Rousseau did, to expose a
private life to public view in order to defend it.

The typical Victorian autobiographer was acutely aware
of his audience. A mutual complicity shaped the genre, and
language became a screen to shelter the vulnerable egos of
writer and reader alike. The very act of creating a persona
through language caused an alienation between self and
non-self. The various versions of John Stuart Mill's autobiography indicate how meticulously Harriet Taylor and

Mill shaped a dual image, acceptable to the public and reassuring to themselves. De Quincey's *Confessions of an English Opium Eater* contain many passages which are in effect a penitential plea to heal the estrangement between his erring self and censorious society—even at the risk of "breaking through those restraints of delicate reserve":

> On the one hand, as my self-accusation does not amount to a confession of guilt, so, on the other, it is possible that, if it did, the benefit resulting to others, from the record of an experience purchased at so heavy a price of suffering and one of self-conquest, might compensate, by a vast overbalance, any violence done to the feelings I have noticed, and justify a breach of the general rule.[5]

Rousseau believed that once men had read the true record of his life, his sincerity and his suffering were such that he would be eternally vindicated. Claiming "I am like no one in the whole world," he did not profess to utilize his life as an object-lesson to other sinners because the whole basis of his self-definition was uniqueness.[6] Such egoism would have been anathema to the Victorians, for whom autobiography had to have an ostensible value for others. Lives of prominent men provided working models for their readers to emulate. "If . . . I were a hero of whatever kind whatever," announces the narrator of the semi-fictional *Autobiography of Mark Rutherford* (1881), "I might perhaps be justified in communicating my success to mankind and stimulating them to do as I have done."[7] In a period when the foundations of orthodox Christianity were revealing alarming cracks, religious leaders constantly urged their flocks to study the lives and works of good men as illustrations of the active virtues. While only a certain enthusiastic coterie embraced the Comtist Religion of Humanity, the majority, in an era in which the Carlylean Hero tended to absorb the qualities of Godhead, erected the lives of great men into a quasi-hagiography. This attempt to create a new system of affirmations might strike a sharp-eyed observer like W. H. Mallock as "a solemn farce," but both autobiographer and average reader regarded the enterprise with deep earnestness.[8]

The word "autobiography" was coined early in the cen-

tury by Southey. The term was used interchangeably with
"biography" by Carlyle, who viewed both genres as inval-
uable records of man, for, he asserted, "Man is perennially
interesting to man; nay, if we look strictly to it, there is
nothing else interesting." Contemptuously dismissing fictional representations as "so many mimic Biographies," he
cries for a magic rod to be thrust into the hands of the
bemused editor of *Fraser's,* in order that he might turn the
"artificial soap-lather, and mere Lying, into the faithful
study of Reality, what knowledge of great everlasting
Nature, and of Man's ways and doings therein, would not
every year bring us in!"[9] In a sense Carlyle achieved his
wish, for in the course of the century the genre became
increasingly respected, and by 1895 James Ashcroft Noble
was praising autobiography as the highest form of truth
because in this medium alone could lives be revealed by
"the only persons who could tell them with absolute truthfulness."[10] In addition, Noble emphasized another concept of
autobiography which was widely held among the Victorians: that it was a means of cementing the bonds of kinship between men. A far cry from the private fantasies of
Rousseau, the solitary *promeneur!*

If the Victorian autobiographer accepted the conventional
image the public demanded from him, at the same time
there were certain areas of his experience which he jeal-
ously guarded as a sacred preserve into which his readers
might not trespass. "The essential part of his life," says J. A.
Froude in his Preface to Carlyle's *Reminiscences,* "was in
his works, which those who chose could read. The private
part of it was a matter in which the world had no concern."[11]
There was one attitude of Trollope's with which his readers
fully concurred: "My marriage," he declared, "was like the
marriage of other people, and of no special interest to any
one except my wife and me," and so he passed on to a discussion of the modest earnings of *The Warden.*[12] Yet,
occasionally, into the most impersonal voice of the public
figure, the anguished cry of private grief breaks through.
Thus John Stuart Mill speaks of his marriage: "For seven
and a-half years that blessing was mine; for seven and a-half

only! I can say nothing which can describe even in the
faintest manner, what that loss was and is."[13] In Carlyle's
fragmented autobiography, he breaks off the narrative to
speak directly to his dead wife: "Thanks, darling, for your
shining words and acts, which were continual in my eyes,
and in no other mortal's. Worthless I was in your divinity,
wrapt in your perpetual love of me and pride in me, in
defiance of all men and things. Oh, was it not beautiful all
this that I have lost forever!"[14] And who can forget the
poignancy of Ruskin's simple summation of his childhood:
"I had nothing to love."[15]

If *Praeterita* (1885-8) is infinitely more self-revealing
than most Victorian autobiographies, it is for the most
pathetic of reasons. The early part, written in periods of
lucidity, flows without rupture; but the onset of madness is
apparent towards the end of the book as it trails off into an
incoherent account of Ruskin's obsession for Rose La
Touche. The writing of his autobiography gave him a measure of temporary relief in the opportunity it provided for
dwelling pleasurably on the past. "I have written
them. . . ," he says of his reminiscences in the Preface,
"frankly, garrulously, and at ease; speaking of what it gives
me joy to remember at any length I like—sometimes very
carefully of what I think it may be useful for others to know;
and in passing in total silence things which I have no pleasure
in reviewing, and which the reader would find no help in
the account of. My described life has thus become more
amusing than I expected, to myself."[16] Still, a life which
held as much personal misery as Ruskin's did, remains only
a truncated version of the truth if it has been edited primarily for public consumption.

The Victorian public seemed more amenable to accepting
anguished introspection if it was of a religious nature. More
questionable matter was admissible if the author was long
since dead. The contemporary *Journal Intime* of Henri-
Frederic Amiel exerted a morbid fascination for the Victorian sensibility, but its English translator, Mrs. Humphry
Ward, was fully aware that the attraction was one which
would not be accepted readily by many readers. In the Pref-

ace, she remarked that "the public which can admit the claims and overlook the inherent defects of introspective life has always been a small one," and she hastened to assure her readers reared on blander stuff that they "will find in it, not a volume of *Memoirs,* but the confidence of a solitary thinker, the meditations of a philosopher for whom the things of the soul were the sovereign realities of existence." She herself had been drawn to Amiel because "while he represents all the intellectual complexities of a time bewildered by the range and number of its own acquisitions, the religious instinct in him is as strong and tenacious as in any of the representative exponents of the life of faith."[17] As she has told us in *A Writer's Recollections,* her remarkably popular three-volume novel *Robert Elsmere* (1888) was conceived in the process of translating Amiel. It is significant that the public found such a tortuously analytic sensibility, closely akin to that of Amiel, easier to accept when it belonged to a fictional character.

Robert Louis Stevenson expressed deep uneasiness that Pepys should have disclosed the more reprehensible side of his character with such candor; it would have been a different matter if the revelations had issued from the pen of a foreigner. John Addington Symonds' translations of the uninhibited memoirs of Count Carlo Gozzi and Benvenuto Cellini were enormously successful; indeed, the latter went through three printings in less than eighteen months. Unrestrained as these memoirs might have appeared in comparison with those to which his readers were accustomed, Symonds felt constrained to explain that although Gozzi's candor was "the candour of a cleanly heart," he had yet felt obliged to remove "those passages and phrases which might have caused offence to some of my readers."[18] In the Preface to his translation of Cellini's autobiography, Symonds ventured to take a poke at his fellow-Victorians: "I hold him for a most veracious man," he said of his subject. "His veracity was not of the sort which is at present current. It had no hypocrisy or simulation in it."[19]

Symonds' own autobiography (published in 1976) was more significantly in the tradition of Rousseau's *Con-*

fessions than any other Victorian document.[20] His description of it as *Memoirs* is rather curious; it is, strictly speaking, a confessional, yet Symonds probably felt that the unobtrusive term "memoir" was far less emotionally charged and hence more appropriate to the quasi-scientific case history that he was attempting to write. Furthermore, even the term "autobiography" would be more appropriate than "memoir" if one accepts the differentiation which Roy Pascal makes in *Design and Truth in Autobiography* (1971). Pascal emphasizes that an autobiography's center of interest must be the narrator's self rather than the outside world, while *Memoirs* minimizes the notion of the narrator's evolving personality, stressing instead events and people external to him.

Symonds has recorded that from an early age he kept Rousseau's *Confessions* by his bed, yet in the *Memoirs* he acknowledges no debt to them. There are probably two reasons for this omission. In the first place, the whole thrust of his argument is that, as a homosexual, he had done nothing of which to be ashamed. With public pressures such as they were, he had been as true to his nature as possible; and even though he had indulged in acts which would not be condoned by the general public, he believed that he had always behaved in an upright and honorable manner. Secondly, unlike many modern Rousseau scholars, he did not recognize the possibility that Rousseau might have been a crypto-homosexual. He simply accepted at face value Rousseau's expressions of horror at homosexuality.

Nevertheless, in his attempt at being utterly sincere, some of his letters reveal that he readily accepted kinship with Rousseau. Although he did not begin to write what he considered the most important work of his life until 1889—that is, in his fiftieth year—as early as 1863, he wrote to a friend while still wrestling with the truth of his emotions: "I have often thought that, if I lived to do nothing else, I should write Confessions which would be better than Rousseau's and not less interesting. I sometimes think that I am being trained for this."[21] Nearly thirty years later,

after he had finally begun to write this long-planned undertaking, he wrote to his most intimate friend, Graham
Dakyns:

> My occupation with Cellini and Gozzi has infected me with their Lues
> Autobiographica; and I have begun scribbling my own reminiscences.
> This is a foolish thing to do, because I do not think they will ever
> be fit to publish. I have nothing to relate except the evolution of
> a character somewhat strangely constituted in its moral and aes-
> thetic qualities. The Study of this evolution, written with the candour
> and precision I feel capable of using, would I am sure be interesting
> to psychologists and not without its utility. There does not exist
> anything like it in print; and I am certain that ninety-nine men
> out of a thousand do not believe in the existence of a personality
> like mine. Still it would be hardly fair to posterity if I were to yield
> up my vile soul to the psychopathical investigators.
>
> I do not know therefore what will come of this undertaking. Very
> likely, I shall lay it aside, though the fragment is already considerable
> in bulk and curious in matter—and I feel it a pity, after acquiring
> the art of the autobiographer through translation of two master-
> pieces, not to employ my skill upon such a rich mine of psycho-
> logical curiosities, as I am conscious of possessing.
>
> This may appear rather conceited. But it is not so. I speak as an
> artist, who sees 'a subject' of which he is confident. *Infin del corti*
> I believe I shall go forward, and leave my executors to deal with
> what will assuredly be the most considerable product of my pen.
>
> You see I have 'never spoken out.' And it is a great temptation
> to speak out, when I have been living for two whole years in lonely
> intimacy with men who spoke out so magnificently as Cellini and
> Gozzi did.[22]

When he finally came to write the *Memoirs,* he was firmly
convinced that its revelations were such that they could
never be published in his lifetime. Rousseau, on the other
hand, gloried in reading aloud from his *Confessions,* sometimes for fifteen hours at a stretch, to a selected audience
in the salons until prohibited by the police: "I concluded
thus my readings, and everyone was silent. Alone Mme
d'Egmont seemed moved; she shuddered visibly; but she
quickly regained her composure; and remained as mute as
the rest of the company. Such was the fruit I harvested
from this reading and from my declaration."[23]

Since there was no such exhibitionism in Symonds, why
then did he abandon all other work for eighteen months,
for an enterprise which involved the evocation of painful

and sad memories? In part, the writing of the *Memoirs* was a therapeutic act—a catharsis and a liberation—as the *Confessions* had been for Rousseau. For each it was also an ordering of the confusion of his existence, and an *apologia pro vita sua*. For Rousseau no one like himself had ever existed. Symonds saw himself as unique in the modern world in his repeated assertions of the "pure" Hellenism of his homosexuality.

Symonds' Proustian recollection of his childhood is perhaps the finest section of the work. The importance he attached to childhood is described in a letter to Horatio Brown, who was destined to be the literary executor of the *Memoirs:* "According to my conception of such a work, the years of growth are the most important, and need the most elaborate analysis. . . . It is a fascinating canvas, this of Lebensschilderung, for a man who has been hitherto so reticent in writing, and who is so naturally egotistical and personal as I am."[24] Nevertheless, apart from the formation of his aesthetic responses, there is little indication that Symonds—writing a decade before Freud's *The Interpretation of Dreams*—recognized that an infantile traumatic fixation might have shaped his sexual proclivities. His two memories of his mother are, first, a terrifying experience of driving in a carriage with her when the horses suddenly bolted downhill, and, second, her death. The combination of the two—the terror engendered by the violent rocking from side to side within an enclosed space, and later a young child's bewilderment by the mystery of death—might well have given him deep psychological scars. But Symonds simply relates the two incidents, adding only that he can remember feeling no grief over his mother's death. Rousseau, on the other hand, recognized that the emotional and sentimental aspects of his nature were influenced irrevocably by his father's tears and caresses. Moreover, he seems within grasp of the fact that his sense of undefined guilt stemmed from his mother's death at his birth.

The celebrated episode in which Symonds was instrumental in ruining the career of the Headmaster of Harrow is revealing of his ambivalent behavior, part punitive and part confessional. Tattling to his father about Vaughan's proclivity for pederasty gave him, at one blow, both revenge against his teacher and mentor, and absolution from his beloved parent. This section of the manuscript is heavily scored, suggesting a general uneasiness; and the revisions were obviously made in an attempt to exculpate himself from direct blame. One is again reminded of that representative Victorian, Trollope: "Who could endure to own the doing of a mean thing?"[25] But Rousseau, in any number of incidents—particularly in blaming the innocent servant for his own theft of the ribbon—has no hesitancy in displaying the meaner aspects of his character, apparently believing that his perfidy was mitigated by the depth of his remorse.

Considering his time and place, Symonds *does* speak frankly about his sexual activities; but there is a generalized character in the description of his mature liasons that robs them of vividness and emotional resonance. While we have a right to demand factual accuracy—and certainly emotional sincerity—from an autobiography, the most compelling autobiographies are those which involve the reader in the same kind of illusion that he experiences while reading a novel. Symonds totally lacked a novelist's gift for creating scenes peopled with characters and their mutual interaction. Narcissistic as Rousseau was, he was able to create unforgettable portraits of Mme. de Warens, Mme. de Houdetot, Grimm, Diderot, and many others. But Symonds' work is claustrophobic in its undeviating concentration on self—wife, children, friends, remain only names on a page, and even his sweethearts are only romanticized extensions of himself. Nothing in life held so much interest for Symonds as the discovery and analysis of his own temperament.

As far as structure is concerned, Symonds was disappointingly unaware of how a narrative should be shaped organically. Unlike the flowing chapters on his early life, the latter part of the work breaks up into disparate chapters on his philosophic beliefs, literary achievement, and so on. Finally, like so many other autobiographies, it trails off to an abrupt end, as though he were uncertain

how to finish it. In his case it was due to the fact that he
had been reading widely among contemporary investigators
of homosexuality, only to discover that he was not unique,
that there were thousands of others like himself. Consequently, he lost interest in the *Memoirs* and turned to the
more practical work of overt polemicism, particularly in
the collaboration with Havelock Ellis on *Sexual Inversion*.

Fundamentally, Symonds' *Memoirs* do not measure up to
Rousseau's *Confessions* because he lacks the skills of a
novelist. Professor C.D.E. Tolton has argued recently that
on the basis of both structure and fictionalization, Rousseau's *Confessions* may indeed be the best French *novel*
of the eighteenth century.[26] Although certain of the Victorians might have admired Rousseau for the depth of his
emotional nature, for his idealism, and for his fervent response to nature, they were not prepared to imitate him in
his most significant contribution to letters: candor.

Even in exile, Symonds could not escape the pressures
and conventions of his background. Steven Marcus has
made the perceptive observation that the Victorians were
terrified of their fantasy life. They could really only face it
in the form of fairy-stories, melodramas, extravaganzas or
classical myth—in the form, that is to say, of distancing
fiction. Rousseau, in his fathomless longing for love and
admiration, was uninhibited about displaying the darker
corners of his psyche. He could, in a sense, be described
as the first contemporary man in the way he pointed forward to the philosophy of Nietzsche and to Freudian
psychoanalysis, both of which presuppose a methodology
of spontaneity inimical to the skeptical pragmatism of the
British.

The milieu of nineteenth-century England, in short, made
it impossible to write an autobiography which would also
have been a true confessional. Perhaps only the novel
provided that.

---

1. *The George Eliot Letters,* ed. Gordon S. Haight, 7 vols. (New Haven:
Yale University Press, 1954-55), I, 277.

2. Letter of June 21, 1862, quoted in E. T. Cook, *The Life of John Ruskin,* 2 vols. (London: George Allen, 1911), II, 549.

3. Letter of May 8, 1866, quoted in Cook, II, 549.

4. Cook, II, 548-49. Ruskin's words are from *Praeterita, Works,* eds. E. T. Cook and Alexander Wedderburn, 39 vols. (London: George Allen, 1903-12), XXXV, 115.

5. "Original Preface to 'The Confessions,'" *Works,* 16 vols. (Edinburgh: Adam and Charles Black, 1862), I, iv.

6. *The Confessions of Jean-Jacques Rousseau,* ed. Lester G. Crocker, (New York: Washington Square Press, 1965), p. 1.

7. William Hale White, *The Autobiography of Mark Rutherford* (London: Trubner, 1881), p. 1.

8. *Memoirs of Life and Literature* (London: Chapman and Hall, 1920), p. 37.

9. "Biography," *Works,* ed. H.D. Traill, 30 vols. (London: Chapman and Hall, 1896-99), XXVIII, 44, 48, 59-60. The essay, ostensibly a review of Boswell's *Life of Johnson,* first appeared in the 1832 *Fraser's.*

10. *Impressions and Memories* (London: J. M. Dent, 1895), p. 37.

11. *Reminiscences,* 2 vols. (London: Longmans, 1881), I, v.

12. Anthony Trollope, *An Autobiography* (New York: J. W. Lovell, 1883), p. 53.

13. John Stuart Mill, *Autobiography* (London, 1873), p. 240.

14. *Reminiscences,* II, 240.

15. *Praeterita, Works,* XXXV, 44.

16. *Works,* XXXV, 11.

17. *Amiel's Journal,* 2 vols. (London: Macmillan, 1885), I, xi.

18. *The Memoirs of Count Carlo Gozzi,* 2 vols. (London: J. C. Nimmo, 1890), I, ix.

19. *The Life of Benvenuto Cellini,* 2 vols (London: J. C. Nimmo, 1888), I, xxiv.

20. J. A. Symonds, *Memoirs.* MS in The London Library; published (1976) by Allen Lane (London).

21. Phyllis Grosskurth, *John Addington Symonds: A Biography* (London: Longman, 1964), p. 276.

22. *Ibid.,* p. 277.

23. *Confessions,* p. 350.

24. Grosskurth, p. 278.

25. *An Autobiography,* p. 3.

26. C.D.E. Tolton, *André Gide and the Art of Autobiography* (Toronto: University of Toronto Press, 1975), p. 58.

HOWARD HELSINGER

Credence and Credibility:
The Concern for Honesty
in Victorian Autobiography

In Book X of the *Confessions* St. Augustine confronts a
problem intrinsic to autobiography when he asks, "What
have I to do with men, that they should hear my confessions . . . ? When they hear me speak about myself, how
do they know if I speak the truth, since none among men
knows 'what goes on within a man but the spirit of man
which is in him.' "[1] Testifying to his own character, the
autobiographer is a suspect witness whom even the least
skeptical auditors might doubt. We know our own tendencies to present ourselves, even to ourselves, as better or
worse than we are, and so inevitably suspect the autobiographer of similarly painting himself in colors too light
or too dark. The more personal his testimony, the less liable to corroboration by public knowledge, and hence the
paradox: the greater the autobiographer's effort at introspective honesty, the more subject he grows to doubt.
Even if he does not consciously suppress or distort information, he may do so unconsciously. But if memory consciously and unconsciously shapes the past to fit the needs
of the present, how then can the autobiographer escape the
imputation of falsehood and lying?

The autobiographer's defense against these charges reveals his conceptions of the nature of autobiography. Augustine, for example, takes autobiography to be a form of
speech which is both intimate and influential—intimate
in that it is both introspective and among friends; influ-

ential in that it shapes both his own life and theirs. He says:

> Because 'charity believes all things' among those whom it unites by binding them to itself, I too, O Lord, will confess to you in such a manner that men may hear, although I cannot prove to them that I confess truly. But those men whose ears charity opens to me believe me. . . . Charity . . . tells them that I do not lie when I make my confessions: it is charity in them that believes in me. (X, 3, 3)

By charity—that is, caritas—Augustine means the love by which men are properly bound to God. According to him, the things of this created world, including our fellow mortals, are to be loved not in themselves, which would be cupidity, but in God, for only God may properly be loved in himself. The *civitas dei* is a society bound together by its common love of God; bound, that is, by charity. As God is Truth, so truth and belief are characteristics of this society. By binding men together in a common love, charity binds them together as brothers enabled to see through potentially deceitful surfaces to the truth within. Charity, in other words, defines a relationship, and it is on the basis of that relationship that Augustine presumes to validate his speech. Augustine's honesty is thus confirmed by his intimacy with his readers, which is in turn a correlate of his intimacy with himself and, ultimately with God.

Few Victorian autobiographers shared Augustine's recognition of the innate difficulties in telling the truth about one's own life. Their response to that suspicion of deceit from which no autobiography can be wholly free suggests they conceived this literary mode not as intimate speech but public discourse. They write not only for themselves and their contemporaries, but for posterity. They grow concerned about propriety, avoid introspection, and produce work which is predominantly memoir. In general they lack self-consciousness. Thus, the embarrassing depths of self-pity and regret which Ruskin reveals to us in *Praeterita* are insights for us, but not for him, because he does not watch himself looking at himself. Carlyle's elaborate framework in *Sartor Resartus* serves as a conscious means of avoiding the appearance of self-consciousness. Due to this lack or avoidance of self-consciousness, the Victorians make a limited and distinctive response to the question of autobiographical honesty. Unlike Augustine, whose claim to belief rests on the relationship he affirms with himself and his audience, most Victorian autobiographers rest their claim to belief on their denial of any such relationship.

The two defenses: *ex vita* and *ex morte.*

We can illustrate the two opposite modes of defense in the writings of David Hume and Edward Gibbon. In April of 1776, four months before he died, the terminally ill David Hume wrote a brief account of his life, intended as a preface to the next edition of his works. This abbreviated autobiography begins:

> It is difficult for a man to speak long of himself without vanity; therefore I shall be short. It may be thought an instance of vanity that I pretend at all to write my life; but this Narrative shall contain little more than the History of my Writing; as indeed, almost all my life his been spent in literary pursuits and occupations.[2]

The fear of seeming vain and thus guilty of self-interest and distortion is almost enough to silence Hume, but by his consciousness of that suspicion he seeks to weaken it. He will, moreover, speak briefly and write factually, a mere "History of my Writings." His strongest defense, however, is that in his debilitated condition "it is difficult to be more detached from life than I am at present" (7). That very detachment from himself, from others, and from life in general is to be the guarantee of his honesty. Thus he says "I am, or rather was (for that is the style I must now use in speaking of myself, which emboldens me the more to speak my sentiments); I was, I say, a man of mild dispositions" (7). By speaking of himself in the past tense, like a voice from the grave, Hume claims to be beyond self-interest, and therefore without motive to distort. We may call this, therefore, the defense *ex morte.* By its aid Hume can treat himself objectively, and by speaking quasi-posthumously, speak frankly. But this is of course pretense, a not very effective rhetorical pose, for since the beginnings of history men seem to have been concerned for their reputations after death. Rather than solving the problem of autobiographical credibility, the defense *ex morte* avoids it. The autobiographer hopes such an approach will transform him into an historian, and hence enable him to escape his difficulties. But, as Hume himself seems to have realized, the escape is impossible, for he concludes, "I cannot say there is no vanity in making this funeral oration of myself, but I hope it is not a misplaced one: and this is a matter of fact which is easily cleared"(8).

Edward Gibbon is less tempted by the pose of historical detachment. He began his autobiography in 1786, and worked on various versions of it until 1791. The earliest version, wherein Gibbon first faced the difficulty of autobiography, opens as follows:

> In the fifty-second year of my age, after the completion of a toilsome and successful work, I now propose to employ some moments of my leisure in reviewing the simple transactions of a private and literary life. Truth—naked unblushing truth, the first virtue of more serious history—must be the sole recommendation of this personal narrative. The style shall be simple and familiar. But style is the image of character, and the habits of correct writing may produce, without labor or design, the appearance of art and study. My own amusement is my motive, and will be my reward; and if these sheets are communicated to some discreet and indulgent friends, they will be secreted from the public eye till the author shall be removed from the reach of criticism or ridicule.[3]

The expectation of posthumous publication allies this to the defense *ex morte*, as does the identification with "more serious history," but Gibbon's sensitivity to style indicates how conscious he is of an audience. He proposes to adopt a "simple and familiar" style fit for both his subject matter and the relationship he seeks with his audience. He aims at "truth—naked unblushing truth," and a simple and familiar style will encourage belief because "style is the image of character." We will believe him because he seems familiar, i.e., intimate and known. But character is constant, and his own may be so habituated to the forms of "correct writing," Gibbon goes on, that strive as he may to be simple, he may yet unwittingly and unintentionally "without labor or design," give the "appearance of art and study," and thereby seem false and deceitful. In short, if his style is true to his character he will be taken for a liar, and only by borrowing a style and thereby masking his character can he be sure of making a truthful impression. Unable to embrace Wilde's paradox that "Truth is entirely and absolutely a matter of style," Gibbon softens the effect of his art by apologizing for it, and thereby takes us further into his confidence. To these means of enhancing his credibility Gibbon can add his reputation as an historian, which lends weight to, and is in turn reinforced by, his tendency to generalize, for as his generalizations ring true, and are confirmed in our experience, we give credence to his account. This reliance on reputation, together with an explicit consciousness of style and its effects, indicate in Gibbon an awareness and acceptance of his relationship to his audience. His words may be published post-humously, but they are spoken by a man in touch with society, and with himself. As a means of affirming autobiographical truth such assertion of relationship, which resembles the brotherhood of charity on which Augustine relies, may be termed the defense *ex vita.*

We will find a clearer example of this defense *ex vita* in Wordsworth's *Prelude,* which was, as McConnell has recently stressed, known in manuscript as "the Poem to Coleridge."[4] The poem's primary claim to our belief is its intimate voice. It is, like Augustine's confession to God, private, privileged discourse on which we are merely eavesdropping. By adopting a private voice the poet can deny all public role-playing. Whereas the defense *ex morte* claims truth by denying relation to living men, the fully realized defender *ex vita,* like Wordsworth, affirms so intimate and immediate a relationship with his audience as to allow no self-conscious separation, no division, no duplicity. He assumes, or if necessary creates, such a community as Wordsworth lauds in *The Recluse:*

> Society is here
> A true community—a genuine frame
> Of many into one incorporate. (11.614–16)

That sense of community seems to have diminished as the century wore on, and by 1850, when the *Prelude* appeared posthumously, the defense *ex vita* had fallen into disuse.

In that year, in the Preface to his *Autobiography*, Leigh Hunt seems to refer to a familiar intimacy with his readers: "I have been so accustomed during the greater part of my life to talk to the reader in my own person . . . that I fall more naturally into this kind of fireside strain than most writers, and therefore do not present the public so abrupt an image of individuality."[5] Hunt's purpose here, however, is not to evoke relationship, but to apologize for personality. Propriety, far more than veracity, concerns Hunt as he admits, to the despair of anyone hoping for frankness, that: "I have lived long enough to discover that autobiography may not only be a very distressing but a very puzzling task, and throw the writer into such doubts as to what he should or should not say, as totally to confuse him" (v–vi). Such statements may stir in the reader doubts about what he should or should not believe. Although Hunt recognizes the value to his undertaking of a charitable sympathy, which he calls intuition, between author and reader, he does little to encourage that relationship, and the prayer with which he closes his Preface suggests only the difficulty of achieving it: "And so Heaven bless the reader, and all of us: and enable us to compare notes some day in some Elysian corner of intuition, where we shall be in no need of prefaces and explanations" (vi). The true community where explanation is unnecessary has withdrawn to an Elysian corner, and the autobiographer withdraws into himself. Whatever influence his work can have is purely reflexive—it makes him feel better: "I will liken myself to an actor, who though commencing his part on the stage with a gout or a headache, or perhaps, even with a bit of a heartache, finds his audience so willing to be pleased, that he forgets his infirmity as he goes, and ends with being glad that he has appeared" (iv–v). Were the issue of honesty and credibility as sharp for Hunt as it is for Augustine, his resemblance to an actor would trouble him. That it does not is an indication of how mute the issue has become.

The autobiographer as gentleman: Trollope.

I have suggested that the autobiographer is compelled to defend himself against the suspicion of falsifying or holding back the details of his life, but this is true only if he desires to seem entirely frank, if his goal is the "naked unblushing truth" Gibbon aimed at. One may aim else where, and when Hunt considers what he "should not say," truth has begun to clothe herself with modesty. To at least one sensitive Victorian autobiographer, the naked truth seemed not merely improper, but unattainable. Writing in 1875, Anthony Trollope opens by asserting, "That I, or any man, should tell everything of himself, I hold to be impossible"[6] and he closes on the same note: "It will not, I trust, be supposed by any reader that I have intended in this so-called autobiography to give a record of my inner life. No man ever did so truly—and no man every will"(261). Trollope asserts here not the rhetorical difficulty of convincing his audience of his honesty, but the prior epistemological impossibility of entirely accurate or honest self-knowledge, and the secondary difficulty of the complete expression of such self-knowledge as can be attained. When he says "who could endure to own the doing of a mean thing? Who is there that has done none?"(1) he seems to embrace modesty as inevitable, but he has more than just conscious modesty in mind. "Rousseau probably attempted," he admits, "a record of [his] inner life," which includes to be sure the doing of mean things, "but who doubts," Trollope goes on, "but that Rousseau has confessed in much the thoughts and convictions rather than the facts of his life?"(261) However honest a man's intentions, "A man does, in truth, remember that which it interests him to remember"(111). The exclamatory "in truth" has full adverbial weight. One cannot report "the facts of his life," because "in our lives we are always weaving novels" (111). In the end there remain no facts at all.

Such thorough skepticism does not, however, relieve the autobiographer of the need to convince his audience that he has at least aimed at such honesty as can be attained. Memory may be determined by interest, but it can be at least undertaken "in truth." Trollope may hold that to tell everything of himself is impossible, but he goes on to say "that nothing that I say shall be untrue." His defenses, however, are strangely limited.

As Trollope had intended, his *Autobiography* was published posthumously, but he uses the defense *ex morte* only to explain and apologize for what would be otherwise socially unacceptable frankness. After speaking fondly of John Everett Millais, he concludes: "These words, should he ever see them, will come to him from the grave, and will tell him of my regard,—as one living man never tells another" (108). As a voice from the grave he "may dare to say what no one now does dare to say in print,—though some of us whisper it occasionally into our friends' ears. There are places in life which can hardly be well filled except by a Gentleman" (2). He excuses his speaking well of the moral influence of his own novels by evoking "that absence of self-personality which the dead may claim" (15). Despite Trollope's awareness of the problem of honesty, he cannot, as a gentleman ("one of us"), manifest "self-personality."

In so far then as Trollope seeks to convince us of his honesty, it should be the defense *ex vita* on which he relies. Even the posthumous voice serves the ends of this defense, by allowing him to speak as if whispering into friends' ears. An expectation that we will believe and trust him because he is known and familiar would be consonant with the *Autobiography* as a whole, which is conceived as an anti-romantic polemic against the idea of writer as genius. Writing, we are to understand, is a profession like others, allied more to hard work than to inspiration. "It is my purpose as I go on," says Trollope,

> to state what to me has been the result of my profession in the ordinary way in which professions are regarded, so that by my example may be seen what prospect there is that a man devoting himself to literature with industry, perseverance, certain necessary

aptitudes, and fair average talents, may succeed in gaining a live-
lihood, as another man does in another profession. (77)

Writers, indeed, will do well to learn from cobblers:

> I had . . . convinced myself that in such work as mine the great
> secret consisted in acknowledging myself to be bound to rules of
> labour similar to those which an artisan or a mechanic is forced to
> obey. A shoemaker when he has finished one pair of shoes does not
> sit down and contemplate this work in idle satisfaction. 'There is
> my pair of shoes finished at last! What a pair of shoes it is!' The
> shoemaker who so indulged himself would be without wages half
> his time. It is the same with a professional writer of books. . . .
> Having thought much of all this, and having made up my mind that
> I could be really happy only when I was at work, I had now quite
> accustomed myself to begin a second pair as soon as the first was
> out of my hands. (230-231)

The writer, in short, is a day-laborer, not a wool-gathering
poet who sits "nibbling his pen, and gazing at the wall before him, till he shall have found the words with which he
wants to express his ideas": "All those I think who have
lived as literary men,—working daily as literary labourers,
—will agree with me that three hours a day will produce as
much as a man ought to write" (195).

If statements such as these convinced us that writers are
just ordinary folk, they might encourage us to trust Trollope
as "one of us," but pride in his own singular achievements
regularly undercuts his claim to be common. Even the
community of "literary men" invited to agree with him is
meant to marvel when Trollope illustrates these precepts
by his own practice: "It had at this time become my custom
. . . to write with my watch before me, and to require from
myself 250 words every quarter of an hour. I have found
that the 250 words have been forthcoming as regularly as
my watch went" (195). We are struck more by the singular-
ity of his diligence than by the familiarity of his effort.
The labor may be common, but the laborer is extraordinary: "I feel confident that in amount no other writer
contributed so much during that time to English literature"
(194). What is to encourage us to share that confidence?
There are "two kinds of confidence which a reader may

have in his author," explains Trollope, "a confidence in facts, and a confidence in vision" (94). (These correspond to the defenses *ex morte* and *ex vita*.) For the first a writer employs research, strives for accuracy, and demands of the reader faith; for the second he employs observation, aims for sensitivity and imagination, and demands judgment. Although Trollope explains that he himself employs the subjective way of vision, his *Autobiography* seems rather more a reporting of facts demanding faith. His account of his schooling is characteristic:

> When I left Harrow I was all but nineteen, and I had at first gone there at seven. During the whole of those twelve years no attempt had been made to teach me anything but Latin and Greek. . . . The assertion will scarcely be credited, but I do assert that I have no recollection of other tuition except that in the dead languages. . . . I feel convinced in my mind that I have been flogged oftener than any human being alive. It was just possible to obtain five scourgings in one day at Winchester, and I have often boasted that I obtained them all. Looking back over half a century, I am not quite certain whether the boast is true; but if I did not, nobody ever did. (14)

These are ostensibly facts, although they are guaranteed only by Trollope's assertion. They are, as it were, subjective facts, for which Trollope's own character, or his reputation as a truthful gentleman, can be the only ground of belief. To support our faith in his facts, we need to judge him, to know him. But his character is unique, as he has been at pains to have us realize, and hence hard to know and difficult to judge.

Trollope's difficulty in establishing a basis for belief stems from his ambivalent desire to be both common and unique, of the masses and above them. Success mattered to him intensely, but he never quite trusted the success he achieved. "To be known as somebody,—to be Anthony Trollope if it be no more,—is to be much" (78), he acknowledges, but he made the extraordinary experiment of publishing several novels anonymously to see if they would sell without his name. Perhaps Trollope's visit with Brigham Young is emblematic. "I called upon him," Trollope says:

sending to him my card, apologising for doing so without an introduction and excusing myself by saying that I did not like to pass
through the territory without seeing a man of whom I had heard
so much. He received me in his doorway, not asking me to enter,
and inquired whether I were not a miner. When I told him that I was
not a miner, he asked me whether I earned my bread. I told him I
did. 'I guess you're a miner,' said he. I again assured him that I was
not. 'Then how do you earn your bread?' I told him that I did so by
writing books. 'I'm sure you're a miner,' said he. Then he turned
upon his heel, went back into the house, and closed the door. I was
properly punished, as I was vain enough to conceive that he would
have heard my name. (249)

Although he can, as here, laugh at his presumption, Trollope nonetheless presumes that we too will have heard his
name, that we will know who he is. He pretends to be a
laborer, but expects to be trusted as a gentleman.

When he seems to really take us into his confidence, he
successfully evokes confidence in turn, but that happens
only once, in the next to last paragraph. Speaking of his
surviving sources of pleasure, he says: "Could I remember,
as some men do, what I read, I should have been able to
call myself an educated man. But that power I have never
possessed. Something is always left—something dim and inaccurate,—but still something sufficient to preserve the taste
for more. I am inclined to think that it is so with most
readers" (262). Most readers at that point may want to say
"ah, one of us at the very last," but the need in Trollope
to seem singular reasserts itself, and he closes his book on
the otherwise inconsequential note that he has been reading
the English dramatists, and that "if I live a few years longer,
I shall, I think, leave in my copies of these dramatists,
down to the close of James I., written criticisms of every
play. No one who has not looked closely into it knows how
many there are" (262).

The sharpness of Trollope's sense of the impossibility of
accurate self-knowledge or honest self-expression may have
contributed to his limited response to the rhetorical problem of creating an appearance of honesty. He tells us once
at the beginning that he shall say nothing untrue, and
relies thereafter on his reputation as a gentleman among

equals, and on our corresponding trust. But by assuming
such an audience, he assumed certain limitations on frankness. There were things he might not say, even if he wished
to. Manifest self-consciousness, for instance, would have
been improper. The community of gentlemen does, in fact,
guarantee Trollope's honesty, but it is an honesty restricted
to a range much narrower than we may hope to find in
autobiography, where politeness is not always a virtue.

The autobiographer as natural historian:
Darwin, Spencer, Mill.

Few Victorian autobiographers share Trollope's skepticism about the possibility of honesty. Darwin, for example,
claims in 1876: "I have attempted to write the following
account of myself as if I were a dead man in another
world looking back at my own life" (7). In Darwin this
defense and its claim to objectivity suggests scientific
method. The principal uncertainty of autobiography rises
from the encounter of living self with deceitful memory,
but Darwin's stance, "as if I were a dead man," fixes for
observation his own life as surely as formaldehyde had
fixed his collection of limpets. Beyond this defense *ex morte*
Darwin's *Autobiography* hints at a community with the
audience of his family: "A German Editor having written
to me to ask for an account of the development of my
mind and character, with some sketch of my autobiography,
I have thought that the attempt would amuse me, and might
possibly interest my children or their children" (8). Later,
when he momentarily adopts the second person, all other
audience than his family seems forgotten: "You all know
well your Mother, and what a good Mother she has ever
been to all of you" (6). Despite his immediate relation
with his audience in this passage, the invocation of community is entirely naive, and made with no sense of its
effects or consequences. As we read further we cannot, I
think, fail to grow skeptical: "She has ever been my greatest
blessing, and I can declare that in my whole life I have
never heard her utter one word which I had rather have
been unsaid. . . . I have indeed been most happy in my

family, and I must say to you my children that not one of
you has ever given me one minute's anxiety, except on the
score of health" (6). That account may, just possibly, be
true in substance, but its style reeks of fiction, of those
novels "which are works of the imagination, though not of a
very high order," of which Darwin says "a surprising number have been read aloud to me, and I like all if moderately
good, and if they do not end unhappily—against which a law
ought to be passed" (138). Darwin is basically unself-
conscious. He doesn't hear himself speak in this passage,
and is unaware of how suspicious we may be of his Polly-
anna tone. It is precisely Gibbon's sensitivity to style, and
the concomitant sense of audience, which Darwin lacks.

Herbert Spencer, writing between 1886 and 1894, continues the scientific tradition and calls his *Autobiography*
a "natural history of myself."[8] He chooses explicitly between modes of defense: "In years to come, when I shall
no longer be conscious, the frankness with which the book
is written may add to whatever value it has, but while I am
alive it would, I think, be out of taste to address the public
as though it consisted of personal friends" (IX). Good taste
does not make good autobiography, but the English sense
of reserve and decorum is at work. Self-exposure is indecent, and vanity is shameful, but some appearance of
vanity is almost inevitable:

> It is a provoking necessity that an autobiography should be ego-
> tistic. A biography is inevitably defective as lacking facts of im-
> portance and still more as giving imperfect or untrue interpretations
> of those facts which it contains; and an autobiography, by exhibiting
> its writer as continually talking about himself, is defective as making
> very salient a trait which may not perhaps be stronger than usual.
> The reader has to discount the impression produced as well as he
> can. (X)

Having expressed his generation's distaste for manifest
egotism, Spencer here goes on to imply that the defects of
biography are rectified in autobiography, which will have
all the facts and interpret them correctly; and that the
autobiographer's (i.e., his own) apparent egotism is a false
impression generated by the medium itself. Although in this

second point he is astutely aware of style, in both points
Spencer reveals his basic unself-consciousness. Regarding
the first, autobiographers such as Augustine have made
clear the elusiveness, even in autobiography, of truth in fact
or interpretation. Regarding the second, which is intended
as self-defense, Darwin gives contrary testimony, having
written of Spencer: "I think that he was extremely egotistical" (108). Spencer's comments may be a response to
Darwin, but if so the defense is even less convincing.

In so far as Darwin and Spencer are writing "natural
history," it seems appropriate that they should adopt
posthumous publication and the associated defense *ex morte*
to establish themselves as disinterested observers objectively reporting the facts. But posthumous publication is
adopted also by John Stuart Mill, for whom subjective experience has major importance. Actually, Mill makes no
defense at all, says nothing about when the book is to be
published, says nothing about the difficulty or inaccuracy of
reminiscence, nothing about vanity, nothing about truth.
Lucid prose and clear intentions go far toward encouraging our belief, but we may still wonder at Mill's apparent
unconsciousness of the imputations to which autobiography
may be subject.

The gloomy crisis in Mill's mental history was first resolved by his reading in Marmontel's *Memoires* a sentimental passage that sounds today highly self-conscious and
artificial. In the aftermath of his emotional response Mill
adopted a theory "having much in common with . . . the
anti-self-consciousness theory of Carlyle": "Ask yourself
whether you are happy, and you cease to be so." He might
also have said, "ask yourself whether you are truthful, and
you cease to be so."[9] In each case self-consciousness is
the canker in the bud. Darwin, Spencer, and Mill avoid
introspection and thus avoid doubts and anxiety about the
veracity of their self-image. It is not surprising that they
should do so, for they are, professionally, men dedicated
to objective truth, to fact. Mill's discovery of the importance
of feeling and emotion, his discovery, that is, of the inner
life, doesn't bring him to doubt the possibility of describ-

ing that life accurately, because he immediately objectifies what he discovers. Mill urges on his friend Roebuck that

> the imaginative emotion which an idea, when vividly conceived, excites in us, is not an illusion but a fact, as real as any of the other qualities of objects; and far from implying anything erroneous and delusive in our mental apprehension of the object, is quite consistent with the most accurate knowledge and most perfect practical recognition of all its physical and intellectual laws and relations. (106-107)

He thus redeems the inner life, imagination, and emotion by identifying them with the real world of objects. If the emotions associated with perception are not erroneous and delusive, the autobiographer's fear that his highly charged memories may falsify experience becomes groundless. Mill is converted to an appreciation of individuality and imagination, but the imagination remains subject to "intellectual laws" and rational analysis and the individual excapes self-consciousness. The extent of Mill's self-consciousness may be his observation, in a letter to Harriet of 1855, that "I know how deficient I am in self-consciousness & self observation."[10]

The autobiographer acused: Newman.

The only Victorian who equals Augustine in his awareness of the difficulty of securing unqualified belief for autobiography, or approaches his sensitivity to the elusiveness of truthful self-expression, is John Henry Newman. But, then, Newman was impelled to write the *Apologia Pro Vita Sua* by Kingsley's accusations, from among which he chose one against which to make his stand: "there is only one about which I much care,—the charge of Untruthfulness."[11] Confronting Kingsley's quotation of his own words that "it is not more than a hyperbole to say, that, in certain cases, a lie is the nearest approach to truth," Newman necessarily makes his defense against the charge of lying detailed, elaborate, and explicit.

Newman was not merely accused of telling a lie, but of being a liar, and the effect, as he observes, is to "poison

the wells" (6). Until that comprehensive charge is dispelled
nothing that Newman says can escape its taint:

> If Mr. Kingsley is able thus to practise upon my readers, the more
> I succeed, the less will be my success. If I am natural, he will tell
> them. 'Ars est celare artem'; if I am convincing, he will suggest that
> I am an able logician; if I show warmth, I am acting the indignant
> innocent; if I am calm, I am thereby detected as a smooth hypocrite;
> if I clear up difficulties, I am too plausible and perfect to be true.
> The more triumphant are my statements, the more certain will be
> my defeat. (7)

Kingsley here serves Newman as the traditional voice of
autobiographical self-doubt, accusing him of artful deceit,
hypocrisy, and acting. "He called me a liar," says Newman,
and "what I needed was a corresponding antagonist unity
in my defence" (11), for his very identity had been challenged. Newman responds to Kingsley's question "What
does Dr. Newman mean?" by pointing out the implications
of his antagonist's question: "He asks what I mean; not
about my words, not about my arguments, not about my
actions, as his ultimate point, but about that living intelligence by which I write, and argue, and act. He asks
about my Mind and its Beliefs and its Sentiments" (12).
Words, arguments, and actions are the stuff of superficial
autobiographies, the "natural histories" of self; but the
charge of lying, whether leveled by an external adversary
like Kingsley or by the adversary in one's own soul, stimu-
lates autobiography of a different sort: "I must, I said,
give the true key to my whole life; I must show what I am
that it may be seen what I am not, and that the phantom
may be extinguished which gibbers instead of me. I wish to
be known as a living man, and not as a scarecrow which
is dressed up in my clothes" (12). Newman's task is to
distinguish surface from substance, to discover the real to
extinguish, as did Augustine, the Manichean phantom of the
false and divided self.

Newman thus faces the familiar autobiographical task
of affirming his own true unity. Like other converts, he must
"distinguish between his past self and his present" (402)
to show that he was not *then* what he is now; not only to

affirm the change, but also to prove that he was not then already converted—was not then lying. At the same time, to make us understand the connection between past and present and their basic unity, he must indicate how minute were the increments of change.

Newman's own self-consciousness fed the suspicions leveled against him. When Tract 90 was published he saw, from the reaction, that "Confidence in me was lost," but he had, he says, "already lost full confidence in myself." "How was I any more to have absolute confidence in myself? how was I to have confidence in my present confidence? how was I to be sure that I should always think as I thought now?" (88) He had, he says, a "secret longing love of Rome, . . . And it was the consciousness of this bias in myself . . . which made me preach so earnestly against the danger of being swayed by our sympathy rather than our reason in religious inquiry" (152). This self-consciousness becomes an element of Newman's defense as it enables him so exactly to express the position of his opponents.

Among the other elements of Newman's self-defense, his articulate style, careful logic, clear ideas, and precise facts, we must also recognize the impression he gives of self-exposure. "I mean," he says, "to be personal . . . to speak out my own heart" (13). It is commonplace to say that "It is not at all pleasant for me to be egotistical; nor to be criticised for being so" (14), but Newman's expressions of distaste are made so elaborate, and placed so significantly once at the end of the Preface, and again at the beginning of the central "History of my Religious Opinions from 1839 to 1841," that we come to credit them. The sense of self-exposure he generates works to suggest an intimacy with his readers, and hence a sense of community with them. Very early he evokes that community by reminding his readers of how well they know him:

Whatever judgment my readers may eventually form of me from these pages, I am confident that they will believe me in what I shall say in the course of them. I have no misgiving at all, that they will be ungenerous or harsh with a man who has been so long before the eyes of the world; who has so many to speak of him from per-

sonal knowledge; whose natural impulse it has ever been to speak
out. . . .(7)

He goes on to characterize himself in such a way as to
impart a sense of precisely such personal knowledge. Our
larger sense of intimacy comes from Newman's meticulous
introspection, which encourages us to believe (as we never
do Gibbon) that he is indeed naked before us. But there is
also at work to encourage our belief a real community,
a brotherhood of auditors, to which Newman directs this
work; and which he invokes on his last page: "my dearest
brothers of this House, the Priests of the Birmingham Oratory," with whom he prays to be "brought at length, by the
Power of the Divine Will, into One Fold under One Shepherd" (252-253).

The affirmation of his veracity can occupy so large a place
in Newman's thought because conversion yields him, as
it did Augustine, a conviction of truth to which both life
and autobiography must testify. Unified in soul, he must be
on guard against the disunity of life. Unlike his contemporaries, he is therefore intimate, introspective, and wholly
conscious of his own style.

The autobiographer as artist: Gosse.

Self-consciousness and sensitivity to the issue of autobiographical honesty are natural correlates. The self-conscious autobiographer recognizes the autobiography itself
as part of his self-characterization; he sees with Gibbon
that "style is the image of character," and is therefore
aware of the artificial element in any image of character
he may create. His task becomes that of convincing us of
the congruence of style and character, and it is to that end
that he aims at a sense of intimacy. The would-be natural
historian of himself, on the other hand, not wanting to admit to watching himself, puts on an objective style, and
pretends to be talking about someone else. He thus presents himself as not only unbiased, but as free of any possible duplicity. Lying speech is always duplicitous, aware
of itself and of the truth it is not. Deceit, in other words,

is always self-conscious, and so the natural historian avoids the appearance of self-consciousness to avoid the suspicion of deceit. But that can only be pretense, and it is really more honest to admit to self-consciousness. The difficulty this creates for an autobiographer like Augustine or Newman who has a personal truth to convince us of is not, as we have seen, insurmountable. Indeed, they find their way to truth through self-knowledge, according to the ancient injunction *nosce te ipsum*.

When self-consciousness becomes an end in itself, as it does for Edmund Gosse, the issue of honesty is transformed. The account which Gosse gives of his education in *Father and Son* is, as he says, "the record of the struggle between two temperaments, two consciences and almost two epochs."[12] In broadest terms it records the struggle between Truth and Imagination, between the rigid Evangelical Puritanism of his father and his own dawning imaginative sensitivity. In the world of his parents all fiction, indeed, all art, was rejected. His mother noted in her diary that from early youth she "considered that to invent a story of any kind was a sin" (19), his father burned Gosse's copy of Jonson and Marlowe, and Gosse reports that ". . . not a single fiction was read or told to me during my infancy" (20). By all their denial of the imagination his parents had, he says, "desired to make me truthful; the tendency was to make me positive and skeptical" (20).

We might imagine that as a skeptic Gosse would deal rigorously with the autobiographical claim to truthfulness, but he raises the issue only once, in his opening sentence:

> At the present hour, when fiction takes forms so ingenious and specious, it is perhaps necessary to say that the following narrative, in all its parts, and so far as the punctilious attention of the writer has been able to keep it so, is scrupulously true. If it were not true, in this strict sense, to publish it would be to trifle with all those who may be induced to read it. (3)

Like the more conventional opposite disclaimer that "any resemblance to persons living or dead is purely coincidental," Gosse's statement acknowledges the similarity of his

account to fiction, but denies the identity. The similarity
seems scarcely to trouble him, and, he shows little sensitivity to the role of style in creating the appearance of
honesty. If this book is, as he claims, "nothing else if it is
not a genuine slice of life," we may wonder how a plum
such as the following got into the loaf from which the
slice was cut:

> This, then, was the scene in which the soul of a little child was
> planted, not as in an ordinary open flower-border or carefully
> tended social parterre, but as on a ledge, split in the granite of some
> mountain. The ledge was hung between night and the snows on one
> hand, and the dizzy depths of the world upon the other; was fur-
> nished with just soil enough for a gentian to struggle skywards and
> open its still azure stars; and offered no lodgment, no hope of salva-
> tion, to any rootlet which should stray behind its inexorable limits. (14)

Like Darwin's idealized account of his family, this is the
stuff of fiction. But the "positive and skeptical" Gosse,
trained to truthfulness, was not stylistically naive, and we
must wonder why he felt no greater need to distinguish his
account from fiction, and affirm his veracity.

The discovery of untruth was the central event in
Gosse's mental history. He confused his father, he says, "in
some sense with God," so that when one morning in his
sixth year, he heard his father say something which "*was
not true*," "the shock to me was as that of a thunderbolt."
"The most curious" and for us most important consequence
of this crisis is that "I had found a companion and confi-
dant in myself. There was a secret in this world and it
belonged to me and to somebody who lived in the same
body with me. There were two of us, and we could talk
with one another" (28). The rest of his childhood is dedicated to the preservation of that secret self: "Through thick
and thin I clung to a hard nut of individuality deep down
in my childish nature. To the pressure from without, I resigned everything else, my thoughts, my words, my anticipations, my assurances, but there was something which
I never resigned, my innate and persistent self." In the
"consciousness of self" Gosse gained through this newly
discovered inner duality we may recognize the potential

for lying. Duality enables duplicity; if you can keep a secret you can choose to not tell the truth. In protecting that
duality Gosse aims at a goal directly opposite to St. Augustine's.

Gosse's deconversion is, in significant detail, just the reverse of Augustine's conversion. Augustine's education
began with literature. As a schoolboy he loved theatre, and
won a prize for his reading of a speech of Juno's from the
Aeneid. His training in rhetoric was training in the surface rather than the substance of words, and he moved
only gradually toward a penetration of the surface and an
insistence on Truth. Augustine was tormented by the duality he discovered in himself, which he refers to as "this
debate within my heart . . . of myself against myself"
(VIII, 11, 27), and he devoted all his effort and prayer to
resolving that duality and restoring his soul's unity in God.
At the climactic moment of conversion he refers to theater
as a temptation away from Truth ("If one of us debates
with himself . . . whether he should go to the theatre or
to our church" [VIII, 10, 33]) and when, finally, he takes
to heart the words of Scripture, "Not in rioting and drunk-
enness, not in chambering and impurities . . . but put
you on the Lord Jesus Christ," he rejects the world of
theater and "all the dark shadows of doubt fled away"
(VIII, 12, 29).

The setting of Gosse's climactic deconversion is an "open
window at the top of the school-house," a sort of tower
from which he "gazed down on a labyrinth of gardens
sloping to the sea" (20), a setting, we may note, remarkably like one in Ostia, "a certain window, where we could
look into the garden" (IX, 10, 23) wherein Augustine and
his mother shared their mystic vision. But for Gosse the
tower is not a way of ascent to God, but a prison, keeping
him from the world. As a child he was, he says, "most
carefully withdrawn, like Princess Blanchefleur in her
marble fortress" (26), and even later "my soul was shut
up, like Fatima, in a tower to which no external influences
could come" (146). Like Augustine at a comparable climax,
Gosse's sense of his double nature is particularly strong:

"I was at one moment devoutly pious, at the next haunted
by visions of material beauty and longing for sensuous
impressions. In my hot and silly brain, Jesus and Pan held
sway together" (209). It is the moment of sunset, and he
prays for Jesus to come "and take me before I have known
the temptations of life, before I have to go to London and
all the dreadful things that happen there." He concludes:

> This was the highest moment of my religious life, the apex of my
> striving after holiness. I waited awhile, watching; and then I had
> a little shame at the theatrical attitude I had adopted, although I
> was alone. Still I gazed and still I hoped. Then a little breeze sprang
> up, and the branches danced. Sounds began to rise from the road
> beneath me. Presently the colour deepened, the evening came on.
> From far below there rose to me the chatter of the boys returning
> home. The tea-bell rang,—the last word of prose to shatter my mys-
> tical poetry. 'The Lord has not come, the Lord will never come,' I
> muttered, and in my heart the artificial edifice of extravagant faith
> began to totter and crumble. From that moment forth my Father
> and I, though the fact was long concealed from him and even from
> myself, walked in opposite hemispheres of the soul, with 'the
> thick o' the world' between us. (210)

What interrupts this would-be ecstasy, this yearning for
surrender and unification, is self-consciousness, "shame at
the theatrical attitude I had adopted," the recognition that
he is acting. The world that had been stilled, stirs, and stirs
desire; the shadows which had fled from Augustine fall;
and the completed separation from his father, as if in "opposite hemispheres of the soul," seems a figure for the confirmed duality of his own nature.

As Gosse moves away from the unity of faith and the
belief in Truth, he moves towards a theatricality which implies not only an acceptance of lying but almost a defense
of it. Not that he advocates dishonesty, but rather such
polite prudence as we have seen in Hunt and Trollope.
"Even at the age of eleven," says Gosse, "one sees that on
certain occasions to press home the truth is not convenient" (155). In the epilogue, as he judges his father who
was a natural historian, Gosse defends "prudence" as part
of the civilized life:

> My Father was entirely devoid of the prudence which turns away
> its eyes and passes as rapidly as possible in the opposite direction.

> The peculiar kind of drama in which every sort of discomfort is welcomed rather than that the characters should be happy when guilty of 'acting a lie' was not invented in those days, and there can hardly be imagined a figure more remote from my Father than Ibsen. Yet when I came, at a far later date, to read 'The Wild Duck' memories of the embarrassing household of my infancy helped me to realise Gregers Warle, with his determination to pull the veil of illusion away from every compromise that makes life bearable. (222)

Gosse comes down in favor of the veil of illusion, in defense of the lie that makes life bearable. Even if complete honesty were possible it would be undesirable, for he wants to preserve the privacy of his hard-won inner world Like Trollope, therefore, he rests his credibility on his identity as a gentleman, one who would not "trifle with all those who may be induced to read," and thereby establishes his right to privacy.

The most celebrated defense of lying is of course Oscar Wilde's essay "The Decay of Lying," where he laments the increasing factuality of novels. Like Gosse, Wilde wants his veil of illusion whole: "What is interesting about people in good society," he says, ". . . is the mask that each one of them wears, not the reality that lies behind the mask."[13] "Truth is . . . a matter of style," and reality and identity matters of appearance, for beneath the surface "we are all of us made out of the same stuff."[14] Wilde nonetheless finds autobiography irresistible: "when people talk to us about others they are usually dull. When they talk to us about themselves they are nearly always interesting."[15] Because autobiography interests Wilde he presumes it to be the work of liars, whose aim he has defined as "simply to charm, to delight, to give pleasure."[16]

Augustine's self-searching pursuit of Truth marks the discovery of the individual. Wilde's defense of lying, which is part of his response to the Victorian avoidance of introspection and transformation of autobiography into public, objective history, is really a reaffirmation of the individual, but it mocks the autobiographical claim to veracity because all the available truths have become truths of imagination. Gosse, speaking of himself in the third person says that "the young man's conscience threw off once for all the yoke of his 'dedication' and, as respectfully as he could, without parade or remonstrance, he took a human being's privilege to fashion his inner life for himself." He might be describing Stephen Dedalus, flying by the "nets of religion, nationality, and language," to "forge in the smithy of my soul the uncreated conscience of my race."[17] Gosse, like Dedalus, has become an artificer, because the inner self is no longer considered a scientific fact but is recognized as an imaginative creation.

It may be, as Trollope suspected, that no autobiographer can tell the whole truth, but no autobiographer can wish to be taken for a liar either. What he writes can have no standing as autobiography if it is not thought to be true, at least as far as it goes. Narratives we know to be untrue we call fictions. Almost all autobiographers make some gesture, therefore, toward affirming their honesty, although some, like Mill, may assume that the identification of their narrative as autobiography is gesture enough. To the Victorian autobiographers who approached themselves objectively the problem of honesty apparently seemed slight, and the defense *ex morte* sufficient. More introspective and self-conscious autobiographers see the claim to objectivity as a rhetorical pose, and aim instead at intimacy and sincerity. But this defense *ex vita* is rhetoric too. Because self-consciousness seems to preclude sincerity, or at least its appearance, even if you could tell the whole truth of your self, you still might be unable to convince people you were doing so. As the objective standards of truth with which Augustine and Newman could identify themselves grew inaccessible, therefore, defenses against the imputation of lying gave way to a defense of lying itself. This is not only the result of an increase in self-consciousness, or the willingness to appear self-conscious, although that plays its part too. There is also a concomitant shift in the conception of the self that autobiography intends to reveal. For the natural historians, the self was an object of description. Gosse, on the other hand, can speak of "fashioning" his inner life because the self has become something discovered, revealed, or created by the autobiographer. The self has come to be seen as the creation of its language. What I have spoken of as Gosse's defense of lying is really therefore a defense of style; a defense of language as the instrument of self-creation, self-discovery, and self-preservation. As some autobiographers embraced once again Buffon's dictum that "le style est l'homme meme," they may have felt that protestations of honesty were unnecessary, since far more effectively than by historical fact, their naked truth would inevitably stand revealed by their very words themselves.

1. *The Confessions of St. Augustine,* trans. John K. Ryan (Image Books: Garden City, 1960). Book X, chapter 3, paragraph 3. Hereafter all citations to Augustine in the text will occur in the following form: X, 3, 3.

2. David Hume, "My Own Life," in *Essays: Moral, Political, and Literary,* ed. T. H. Green (London: Longmans, Green, 1898), I, 1. Hereafter cited in text.

3. *The Autobiography of Edward Gibbon,* ed. Dero A. Saunders (New York: Meridian Books, 1961), p. 27. Hereafter cited in text.

4. Frank D. McConnell, *The Confessional Imagination* (Baltimore: The Johns Hopkins University Press, 1974).

5. Leigh Hunt, *Autobiography* (New York: Harper Brothers, 1850), p. v. Hereafter cited in text.

6. Anthony Trollope, *An Autobiography,* volume 1 of "The Shakespeare Head Trollope," (Oxford: Blackwell, 1929), p. 1. Hereafter cited in text.

7. *The Autobiography of Charles Darwin,* ed. Nora Barlow (London: Collins, 1958), p. 21. Hereafter cited in text.

8. Herbert Spencer, *An Autobiography* (New York: Appleton, 1904), p. vii.

9. John Stuart Mill, *Autobiography,* ed. John Jacob Coss (New York: Columbia University Press, 1924), p. 100. Hereafter cited in text.

10. *The Later Letters of John Stuart Mill, 1849-1873,* ed. Francis E. Mineka (Toronto: University of Toronto Press, 1972), p. 476.

11. John Henry Newman, *Apologia Pro Vita Sua,* ed. Martin J. Svaglic (Oxford: Clarendon Press, 1967), p. 8. Hereafter cited in text.

12. Edmund Gosse, *Father and Son,* ed. William Irvine (Boston: Houghton Mifflin, 1965), p. 3. Hereafter cited in text.

13. Oscar Wilde, "The Decay of Lying," *Intentions* (London: Osgood, McIlvaine, 1891), p. 14.

14. "The Decay of Lying," p. 29.

15. "The Critic as Artist," *Intentions,* pp. 97-98.

16. "The Decay of Lying," p. 28.

17. James Joyce, *A Portrait of the Artist as a Young Man* (New York: Viking, 1964), p. 253.

LUANN WALTHER

The Invention of Childhood
in Victorian Autobiography

Yeats, in his autobiography, said that he could remember
little of childhood but its pain; Gide, in his, that he could
recall nothing in his childhood soul that was not "ugly,
dark, and deceitful."[1] Neither man was subjected to any
extraordinary unpleasantness or to the rigors of that infamous Victorian method of upbringing, "the breaking of
the will." Ruskin, on the other hand, to whom denial and
deprivation were central in his early life, who was whipped
summarily for crying or tumbling on the stairs, thought
that childhood was a blessed time, the happiest time of
life.[2] Augustus J. C. Hare's adoptive mother approved of
and often aided her pious sister-in-law in treating Augustus
in a way which can only be described as abominable (in
order to teach him to "give up my way and pleasure to
others", for example, his mother made him sacrifice his
adored cat Selma to the formidable Aunt Esther, who
promptly had it hanged), yet in later life Hare wrote of
his relationship with this strange mother with a sincere
overflow of love and affection, with, it is not unfair to say,
a sadly maudlin nostalgia.[3]

Clearly not only the conditions of but the attitudes
toward childhood change considerably from age to age.
Childhood, the invention of adults, reflects adult needs
and adult fears quite as much as it signifies the absence
of adulthood. In the course of history children have been
glorified, patronized, ignored, or held in contempt, depending upon the cultural assumptions of adults. The

64

autobiographical evaluation of one's early life has in turn reflected these assumptions. In an age like the seventeenth century, when babies were wrapped tightly in swaddling bands in order that they might grow not only physically but morally straight, and might not, moreover, crawl on all fours like distasteful little animals,[4] we should hardly expect an autobiographer to dwell at length upon the particular details of his early life; infancy, except in the abstract, was a kind of larval stage to be passed through as quickly as possible.[5] Modern autobiographers, in contrast, often examine the events of their first years for insights into their adult selves: Gide's account of having bitten the beautiful white neck of a cousin whom he was supposed to kiss, or his description of having acquired "bad habits" with the concierge's son as early as he could remember, are meant to serve as signals of the pleasures and perversities he was to find in his later life. Victorians, for whom the realities of early life were sometimes brutal or at least unpleasant, nevertheless participated in a culture which regarded childhood so ambivalently that many autobiographers praised parents whom they might have blamed, and recalled comfort and happiness when they had reason to remember otherwise.

If childhood is in one sense a historical "invention,"[6] the Victorian autobiographical childhood is in another sense a literary one, since never before this period had so many English writers been interested in recalling their early lives at length within the form of sustained prose autobiography. I would like to look at Victorian autobiography as having developed within a culture in which to be a child was both a privilege and a hardship. In so doing I hope to illustrate certain inter-relations between the history of childhood and the development of the autobiographical child figure, and to demonstrate the literary uses to which this relatively new creature was put. Autobiography is neither fiction nor history, yet it is often read as if it were fiction and cited as if it were history. Among other things the discussion will show that, as historical evidence, autobiography is unreliable; no autobiographer can be free of

the fictionalizing impulse, and, even if he were, his memory
itself is creative. At the same time I wish to note the very
real effects which Victorian cultural attitudes had upon
the development of a literary genre and its conventions.
Finally I would like to ask what one can generalize about
the role of the "self as child" in the Victorian adult imagination, if one can generalize at all.

* * *

Family is the first, the permanent, the elemental sphere of social
life, of morality; and consequently, it is the source of religion. . . .
Here and there a few single men and women with intellectual
aspirations, and here and there a few childless and unencumbered
adults, may nurse the idea that they are living for themselves alone:
but their condition is so abnormal, so unnatural, and their mental
and moral constitution so morbid, that their opinion is not worth
considering, and their demands should excite nothing but pity.[7]

These remarks were delivered by Frederic Harrison in
1893 in a lecture entitled "Family Life." Though he speaks
with the passion of a man who almost seems to know that
he is supporting a losing cause, Harrison represents attitudes toward the home and the family which were by no
means uncommon throughout much of the Victorian period.
Without the family unit, it was feared, society would be
endangered, religion would crumble, individuals would fall
into unrestrained and base activity: in short, anarchy would
result. The childless adult was unnatural, "morbid," a threat
to the order of society. At the same time, however, he was
admittedly "unencumbered," and, at least potentially,
intellectual. That Harrison did not see a conflict here is
typical of the way in which many Victorians were able to
maintain, simultaneously, two contradictory notions of
"home," and, more specifically, of the place of the child in
it. On the one hand the child was a source of hope, of
virtue, of emotion: along with the angelic wife, he was the
repository of family values which seemed otherwise to be
disappearing from an increasingly secular and brutal world.
"Household happiness, gracious children, debtless compe-
tence, golden mean"[8]: these were ideals. But at the same
time, and of course much less obviously, the child was a

hardship, an obstacle to adult pleasure, and a reminder of one's baser self.[9] He might be innocent, untainted by sexual knowledge, uncorrupted by the world of business, free from the agony of religious doubt; yet he was also potentially wicked and needed constant guidance and discipline. These contradictions are apparent throughout the children's literature of the period: while there is much sentimentality about the natural goodness of children and their clear, unspoiled view of things ("Sweetheart Travellers," "Little Lord Fauntleroy"), there is also a strong element of admonition against following natural desires because they are likely to be selfish or sinful ("Rosamund and the Purple Jar," "The Fairchild Family").

In this context it is not surprising that children were much favored while they were much denied. It was during Victoria's reign that the Christmas tree was introduced to England, that penny and halfpenny and farthing toys became popularly available, that the children's book trade reached previously unparalleled heights in volume and quality. It was also the age in which the early isolation of children from their parents through the growth of the nursery and Nanny traditions became established and acceptable in middle class homes;[10] and the child for whom new games and amusements were being created was also painfully familiar with the cane, the strap, and the riding whip as disciplinary methods. As children became the focus of more attention due to the increased emphasis on "family life," the large injustices they had suffered for centuries were attacked by many legal and philanthropical reforms (such as Lord Shaftesbury's Factory Acts or his "Ragged Schools" for the poor), yet the more disguised kinds of abuse seem to have increased. There was common use of Godfrey's Cordial and other opiates to keep babies quiet; there was administering of horrifying punishments "for the child's own good" (in "The Fairchild Family," for example, the children are taken to the gibbet to see the hanged criminals in order to teach them respect for the law; real-life Nannies sometimes did this too, and seem very often to have used bedtime horror stories as preventive discipline);[11] there was a general burdening of small children

with overbearing moral expectations and religious demands.
Illustrating the disparities of freedom for the Victorian
child, A. O. J. Cockshut noted that "the child was free to
find God for himself, but not to leave the prunes upon his
plate, to criticise his father, or to choose his own books."[12]

Thus, while one social historian can say that for the nineteenth century the "privileged age" is childhood (as is
"adolescence" for the twentieth and "youth" for the seventeenth),[13] another can dwell grimly upon the difficulties
through which children had to pass (floggings, malnutri-
tion, and the like),[14] and both can be right. There was
indeed a strong tendency to idealize childhood—to see in the
child such qualities as an enviable imagination, a naive
spontaneity, an unspoiled sense of beauty.[15] There was
great popular sentiment for the child's innocent vulnerabil-
ity—poor little Nell!—and great praise for his innocent
goodness—perfect little Fauntleroy! "I love thee . . . with
my childhood's faith," says the speaker in Elizabeth Barrett
Browning's famous sonnet, thus granting superiority to the
child's pure ability to believe over that of the polluted
adult. The simplification and dilution of Romantic child-
images to their sentimental extremes became a staple of
the popular novel.[16] And melodrama was not the only
literary product of this concentration on childhood perception: Lewis Carroll's Alice, in addition to being a nice and
mannerly middle-class girl, was allowed to become a complex (if unrecognized) spokesman for her time.

But despite the wave of interest and solicitude toward
children which can be found in the literature and the social
movements of the period, one can understand why Peter
Pan's "I'll never grow up" was not heard until after 1901:
the fun was too often complemented by discomfort and fear.
Icy cold baths, distasteful medicines, long sermons, and
teachers who flogged their students are typical memories
in accounts of the period, and all took place in the name
of healthy upbringing. Popular Victorian attitudes toward
the amusement of children were similar to the attitudes
toward sex described by Steven Marcus in *The Other
Victorians*: the vital supply was limited, therefore one must

be economical, one mustn't have too much. Alice Meynell advises her readers that

> . . . the evil to be feared is not that of making the child too happy; it is that of using up the capital estate of pleasure. If a child is to continue happy, to continue amused and gay, he must be entertained upon the usufruct and not upon the capital of pleasures. . . . The child over-amused is in peril of losing amusement itself within his own heart. . . .[17]

If the child was in some ways superior to the man and in other ways his pet or his slave, if he was sometimes God's spokesman (as in certain Evangelical story books)[18] and sometimes the object of cruel yet "necessary" punishments (as in fairy-tales by Knatchbull-Hugesson and Christina Rossetti), if, in short, he was both an ideal innocent and a selfish fallen creature, how did this cultural double standard affect the writing of the autobiographical childhood? Without wishing to draw any simple lines between large cultural motifs and the writing of specific books of literature, I would yet like to suggest two impulses which these attitudes may have encouraged in autobiographers. First is the need to emphasize childhood adversity, to portray oneself as not having been spoiled by overindulgence, even, in some cases, to have deserved hardship. Second, and in conflict with this, is the desire to present childhood as an Edenic, blissful state, a time of past blessedness, a world completely different from the grating present.

The first tendency has in some ways created a false view of the period, and since the interpretation of history through the "history of childhood" has in recent years become more and more popular, this is an important area for examination. The second tendency had a special function. It provided the autobiographer with a workable approach to the past and it allowed him to create, in the richness of memory, a place of repose from the harsh, indifferent "fast-hurrying stream of Time" which threatened him. In his vacillation between the need to have suffered and the need to have been blissfully innocent, the Victorian autobiographer reflected the cultural ambivalence of his age regarding children, yet at the same time discovered facets of himself which were emotionally restorative and which ultimately had their own literary power.

* * *

Though English autobiographers are generally more reticent about personal matters than, for example, their French counterparts, they do exhibit a willingness to discuss their early sufferings in print. When the military man William Butler wrote his autobiography he spent little time on his childhood; after all, it had nothing to do with the battles past and battles to come, the politics, and the impersonal events of history which were his primary concern, his "life." This is predictable in autobiographies of men of state. Butler did, however, manage to pause long enough to express admiration for his hardworking parents, and to describe certain of the early hardships of their family.[19] Anthony Trollope, writing for entirely different reasons yet with a similar desire for objectivity, also felt that the miseries endured by his family could and must be told: the poverty of his father, the hopeless depression of his schooldays, the unceasing efforts of his mother to save the family from the creditors. "Ah! how well I remember all the agonies of my young heart," he confesses.[20] Thomas Carlyle chose to portray his strict father as a hero in *Reminiscences* (he was "perhaps among Scottish peasants what Samuel Johnson was among English authors," his "noble head" was like Goethe's, his "natural faculty" like Burns'); yet a different view of this stern man emerges out of the loose fictional disguises of *Sartor Resartus*, as Carlyle allows himself to reveal his own childhood unhappiness. Teufelsdröckh "wept often; indeed to such a degree that he was nicknamed *Der Weinende* (the Tearful)"; the same was true of Carlyle. And in the first person: "I was forbid much: wishes in any measure bold I had to renounce; everywhere a straight bond of Obedience inflexibly held me down . . . my tears flowed. . . ."[21] Sara Coleridge, the daughter of Samuel Taylor Coleridge, began her autobiographical recollections with the intention of pointing out whatever "chief moral or reflexion" the various stages of her life might illustrate, but she only got so far as describing such things as the displeasure Coleridge showed when she preferred her mother to him, the "nervous sensitiveness and morbid imaginativeness" she developed early in life, the nightmares she had, at Grasmere, of terrible lions, of the ghost of Hamlet, of Death at Hell's Gate.[22] The ability to remember and describe the painfulness of family struggle and childhood isolation was perhaps best accomplished at the end of the period in Edmund Gosse's *Father and Son*, in which the melancholy details of his mother's death, and the seemingly interminable dullness of his father's narrow religious life afterward, are painstakingly told.

What is striking in many of these accounts is the autobiographer's willingness to accept the blame for his own unhappiness or to see his suffering as having been, in retrospect, "good for him." Trollope said that his misfortunes were caused not only by his gentleman father's poverty but also by "an utter want on my own part of that juvenile manhood which enables some boys to hold up their heads even among the distresses which such a position is sure to produce." Though his father "knew not what he did" in passion, and in that state "knocked me down with the great folio Bible which he always used," Trollope insists that this form of punishment was simply the result of ignorance: "no father was ever more anxious for the education of his children, though I think none ever knew less how to go about the work."[23] Samuel Smiles, the writer of self-help books, revealed his old schoolteacher Hardie to have been a tyrant and an indefatigable flogger, but then praised him for his "fairness."[24] Similarly, Leigh Hunt described the humiliating methods of "Old Boyer," the famous teacher at Christ Hospital school. Though Boyer knocked Hunt's tooth out with the back of a Homer, and ridiculed his essays by "contemptuously crumpling them up in his hand, and calling out, 'Here, children, there is something to amuse you,' " Hunt saw him in retrospect as a "conscientious" and "laborious" man, and Christ Hospital school remained a dear memory.[25]

Evidently a child was expected to be stoical when misfortune befell him. In Victorian popular novels there are many pathetic orphans, dying children, and neglected waifs; these young martyrs were attractive for various reasons, not the least of which was a horror of that worst and most dreaded alternative, the "spoilt" child.[26] It would seem that any child who was poor and abused was superior to one overly coddled. When the illustrator Dorothy Tennant Stanley decided to reject, for her "ragged life" drawings, the very widespread and popular images of "pale, whining children with sunken eyes, holding up bunches of violets to heedless passers-by; dying match girls, sorrowful watercress girls, emaciated mothers clasping weeping babes," in favor of more robust and happy urchins and "street Arabs," she too was operating under the assumption that the most interesting children in London were those whose "ingenuity" and "charm" were born of extreme adversity, in this case poverty.[27] The feeling against spoilt children was so common that even so unlikely (and confessedly spoilt) a person as Lord Alfred Douglas echoed the general disapproval: "I would rather see a child badly treated than spoilt," he said; "suffering is good for the soul."[28]

This may account in part for the lack of autobiographical reticence regarding childhood troubles. Victorians did not wish to think of themselves as having been "over-amused" as children. They were moreover quite ready to feel guilty for not having been strong or "manly" enough in times of distress. Childhood suffering was bracing; it was good for you. Learning obedience at the point of the rod was cause for tears, perhaps, but, as Teufelsdröckh says, "it was beyond measure safer to err by excess than by defect. Obedience is our universal duty and destiny; wherein whoso will not bend must break: too early and too thoroughly we cannot be trained to know that Would, in this world of ours, is as mere zero to Should, and for the most part as the smallest of fractions even to Shall."[29]

Hence the harshness of parents and other authorities was forgiven and justified. Though Ruskin portrayed himself as a lonely, suppressed child, often whipped, who was denied all toys, sweets, and even companions, he rationalized each of these denials by praising its beneficial result. The "utter prohibition" of wine and sweets, he said, had left him with "an extreme perfection in palate and in all other bodily senses." The whipping had given him "serene and secure methods of life and motion." The lack of toys and other distractions had given him a "formed habit of serenity," an ability to concentrate contentedly upon the patterns in the carpet or the wallpaper and thereby to learn "the main practical faculty" of his life, "the habit of fixed attention with both eyes and mind" through which his future in art was established.[30] Gosse too felt that parental severity had had its value. Even though the zoological illustrations which his father helped him paint had been "wrung" from him, "touch by touch, pigment by pigment, under the orders of a taskmaster," the mental discipline gained by working according to the strict requirements of his father had finally been worth the agony: "It taught me to concentrate my attention, to define the nature of distinctions, to see accurately, and to name what I saw."[31]

Neither man protested, as a modern autobiographer might, that his talent had been damaged or his creativity stifled by such restrictions. Ruskin in fact wondered whether his childhood had not been *too* luxurious; perhaps, he thought, his mother had been right in suggesting that he had been "too much indulged." Mill also thought that he might have had too much too soon in his boyhood, and that easy success had spoiled his appetite for living: "I had had (as I reflected) some gratification of vanity at too early an age . . . little as it was which I had attained, yet having been attained too early, like all pleasures enjoyed too soon, it had made me *blasé* and indifferent to the pursuit." Like Meynell's "child over-amused," he felt that he had lost the very capacity for enjoyment: ". . . neither selfish nor unselfish pleasures were pleasures to me."[32]

In a reaction against overindulgence some autobiographers not only did not judge their parents as harshly as they might have done, but tended to select details which suggested more hardship than may necessarily have been the case. Ruskin, for example, gives his readers some slightly exaggerated impressions of how much he was denied. He was, no doubt, called upon to crack nuts slavishly for the guests at dinner without being allowed to eat any himself; he did, probably, remember after sixty or more years the first three raisins he was given to eat, so rare a treat were they; he must certainly have had to grow up without elaborate toys and, as he relates, to give up the beautiful Punch and Judy dolls which his aunt had given him because it was "not right" that he should own such things. Yet occasionally a glimmer of luxury peeps through all this grey suppression, and causes one to wonder. The dolls were forbidden, but we soon enough learn of the rather splendid gift of a silver-mounted postilion's whip from the young traveller's increasingly well-off father. Food being so important to children, we marvel at the poor boy's misfortune to have had no sweets, nuts, "nor anything else of dainty kind" to eat, but we then read of the "ethereal flavor" of cherry pies which were cooked from the cherries he himself had chosen—in the very garden of which he had said earlier that "*all* the fruit was forbidden."[33] It is not that Ruskin deliberately wishes to mislead but that like many others he selectively remembers the difficulties of his "poor little life" with a kind of unconscious pride; he creates of himself a character worthy to stand beside the rest of the unspoilt, brave, heroic children of collective Victorian fantasy.

If there was, as I am suggesting, a certain cultural encouragement to feel that one had suffered, then there is some question as to how to read a book like Augustus J. C. Hare's *The Story of My Life*. This six-volume autobiography is a mine for anyone looking for incriminating testimony against Victorian authority figures and the "breaking-of-the-will" school of upbringing. It begins with the story of how Augustus, an unwelcome birth, was shipped off by his parents to his widowed aunt Maria when she offered to raise him as her own. ("My dear Maria, how very kind of you! Yes, certainly, the baby shall be sent as

soon as it is weaned; and, if any one else would like one,
would you kindly recollect that we have others," Mrs. Hare
wrote.)[34] Then starts the long and pitiful account of Maria's
sincere but clumsy campaign to teach him obedience and
unselfishness. There was the lesson of the puddings:

> The most delicious puddings were talked of—*dilated* on—until I be-
> came, not greedy, but exceedingly curious about them. At length
> 'le grand moment' arrived. They were put on the table before me,
> and then, just as I was going to eat some of them, they were snatched
> away, and I was told to get up and carry them off to some poor per-
> son in the village.[35]

There was the hanging of Selma. There was, alas, the all-
too-frequent presence of Selma's murderess, Aunt Esther.
This woman made Augustus sleep in an austere, freezing
cold back room *because* he had chilblains and gave him
sauerkraut to eat *because* it made him sick. (Esther said of
another aunt's children when they were ill with measles:
"I am *very glad* they are so ill: it is a well-deserved punishment because their mother would not let them go to
church for fear they should catch it there." "She had the
inflexible cruelty of a Dominican," Hare wrote.)[36]

The horrors go on and on. Augustus was made to wear a
miserable and unnecessary back brace—"a terrible iron
frame"—when he went to Harrow. Christmas at home meant
"having to sit for hours and hours pretending to be deeply
interested in the six huge volumes of Foxe's 'Book of Martyrs,' " and "being compelled—usually with agonizing chilblains—to walk twice to church, eight miles through the
snow or piercing marsh winds, and sit for hours in mute
anguish of congelation, with one of Uncle Julius's interminable sermons in the afternoon. . . ."[37] In the midst
of all this anguish burns an undying flame of affection for
Maria, "my darling mother." Hare justifies all her complicity with his more-than-Murdstonian aunts by referring to
Maria's high religious principles: when persecuted, one
must turn the other cheek; it grieved her that Augustus had
to suffer, but as a good Christian he too must follow Christ's
meek example. And so Aunt Esther's tyranny prevailed,
year after miserable year.

Multitudes of questions arise from a reading of Hare's book, but the one which concerns us here is how to read it in light of the autobiographer's impulse to entertain, at some level, the vision of himself as a child of adversity. With Hare, one senses a definite authorial relish in the description of family eccentricities and calamities. There are some very humorous passages, and there are moments when a character may be perfectly captured in a laughably grotesque image: at one point Esther is seen, spade in hand, marching off to the church-yard to bury two grinning skulls which have interested Augustus during his imprisonment in the church vestry. Dickens might have written it better, but the image itself cannot be improved upon for its delightfully apt placing of Esther in her proper setting. When social historians use Hare's book as factual evidence of the kind of discipline which Victorian parents were capable of inflcting, are they not misunderstanding the workings of a literary imagination? The young Hare, one is bound to note, often bears an uncanny resemblance to David Copperfield in *The Story of My Life*; one can also find echoes of *Praeterita* in the book. Hare was an experienced travel book writer who loved to repeat quaint stories and eerie legends to enhance his factual material. I do not mean here to claim that autobiography and fiction are one, or that Hare was a marvelous liar, but simply to suggest that in the case of an autobiography like this one, it ought to be read as existing within literary and cultural traditions which encouraged the selection of certain memories over others. In addition to noting Hare's habit of storytelling and his eye for the macabre and the unusual, we have to remember the increasing ease with which his culture allowed him to discuss the severity of former generations. Just as the claim that "I was the chief of sinners" became a kind of convention in Puritan autobiography, so the retelling of childhood woe became, if not conventional, at least common enough to be seen as part of a pattern.[38] A man whose will had truly been broken, of course, would not have written the book at all.

The willingness to have suffered may perhaps be more

clearly seen when viewed in contrast with its equally strong opposite: the desire to have inhabited an Edenic "other world" as a child. The ideological struggle in nineteenth-century children's literature between the didactic tale and the fairy-tale parallels this division. A fairytale need not have any relation to the world of Would, Should and Shall; its eventual triumph over the moralistic stories of writers like Mrs. Sherwood and Charlotte Mary Yonge is an indication of the adult writers' recognition that the realm of childhood fantasy could be as real and necessary as the world of adult rules and restrictions. Alongside the child as martyr, the Victorian mind was able to see the child as a free spirit, sporting idyllically on Echoing Greens, drinking in perceptions with a power which would later be lost. Ruskin praised the "large eyes of children," equating the child with the man of genius in having "infinite ignorance, and yet infinite power; a fountain of eternal admiration, delight, and creative force within him, meeting the ocean of visible and governable things around him."[39] Froude thought that the child's simple ability to believe was worth all the world's knowledge. He would gladly give away all he was, he said, "but for one week of my old child's faith, to go back to calm and peace again, and then to die in hope."[40]

In this spirit, then, though somewhat less dramatically, autobiographers called forth memories of early happiness. Frances Power Cobbe describes a pleasant nursery, a mother who often cuddled up close to her on the sofa, a house full of relatives at Christmas with all the children playing "romping games" through the halls and corridors. In her childhood drawing room "the happiest hours of my life were passed."[41] Lord Alfred Douglas also passed his "happiest days" in a family country house and remarked that "when you go to heaven you can be what you like, and I intend to be a child." Douglas, like Hare, idealized his mother as she had appeared to him in the early days, remembering that she had had an "angel's beauty"; she was so beautiful, he said, that when she and her sister went driving in the Park, "people stood on chairs to see them."[42]

Angelic mothers, paradise in the form of a childhood garden—these are images which appear to have been very important to the formation of one's concept of early childhood. Frances Hodgson Burnett remembered an "enchanted garden which, out of a whole world, has remained, throughout a lifetime, the Garden of Eden."[43] Her biographer could not place this garden, since the most likely spot housed only a small garden, not the "imposing mansion ensconced in trees" described by her son and first biographer, but the image was nevertheless real enough to Mrs. Hodgson Burnett, who transformed it into *The Secret Garden*, her best children's book. Ruskin of course began and ended *Praeterita* with images of "Eden-land" and "the rivers of Paradise."[44] William Michael Rossetti grew up in the dinginess of Charlotte Street, Portland Place, but found that his earliest recollections were of his grandfather's country cottage in Buckinghamshire: though he was there only about three times after his infancy, he still clearly remembered as an adult the pigs, dogs, spiders, earwigs, and slugs of those early rural visits.[45]

Sometimes it is not so much the content of the memory which is important in the establishment of an idyllic feeling. The very act of remembering can also be a source of unusual pleasure. As "the past grows holier the farther we leave it,"[46] so the recapturing of lost time through memory may seem to carry an almost mystical significance. Leigh Hunt found that the accidental appearance in a music stall of songs he had sung as a boy caused him to remember the intensity, the reality of the past; this moment of childhood clarity made all his adult life seem stale and unreal:

> What a difference between the little smooth-faced boy at his mother's knee, encouraged to lift up his voice to the pianoforte, and the battered grey-headed senior, looking again, for the first time, at what he had sung at the distance of more than half a century! Life often seems a dream; but there are occasions when the sudden reappearance of early objects, by the intensity of their presence, not only renders the interval less present to the consciousness than a very dream, but makes the portion of life which preceded it seem to have been the most real of all things, and our only undreaming time.[47]

This perhaps describes the kind of pleasure which Dickens felt while writing *David Copperfield*, and which made him so regretful finally to put his pen down when the book was finished. The memorialization of the past, through objects (Hunt's songbooks) or through narration (Dickens' story), creates not only a pleasant sense of nostalgia, but can also confer the energy and the purity of the former time to the present. The following passage on David's reaction to his mother's death is interesting because it seems also to describe the process by which the autobiographer is able to revive those images which seem most pure and eternal:

> From the time of knowing of the death of my mother, the idea of her as she had been of late vanished from me. I remembered her, from that instant, only as the young mother of my earliest impressions, who had been used to wind her bright curls round and round her finger, and to dance with me at twilight in the parlour. . . . In her death she winged her way back to her calm untroubled youth, and cancelled all the rest.[48]

The ability to write *David Copperfield* must have begun with a similar cancellation, imaginatively, of Dickens' grown-up life; this then opened the door to the past, that fascinating other world, in all its seeming innocence and clarity.

Though the psychologist Emma Plank found that, of all the autobiographies she studied, only those written by "men of letters" revealed "genuine recollections" of very early memories (as opposed to "screen memories," or to repetitions of what an author had heard from other people about himself as a child), one should also note that men of letters can recollect things that may never have happened at all.[49] Memory is not only creative in that it may "screen" or "conceal," in the Freudian sense, the significant event; a writer's memory, especially, may easily blend the real and the written event. Thus when Matilda Betham-Edwards describes her "first recollection" as a baby in her nurse's arms, she may simply be inadvertently revealing her admiration for the work of Thomas Hardy:

> The scarlet coat so strikingly contrasted with the blue sky and green hedges, the ingratiating smiles of the wearer, who, whilst making

love to the maid, warily ministered to the good humor of her charge,
the animation of the pair, all these things make up a clear, inefface-
able whole.[50]

For Betham-Edwards, this pleasant scene is clear and inef-
faceable; but the fact that it is so like the famous appearance of Sergeant Troy in *Far From the Madding Crowd,*
which she has read, suggests the effect other writers may
have on autobiographers. The "other world" of childhood
may also be a literary world.

Whether the autobiographer chooses to describe his
former happiness in metaphors of enchanted gardens or
visions of mother, whether his memories are "genuine" or
screened or second-hand, the important point is that the
tendency toward the idyllic is as common in descriptions
of childhood as the previously discussed portrayal of adversity. Both are in part the result of cultural attitudes,
though of course it would be much too limiting to see them
only in this light. Both tendencies may exist side by side
in the same writer, as when Hare portrays himself as a
persecuted child raised by an angelic mother. The inclina-
tion is to swing from one to another, but never to reverse
them; so far as I know, there are no spoilt children nor
ugly mothers in Victorian autobiography.[51] Each form of
selection has its function for the writer. He is able, through
the recounting of troubled times, to relieve his own sense
of guilt, to reassure himself of his worth, and to implicate,
without actually accusing, those who may have persecuted
him or failed to help him. More importantly, the journey
back to the imagination's "fair Life-garden" of childhood,
where "everywhere is dewy fragrance, and the budding of
Hope" allows the writer to escape his grown-up world of
anxiety and limitation and to participate in an ideal which
nevertheless seems "the most real of all things, and our
only undreaming time."[52] In the furthest reaches of memory
he finds a measure of repose.

. . . as yet Time is no fast-hurrying stream, but a sportful sunlit
ocean, years to the child are as ages: ah! the secret of Vicissitude,
of that slower or quicker decay and ceaseless down-rushing of the
universal World-fabric, from the granite mountain to the man or day-

moth, is yet unknown; and in a motionless Universe, we taste, what afterwards in this quick-whirling Universe, is forever denied us, the balm of Rest.[53]

1. William Butler Yeats, *Autobiography* (New York: Collier, 1965), p. 5; André Gide, *If It Die* (New York: Vintage, 1935), p. 4.

2. John Ruskin, *Works,* ed. E. T. Cook and Alexander Wedderburn (London: George Allen, 1903-1912), II, 66. "[All men] look back to the days of childhood as of greatest happiness, because those were the days of greatest wonder, greatest simplicity, and most vigorous imagination. . . ."

3. Augustus J. C. Hare, *The Story of My Life* (London: George Allen, 1896-1900), 6 vols. All subsequent notes refer to Volume I.

4. *See* David Hunt, *Parents and Children in History: The Psychology of Family Life in Early Modern France* (New York: Basic Books, 1970), p. 130 and *passim*

5. What Traherne and Vaughan describe in poems like "Childehood" and "Wonder" is a religious or metaphysical idea: "I cannot reach it; and my striving eye/ Dazles at it, as at eternity." ("Childehood".)

6. *See* Philippe Ariès, *Centuries of Childhood: A Social History of Family Life,* tr. Robert Baldick (New York: Vintage, 1962).

7. Frederic Harrison, *On Society* (London: Macmillan, 1918), pp. 33 and 40.

8. Alfred Lord Tennyson, "Vastness."

9. Thomas Hardy illustrates the extremities of this darker view through several characters whose illegitimate babies become their curse. Tess Durbeyfield loves her child and hates him: "When the infant had taken its fill the young mother sat it upright in her lap, and looking into the far distance dandled it with a gloomy indifference that was almost dislike; then all of a sudden she fell to violently kissing it some dozens of times, as if she could never leave off, the child crying at the vehemence of an onset which strangely combined passionateness with contempt." (*Tess of the D'Urbervilles,* New York: Modern Library, 1951, pp. 113-14).

10. *See* Jonathan Gathorne-Hardy, *The Rise and Fall of the British Nanny* (London: Hodder and Stoughton, 1972).

11. *See* Gathorne-Hardy pp. 282-88 and Lloyd deMause, "The Evolution of Childhood," in *The History of Childhood* ed. Lloyd deMause (New York: Psychohistory Press, 1974), pp. 11-13.

12. A. O. J. Cockshut, *Truth to Life: The Art of Biography in the Nineteenth Century* (New York: Harcourt Brace Jovanovich, 1974), p. 67.

13. Ariès, *op. cit.,* p. 32.

14. deMause, *op cit., passim.*

15. *See* George Boas, *The Cult of Childhood* (London: Warburg Institute, 1966).

16. *See* Peter Coveney, *The Image of Childhood* (Baltimore, Md.: Penguin Books, 1967).

17. Alice Meynell, *Childhood* (New York: Dutton, 1913), pp. 61-62.

18. *See* Gillian Avery, *Nineteenth Century Children* (London: Hodder and Stoughton, 1965), pp. 81-104.

19. William Butler, *Autobiography* (London: Constable & Company, 1911).

20. Anthony Trollope, *An Autobiography* (London: Williams and Northgate, 1946), p. 28.

21. Thomas Carlyle, *Sartor Resartus* (New York: Odyssey, 1937), pp. 98, 104.

22. Sara Coleridge, *Memoir and Letters of Sara Coleridge* ed. by her daughter (London: Henry S. King & Company, 1873).

23. Trollope, pp. 21-22, 32.

24. Samuel Smiles, *Autobiography* ed. Thomas Mackay (New York: Dutton, 1905).

25. Leigh Hunt, *Autobiography* ed. J. E. Morpurgo (London: Cresset Press, 1949), p. 78.

26. *See* Coveney, pp. 179-93.

27. Dorothy Tennant Stanley, *London Street Arabs* (London: Cassell, 1890). p. 5.

28. Lord Alfred Douglas, *Autobiography* (London: Martin Secker, 1929), p. 16.

29. Carlyle, *op. cit.*, pp. 98-99.

30. Ruskin, *Praeterita, Works,* XXXV, 44, 21, 22.

31. Edmund Gosse, *Father and Son* (Baltimore, Md.: Penguin, 1970), pp. 120-121.

32. John Stuart Mill, *Autobiography* ed. Jack Stillinger (Boston: Riverside, 1969), p. 84.

33. Ruskin, *Praeterita, Works,* XXXV, 26, 50, 36.

34. Hare, p. 51.

35. *Ibid.,* p. 112.

36. *Ibid.,* p. 202-03.

37. *Ibid.,* pp. 239-40.

38. L. D. Lerner, "Puritanism and the Spiritual Autobiography," *The Hibbert Journal* LV (1956-57), 373-86.

39. Ruskin, *Works,* II, 66.

40. James Anthony Froude, *The Nemesis of Faith* (1940), pp. 30-1. Quoted in Walter Houghton, *The Victorian Frame of Mind* (New Haven: Yale University Press, 1957), p. 86.

41. Frances Power Cobbe, *Life,* 2 vol. (London: Richard Bentley and Son, 1894), p. 10.

42. Douglas, *op. cit.,* pp. 9-10.

43. Ann Thwaite, *Waiting for the Party: The Life of Frances Hodgson Burnett* (New York: Scribner's, 1974), p. 8.

44. Ruskin, *Praeterita, Works,* XXXV, 561, 20.

45. William Michael Rossetti, *Some Reminiscences* (New York: Scribner's 1906).

46. Carlyle, "James Carlyle," *Selected Works, Reminiscences, and Letters* ed. Julian Symons (Cambridge, Mass.: Harvard University Press, 1970), p. 517.

47. Hunt, p. 45.

48. Charles Dickens, *David Copperfield* (Boston: Riverside, 1958), p. 109.

49. Emma N. Plank, "Memories of Early Childhood in Autobiographies," *The Psychoanalytic Study of the Child* (New York: International Universities Press, 1945-54), VII, 381-393.

50. Matilda Betham-Edwards, *Reminiscences* (London: G. Redway, 1898), p. 2.

51. Lord Alfred Douglas said that he had been spoilt, but then portrayed himself as being naturally generous and self-sacrificing. This he attributed to his aristocratic instinct.

52. Carlyle, *Sartor*, p. 91.

53. *Sartor*, p. 90.

PART TWO

Essays on Individual Autobiographers

ELIZABETH K. HELSINGER

The Structure of Ruskin's *Praeterita*

Ruskin's *Praeterita* is a strangely self-destructive autobiography. It was evidently written by a man who did not like himself. He measures his achievements, professional and personal, and concludes he is a failure. The book seems deliberately to refuse the minimum we expect from autobiography: a retrospective account of the writer's life which discovers some order, consistency, and purpose in past actions, a progress towards his present self. *Praeterita* lacks focus. There are no definable principles of inclusion. It is digressive in form. Unimportant people provide subjects for much anecdotal reminiscence, while many people of particular importance to Ruskin are barely mentioned or entirely omitted. The absence of introspection in all his memories is striking. Regret for lost opportunities is so frequent that it becomes obtrusive. The tone of discontent is pervasive. *Praeterita* is hardly adequate as personal history or apology. It is an apparently perverse undertaking, almost a sabotage of the self.

In place of a completed self Ruskin offers something much more tentative: a peculiar sensibility. A sensibility is not an achieved identity, but a given receptiveness. Friendships and accomplishments, even education, seem to have affected this core of identity very little. This, I think, is one reason why the expected autobiographical content of *Praeterita*, presented in chronological fashion, is often so unsatisfactory. Ruskin's minimal sense of self was powerfully touched by places, not people, and his accounts of certain scenes are the most emotionally charged passages in the book. These experiences do not, however, form a pattern of growth, a progressive development toward the achieved self of the moment of writing. They give us instead a series of repetitions and returns through which Ruskin's sense of his original identity, the peculiar sensibility of his "tadpole" self, is steadily intensified. These descriptive passages, closely linked by imagery and by conscious recall, give *Praeterita* a definite structure it first seems to lack.

That structure, depending on the metaphoric and affective connections between place and state of mind, is potentially a powerful one for autobiography—we think of Proust, of course. It was also closely fitted to Ruskin's habits of mind and attitudes toward himself. He had successfully used a similar structure in his critical writing for thirty years. But in the process of writing *Praeterita* Ruskin seems to have tried to follow two conflicting models for autobiography. On the one hand, he was drawing a portrait of a sensibility reflected in the scenes to which it characteristically responded. At the same time he was also attempting to discern a more traditional historical pattern: the growth of a mind in a single direction, marked by spiritual crisis revealing that direction, and culminating in a present identity confirmed by achievement. Ruskin's efforts to find a satisfactory form for his autobiography can be traced through three successive stages. Two opening chapters use landscapes to present characteristic mental states. In the body of the book, Ruskin writes a narrative or narratives which are intended to conform to a chronological scheme of development, but which are also structured by repeated ascents to the same emblematic view. Narrative breaks down in the final chapters, and place is again the principle focus. Threatened by madness, Ruskin nonetheless completes the formal structure of his book in two paragraphs which brilliantly recapitulate his presentation of a self defined by what it sees.

Ruskin is reluctant to assume the role of the self-conscious autobiographer. Like many of his contemporaries—Tennyson and Browning, for example—he condemns the self-absorption of his own childhood and the introspective habits that he and his contemporaries inherited from the romantics. In place of the ascent to vision through a voyage of self-exploration, he prefers "the science of aspects,"[1] visual study of the outside world. But autobiography demands both introspective and retrospective study. Ruskin's narrative in *Praeterita*, discontinuous and incomplete, especially cries out for the shaping presence of a self-reflective author. On rare occasions, he does allow his readers to glimpse his present self reflecting on the past, but even then he is almost always calling attention to the apparent shapelessness of his life. At the end of the first book of *Praeterita*, for example, he comments on the peculiar blend of feeling and ability in his eighteen-year-old self:

> But so stubborn and chemically inalterable the laws of the prescription were, that now, looking back from 1886 to that brook shore of 1837, whence I could see the whole of my youth, I find myself in nothing whatsoever *changed*. Some of me is dead, more of me stronger. I have learned a few things, forgotten many; in the total of me, I am but the same youth, disappointed and rheumatic. (220)

Nearly fifty years are wiped out; there is no growth, no progress, no change. Ruskin at sixty-seven and Ruskin at eighteen are like Childe Roland; the aging youth, disappointed when he arrives at a viewpoint, discovers only a heart which, if not blind, is at least diseased. "Looking back" is not illuminating; the distance travelled between past and present disappears. Identity is not life shaped by time, but something else whose "laws" are "chemically inalterable" by temporal or spatial journeying.

Ruskin's complaints of shapelessness, isolation, lost ways, stopped progress, and unreached goals go on to imply a criticism of the linear view of life as progress and achievement, and to suggest an alternative. Ruskin characteristically approached both literal and metaphorical paths as more than the shortest distance between two points. Disgressing from a description of Herne Hill, in the second chapter of *Praeterita*, he laments the loss of a favorite walk down the ridge from his old home. The field

through which it passed has been walled off, though the
path itself remains. He remarks that "questions of right-
of-way are now of constant occurrence; and in most cases,
the mere *path* is the smallest part of the old Right, truly
understood. The Right is of the cheerful view and sweet
air which the path commanded"(49). Ruskin cares far
more for his view of the field than for his progress through
it. He takes the same attitude in all his longer travels—
which is why he prefers the more leisurely pace of the carriage to the efficient speed of the railroad. "We did not
travel for adventures, nor for company," he says of his
first trips to the Alps, "but to see with our eyes, and to
measure with our hearts . . . even in my own land, the
things in which I have been least deceived are those which
I have learned as their Spectator" (119). When Ruskin
envisions the course of his own life, he speaks not of roads,
tracks, paths, or streams, but of fruitful fields: "my granted
fields of fruitful exertion" (372), "the Holy Land of my
future work" (167). Like Tennyson (*In Memoriam*, Sections 23-46), he finds it oppressive or impossible to pursue
a single dreary way, and gives up the quest. He chooses instead the flowers and fruits of landscapes glimpsed by the
way, and secured to him not as traveler but as Spectator.

The life described in *Praeterita* is a domain which Ruskin possesses visually, that he may labor to cultivate it by
articulating his experience to others. That domain is first
glimpsed in 1833 and not complete for several years, but
it has already been imagined as the proper field of his
vision by the child who watches the glittering springs of
Wandel and asks to be painted in a landscape of blue
hills. Ruskin's constant travelling is never progress;
it is the means by which he revisits the territory of a visually
extended self. *Praeterita* follows the course both of real
journeys and of the voyages of memory that each new visit
provokes. It is a history of continual return, of constant
circling, a circumscription of a self identified with what it
saw. Except for its dedication to his parents, Ruskin wrote
in the preface, *Praeterita* would "have been little more
than an old man's recreation in gathering visionary flowers

in fields of youth" (11-12). The description is just, but it
needs no apology. The fields of Ruskin's youth are the
fields of his maturity and his old age, and he recreated
their flowers and "sweet air" by a life-long series of
mental and physical returns. The last of these revisits
were accomplished in *Praeterita*.

Ruskin had no real model for an unprogressive autobiography. Even *In Memoriam*, with its wandering lyrics
and self-enclosing rhymes, is a protest against an old mode
rather than the straightforward creation of a new. *Praeterita* reflects several stages in Ruskin's struggle to make
his book conform to the shape of his life and yet meet the
demands of the older form of autobiography. The first
two chapters were not written as part of an autobiography
at all, but as illustrations for *Fors Clavigera*. Ruskin incor-
porated them into *Praeterita* with the addition only of
titles and closing paragraphs. He commented on what he
had done, pointing out the differences between these chapters and the body of his book:

> . . . I fear the sequel may be more trivial, because much is con-
> centrated in the foregoing broad statement, which I have now to
> continue by slower steps;—and yet less amusing, because I tried al-
> ways in *Fors* to say things, if I could, a little piquantly; and the
> rest of the things related in this book will be told as plainly as I can.
> But whether I succeeded in writing piquantly in *Fors* or not, I cer-
> tainly wrote often obscurely; and the description above given of
> Herne Hill seems to me to need at once some reduction to plainer
> terms. (46-7)

Ruskin was aware that the two chapters bear an almost
emblematic relationship to the life he must go on to recount "by slower steps" and in "plainer terms." They are
remarkably unspecific about actual dates or chronology of
events, recounting scenes from various periods of early
childhood. And they clearly attempt to represent the essential experiences, not only of childhood, but of Ruskin's
adult life as well: his fascination with water, his delight
in the garden, his patient visual exploration of the patterns
on his carpet, his role as removed spectator looking out
at the world. Joining these chapters to a full account of

his life, Ruskin is careful to note that not only will the rest
of the account, progressive rather than emblematic, be
slower and less "piquant," it will also, to some extent, be
unnecessary. He said of his early travels that "although,
in the course of these many worshipful pilgrimages, I gathered curiously extensive knowledge, both of art and natural
scenery, afterwards infinitely useful, it is evident to me in
retrospect that my own character and affections were little
altered by them" (33). At this point in *Praeterita* Ruskin
is clear that a progressive model will not reflect what is of
most importance about him—the peculiar sensibility which
time and events will not change.

He uses the new titles and conclusions to the first two
chapters to further underline their emblematic status.
The method of composition was one which he had used
often in his critical writing. "The Springs of Wandel" (as
the first chapter is called) refers in the first place to the
stream behind his aunt's house in Croydon. The chapter's
concluding sentence, in characteristic fashion, moves from
an incident in the past (the Ruskins' early carriage travels
in England) through an indefinitely extending future of repeated travels ("in the course of these many worshipful
pilgrimages") up to the present ("it is evident to me
in retrospect" 33). The sentence goes on with a return to
the early time, where "the personal feeling and native
instinct of me had been fastened, irrevocably, long before," and comes to rest, finally, on a single detail, "the
cress-set rivulets in which the sand danced and minnows
darted above the Springs of Wandel." The focus on this
detail is not entirely unprepared; the Croydon spring has
been mentioned only once, in passing, but there are several other watery memories through which Ruskin has
presented his childish fascination with watching water,
in particular that of "the filling of the water-cart, through
its leathern pipe, from the dripping iron post at the pave-
ment edge; or the still more admirable proceedings of the
turncock, when he turned and turned till a fountain sprang
up in the middle of the street" (21). Ruskin's responses
to the Croydon spring and the water-cart are picked up

and woven together in the final image of the springs of Wandel, which becomes emblematic of one aspect of the visual domain which his sensibility established. "The Springs of Wandel"—and puns are always intentional with this most word-conscious of writers—describes both source and spring-time of Ruskin's unique sensibility.

Chapter Two, "Herne Hill Almond Blossoms," ties an apparently loose collection of reminiscences to a single significant image of multiple repercussions by a similar procedure. The Herne Hill garden has been described earlier in the chapter as an Eden where all fruits were forbidden, and Ruskin returns in the last paragraph to state, in "plainer terms," what those fruits were and when they could be eaten. But he does not stop with the literal description. The forbidden fruits remind him "that the seeds and fruits . . . were for the sake of the flowers, not the flowers for the fruit" (50). The childhood experience is the seed of the adult love of visual beauty for its own sake. The fully-flowered thought dominates the concluding sentence, which makes the same imaginative excursion as the last sentence of the first chapter. The almond blossoms are part of "an unbroken order" of constant seasonal change repeated "for many and many a year to come." Memory moves forward on that wave of natural change to the present, and returns again to the past, praying for the protection of the fragile almond blossom.

> The first joy of the year being in its snowdrops, the second, and cardinal one, was in the almond blossom,—every other garden and woodland gladness following from that in an unbroken order of kindling flower and shadowy leaf; and for many and many a year to come,—until indeed, the whole of life became autumn to me—my chief prayer for the kindness of heaven, in its flowerful seasons, was that the frost might not touch the almond blossom. (50)

The sentence combines temporal change with the stasis of perpetual motion, rhythmic progression with circular return. It summarizes neither life nor chapter, but it connects them to an image which it fills with new significance gathered in the course of a journey of circumspection. The structure reminds us of Proust, who recognized in

Ruskin's prose many of his own strategies. Proust constructs even longer sentences, where a word or an image echoes repeatedly while it accumulates meaning, and repeats in miniature the process of affective memory which the book recreates.

Although Ruskin declares his intention to continue *Praeterita* in a different manner, the titles of most of his subsequent chapters also focus attention on a single scene. Usually the experience is one which is repeated many times—typically, a place which Ruskin visits often, like "The Simplon," or "L'Hôtel du Mont Blanc." The responses Ruskin describes on any one visit are also habitual. Of the Hôtel du Mont Blanc, he confesses "How to begin speaking of it, I do not know, still less how to end" (433). *Where* to begin or end is also a problem, for the chronological narrative itself is constantly interrupted by references to other visits at other times. The chapter's subject is less what happened in 1849, the point which Ruskin has reached in his narrative, than what the hotel means to him after many revisits. The place of the title becomes, in the course of the chapter, first the stimulus and then the emblem for a recurring state of mind. The cumulative effect of these chapters, where places become images for the responses they evoke, is to establish a discontinuous mental geography which takes the place of direct introspective analysis, the guided tour from past to present.

The mental landscape of individual views, flowery fields seen from the Right-of-Way, does not provide Ruskin with a sufficient structure for his book, however. He acknowledges that an autobiography must above all be a chronological narrative. It is, he maintains, "my needful and fixed resolve to set the facts down continuously" (279). After his indulgence in "piquant" style in the first two chapters, he was determined to set his life out as a path and follow it. *Praeterita* was to consist of three books of twelve chapters, each book covering roughly twenty years. For the remaining ten chapters of Book I and most of Book II, Ruskin keeps his narrative plan very much in mind. Yet in spite of the pressure of the genre to select a single line of development, he cannot make his own life conform to that pattern. *Praeterita*'s central chapters are peppered with apologies for narrative deviations. "Whether in the biography of a nation, or of a single person," Ruskin confesses,

> it is alike impossible to trace it steadily through successive years. Some forces are failing while others strengthen, and most act irregularly, or else at uncorresponding periods of renewed enthusiasm after intervals of lassitude. For all clearness of exposition, it is necessary to follow first one, then another, without confusing notices of what is happening in other directions. (169)

In place of a single life, Ruskin discovers many different lives, each with its own time scheme. Autobiography threatens to splinter into multiple temporal narratives. Chronological structure is clearly disintegrating, with no very satisfactory substitute for the vital and literary unity it provided. And even multiple narratives may not be enough to cover everything essential. "I shall have to return over the ground of these early years," Ruskin warns, "to fill gaps, after getting on a little first" (49-50). A proliferation of paths is only a temporary expedient. Ruskin's real desire is to cover *all* the ground of these early years. He is most successful when he digresses from narrative travelling to take emblematic views like those his chapter titles suggest.

The record of facts continues, in spite of the signs directing us to broader views, but it is accompanied by notices of Ruskin's increasing discontent. He complains at the beginning of Book II that "for any account of my real life, the gossip hitherto given to its codling or cocoon condition has brought us but a little way." But progress still seems to promise the best solution, and Ruskin goads himself to run faster: "I must get on . . ." (261). A few chapters later he expresses more serious dissatisfaction:

> In my needful and fixed resolve to set the facts down continuously, leaving the reader to his reflections on them, I am slipping a little too fast over the surfaces of things; and it becomes at this point desirable that I should know, or at least try to guess, something of

what the reader's reflections *are*! and whether in the main he is getting at the sense of the facts I tell him. (279)

Chronological narrative gives us the facts, but not what the facts mean. Ordinarily we would expect the self-reflective author to help us, and Ruskin seems to announce just that: "I think it, however, quite time to say a little more fully, not only what happened to me, now of age, but what was *in* me" (281). But what follows is a series of passages from his diary contemporary with the events he is recording, not a statement of progress and direction from the perspective of the present. Eager to avoid the dangers of morbid introspection, the author refuses to speak up.

Even without the author's guiding presence, however, the narrative of his life can convey direction and purpose by recounting a moment of insight, the traditional resolution to a crisis of indirection in spiritual autobiography. Ruskin's letters and diaries indicate how ardently he had looked forward to such a moment, and how often he had been disappointed. On at least seven different occasions between 1845 and 1882 he thought he had achieved religious conversion, only to discover, in retrospect, that the turning had not been definitive.[2] The middle chapters of *Praeterita* present a different series of illuminative moments. They are aesthetic rather than religious revelations in any traditional sense: Ruskin's first sight of the Alps at Schaffhausen in 1833; insights into leaf and branch design achieved at Norwood and Fontainebleau; his first real understanding of early Italian religious art at Lucca and Pisa, in 1845; further significant mountain walks in 1841, 1849, and 1860; and the blended impressions of music and color received in the Veronese gallery at Turin in 1858. Each experience stands out from the narrative by the intensity with which it is rendered. Ruskin himself also tells us we have reached a critical point, and his language on each occasion is very nearly the same: "blessed entrance into life" (115), "I had found my life again" (297), "I began the best work of my life" (474), "a new epoch of life and death begins" (485). Yet these passages span a period of seventeen years and refer to eight different occasions on which Ruskin says his "true" (167, 437), "best" (474), or "new" (485) life began. The conversion or turning point we expected has multiplied. Ruskin climbs the mount of contemplation again and again—"my most intense happinesses have of course been among mountains" (157)—but once there, he gains no simple prospect of the past or future course of his life. He knows only that it must lie among mountains. His vision is not of the road he will follow, but of the view he will continue to enjoy. That view is, it is true, progressively enriched with new details of fore- and middle ground. In the aftermath of each new revelation, Ruskin was disappointed to discover how limited the view, how small the change in the direction of his life. In writing *Praeterita,* however, he arranges this series of views to suggest, if not a linear pattern of development, at least a spiral movement rather than a totally unprogressive series of returns. With each repeated vision, the familiar view is amplified—and Ruskin sees himself closer to a sense of his identity. The revelation is painfully gradual, not wonderfully sudden. The sequence of visionary moments in *Praeterita* does not show a dramatic development of identity or self-consciousness. It reveals instead a sensibility which remains fundamentally unchanged.

Ruskin also includes in Praeterita a number of false visions, similar experiences among mountains or before paintings which proved misleading. He describes, for example, an abortive conversion at Nyon in 1845 (378). He puts special emphasis on his early passion for Venice, as he quotes from an 1841 diary.

> Thank God I am here; it is the Paradise of cities.
> This, and Chamouni, are my two homes of Earth. (296)

But the Byronic vision of Venice is given only to be retracted as false. "Venice I regard more and more as a vain temptation" (296). The false visions cast further doubt on the usefulness of the "true" visions at Schaffhausen and elsewhere. Ruskin is too honest to leave out his wrong turnings, the roads which peter out, but by including them he blurs our sense of his progress or purpose.

In the last third of *Praeterita* the narrative structure

breaks down. "This gossip has beguiled me till I have no time left to tell what in proper sequence should have been chiefly dwelt on in this number" (508), he confesses. Scattered memories of people and places distract him from his chosen course as he nears the end of Book II. The decision to give up his sequential plan was nevertheless deliberate. He recognized the signs of imminent mental collapse and felt himself running out of time. "Lest I should not be spared to write another [number of] *Praeterita*" (460), he determined to indulge "an old man's visionary recreation" without regard for further progress towards the present.

Except for the masterful account of his unconversion ("The Grande Chartreuse"), the last chapters of *Praeterita* are diffuse, even chaotic, but in them we find repeated an exchange of vividly seen space for chronologically reconstructed time as a principle of order. When Ruskin surrenders the artistic control he had exercised in the middle of the book he returns to something like the emblematic method of his opening chapters. Places continue to provide the connections, the guides for memory. Ruskin seems to have lost track of time, but he recurs again and again to the hills of Scotland. "And there is no other country in which the roots of memory are so entwined with the beauty of nature" (466), he explains. Such rooted memories, entwined with place, give "design and fixed boundaries" (636) to Ruskin's wandering. But the scenes he revisits do not become emblems—not, that is, until the brilliant last paragraphs of *Praeterita*. Before we reach these, however, we should take another look at the intended and actual structures of the book as a whole.

Ruskin originally planned to take his narrative down to the 1880's, but at an early stage in his writing he decided to end the account with the 1860s. The actual *Praeterita* follows this second plan through the first four chapters of Book III, when Ruskin was permanently silenced by a final attack of madness. The book remains, in one sense, unfinished. Yet according to his second plan, the story would not have continued much beyond the point where he was

forced to end it. The last chapters of Book III were to
have been a series of farewells to the places to which he
felt himself most closely tied (634). They would effectively
have turned the linear movement of the narrative back on
itself, returning to the scenes of Ruskin's youth. They would
also have shifted the book's emphasis from temporal progression to spatial views and reviews.

But place, not time, had determined the parts of *Praeterita* all along: all but seven of the 28 chapter titles—or
36 intended titles—are place names. And Ruskin found his
titles before he wrote his chapters, as we see from the
plans for the unfinished Book III. On the rare occasions
when he directs his readers how to see his life, he gives
them what was evidently his own procedure, suggesting
emblematic views, not setting out road maps. "I must here,
in advance, tell the general reader," he warns in Book I,
"that there have been, in sum, three centres of my life's
thought: Rouen, Geneva, and Pisa" (156; also 296, 371).
The projected final chapters return to these scenes, Rouen
in France, Geneva in Switzerland, and Pisa in Italy. They
also include a return to a fourth "home," though at Dover
he barely sets foot on English soil. The conclusion would
not have altered the structure of *Praeterita*. It would have
clarified a pattern which, though submerged in the chronological narrative, is already present.

Granted that Ruskin designs chapters around significant
places, generally prefers views to paths, and tells us we
should look for geographical centers of his thought; a string
of 21 locales organizes but does not structure the autobiography. There are, however, five chapters which receive
special emphasis. "Schaffhausen and Milan," "The Col de la
Faucille," "The Simplon," "The Campo Santo," and "The
Grande Chartreuse" each present an experience of height-
tened visual and emotional intensity which gives the chapter
its title, and is the subject of its opening or concluding paragraphs. No other chapters combine formal emphases with
the same visual and affective intensity of description.

If we examine those views to which Ruskin gives special
weight, we discover that although they are geographically

distinct, they are visually almost identical. "Schaffhausen
and Milan" is memorable for its description of Ruskin's first
sight of the Alps:

> We must still have spent some time in town-seeing, for it was
> drawing towards sunset, when we got up to some sort of garden
> promenade—west of the town, I believe; and high above the Rhine,
> so as to command the open country across it to the south and west.
> At which open country of low undulation, far into blue,—gazing as
> at one of our own distances from Malvern of Worcestershire, or
> Dorking of Kent,—suddenly—behold—beyond!
>   There was no thought in any of us for a moment of their
> being clouds. They were clear as crystal, sharp on the pure horizon
> sky, and already tinged with rose by the sinking sun. Infinitely
> beyond all that we had ever thought or dreamed,—the seen walls of
> lost Eden could not have been more beautiful to us; not more awful,
> round heaven, the walls of sacred Death. (115)

Though the mountains dominate this view, the city's "garden promenade" in the foreground, and the river and plain
across which the unsuspecting eye travels, are essential
elements in Ruskin's visual experience of Alpine glory. At
Milan, later in the chapter, the experience is twice repeated: the distant Alps are seen once through the ornate
pinnacles of the cathedral, and a second time, at sunset,
from a park which looks across the town. "The Col de la
Faucille" concludes with a magnificent prospect of the
Alps across the lake and valley of Geneva—a vision, Ruskin
says, of his Holy Land. The foreground of garden and city
and Gothic tracery, missing from this prospect, is supplied
by a lenthy, almost cinematic exploration of the town of
Abbeville at the beginning of the chapter. The reader,
traversing the intervening time and space imaginatively as
"the modern fashionable traveller" (153), forms a composite prospect. When Ruskin reaches "The Campo Santo"
—literally the holy land—he discovers a familiar and satisfying view at both Lucca and Pisa: sunset walks, marble
towers, a city at his feet, and clouds and mountains in the
distance. "The Grande Chartreuse," recounting Ruskin's
unconversion, opens with his disappointed expectations of
the same scene at the Carthusian monastery, and closes
with his discovery of it in an unexpected place, the city of

Turin. There, when Ruskin leaves the viewless grey Waldensian chapel, he climbs to an upper gallery with an open window. The afternoon light brings out a glow of "perfect colour" (496) in the Veronese painting which is his richly sensuous foreground. Accompanied by music, bathed in rosy light, opening on a view of remembered, if not literally seen mountains, the secular Veronese painting in the gallery of Turin is justified and sanctified as it takes the place of natural and religious art in the foreground of Ruskin's visual domain.

The most extensive description of that domain occurs in the chapter which would have fallen almost at the center of *Praeterita*. "The Simplon," third in order of the five chapters which present this landscape most intensely, describes the prospect of and from Geneva. Our first view of it is from the Simplon, "that mighty central pass" through the Alps (320), and it reveals

> this bird's-nest of a place, to be the centre of religious and social thought, and of physical beauty, to all living Europe! . . . . It rules them,—is the focus of thought to them, and of passion, of science, and of *contrat social* . . . . Saussure's school and Calvin's— Rousseau's and Byron's, —Turner's,—
> And of course, I was going to say, mine . . . . (321)

There is no mistaking Ruskin's intention. We are to see Geneva as more than geographically central; to regard it as the focus of a mental landscape which is both public ("to all living Europe") and personal. The seven pages that follow present the city exclusively in visual terms, but Ruskin's description is charged with such energy that we read it as a mythical landscape of desire.[3]

On every side of this island city, surrounded by gardens and approached by "the delicatest of filiform suspension bridges" (323), he discovers variations of an ideal view. From bridge, terrace, or "sycamore-shaded walk," he shows us now an expanse of lake, now of orchard and vineyard, which carry the eye up to more "ghostly ranges of incredible mountains" (325). Finishing his circuit of the town, he turns inward to examine the foreground of this

visual feast more closely. In the high, dark, secluded center
of the town, we are admitted to Mr. Bautte's, the jeweler
whose workmanship in "purest gold" achieves a unique
"subtlety of linked and wreathed design" (326). We come
away from this *sanctum sanctorum* "of treasure possessed"
—the visual treasure of intricate pattern which was the first
and nearest of Ruskin's private domains. From there we
move outward to the great river which encircles the town.
The "not flowing, but flying water" has in it "the con-
tinuance of Time" (326). But this is time which is never
wasted, never exhausted, motion which is constant and
therefore never progresses, and never ends.

> But here was one mighty wave that was always itself, and every
> fluted swirl of it, constant as the wreathing of a shell. No wasting
> away of the fallen foam, no pause for gathering of power, no help-
> less ebb of discouraged recoil; but alike through bright day and
> lulling night, the never-pausing plunge, and never-fading flash,
> and never-hushing whisper, and, while the sun was up, the ever-
> answering glow of unearthly aquamarine, ultramarine, violet-blue,
> gentian-blue, peacock-blue, river-of-paradise blue, glass of a painted
> window melted in the sun, and the witch of the Alps flinging the
> spun tresses of it for ever from her snow. (327)

It is the perfect visual stasis of living natural design, as
Mr. Bautte's gold and enamel brooches are a Byzantine
perfection of artistic invention. In this ideal city, art and
nature are interchangeable: the river has "currents that
twisted the light into golden braids, and inlaid the threads
with turquoise enamel" (327). It is itself "one lambent
jewel" (326). And here the jewel and gold change places,
and "the dear old decrepit town" with its golden center is
embraced by the river "as if it were set in a brooch of
sapphire" (327-8).

   At the center of his book, Ruskin's landscape of desire
is realized in its most perfect form. "Foreground" and
"background" are no longer adequate to describe it, for the
spectator is now at the center of a view which extends
outward in every direction: from the city, the nearest perfection of timeless natural and artistic design, across the
plains of human dwelling and cultivated garden, and up and
out into the infinite rosy distance of mountain, cloud, and

open sky. The eye finds no limits to its motion, but the spectator remains fixed and motionless. From Geneva one travels everywhere, but need never leave home. It is the perfect image for Ruskin's life, and the antithesis of Christian or romantic pilgrimages: perpetual travelling, for the sake of the view; a series of circular journeys, with no direction and no goal; total visual possession of a universe whose center is completely human, yet completely impersonal. The unseen spectator loves what he sees passionately, and he becomes what he loves. In *Praeterita*, he is what he sees, and the landscape of "The Simplon" is the geography of a self, a geography perhaps not wholly conscious, but quite consciously placed at the center of the autobiography.

Had Ruskin ended *Praeterita* as he wished, he would evidently have given us four more views of his visual universe, returning to the landscapes he had come to possess since his first European trip in 1833. The larger structure of the book, with its center at Geneva, would have been a circle connecting the end of Part III with the middle of Part I, abolishing the temporal distance between the 1830s and the 1860s or '80s. The intended design could not be completed; perhaps, I am tempted to propose, it would have been left without conclusion even had madness not intervened. Ruskin had encountered the same difficulty bringing an equally digressive work to an end twenty-nine years earlier. "Looking back over what I have written," he began the last chapter of *Modern Painters*,

> I find that I have only now the power of ending this work,—it being time that it should end, but not of "concluding" it; for it has led me into fields of infinite inquiry, where it is only possible to break off with such imperfect result as may, at any given moment, have been attained. (7.441)

Ruskin's life had led him into fields of infinite inquiry too, and though it was time that it should end, its unprogressive course so far suggested no point at which it could arrive which would feel properly final. But Ruskin did end his autobiography. *Praeterita*'s two closing paragraphs give it a formal completeness which the planned four chapters of review would not, for in the actual *Praeterita* Ruskin finds his way back, not only to the familiar European landscapes of his middle years, but to the founts and springs of perception emblematically presented in the first two chapters.

"I draw back to my own home . . . permitted to thank Heaven once more for the peace, and hope, and loveliness of it," the first of these last paragraphs begins (560). The home to which he now returns is Denmark Hill in 1869, but the scene which he recalls combines the crystal waters of "The Springs of Wandel" with the pink-blossomed garden at Herne Hill. Combines—but improves; the child was lonely in his Eden of forbidden fruit, but in this return Ruskin takes his

> Elysian walks with Joanie, and Paradisiacal with Rosie, under the peach-blossom branches by the little glittering stream which I had paved with crystal for them. I had built behind the highest cluster of laurels a reservoir, from which, on sunny afternoons, I could let a quiet rippling film of water run for a couple of hours down behind the hayfield, where the grass in spring still grew fresh and deep. There used to be always a corncrake or two in it. Twilight after twilight I have hunted that bird, and never once got glimpse of it: the voice was always at the other side of the field, or in the inscrutable air or earth. And the little stream had its falls, and pools, and imaginary lakes. Here and there it laid for itself lines of graceful sand; there and here it lost itself under beads of chalcedony. . . . Happiest times, for all of us, that ever were to be. (560-1)

The glittering stream absorbs Ruskin's gaze like "the gay glittering" Rhone of his Geneva landscape (327). But the lovely peace of this paradise is nearly all foreground. Only the voice of the unseen bird for an instant leads the eye to "the other side of the field, or in the inscrutable air or earth"; it returns to lose itself in the "falls, and pools, and imaginary lakes" of the little stream under the peach-blossoms. Vision is contracted, as if to the child's perspective; the stream forms a landscape in miniature. The distant heights to which the man's eye travels exist as yet only in the child's imagination. We remember what Ruskin told us at the end of his first chapter:

> . . . that the personal feeling and native instinct of me had been fastened, irrevocably, long before, to things modest, humble, and pure

in peace, . . . by the cress-set rivulets in which the sand danced and
minnows darted above the Springs of Wandel. (33)

From 1889, by way of 1869, Ruskin has returned to his
earliest memories, the peaceful foreground of his visual
domain.

But the book does not end here. There is no single completed circle, no simple joining of end and beginning, in
memory. "How things bind and blend themselves together!" the second of these last paragraphs opens. The
"glittering stream" at Denmark Hill led him back to the
"spring of crystal water" at Croydon, but memory does not
stop when it has found its source. The last paragraph of
Praeterita recapitulates the process it has just articulated.
Memories of fountains and crystal waters multiply: Trevi
of Rome, 1872; Brande of Siena, 1870; the Brande of
Dante's poetry; "the crystal and ruby glittering" of water
changing into wine in Joseph Severn's unfinished "Marriage at Cana." Visual similarities—light playing on water in
the foreground of a larger scene—bind and blend together
disparate experiences which neither simple chronology nor
purposeful progression can adequately connect. The visible
fountains accumulate emotional significance. When their
source is discovered and all are revisited, they come to
designate an aspect of the self: "the personal feeling"
which is "fastened . . . to things modest, humble, and pure
in peace." But behind that single foreground feature, Ruskin
recreates a familiar view, a landscape which places "the
personal feeling" attached to sunlit water in a perspective
we now recognize. From the Fonte Brande Ruskin walks
to the hills above Siena. Glitter and movement continue to
occupy his foreground, though now they come not from
light on water but from fireflies at sunset in nearby dark
thickets. Beyond this living design the town of Siena is
seen through its gates. Behind gates and city rise "moun-
tainous clouds still lighted from the west, and the openly
golden sky," the furthest reaches of the Holy Land which
Ruskin visually occupies.

As Ruskin again creates the same view, Pater's description of the only possible self-consciousness is graphically

realized.[4] The fabric which is perpetually woven and unwoven has a visual counterpart in *Praeterita*: the landscape
which Ruskin dissolves into its elements, so that he may
trace them to their sources in memory and recompose them
into landscape again. The web of consciousness which
emerges is always the same. Pattern and self correspond,
but they can be known only through the process by which
they recreate themselves.

There is a change in the Siena view, however, and it
brings autobiographical recreation of the Paterian kind to its
only possible end. Ruskin's eye moves from fireflies to
clouds and sky, but it also returns, by Siena's gate, to his
foreground, if not to his heart, there to lose itself forever
among those tiny, glittering lights. For the first time, foreground overwhelms background; perspective disappears.
Ruskin's visual space collapses to a single plane of moving
lights. How like, and yet how different, from the sun that
Turner saw at his death, or the stars that close Dante's
great visions.

> *How* they shone! moving like fine-broken starlight through the pur-
> ple leaves. How they shone! through the sunset that faded into thun-
> derous night as I entered Siena three days before, the white edges of
> the mountainous clouds still lighted from the west, and the openly
> golden sky calm behind the Gate of Siena's heart, with its still golden
> words, "Cor magis tibi Sena pandit," and the fireflies everywhere in
> sky and cloud rising and falling, mixed with the lightening, and more
> intense than the stars. (562)

For all their wonderful brilliance, the fireflies are very small,
and very near.

Ruskin was what he saw; *Praeterita* continually recreates
that self as he sees again all that he loves most deeply. As long
as memory leads and the eye responds, there can be no end
to that perpetual recreation. But in *Praeterita's* last paragraph, Ruskin reverses the visual movements of a lifetime.
From background, he returns to foreground; from the brilliance of sunset cloud, to the tiny lights of fireflies; from the
intense happinesses of mountains, to the pure peace—perhaps—of home. The Spectator has lost his view, and with it
his hold on self-consciousness.

The record of Ruskin's development and achievements is unfinished, but the formal symmetry of *Praeterita* is completed in its brilliant ending. In the Paradisiacal walks we have already returned to the emblematic scenes of the book's beginning. The fireflies of Siena take us there too, but only after we have seen the child's foreground placed in the larger visual domain of the book's middle chapters. The last two scenes perfectly balance the first two chapters, but they revolve no less about the book's real center, Geneva, and the landscapes which resemble it.

Like Arnold, Browning, and Tennyson, Ruskin had for years pursued in imagination the questing Ulysses. *Praeterita* bears the marks of his long vigil for the Ulysses in himself. But like the poets, again, Ruskin was not faithful to a marriage which proved uncongenial. *Praeterita* abandons purpose and chronology, and when it does a new kind of self-consciousness takes over. The patterns it creates may not have fulfilled Ruskin's expectations, but they are none the less there. The man reviewing his life still looked for the wandering Ulysses, but the artist, bringing his book to an abrupt close, was sufficiently aware of the form he had created to tie up the threads of his Penelopean web and leave it whole.

---

1. *The Works of John Ruskin, Library Edition*, ed. E. T. Cook and Alexander Wedderburn. (London, 1903–1912), 39 vols. Vol. 5, 387. Further references to Ruskin's works will be given in the text by volume and page (5.387) or by page alone in the case of *Praeterita*, volume 35 of the *Works*.

2. (1) Nyon, 1845: *The Diaries of John Ruskin*, ed. Joan Evans and John Howard Whitehouse. (Oxford: Clarendon Press, 1958), pp. 321–2, 364, and *Ruskin's Letters from Venice, 1851–2*, ed. John Lewis Bradley. New Haven: Yale University Press, 1955, p. 245.

   (2) Cormayeur, 1849: Bradley, 245.

   (3) Venice, 1852: Bradley, 245.

   (4) Lucerne, 1854: *Diaries*, 497–8.

   (5) Assisi, 1874: *Diaries*, 795–802, and *Works* 23.xlvii.

   (6) Venice, 1877–8: *Diaries*, 921–26.

   (7) Nyon, 1882: *Diaries* 1020.

3. Pierre Fontaney gives the Geneva description such a reading in an excellent and suggestive article, "Ruskin and Paradise Regained," *Victorian Studies* 12 (March, 1969), 347–56. But Fontaney concludes that Ruskin does not know what he is doing: "This happened in an entirely spontaneous way. There is no

doubt Ruskin was not aware of the imaginative structure of these pages as I have reconstructed it, and that he did not know that his relaxed, rambling narrative ran in the time-honored grooves of ancient motifs and myths" (356). Fontaney does not relate "The Simplon" to a larger structure in the book.

4. "To such a tremulous wisp constantly reforming itself on the stream, to a single sharp impression, with a sense in it, a relic more or less fleeting, of such moments gone by, what is real in our life fines itself down. It is with this movement, with the passage and dissolution of impressions, images, sensations, that analysis leaves off—that continual vanishing away, that strange perpetual weaving and unweaving of ourselves." "Conclusion," *The Renaissance*, (London: Macmillan, 1910), p. 236.

CLAUDETTE KEMPER COLUMBUS

Ruskin's *Praeterita* as Thanatography

In *Praeterita* Ruskin writes that he means to describe his visit to the Grande Chartreuse during which "a word was said of significance enough to alter the course of religious life in me, afterward forever."[1] This introduction would seem to be followed by meaningful language, a decisive confrontation. But what immediately follows, in fact, is a failed encounter with a monk to whom Ruskin addresses no significant word, and from whom he receives none. That is the first of a series of encounters which show Ruskin, who refuses to allow that the words of others have significance, himself resorting to silence at moments when he could communicate with another person. This encounter further serves to show the hollowness of that language which he does employ. For example, his tribute to the restorative powers of mountains is not only described as a tribute to an outworn power, but he had himself been "totally disappointed" with the mountains around the monastery. Another potential restorative, the ideal character of a nun (whose prototype Ruskin had found in a tale) is followed by descriptions of a "never forgotten" experience of a nun to whose exhortations he responds years later in his autobiography (while remaining silent at the time): "it has always seemed to me that there was no entering into that rest of hers" (XXXV, 478). Again, Ruskin shows himself lapsing into wordlessness. A negative narrative—and a negative Ruskin—gradually dominates the positive version of his life.

For example, in relating his unconversion, his estrangement from organized religion, he provides no indication of what he was converted *to*. Nor does Ruskin support his hyperbolic estimate of his own "best" work. Although he names the years 1840-1860 as those in which he did this work, he also presents it as meaningless—as he also does on occasion in letters, diaries, *Fors Clavigera*, and other chapters of *Praeterita*: the ten years from 1850 to 1860 were "for the most part wasted in useless work."[2] In brief, negations of any positive valuation seem to be *Praeterita's* recurrent pattern: méconnaissance in conversion, emptiness in excellence, death in the print of life. By remaining persistently unspoken, the promised Word communicates his psychogiobraphy more powerfully than the confidence he expresses in his own opinions. The compulsions of negation override the record of his achievements.

D. W. Winnicott discovered that what had become real to one of his patients were the blanks, the gaps in life. What was not there, what was lost, what was negative obviated for her any positive therapeutic interanimation. Winnicott imagined his patient saying, "The negative [of things which had gone before; the memory of things that yet had never even then been satisfactory] is more real than the positive of you."[3] Jacques Lacan postulates a similar "two body" psychology, arguing that the *moi* of the speaking subject differs from the presence which is speaking According to him, the two "bodies" are out of touch with each other, each remaining unconscious of both its own and the other's sphere of awareness.[4]

Although my discussion of Ruskin owes much to Lacan, I nonetheless argue that in *Praeterita* the speaking presence does in fact reveal the repressed *moi*. Through mechanical patterns of reptition which are imagistic, verbal, and behavioral the second body, the *moi*, appears. Moreover, this second body "runs" the speaking presence. Rhetorical skills of so especially high an order as Ruskin's illustrate the incipiently robotic nature of language. Rote figures of speech induce predictable turns in the meaning. The mechanics of a verbal pattern in *Praeterita* so consistent as hyperbole sketches the nature of more than the positive Ruskin; it also sketches the destructive dynamic of the silent and negating *moi*.

It is not easy to assess the extent to which Ruskin as rhetor was conscious of depicting repression, the death-in-life conveyed in his verbal and behavioral patterns. In his letters, he notes that an encapsulated lucid self witnessed his insanity, and possibly the negative *moi* likewise bears witness to its own destructive presence. *Witnessing* is not, of course, the same as consciously expressing the operation of the repressed psyche in a text. Yet Ruskin must in some mode have understood the nature and consequences of that repression which by definition is not accessible to the conscious, reflective mind. By means of a mastery of language so complete that it no longer required conscious fashioning, Ruskin expresses what his consciousness would have censored. As if deliberately, he diverted the attention of his critical intelligence to the enterprise of mapping the external world. He thus permitted a portrait of his psychic world to emerge while his "back was turned."

One of the chief means by which he thus portrays his psychic world is hyperbole, which is an especially apt trope for placing unconscious perceptions in a text.[5] Symptomatic of repression so resistant to acknowledgement that it constitutes a third primal scene, hyperbole enacts the violence of the negative self, the *moi*, against any positive possibility.[6] By eliminating the middle or mediating ground, hyperbole insures the continuing separation of the speaking presence and the *moi*. But it also disrupts communication between the speaking presence and the other as well, so that the significant Word is never constituted and never spoken. A hyperbolic statement, even in day-to-day experience—"Isn't this the most marvellous dinner you've ever tasted?"—is, if seriously taken, subtly tyrannical. The hearer is perceptually and emotionally challenged. If he doesn't "rise" to the remark, some flaw in his sensibility is indicated. And the speaker is threatened, since anything so exceptional is rare; hence, the unrestorable is being consumed.

Many of Ruskin's essentially hyperbolic statements enact mutually annihilating contradictions. These contradictions go beyond disparity, beyond such conflict of meaning that might in more normative instances invite creative

resolution. They even go beyond what John Rosenberg
terms Ruskin's Manichean habit of thought, for they obviate
completion of a hermeneutic circle.[7] The polar separation is
doubly negative because each side is shown to be unten-
able. Because hyperbole excludes the middle ground, tension operates only destructively.

One such powerful polar opposition that informs *Praeterita* is between Ruskin's drive toward an eremtic solitude and his drive toward social action. In the chapter entitled "Macugnana," the solitude so intensely desired is
unendurable, an illusion. And in "The Col de la Faucille"
Ruskin refuses Carlyle's vision of Eden as a "peopled garden"; he argues he is happy only when nobody (in particular neither his mother nor the gardener) is thinking of him.
Yet Ruskin proposes communal life with equal intensity and
chastises those who, eremitically monkish, had withdrawn
"from their direct and familiar duties, and ceased, whether
in ascetic or self-indulgent lives, to honour and love their
neighbor as themselves" ("The Grande Chartreuse" XXV,
481). The intensity generated by the alternating pull between
negated solitude and negated society, between absence and
absence, destroys Ruskin's ontological, operational, and
evaluational space. In its judgmental extremism—instant
exaltation, instant degradation; best work, wasted work;
mountain gloom, mountain glory—hyperbole makes self-
representation always a half-truth since any over-inflated
or deflated portrait of the self cannot find corresponding
reflection in the outside world: the valuations one makes
of oneself and others are inevitably disproportionate.
Ruskin thus appears either in miniaturization as Granny's
little boy, as St. Crumpet, or in magnification as Bishop
Ruskin, as an old lady in a household of wicked children.

The monk who shows Ruskin through the Grande Chartreuse provides him with an opportunity to find his eremitic
reflection in another. Ruskin asks "about the effect of the
scene outside upon religious minds. Whereupon, with a curl
of his lip, 'We do not come here,' said the monk, 'to look
at the mountains.' Under which rebuke I bent my head
silently, thinking however all the same, 'What then, by all

that's stupid, do you come here for at all?' " (XXXV, 477)
In his devastated and devastating silence, Ruskin finds
the other crucially lacking, so much so there is No Word
to be said.

This initial encounter produces four major charges
against the monk, yet each implicitly constitutes a charge
against Ruskin himself. First, the monk did not look out
the window at the mountains—that is, he had no eyes for the
moral lessons of nature—and yet in this chapter, Ruskin
himself does not describe anything outside the window; he
leans on the sill, but does not allow the mountain to elevate and solemnize his own thoughts. Second, the monk
had abandoned societal duties in exchange for solitude
and meditation. But, starting in 1858, Ruskin, who repeatedly referred to himself as miserably benevolent, suffered
greatly from the social responsibility he assumed to be obli-
gatory, until finally in 1873 he wrote that heroical self-denial
in the service of others had issued in catastrophe and disappointment, and had upset all his moral principles. Third,
the monk persisted in copying old books in the same patterns for his own pleasure, instead of attempting to draw
a bird or a leaf rightly. But in this chapter Ruskin expresses
his loss of confidence in his powers to draw, and he introduces the chapter by copying out word for word an old poem
of his own. He even asserts that this patently "old pattern"
is not only as good but even better than attempting to re-
draw his feelings during that period. This is reptition in
the most valueless sense, writing as replication. Fourth,
the monk, who is narrowly doctrinaire, teaches what he
does not understand (an inference drawn by association
with other representatives of the Catholic faith in the chapter). But, interestingly, Ruskin himself takes a strict, if
tacit, authoritarian, doctrinaire position vis-à-vis the monk
(and the nun). Without fellowship in language or companionship in seeing, the loss is in part the bitter death of
narcissism, the self drawning in its own projected beauty.
The monk, the accused other, is also an unacknowledged
altar ego, a negative *moi* appearing through Ruskin's
speaking presence and indirectly revealing Ruskin to be the

other. Rejecting the other's likenesses to the negative *moi*, the speaking presence terms them differences, while indirectly revealing himself to be like the other whom he is denying. So Ruskin illustrates Lacan's double impulse: to tell and not to tell; to see and not to see; to hide and yet confess.[8]

Before exploring the fatal discontinuities in the encounters that ensue, I want first to look at hyperbole's obliteration of value for Ruskin in the works of art in the chapter: the potential art gallery that is the Grande Chartreuse, his copied-out opening poem, an Hours of the Virgin, and Veronese's *Solomon and the Queen of Sheba*.

The word "Grande" indicates magnitude, but Ruskin cancels the indicated magnitude by a lengthy series of negatives: the monastery is "utterly disappointing," shows "nothing," "not a picture, not a statue, not a bit of old glass, or well-wrought vestment or jewellery; nor any architectural feature" (XXXV, 476). Eclipsed magnitude also characterizes the prayerlike opening poem, originally entitled "Mont Blanc Revisited," written in 1845 and so revisited in the 1880s. Ruskin recopies the poem, he tells us, because he does not feel able to recover the boldness and simplicity that prompted the original composition, a remark which indicates that the inner magnitude which was a source of value in the forties was near extinction by the eighties. The thoughts that the peaks in the poem had brought him in 1845 were such as experienced by holy desert eremites of old, extinct, solitary men in the darkness, absolutely dependent upon God. But Ruskin then erases this positive significance. The valuable hermit is extinct; and the "hermit" monk in the more recent past is valueless. Moreover, even the hermits of old at a lower elevation yet greater than himself transform Ruskin's "high" —his boldness, simplicity, the real temper in which he began his best work—into a low. The "lowness" behind the expression of his highness is also brought out in the body of the poem:

> Ah, happy, if His will were so,
> To give me manna here for snow. (XXXV, 473)

Ruskin's use of the subjunctive tense, the condition contrary
to fact, makes it seem that God intends to feed Ruskin
snow. So, not only at the initiatory peak of what Ruskin
recalls as his best work were his circumstances less and
lower than the past's, but God had already absented Himself from his dependent to the point that

> . . . all God's love can scarcely win
> One soul from taking pride in sin,
>   And pleasure over graves.

> Yet teach me, God, a milder thought,
> Lest I, of all Thy blood has bought,
>   *Least* honourable be.
>   (XXXV, 474 [italics mine])

   Since Ruskin associated mountains with concepts of sublimity, and since, dismal as it is, the poem strives after a
large effect, it may not be wholly illicit to cite Ruskin's
description of the sublime:

> There are few things so great as death; and there is perhaps nothing
> which banishes all littleness of thought and feeling in an equal de-
> gree with its contemplation. Everything, therefore, which in any
> way points to it . . . [is] in some degree sublime. But it is not the
> fear, observe, but the contemplation of death; not the instinctive
> shudder and struggle of self-preservation, but the deliberate mea-
> surement of the doom, which is really great or sublime in feeling.
> . . . Whether do we trace it most in the cry to the mountains, 'Fall
> on us,' and to the hills, 'Cover us' . . . ?
>   (*Modern Painters*, Vol. 1, III, 128–29)

   The definition of sublimity, the cry to the mountains to
fall on him, offers a negative measure of "magnitude," just
as do the Biblical echoes of the "least" who shall be most
in the poem. To the extent that Ruskin faces a doom so
vast as to be universal he is great, Christlike, purchasing
grace for others by shedding his blood symbolically (his
mother at once found fault with the words "sanguine stain"
as "painful / and untrue of the rose-colour on show" XXXV,
474).
   The potential for magnificence in self-abasement is a commonplace of a saint-martyr complex, but I am arguing that
Ruskin was aware he was describing a pathological con-

dition. Having depicted an inner, past (but unchanging) self with eremitic longings, he accuses himself as Other in criticizing eremite existence, making a catachretic displacement of Self and of value. Having warned his reader against the ascetic monk, he draws himself as an ascetic in the pages that follow, as indelibly Scottish and Puritan by birth and training. Yet his "ordained business," his "ordained" mental gifts "lay elsewhere." His use of the vocabulary of election in the unorthodox context of not-I, not-Mine-of non-election-typifies his crisscrossing of linguistic and categorical properties to depict psychological paralysis. For the worthy, desiring self eating snow rather than manna reverses magnitude, in a way not cathartic in any orthodox Christian sense. What Ruskin's poem and "The Grande Chartreuse" as negative self-portraiture bring to mind is, however, not Wallace Stevens' "A Weak Mind in the Mountains," but a powerful mind with a prospect neither of communication nor of self-realization. Yet in not succeeding as a poem, Ruskin's poem is Stevens' subject matter: Ruskin's poem takes the place of the mountain. The cost of the substitution of poem for mountain is evident in that these lines of verse lay for years in the "dust" of Ruskin's table, a bold and simple work of his own creation that did not work, yet is recopied.

The scene of Ruskin as a child, over-framed and under-depicted by the world around him, repeatedly watching his father shave and asking him repeatedly to explain or complete yet again the meaning of the insatiable picture on the wall shows how the excessively rich signifying of any object or personage that offers a possible *stade de miroir* all signal Ruskin's fate.[9] In "The Grande Chartreuse," the two works of art important to him re-present the dynamics of self-estrangement. One was a fourteenth-century "Hours of the Virgin" which gave him a joy that "-cannot be told, any more than-everything else of good, that I wanted to tell." His "Hours of the Virgin" was "extremely rich, grotesque, and full of pure color," and Ruskin saw in it palaces of Aladdin with "jewel windows," and a "fairy cathedral full of painted windows" (XXXV, 491), incalculable splen-

dors-in miniature. The other work, Veronese's "Solomon
and the Queen of Sheba," glowed with animal vigor in the
full afternoon light in a Turin gallery whose open windows
let in warm air.

The oppositions between these works of art are practically speaking innumerable. The Christian and sacred Virgin represents spiritual serenity and resourcefulness, yet
also suggests Arabian and Gothic architecture. For Ruskin,
Gothic is characterized by savageness, changefulness,
grotesqueness, rigidity, redundancy, imperfectness, domes-
ticity; in short, by terrible tensions. At the same time, the
little book is a pocketable collector's item, to be possessed
(in Ruskin's appalling analogy) as a seven-year-old possesses a doll. The Virgin's archetypical opposite, Sheba,
pagan and profane, represents gratified, carnal sexuality
and the skin of things luxuriously, languidly in bloom. The
painting of her is beyond Ruskin's encompassing. Too big
for the Virgin, Ruskin is dwarfed by Sheba.

Yeats' "Solomon and the Witch" proposes that "each an
imagined image brings/And finds a real image there."
But, in Yeats' poem fantasy transforms itself into real
images that achieve sexual and artistic contact between
self and other, and validation issues from difference. No
images in the painting validate Ruskin's potency. The
differences between himself and Solomon indirectly unmask
Ruskin's incapacities. These external images to which Ruskin responds so positively do not suit, because they do not
reflect him. They negate him, drawing his psychic eclipse.
In superimposing the image of Sheba on the Virgin's,
Ruskin's loss is shown as inescapable. If for Ruskin the
tiny pocketable Virgin is rife with discord beyond resolving, and the Sheba upon the wall not only magnifies but
alters the nature of the tensions that ravage his life, there
is no scale remaining for him to perform. His sexual potency a matter of public question, and reticent concerning
his personal fears, Ruskin nevertheless indicates how the
sexual and psychic dimensions represented by the two
works were closed to him forever.

Discrepancies in psychological size and affectiveness

aside, differences in sensibility, in culture, in nature between Ruskin and the Catholic "Hours," and between Ruskin and the hour of the painting isolate him in direct proportion to how well he appreciates them. Ruskin could not have been a Catholic. " 'But why did you not become a Catholic at once, then?' It might as well be asked, Why did not I become a fire-worshipper? I *could* become nothing but what I was" (XXXV, 492). And the Veronese so dispossessed him that he relegated his evangelical and Puritan belief to silence, supposedly "To be debated of no more" (XXXV, 496).

These objects of contrasting values share one quality: they express for Ruskin the defeat of the pleasure principle and the triumph of the death instinct (no more debate). His impotence appears in the emptiness that objects of overt plenitude have for him.

Repeating his response to the monk, Ruskin recounts two further instances in which he evades another by terming likenesses to himself differences. Such unself-reflexive, "mechanical" encounters emphasize the loss of self-articulation. While appearing to reinforce the self, the devaluation of the other in fact reflects an irreparable lack of self-realization.[10] For example, he speaks of Frederick Maurice as a man whom he loved, but Ruskin "only went once to a Bible lesson of his; and the meeting was significant, and conclusive." The subject of Maurice's lesson was Jael's slaying of Sisera, and Maurice denounced her violence and Deborah's exultant song.

> At the close of the instruction, through which I sat silent, I ventured to inquire, why then had Deborah the prophetess declared of Jael, "Blessed above women shall the wife of Heber the Kenite be?" On which Maurice, with startled and flashing eyes, burst into partly scornful, partly alarmed, denunciation of Deborah the prophetess, as a mere blazing Amazon; and of her Song as a merely rhythmic storm of battlerage, no more to be listened to with edification or faith. (XXXV, 486-87)

With hyperbole Maurice cuts the lines of communication, and Ruskin, reporting the scene in hyperbole, replicates the mechanics of severance, the constriction in dogmatism:

Whereupon there remained nothing for me,–to whom the Song of
Deborah was as sacred as the Magnificat,–but total collapse in sorrow
and astonishment; the eyes of all the class being also bent on me in
amazed reprobation of my benighted views, and unchristian sentiments. And I got away how I could and never went back. (XXXV,
486–87)

Most of the significant scenes in *Praeterita* are similarly
organized so that the crises in the text collapse into negation, withdrawal, silence.

Ruskin's refrain that he has vision and the Other is blind
in turn reflects his own blindness. He sees only himself seeing, and he only sees himself seeing. In his *Dairies* he thus
complains that he is the only person who raises eyes to the
most glorious sunset he had ever seen (I, 352), and he
remarks in *Praeterita:* "I don't think anybody who goes to
Geneva ever sees the Salève" (XXXV, 320). The "wonder
grows" on him, he tells us, "what Heaven made the Alps
for . . . yet gave no one the heart to love them" (XXXV,
320). What is true of nature is true of great art and literature
—all except Ruskin are blind to their beauty and value. Com-
plaining of his countrymen, he can thus claim "I know not
one who shows a trace of ever having felt a passion of
Shakespeare's, or learnt a lesson from him" (XXXV, 369).

Ruskin repeatedly isolates himself by feeling that he is
in the right—"the most terrific personal state that nobody else
is interested in," as a twentieth-century painter has put it.[11]
Ruskin, feeling in the right, and in silence a preacher, singularly unable to witness himself in the Other, repeatedly
un-other-self-reflexive, praises an act of rage in Jael which
he fails to enact himself. In the context of praising violence,
he reveals his repression of it. And hence, he goes further
than Jael; he violates himself. He turns to the distancing
silence of writing, and he uses tropes that do not mediate.

Unable to communicate with others, unable to act with
them in a fully human way, he falls into mechanical repetition. Thus, the same patterns inform his description of a
"fashionable séance of Evangelical doctrine" (XXXV, 489)
at which the Rev. Molyneux presided. In reply to one of
Ruskin's questions that popular minister excited himself on

the subject of the temptation to self-righteousness. Self-
righteously, Ruskin writes, "Under the fulmination of which
answer I retired . . . in silence; nor ever attended another
of the kind from that day to this" (XXXV, 490). Just as in
his 1874 diaries Ruskin reports a dream of concealing from
his mother the bones of the dead, so in his autobiography
the silence in which he writes reveals his repressive ways of
not coming alive. The repeated "silent" dyings of the *moi*
paradoxically pronounce its ontological *difference* from the
hyper-verbal, eloquent, positive pen.[12]

Spatial and interpersonal annihilations are augmented by
temporal ones. At least three temporalities are simultaneously at work in the autobiography. The events of his
life that occurred in actual time along the route of time's
one-directional arrow reappear diachronically in Ruskin's
roughly correspondent life story. That is, the selection of
those events and the mode of presentation which must distort them nevertheless generally attempt to follow time's
flow. Yet a latent, negative time, a suppressed and spec-
tral diachronic tracking is at work. As in the division of his
diaries into two, one a book of pain, old Ruskin alerts his
reader in his preface to the phantom diachronic sequence
haunting the pleasurable one; he says he will pass over "in
total silence" (XXXV, 11) things which give him no pleasure
to review. Apparently shearing off the negative, he alerts the
reader to its absence and hence to its existence. The more
alert and informed that reader, the more he will see the
book of pain in that of pleasure. One can conclude that the
oppositional effect must have been alive in Ruskin's retrospective view of his life. He could not have been unaware as
he wrote that the Ruskin of "The Grande Chartreuse" and
the "un"-conversion to life, to force, to work always created through "a simple act of love" was in those years also
the Ruskin who wrote of having no attachment to living
things (1851), and who thought the true secret of happiness
was to bolt one's gates (1855).

The title of Ruskin's autobiography indicates that he felt
his history to be one of death, for *praeterita*, customary on
tombstones, states, perhaps needlessly, that the deeds of the

buried man are done with, over. The effect of entitling a life's account with a tombstone term seems even more withering if the title is additionally interpreted to read "beyond" as well.[13] Etymological probes are characteristic of Ruskin, who in *Praeterita* plays with "pre-judiced" and "post-judiced" (XXXV, 104) and with *fors* and *clavigera* in the work they title (XXVII, 28). He may therefore be referring not only to things completely in the past, but—if *praeterita* also signifies things having always been beyond the individual's personal doing—to a pattern of life pre-frozen in the "realm of figuration."[14] Ruskin may be engraving the record of his past as having been from the beginning an entombment. Indeed, he may have attempted physically to emblematize this predestination (his particular life engraved on the tombstone of his birth) by electing as an old man to return to his nursery to write his autobiography. He makes graphic origin as ending, nursery as sepulchre, education not as leading-out but as a repression of death.[15]

His title also shows that he is conscious that the reckoning of life in language is a loss, a feminization, a death. He writes of his writing: "I knew exactly what I had got to say, put the words firmly in their places like so many stitches . . . and read the work to papa and mamma . . . as a girl shows her sampler. Drudgery may be a hard word for this often complacent, and entirely painless occupation. . . . but how great work is done, under what burden of sorrow, or with what expense of life has not been told hitherto" (XXXV, 368). Ruskin's dilemma is obvious: whether he writes for pleasure, complacently, as he says he is writing *Praeterita*, or whether he writes a great work under a burden of sorrow, the field of loss remains a constant.

In his preface, Ruskin says that he is gathering visionary flowers from the fields of his youthful life, not simply for "recreation" but to lay upon the graves of his parents. He presents these tomb offerings, the visionary flowers of his past, to his reader positively, that is, in consummate tactile density and as apparently pleasurable. Yet he is aware that the flowers are antibiotic, the "pulsations of death."[16] As early as 1843, in a letter to a college friend, Ruskin writes, "when you say a preparing thing, a fructifying thing, mean a *dying* thing. Therefore, whenever you speak of a tree, you speak of death. That which has not in it the beginning and germ of death, is not a tree. Consequently, if there were trees in the Garden of Eden, there was death; . . . the very meaning of the word flower is—something to supply death" (I, 476).

The *perdu* in Proust's title, *en recherche du temps perdu*, tolls loss so absolute that it negates search; memory "re-covers" and "re-dresses"—homonyms that contain the ambiguous operation of remembrance. In the process of reconstituting itself, restoration of the past demonstrates itself impossible, for one remembers what no longer exists or, possibly, as in Swann's case, one remembers what never existed. Yet though sensually enveloped, unlike Marcel, Ruskin provides no overt semiology for what is sensed. And, unlike *recherche*, *praeterita* implies loss so total that the equilibrium *au fond* offers no counter-constructs; it only traces death. For example, he does not seek moments from the past, but presents them as sealed. He speaks obliquely of the motionless, in that, instead of retrieving the past, he repeats his writing of it; *Fors*, his personal correspondence, *Proserpina, Sesame and Lilies*, his diaries, *Praeterita*, *Delicta relicta*, and others contain echoes, acoustical traces of one another, recapitulations of subject matter and sentence structure whatever the differences in tone and intent. As a result of this endless repetitiveness, Ruskin is seen to "go" nowehere; his writing of *Praeterita* is a re-engraving. Similarly, every trip in *Praeterita*, although it superficially records changes of environment and psychology, secondly bespeaks changelessness, stasis.

The determinism of destiny in *Fors Clavigera*, the idea of the end in the origin,[17] "the utter *unchangeableness* of people,"[18] evince Ruskin's sense that all origin is both ineluctable and "beyond," driving and static. What Mehlman terms a "self-regulating series of transformations of a constant system of relationships"[19] shows absence as life, for it reveals loss to be what Ruskin "has" by way of a personal "life" story.[20]

Writing for "pleasure," Ruskin does not directly proclaim his sense that he has missed life. Yet the realm for
being through *alterité* even in miniature is shown impossible: not that the object is too small for Ruskin, but that
even into smallness he hypostasizes grandeur too large for
the psychological Ruskin. The shrivelling of his extensional
existence is dramatized in his attempt to draw Bellinzona,
his will "gradually taming and contracting itself into a
meekly obstinate resolve that at least I would draw every
stone of the roof right in one tower of the vinyards"
(XXXV, 494).

But occasionally Ruskin openly discusses his sense of
"uncreation" and its relationship to writing and to reading.
"I looked for another world, and find there is only this, and
that is past for me: what message I have given is all wrong"
(XXXVI, 38). "I have *no* affections, having had them, three
times over, torn out of me by the roots—most fatally last
time, within the last year. I hope to be kind and just to all
persons, and of course I *like* and dislike; but my word 'affec-
tionately' means only—that I *should* have loved people, if I
were not dead." (1868)[21] "And as I transpose myself back
through the forty years of desultory, yet careful reading. . . , it becomes a yet more pertinent question to me
how much life has been also wasted in that manner, and
what was not wasted, extremely weakened and saddened"
(XXXV, 368–69). On June 19, 1874, a decade before *Praeterita*, Ruskin jotted down in his diary some reflections on
"uncreation" by God's anger. "The earth becomes void
again; the word goes forth: 'let there be no light!' There is no
man, but only dust, and the birds of heaven are fled"
(*Diaries,* III, 796). His practise of compressing decades into
a page and dismissing them as he does in "The Grande
Chartreuse": The assertion that "The events of the ten years
1850–1860, for the most part [were] wasted in useless work"
(XXXV, 483) (i.e., in writing) is a corollary of his often
expressed sense that writing eclipses meaning. "The more I
see of writing, the less I care for it: one may do more with a
man by getting ten words spoken with him face to face than
by the black lettering of a whole life's thought," appears in

grandiloquent letter XVII of the ninety-six that "compose" *Fors Clavigera*. In this letter, he quotes Plato's *Phaedrus*, where the king of Egypt upbraids Thoth, the inventor of writing:

> . . . you, the father of letters, are yet so simple-minded that you fancy their power just the contrary of what it really is: for this art of writing will bring forgetfulness into the souls of those who learn it, because, trusting to the external power of the scripture, and stamp of other men's minds, and not themselves putting themselves in mind, within themselves, it is not medicine of divine memory, but a drug of memorandum. (XXVII, 295)

Ruskin defines the spirit in which he writes this letter as one of "war with the Lord of Decomposition, the old Dragon himself,—St. George's war." As he had seen, the dragon of decomposition is the pen, the letter describing "this broken life of mine." A few months later, in Letter XXVI he writes that the Dragon is too true a creature, an indisputably living and venomous creature, the "marvel of the world," which does not know

> what to think of the terrible worm; nor whether to worship it, as the Rod of their law-giving or to abhor it as the visible symbol of the everlasting Disobedience.
> Touching which mystery, you must learn one or two main facts.
> The word "Dragon," means "the Seeing Creature," and I believe the Greeks had the same notion in their other word for a serpent, "ophis." There were many other creeping, and crawling, and rampant things; the olive stem and the ivy were serpentine enough, blindly; but here was a creeping thing that *saw*! (XXXVII, 483)

The greatest danger to St. George, Ruskin says, is of not seeing the dragon, the "seeing" "death worm" responsible for the decay of contact with the Living Word, of the signifier with the signified; and pen and penis are associatively creeping "seeing" things that prevent noticing. Ruskin's consciousness of the structures of meaning within a word, within word structures, within images, his "semiotic" habit of mind in other areas, the very care with which he "peeled" his life indicate that he grasped writing as hostile to life, mute death's ally, its vocal camouflage.

A constellation of associations already wheels through the

Ruskin cited in this essay; but he adds to the early letter
that tells of the seeds of death in the tree in the Garden of
Eden the cankerworm with the rose, the one "never separate
from the other" (VII, 422), an idea he attributes to Turner.
In Ruskin, rustic, Rose (flower, unenjoyed woman), Mont
Rose (an ideal, unattempted community that Ruskin envi-
sioned), R appears as a typographical character and a
typology of psychic structures of disappointed desire. The
letter interknits conscious statements with repressed ones
(mounting Rose) until planes of signification "slide" in-
satiably from one to the other and become "empty," unable
to fill the void, achieve a Word, the only Word: the plural
"I."

Carlyle describes biography as "Invention of Reality,"
"for which Understanding, a loving heart, vivid uttering
forths are required." "Looking with the eyes of every new
neighbour, he can discern a new world different for each:
feeling with the heart of every neighbour, he lives with every
neighbour's life, even as with his own. Of these millions of
living men, each individual is a mirror to us; a mirror both
scientific and poetic; or, if you will, both natural and magical."[22] But Ruskin, who had said that the "greatest thing a
human soul ever does in ths world is to see something" sees
no natural or magical mirrors to match him, but such irre-
soluble, hyperbolic contradictions as an "entirely right
upbringing" with "nothing to love" as its "chief calamity,"
and with *all* the fruit in the garden forbidden. However
influential and recognized he became, his feeling that he
had initiated nothing vital brought him not to the invention
of reality, the art of autobiography, but to thanatography,
the re-expression of repressions of original and static
death.

1. "The Grande Chartreuse" chapter in *Praeterita, Works*, eds. E. T. Cook and
Alexander Wedderburn (London: George Allen, 1903–1912), XXXV, 475, serves
as the focal point of this essay. Unless otherwise indicated citations to Ruskin in
the text will be to this edition.

2. On April 11, 1873 Ruskin records in his dairy: "It is curious I have so little
satisfaction in work done: only a wild longing to do more, and always thinking of

beginning life—when I am drawing so fast towards its end" (*Diaries*, ed. Joan Evans and J. H. Whitehouse, 3 vols.) [Oxford: Clarendon Press, 1956], II, 743). Herafter cited in text as *Diaries*.

3. *D. W. Winnicott, Playing and Reality* (New York: Basic Books, 1971), p. 23.

4. Jacques Lacan, *The Language of the Self*, trans. Anthony Wilden (Baltimore and London: The Johns Hopkins University Press, 1968), pp. 68–69. In drawing upon the vocabulary of professional psychoanalytic critics, I am left with ambiguous inherited terms such as "consciousness," "self," "the unconscious," and "body." Nevertheless, since there is no way to avoid these terms, I resign myself to working with them in the hope that they will become meaningful in context.

5. Jacques Derrida in "Freud and the Scene of Writing," *Yale Frech Studies*, 48 (1972), 74–117, discusses the mechanics of metaphor in relation to the psyche. According to him, when the "metaphoric machine" is not adapted to scriptural analogy, it remains an *optical machine* (author's emphasis). At that point, writing as a system of relationships between strata does not have a "subject," for what is verbalized has no reader within the psyche. Ruskin's text does, however, indirectly present the author as such a reader.

6. *See* Harold Bloom's analysis of hyperbole as defense of repression in *A Map of Misreading* (New York: Oxford University Press, 1975), pp. 48–51.

7. John D. Rosenberg, "Style and Sensibility in Ruskin's Prose," *The Art of Victorian Prose*, eds. George Levine and William Madden (New York: Oxford University Press, 1968), pp. 177–220.

8. Although I share some terminology with Jay Fellows, *The Failing Distance: The Autobiographical Impulse in John Ruskin* (Baltimore and London: The Johns Hopkins University Press, 1975), we work ultimately from wholly dissimilar contexts, and what Fellows argues as Ruskin's need for "doubleness" (pp. 124–26) has no bearing on a "two-body" psychology.

9. Lacan, pp. 163–66. Lacan argues that for the object to be discovered by the child it must be absent. Yet for the child to develop, the object cannot be excessively absent, continually in need of completion (perhaps especially by a father or the search for it will become pathological).

10. Jeffrey Mehlman's chapter, "Proust's Counterplot: Portrait of the Artist an Old Lady," in *A Structural Study of Autobiography* (Ithaca: Cornell University Press, 1974), pp. 20–64, analyzes the hidden complicity between fictions of autonomy and settings of dependency that are crucially lacking.

11. Frans Kline in a 1958 interview with Frank O'Hara.

12. In "Afloat with Jacques Lacan," *Diacritics* 30 (1971), Stuart Schneiderman observes: "The basic concept of castration asserts that the greatest anxiety derives not from the possibility of dying but from the possibility of never-having-lived. Symbolically this is the state of being buried in an unmarked grave—a fate that met two figures who are central to psycho-analysis, Moses and Oedipus. [The anxiety results from the possibility of not being represented by the word, of being cut off from the discourse of the community]. In the face of this anxiety man builds monuments; he writes poems, creates history, philosophizes. Each of these 'guarantees' a marker or a head stone. Yet all that is preserved in the market at the head of the grave is a lack of being present."

13. I have consulted *Harper's Latin Dictionary* (1879) which was translated from Dr. William Freund's Latin-German work of 1850 and later issued by the Clarendon Press in 1884. Citation B, center column, p. 1434 is especially haunting: "*To be lost, disregarded, perish, pass away, pass without attention or fulfillment.*"

14. George P. Landow, *The Aesthetic and Critical Theories of John Ruskin* (Princeton: Princeton University Press, 1971), pp. 329–56, presents a more optimistic view of the effects of typological (or prefigurative) symbolism on Ruskin.

According to that orthodox Christian typology which Ruskin knew, Moses although prefiguring Christ, does not *experience* Him. The anaological prospects which figuration opened for Ruskin contain value, for being like Christ is compensatory if one looks at the positive possibilities of the analogy. But, I would add, if the likeness exacerbates the awareness of the difference between the model and the living man, the consequences are negative.

15. Mehlman argues that there is a general "impossibility of becoming alive (*bio*) to oneself (*auto*) in the elusive realm which the French call *écriture* (*graphie*)" (p. 12).

16. The term is that of Jean Laplanche, "*Pourquoi la pulsion de mort?*" *Vie et Mort en Psychoanalyse* (Paris: Flammarion, 1970). He proposes an "economy" of "negative" psychological and biological energies: "*Le primat du zero sur la constance*" (p. 196).

17. Jean Laplanche and Serge Leclaire, "The Unconscious: a Psychoanalytic Study," *Yale French Studies*, 48 (1972), 133, connect childhood and origin university with the "myth of *Genesis*: in a single motion, the separation and the naming of heaven and earth occur." Old Ruskin's return to his nursery provides its own obverse. *Praeterita* habitually separates its Edenic landscapes from heaven by showing the roots of death in every garden. The positive—but hyperbolically dangerous—"high" reconstruction of Genesis observed by John Rosenberg in *Modern Painters* has become a husk by *Praeterita* (*The Darkening Glass: A Portrait of Ruskin's Genius* [New York: Columbia University Press, 1961], p. 7).

18. Letter of 1853, quoted in Derrick Leon, *Ruskin the Great Victorian* (London: Routledge and Kegan Paul, 1949), p. 190.

19. Mehlman, p. 13.

20. One may take this notion of prefigural determinism even farther, seeing his life as a repetition not only of childhood but of his father's life-as-living-death as well. The following letter which John James Ruskin wrote to Mrs. Ruskin when his son was twenty, suggests that the son's psychic stasis recapitulates that of his father. "I would to God," wrote the elder Ruskin, "I could . . . search out of my way into regions of Light & life & be even in this world at peace . . . but I live from day to day—without the power to will or to act: .

. . I am a most incorrigible
from day to day—without the power to will or to act: . . . I am a most incorrigible compound of Animal—a Rebel against my own poor aspirings. I have a sort of a Schoolmaster within that seems to scorn his pupil that can neither lead me nor whip me toward [,] that goads & soothes & flatters & reprimands but all in vain.
. . . I am composed of absolute mud, incapable of shaping or moulding into anything tolerable or decent. . . . I can neither recollect the past nor reflect on the present with the least Satisfaction. In short something is wanting" (*The Ruskin Family Letters*, ed. Van Akin Burd, 2 vols. [Ithaca: Cornell University Press, 1973], II, 558–60). Ruskin might have intuited why he began writing *Praeterita* on his father's birthday.

21. Leon, p. 402.

22. Thomas Carlyle, "Biography," Works, ed. H. D. Traill (London: Chapman and Hall, 1889), XXVIII, 45.

MICHAEL RYAN

A Grammatology of Assent:
Cardinal Newman's *Apologia pro vita sua*

The bow and life seem to be called by the same name, 'bios,' by the men of old; so Heraclitus the Obscure said: For the bow the name is life, but the work is death.

—*Etymologicum Magnum*

The story is a familiar one to students of the English Victorian period: In the early 1830s, John Henry Newman, a young tutor at Oxford, led a movement in reaction to the increasing influence and power of liberals, dissenters, and Roman Catholics in Government, Church, and Society. He guided his at times over-zealous, conservative followers back, not to the Caroline divines of the 17th century—the fathers of the Anglican Church—but to the Patristic Age, to Clement and Origen—the fathers of the Catholic Church. In so doing he came to question (especially in Tract XL) the very principles upon which the Anglican Church was founded, the Thirty-nine Articles, because they were not sufficiently catholic in the sense of the Alexandrian fathers. He was criticized harshly for this and forced, by the Anglican bishops, to terminate the *Tracts for the Times.* In 1845, he converted to the Roman Catholic Church, hoping to find there an embodiment of the principles he found lacking in the Anglican. The man who was too conservative and traditional for the Anglicans now became too liberal and heretical for the dogmatic Roman cardinals. Once again, he met with criticism and accusation. In 1864, a gratuitous attack against him by Charles Kingsley in *MacMillan's Magazine* provided the occasion for his *Apologia pro Vita Sua,* the autobiography whose ostensible purpose was to refute Kingsley's charge that Newman's description of the "Economy," the way in which religious truth is conveyed to man, either by God or by his earthly ministers, condones lying. The book was, in fact, a justification of his entire religious life to all of his judges and critics. In it he explained why he had ended the *Tracts* and why he had converted to Rome. This self-examination and the assertion of faith on the basis of private judgment and conscience with which it concludes provided the impetus for his most important theological work, *A Grammar of Assent* (1870), in which he sets forth his theory of religious faith with its emphasis on the individual's private sense of God's presence in his conscience. It is in the *Apologia,* however, that the theory of assent finds its most powerful expression, since there it provides the grounds for Newman's self-defense. The autobiography is the practice for which the *Grammar* would be the theoretical exposition.

Theologians have often used the metaphor of writing for God's voice in man's conscience. Jacques Derrida points out that they invariably present this as "good" writing in opposition to "bad" writing, or writing in the literal sense.[1] This distinction rests on a series of oppositions which, according to Derrida, are borrowed from Western metaphysics—presence/absence, speech/writing, interiority/exteriority, soul/body, life/death. Good writing means self-presence, the soul, voice, interiority, life, while bad writing is the carrier of death, the sign of non-self-presence (*la non-presence à soi*), the body, exteriority. For someone like Rousseau, good writing indicates the divine inscription in the heart, and for this reason it is "equal in dignity to the origin of value, to the voice to conscience as divine law."[2] Bad writing, on the other hand, is perverse, artificial, a technical representation which has more to do with the passions of the body than with spiritual laws. In the *Grammatology,* Derrida undertakes a deconstruction of the opposition between good and bad writing (and, consequently, of all of the metaphysical oppositions which lie behind it) by showing how the two, rather than being distinct poles, are instead supplements of each other. Each

member of the opposition is as much the other as it is itself. To be "itself" it must also carry the trace of the
other. Good writing is at the same time bad writing. I shall
attempt to show how, in the *Apologia*, Cardinal Newman's
self-defense rests on the theological distinction between
good and bad writing, and how the two terms, far from
remaining in opposition, and in spite of the Cardinal's apparent argument, become accomplices of each other. I shall
then draw some conclusions about the nature of autobiography.

As a response to Charles Kingsley's charge of "Untruthfulness," the *Apologia* consists of an apparently successful
search for an authority which would guarantee Newman's
truthfulness, the truthfulness of the *Apologia* itself as a
self-defense. The movement towards this authority passes
through dilemma and doubt before reaching resolution and
certitude. In a certain sense, the defense mimics the pattern of the conversion Newman describes. Both involve giving up hope in one direction in order to turn to another for
help. The term in classical rhetoric for this turning is *apocarteresis.*

The moment of turning in the conversion coincides with
that in the defense. Both occur at the beginning of the fifth
chapter. There, Newman asserts his faith in his new religion, and there also, his self-defense finds a justification
for the truthfulness of its own language. The fourth chapter, which marks the dark night of the soul in the conversion pattern, is also the low point of the defense. The narrative voice is there replaced almost exclusively by letters
out of the past. In this sense, actual writing becomes "bad"
writing; its predominance coincides with the moment of
greatest doubt in the struggle of faith Newman is relating.
The giving up and turning in another direction which occurs between the end of the fourth and the beginning of
the fifth chapters thus consists not only of a turning from
Anglicanism to Roman Catholicism, from doubt to certainty,
but also of a turning from "bad" to "good" writing as the
foundation of his defense. At that moment of turning, the
defense on the grounds of written proof—letters—reaches its

limit and is forsaken in favor of a defense, presented in the narrative voice, which rests on a faith in the voice of conscience, the good writing of the divine inscription in the mind.

Before entering into a more detailed account of the functioning of the *apocarteresis* in the *Apologia,* I will look at the "Preface," which offers a paradigm of the defense.

According to Newman, his well-poisoning Accuser has him in a classic dilemma:

> Here I will but say that I scorn and detest lying, and quibbling, and double-tongued practice . . . and I pray to be kept from the snare of them. But all this is just now by the bye; my present subject is my Accuser; what I insist upon here is this unmanly attempt of his, in his concluding pages, to cut the ground from under my feet,—to poison by anticipation the public mind against me, John Henry Newman, and to infuse into the imaginations of my readers, suspicion and mistrust of everything that I may say in reply to him. This I call *poisoning the wells.* 'I am hence forth in *doubt and fear,'* he says, 'as much as any *honest* man can be, *concerning every word* Dr. Newman may write. *How can I tell that I shall not be the dupe of some cunning equivocation?'* . . . Anyhow, if my accuser is thus to practise upon my readers, the more I succeed, the less will be my success. If I am natural, he will tell them 'Ars est celare artem;' . . . The more triumphant are my statements, the more certain will be my defeat.[3]

We can see why the "charge of Untruthfulness" is of such importance to Newman. If he is to defend himself at all, he must also at the same time justify the truthfulness of the language of his defense. Like Wordsworth's *Prelude*[4] or Rousseau's *Confessions,* the history of the self in Newman's autobiography must also relate the story of how the language of that history was discovered. Newman wishes to prove his own truthfulness and to avoid the snare of lying. And yet all of his proofs will be interpreted as snares. How can he escape this dilemma? Apparently, he does so without great difficulty:

> So it will be if my Accuser succeeds in his maneouvre; but I do not for an instant believe that he will. . . . I have never doubted, that *in my hour, in God's hour,* my avenger will appear, and the world will acquit me of untruthfulness, even though it be not while I live. (p. 8 [italics mine])

Newman first seems to give up hope, but, as we see, he has simply created a wave in order to ride it safely to shore. His Accuser prepares the way for his avenger. But who is this avenger? We are at least given the time of his appearance in the two nearly isomorphic phrases "in my hour" and "in God's hour." The appositional mirroring implies that God will be there at the moment of crisis. If Kingsley has cut the ground out from under Newman's feet, it is God who will break his fall and restore a secure foundation. This is the apparent logic of the phrasing, but there is another, more literal interpretation which would equate the self and God—my hour is His hour; I possess time as he possesses time, and to that extent, in that property I am He. The avenger would be both God and the self. We shall see how this provides a model for Newman's entire defense—a turning from dilemma to an authority founded on *martyria,* confirming something by one's own experience, and a version of *oraculum,* not only becoming a vehicle for God's Word, but also approaching an identity with God. Doubt becomes certitude because the self is inhabited and displaced by God. This should help shed light on Newman's epigraph: "Commit thy way to the Lord and trust in Him, and He will do it. And He will bring forth thy justice as the light, and thy judgment as the noon day."

Using terms like "Accuser" and "avenger," Newman creates a scenario whose pre-text is the Book of Job.[5] Kingsley seems slightly less diabolical than the biblical Satan, but Newman's repetitive characterization of him as the "Accuser" could be a deliberate attempt to relate him to the Satan of the Old Testament. Not only does Satan play the role of Job's accuser, but also the Aramaic word "śâtân" derives from a verb which means "to accuse," and by some commentators, the Satan is thought to have been modelled on the Persian secret police, one of whose functions was to accuse victims in court.[6] Newman's "avenger" also finds a parallel in Job's "witness" and his "vindicator":

> Even now, behold, my witness is in heaven,
> and he that vouches for me is on high . . .
> I know my Redeemer or vindicator lives,
> and at last he will stand upon the earth. (16:19–20; 19:25–6)

Like Job's "gô'ēl," Newman's "avenger" is God. By placing his faith in God's deliverance, Newman establishes a
resonance with the biblical text. The question of language,
of the truth or falsity of Newman's testimony about himself, seems to echo *Job*. As we have seen, Kingsley's
accusations assure Newman's "defeat" even if he "tri-
umphes." So the kinsman accused Job:

> How long will you hunt for words? (18:2)

Or, as another translation has it:

> Your own mouth condemns you—not I;
> Your own lips testify against you. (Anchor Bible, 18:2)

And Newman might answer with Job:

> My lips will not speak falsehood,
> And my tongue will not utter deceit. . .
> Til I die I will not put away my integrity from me (27:4–5)

It is, of course, Newman's stance of long-suffering combined
with righteousness which seems most Job-like. By establishing a parallel with the Bible, he implicitly undermines
Kingsley, and also suggests a strong precedent for his
defense on the grounds of faith.

Similarly, his giving up hope in one direction merely prepares a turning in another for aid. This is Newman's *apocarteresis*. As we see in the "Preface," he seems to emphasize the Job-like hopelessness of his dilemma in order to
reinforce the authority towards which he subsequently
turns. He will employ the same maneuver in the *Apologia*
itself. In the Preface he projects a two-part defense:

> I mean to be simply *personal* and *historical* . . . I must show what I
> am, that it may be seen what I am not. . . . I will draw out, as far
> as may be, the history of my mind. (pp. 13, 12 [italics mine])

In each case, the projected defense will be placed in doubt
during its exposition in Chapters I through IV. While performing autobiography, Newman will question the possibility
of autobiography. But, as I shall try to show, he does so in

order finally to serve the ends of his own autobiography.

A brief consideration of the historical defense will prepare the way for a more detailed discussion of the problem of writing in the personal defense. When he states the intention of his historical defense, Newman carefully limits its scope —"as far as may be." He goes on to apologize for the historical incompleteness of his "sketch":

> However, I have many difficulties in fulfilling my design. How can I say all that has to be said in a reasonable compass? And then as to the materials of my narrative; I have no autobiographical notes to consult, . . . Under these circumstances my sketch will of course be incomplete. (pp. 12–13)

The qualifications become more explicitly pessimistic as the text progresses:

> For who can know himself, and the multitudes of subtle influences which act upon him? And who can recollect, at the distance of twenty-five years, all that he once knew about his thoughts and his deeds, and that, during a portion of his life, when even at the time, his observation, whether of himself or of the external world, was less than before or after. (p. 81)

Newman's insight—that the self's supposed interiority is inseparable from the exteriority of the world—dictates the impossibility of an internal history of a sovereign self. He conceives of autobiography, the "history" of a "mind," in such a way that it would be ultimately impossible to write it. The "truth" he proposes to "show" is far more complicated than the word suggests:

> I will state the point at which I began, in what external suggestion or accident each opinion had its rise, how far and how they *developed* from within, how they grew, more modified, were combined, were in collision with each other, and were changed; . . . I must show,— what is the very truth,—that the doctrines which I held, and have held for so many years, have been taught me (speaking humanly) partly by the suggestions of Protestant friends, partly by the teaching of books, and partly by the action of my own mind. (p. 12 [italics mine])

The word "developed" suggests that Newman thinks of personal history in the same way that he thinks of ecclesiastical history—as a development. As Christian doctrine derives its authority from its progression or succession from Antiquity, so Newman's history, his self-defense, might gain an authority by tracing the development of his "religious opinions" from the antiquity of childhood to the present of writing. The fact that Antiquity holds sway over all history that follows would give particular importance to Newman's childhood feeling of predestined personal salvation:

> I thought life might be a dream, or I an Angel, and all this world a deception, my fellow-angels by a playful device concealing themselves from me, and deceiving me with the semblance of a material world . . . I believe that [the inward conversion] had some influence on my opinions, in the direction of those childish imaginings which I have already mentioned, viz. in isolating me from the objects which surround me, in confirming me in my mistrust of the reality of material phenomena, and making me rest in the thought of two and two only absolute and luminously self-evident beings, myself and my Creator. (pp. 14, 16)

In the sense of autobiographical development, Newman never ceases to think of himself as an Angel and of the material world as a semblance, and his self-justification in Chapter V will rest on this antique "childish" feeling of divine justification: "I considered myself predestined to personal salvation . . . elected to eternal glory" (p. 16).

By questioning the possibility of autobiography as history, Newman prepares the way for a more successful "personal" part of his defense. Yet, he undermines the personal as much as the historical defense, and we see this particularly in his attitude towards writing. While he describes historical writing as an inevitable contraction which is necessarily incomplete, he also implies that all writing is merely a substitute representation which does not convey or retain the self's presence. Just as in the historical defense, doubt cohabits with certitude, so also in the personal defense, Newman's doubt and ambivalence concerning writing's autobiographic status seems in the end to further his defense.

Newman desires "to be known as a *living man*, not as a *scarecrow* which is dressed up in my clothes" (p. 12 [italics mine]). The oppositions implied in this desire are those between life and death, truth and falsity, presence and absence, thing and representation. To the scarecrow belongs the second member of each pair. As the sign of non-self-presence and death, it might be comparable to what we have called bad writing. The scarecrow resembles the self ("dressed up in my clothes"),[7] but it also takes the place of the self ("the phantom . . . which gibbers instead of me"). In addition to the distorted verbal representation ("gibbers"), it, like writing, is a form of visible representation ("my clothes"). And also like writing, it represents death for the "living" self-presence of the represented thing. To this implied chain of oppositions should be added that between meaning and words, for it is Newman's "meaning," or the meaning of "Newman," which Kingsley questions:

> Yes, I said to myself, his very question is about my *meaning*; 'What does Dr. Newman mean?' . . . He asks about what I *mean*; not about my words, not about my arguments, not about my actions, as his ultimate point, but about that living intelligence, by which I write, and argue, and act. (p. 11)

Like the "living man," the "living intelligence" is separate from its representations. The "Mind," the residence of meaning and the origin of words, is distinguished by Newman from the words which are its vehicles and its products. As external signs of an internal intelligence, words are like scarecrows: they clothe but are not the "living" thing. Newman privileges the internal self-presence of meaning to the mind over external representation. In this valorization we find the pattern for all of the hierarchical oppositions contained in the "Preface"—truth is desired over falsity, presence over absence, the living over the dead.

If words are scarecrows, carriers of death for the living interiority of consciousness, how is Newman's personal defense defined as a desire to present the living man by means of language, possible? At one point in the "Preface," Newman refers to a letter as a "written memorial"—tombstone as well as remembrance. Words may not be the "living," but they might *remember*, or signify, the living. In *The Idea of a University*, Newman describes how "literary" writing remembers its origin in speech, which is superior to writing because it is linked directly to consciousness. The terms which we use to describe literature, he writes,

> belong to its exhibition by means of the voice, not of handwriting.
> . . . We call it the power of speech . . . and, even when we write, we
> still keep in mind what was its original instrument, for we use freely
> such terms in our books as 'saying,' 'telling'. . .[8]

At the same time, because "thought and speech are in inseparable from each other . . . literature is the personal use of language" (*Idea*, 207). The written page, because it is the receptacle for an external repetition which remembers speech, is, for the writer, "the lucid mirror of his mind and life" (*Idea*, 221). Literary writing, therefore, is essentially autobiographical, and for this reason Newman can write in the "Notes" to one of his "Early Journals": "For what we know (considering how much character lies in little things, e.g. handwriting) any one act concentrates the man."[9]

This writing, however, is autobiographical only in that it mirrors speech which is bound up with thought—"the two-fold Logos." Newman's theory of the Economy helps account for this logocentric conception of language. In the Economy, the representation is secondary to the thing represented, whose "substantial truth" is nevertheless preserved and conveyed in its re-presentation, which Newman calls a "shadow . . . economical; necessarily imperfect, as being exhibited in a foreign medium."[10] In the divine scheme of things, Newman argues, the Son is an Economy, or "repetition," of the Father. Using the model of the Economy, we might say that writing is the son of the fathering self; it is an Economy, or repetition-in-difference, of speech/ thought. As a mirror-image, it is external, foreign, a shadow, imperfect, but it nevertheless preserves and remembers the truth of that which it represents.

Newman is not always consistent on this point, and there are times when he seems to contradict himself by arguing against the autobiographic potential of literary writing and of language in general. The son might be capable of forget-fulness. Of quoting his own words, Newman writes in the *Grammar of Assent:*

> I quote them, because . . . they represent the doctrine upon which I
> have been insisting, *from a second point of view*, and with a freshness
> and force which I cannot now command, and moreover, (though they
> are my own, nevertheless, from the length of time which has elapsed
> since their publication), *almost with the cogency of an independent
> testimony.*[11]

This writing has—almost—ceased to be autobiographical. It
has almost relinquished that one referent which all writing
is supposed to have—the originating consciousness. A similar
undermining of writing's autobiographic status occurs in the
Apologia where Newman, who defines writing in the
Grammer as a "*logic* of memory, a *memoria technica*"
(*Gram*, 337), an aid to memory which in fact aids forgetfulness, writes:[12]

> It is the concrete being that reasons; pass a number of years, and I find
> my mind in a new place; how? the whole man moves; *paper logic* is
> but the record of it. (p. 136 [italics mine])

Time's differentiating movement gives writing its authority
as "independent testimony," but it also betrays a certain
expropriation of subjectivity in writing.

Bad writing, for Newman, is *technè*, the artificial arrangement of words, and one version of it is logic, the technical
apparatus for reasoning by external propositions. This is
most evident in the *Grammar* where Newman debunks writing and logic as principles of exteriority in favor of speech
and conscience as principles of interiority. He defines
"notions" as metonymies of the things they represent:

> Our notions of things are never simply commensurate with the things
> themselves. . . . This, then, is another instance in which the juxta-
> position of notions by the *logical* faculty lands us in what are
> commonly called mysteries. Notions are but aspects of things. (*Gram*,
> 52 [italics mine])

In Newman's system of assent, notional assent, distinguished from real assent by being an abstraction of concrete
things, belongs with inference, "Verbal reasoning, of whatever kind, as opposed to mental" (*Gram*. 263). Logic, the
"regulating principle" of inference, makes language
abstract by starving

each term down till it has become the ghost of itself . . . so that it
may stand for just one unreal aspect of the concrete thing to which it
properly belongs. (*Gram*, 267)

At times, Newman seems to ascribe this metonymizing tendency to language when he refers to the "logic of words"
(*Gram*. 359) and the "logic of language" (*Gram*. 345). In
the *Grammar*, both logic and language, logic as a system of
language and language as a logical system, seem equally
bad, equally subordinate to conscience and the illative
sense, "the power of judging and concluding."[13] The rejection of logic in favor of conscience inevitably takes the form
of the opposition between speech and writing. The divine
speech in conscience is

a higher source than *logical* rule, an intrinsic and personal power, not
a conscious adaptation of an *artificial* instrument . . . not a *mechanism* . . . not the *formulas* and *contrivances* of language . . . not
any *technical appratus* of words and propositions. (*Gram*, 331, 345,
350, 353 [italics mine])

Artificial, mechanical, contrived, technical—these are the
characteristics of bad writing. In fact, in order to privilege
the voice of conscience, Newman must explicitly "reject"
both writing and logic:

He who has once detected in his conscience the *outline* of a Lawgiver
and Judge, needs no definition of Him . . . and *rejects* the mechanism of *logic*, which cannot contain in its grasp matters so real and so
recondite . . . Such a living *organon* is a personal gift, and not a
mere method or calculus . . . whither can we go, except to the living
intellect, our own, or anothers'? What is *written* is too vague, too negative for our need . . . each individual must have recourse to his own
rule; and if his rule is not sufficiently developed in his intellect for his
need, then he goes to some other *living*, present authority, to supply it
for him, not to the *dead letter* of a treatise or a code. (*Gram*, 315,
354, 356 [English italics mine])

In the *Grammar*, writing and logic are almost intersubsti-
tutable words, and we would not disturb Newman's system
if each time he wrote "logic" we inserted "writing" instead.
Like the scarecrow, each one is a scapegoat, opposed to the
living interiority of the voice of conscience as the carrier of
death.

Hence, Newman's opposition between "paper logic" and the "concrete being" in the *Apologia* belongs in the same series with the scarecrow and the living man, word and meaning, writing and speech.[14] In the final chapter of the *Apologia,* logic is once again associated with a writing that might not be autobiographical, might not be a full record of the living subject:

> But further still: you must not suppose that a philosopher or moralist uses in his own case the license which his own theory itself would allow him. A man in his own person is guided by his own *conscience;* but in drawing out a system of rules he is obliged to go by *logic,* and follow the exact deduction of conclusion from conclusion, and must be sure that the whole system is coherent and one. You hear of even immoral or irreligious books being written by men of decent character; there is a late writer who says that David Hume's skeptical works are not at all the picture of the man. (p. 211)

It is at this point that Newman's ambivalence towards the autobiographic status of writing seems most clear. In order to defend the truthfulness of his own defense, he must argue that a writer can condone lying while not lying himself, or that he can lie in writing while not being a liar. Newman desires a writing which would present the living man, and yet one of the ostensible arguments of the book, the defense of the Economy, sets out to prove that writing is neither a "lucid mirror" of the mind, nor a "picture of the man."

Newman's ambivalence towards writing, if followed rigorously, would place his personal defense in doubt. How can one argue that writing is non-autobiographical in a text which purports to be autobiographical? But this contradiction might also further Newman's self-defense, in the long run, by a certain detour. His seeming ambivalence might rest on the distinction he seems to make between the writing in which the writer "is guided by his own conscience" and that in which "he is obliged to go by logic." The first is autobiographical because it derives from the internal voice, the second is not because it is merely a technical arrangement of external signs. In the *Idea,* Newman distinguishes between the language of Literature, which is "of a personal character," and that of Science, which "treats of what is universal or eternal" and is "in no sense personal" (*Idea,* 218). The *Apologia* is obviously meant to be a work of conscience or Literature, not of logic or Science. And yet, it seems to aspire towards Science—"I wish . . . simply to state facts" (p. 13)—while at the same time placing in question Literature, the personal defense—"as far as I dare witness about myself" (p. 144). By arguing against the autobiographic status of writing and by questioning the capacity of his mind to know itself, Newman, in the *Apologia,* deliberately undermines his own defense. But by so doing, he also creates a need, and prepares the way, for a defense which is uncontaminated by ambivalence and aporia. This, perhaps, is the detour which allows him to accede to the seemingly infallible authority which he assumes in the "Preface."

Good writing and bad writing. We have seen how Newman condemns the latter and relegates it to a secondary position in relationship to the former. His grounds for doing so in the *Grammar* are epistemological—the writing of logic helps us to know, but only the writing of conscience gives us absolute certitude. Since the *Apologia* seeks certitude it relies less on logical argument than on a laying bare of Newman's conscience—"my most personal thoughts, I might even say the intercourse between myself and my Maker" (p. 13)—in order to prove its case. While recapitulating his early arguments on assent in the *Apologia,* Newman writes of a kind of personal authority founded upon "the constitution of the human mind and the will of its Maker," and he distinguishes between "certitude," which is a "habit of mind," and "certainty," which is a "quality of propositions" (p. 29). The "habit of mind" upon which Newman's certitude at the end of the *Apologia* is founded is the habit of conscience, "the connecting principle between the creature and his Creator" (*Gram.* 118). Logic is linked by Newman to the forgetfulness, lack of consciousness, and non-self-presence of bad writing. Its opposite, conscience, is associated with good writing, which shares the qualities of a never-fallen speech, that form of representation which, in Newman's theological metaphysics, always remembers the represented, which makes immediately present the full self-presence of consciousness:

> Were it not for this *voice,* speaking so clearly in my *conscience* and my heart, I should be an atheist . . . and if I am asked why I believe in God, I answer that it is because I believe in myself, for I feel it impossible to believe in my own existence (and of that I am quite sure) without believing also in the existence of Him, who lives a Personal, All-seeing, All-judging Being in my *conscience.* (pp. 186, 156)

The connecting principle between self and Other is spoken intercourse, "being able to hold *converse* with Him" (*Gram,* 118 [italics mine]). It is also writing, a divine inscription. In the *Grammar,* the "universal Deliverer" is described as having "*imprinted* the Image or idea of Himself in the minds of His subjects" (*Gram,* 464 [italics mine]). In the earlier *Lectures on Justification* (1838), Newman had resorted to similar metaphors of inscription—"copy," "mark," "Image"—arguing that the fact that the words stand both "for the instrument marking, and the figure which it marks" is a sign of the "indivisible union between the justifying gift of the Divine Presence and the inherent sanctity which is its token."[15] This is the good writing, the conveyor of God's Presence in the self, which Newman sets against the bad writing of logic.

It would seem, then, that the infallibility Newman assumes in the "Preface" rests on the autobiographical act understood not as being *autographical,* but as being *autobiological*—not as a self-recording in writing, but as a knowledge of oneself as a living being. That knowledge guarantees God's existence, while also confirming his Presence in the self as the voice of conscience.[16] It is this knowledge which is presented in and lends authority to Newman's defense. Just prior to the assertion in Chapter IV that his belief in God is founded on his belief in himself, Newman reminds us that

> from a boy I had been led to consider that my Maker and I, His creature, were the two beings, luminously such, *in rerum natura.* (p. 154)

In deciphering the structure of authority which upholds

Newman's defense, we cannot discount this continuing sense of divine justification. For justification, at least as Newman describes it in the *Lectures,* would supply an avenger, a guarantor of truth for the language of the self-defense. In justification, God makes man righteous "like Himself" (*Lect, 98).* The vehicle of justification is the "in-grafted Word":

> It is a Word having a work for its complement. Such is the charac-teristic of God's doings, as manifested in Scripture, that what man does by working, God does by speaking. Man labours, and a work follows: God speaks, and a work follows. . . . He does not make, He says 'Let it be made,' . . . He does not make us righteous, but He *calls* us righteous, and we are forthwith *made* righteous. *(Lect,* 98)

Unlike man's speech which is separate from the thing it names, God's speech is absolutely proper to the thing; the thing is made present in the naming. If autobiography con-firms justification, "the Divine Presence within," then like the language of justification, the language of autobiography is also necessarily true. To become "like Himself" is to as-sume the power of his speech. It is as if Newman has this in mind when he writes in the "Preface": "Natural virtues may also become supernatural; Truthfulness is such" (p. 8). Might a supernatural virtue also be naturalized? "In my hour, in God's hour"—in a curiously worded passage New-man describes the mixture of activity and passivity involved in the cohabitation of "I" and "He":

> He has willed, I say, that we should so act, and, as willing. He co-operates with us in our acting, and thereby enables us to do that which He wills us to do, and carries us on, if our will does but co-operate with His, to a certitude which rises higher than the *logical* force of our conclusions. (p. 157)

The certitude of justification rises above logic. This would seem to lead to a new version of Newman's original di-lemma—how to convey the certitude of His Presence in the self-presence of the self, what we have called good writing, by means of bad writing, the sign of His Absence and of non-self-presence? But in guaranteeing the truthfulness of Newman's language, justification provides one other important assurance. It sublates the problematic of bad writing by eliminating metaphoricity, the Economy, difference, the possibility of absence. The absolute properness of God's Word to the thing it names makes metaphor impossible— "it follows that the *thing* as well as the *word* righteousness is ours" (*Lect,* 108). If, through justification, Newman believes himself to have become "like Himself," then he avoids the scarecrow and can present instead the "living man" in a language of "fact" uncontaminated by the difference-deferment of metaphor. Economical representation, which has been called a "shadow," would in this way become substance:

> For such a transformation of shadows into substances, and human acts into divine endowments, far from being anomalous, is the very rule of the New Covenant. *(Lect,* 193)

So it would seem. But this would be to protect the text, by reading Newman with Newman, accepting the resident hierarchical oppositions which place good writing above bad writing, conscience above logic, truth above falsity, meaning above words, presence above absence, the living man above the scarecrow, fact above figure. If we are to believe Derrida, metaphysics is founded on such oppositions and hierarchies. To create a hierarchy by privileging one member of an opposition implies repressing the other. As I have pointed out, Derrida's gesture is to show how the two terms are in fact accomplices of each other.

> We could thus take up all the coupled oppositions [*couples d'opposition*] on which philosophy is constructed, and from which our language lives, not in order to see opposition vanish but to see the emergence of a necessity such that one of the terms appears as the difference of the other, the other as 'differed' within the economy of the same [*comme l'autre differé dans l'economie du même*] (e.g., the intelligible as differing from the sensible, as sensible differed; the concept as differed-differing intuition, life as differing-differed matter).[17]

Each term carries within itself the trace of the other; inasmuch as it is itself, it is also the other. The difference-deferment process constitutes all things, but it also at the same time deconstitutes them as things in themselves. As such the process cannot help but deconstitute itself even as it is constituted by/as itself. It has no "as-such-ness" because it disappears even as it appears, erases itself even as it inscribes "itself." Any text, therefore, be it philosophical or literary, or both, as is always also the case, forgets and conceals the difference-deferment which constitutes (while deconstituting) it. But the text always also reveals what it conceals; it cannot hide its own (de-)constitution. The concealment is itself a difference-deferment of what it hides, and therefore it is never complete in itself, never successfully carried out. A reading which produces this deconstruction, rather than protecting the text's system of concealment, would locate the moment or moments in the text when it reveals itself to be a structure of concealment and forgetfulness. Gayatri Spivak puts it this way:

A reading that *produces* rather than *protects*. That description of deconstruction we have already entertained. Here is another: . . . the task is . . . to dismantle [*déconstruire*] the metaphysical and rhetorical structures which are at work in the text, not in order to reject or discard them, but to reinscribe them in another way . . .' (*MP* 256, *WM* 13)

How to dismantle these structures? By using a signifier not as a transcendental key that will unlock the way to truth but as a *bricoleur's* or tinker's tool—'a positive lever' (Pos F 109, Pos E II, 41). If in the process of deciphering a text in the traditional way we come across a word that seems to harbor an unresolvable contradiction, and by virtue of being *one* word is made sometimes to work in one way and sometimes in another and thus is made to point away from the absence of a unified meaning, we shall catch at that word. If a metaphor seems to suppress its implications, we shall catch at that metaphor. We shall follow its adventures through the text and see the text coming undone as a structure of concealment, revealing its self-transgression, its undecidability . . . It is not enough 'simply to *neutralize* the binary oppositions of metaphysics.' We must recognize that, within the familiar philosophical oppositions, there is always 'a violent hierarchy. One of the two terms controls the other (axiologically, logically, etc.), holds the superior position. To deconstruct the opposition is first . . . to overthrow [*rénverser*] the hierarchy.' (Pos F 57, Pos E I. 36) . . . But in the next phase of deconstruction, this reversal must be displaced, the winning term put under erasure. The critic must make room for 'the irruptive emergence of a new "concept," a concept which no longer allows itself to be understood in terms of the previous regime [system of oppositions].[18]

In the system of oppositions which governs Newman's text, we have recognized a "violent hierarchy." Good writing is privileged at the expense of bad; truth at the expense of falsity; the living man at the expense of the scarecrow, etc. It will be possible not only to reverse but also to displace this hierarchy by considering one important metaphor in the text, that of the empty mirror in Chapter V. There, the text seems to exceed the logic of its argument and transgress the seemingly solipsistic, while at the same time divine, authority which Newman has evoked.

As a first step, it will be necessary to look at what the *Lectures* and the *Grammar,*[19] the two most important books for reading the *Apologia,* contribute to its deconstruction. I have suggested that the authority which Newsman assumes in his defense is founded on his sense of justification, of being an "angel," of having God present in his mind as the voice of conscience.

Let us begin with the notion of conscience as a voice. Newman has called it a sign of His Presence, but in the *Grammar* the grammar of his description of conscience leads to an altogether different conclusion. Because it reposes on "a sanction higher than itself for its decisions," one is "accustomed to speak of conscience as a voice . . . or the *echo* of a voice" (*Gram,* 107 [italics mine]). The last qualification (which occurs twice) is significant, for the seemingly slight difference between the actual voice of God and the echo which is heard in the conscience would imply that conscience is as much the sign of an Absence as a Presence. By being different from, yet at the same time the "same" as voice, the echo is constituted as the structure of writing. Like writing, the echo is without consciousness. Always subordinate to voice in Newman's hierarchy, writing seems to inhabit voice as that deferred difference which is the echo. In this regard, we should remind ourselves that Newman, even as he describes the very Presence of Him as a voice in conscience, resorts to a metaphor of writing or inscribing: "He who has once detected the *outline* of a Lawgiver and Judge."

I have already pointed to Newman's argument that

words like "copy," "image," and "mark," indicating both the instrument which figures and the figure made, describe the Divine Presence in the mind and signify the indivisible unity between that Presence and the sanctity it imparts. We might argue against Newman that it is the very undecidability of these words, that they signify two different things at the same time, which undermines the possibility of their referring to any indivisible unity. By pointing away from a unified meaning, they might also point away from the possibility of an undivided Presence.

The power of divine speech in justification seemed to constitute a norm of truthfulness for the language of Newman's defense. God's words, we noted, are proper to the things they name. Being able to claim this nominative power as within one in the voice of conscience, at once one's own and an-Other's, through justification, would seem to overcome Newman's distrust of words as shadows of real things. But at the same time that he makes this claim for divine speech, Newman cannot help but describe the arbitrary nature of language at work within divine speech. In fact, the speech which seems to overcome the economical character of language is at the same time itself economical:

> God treats us *as if* that had not been which has been; that is, by a merciful economy or representation, He says of us, as to the past, what in fact is otherwise than what He says it is. *Lect*, 67)

In short, God lies—justifiably, economically. The voice of conscience might not only be an echo, but the echo of a lie. The word "economy," then, here could mean not only representation, but also undecidability, in the sense that God's speech is both truth and falsity, both good and bad writing, neither one nor the other alone.

One other potential contradiction must be considered before we return to the *Apologia*. Newman's defense seemed to rest on autobiography itself, on the notion that self-contemplation confirmed justification, that God was present in the self as the voice of conscience. But in the *Grammar,* in an argument which repeats similar arguments

in the *Lectures* and the *Apologia,* Newman speaks of "a
chronic alienation between God and man" (*Gram.* 399). If
conscience assures God's identity with oneself, it also testifies to his difference from the self:

> My true informant, my burdened conscience . . . pronounces . . .
> that God exists:—and it pronounces quite as surely that I am alienated
> from Him. (*Gram,* 398)

This "heart-piercing, reason-bewildering fact" (p. 187)
supplies the ground for an argument for Papal Infallibility
in the final chapter of the *Apologia.* But this reason-bewildering fact would also seem to take apart the infallibility of
Newman's defense on the basis of conscience. Instead of
being the sign of pure presence, conscience might be
inscribed in a play of God's presence and absence; instead
of voice, in other words, it might have the structure of writing. With this, Newman's hierarchy would seem to be
reversed; bad writing might dominate, by constituting, good
writing.

I have suggested that, in a characteristic *apocarteresis,*
Newman prepares the way for his final defense on the
grounds of faith by deliberately placing in doubt all other
alternatives, personal and historical. The apocarteretic turning takes place at the beginning of Chapter V where he
writes: "I have never had one doubt" (p. 184). In terms of
his conversion and his defense, certitude is reached and
aporia is apparently overcome. The two major themes of the
chapter are the Economy and Infallibility. We have already
looked at his argument on the Economy—that a man's "logical" writings need not be a picture of the man because in
them he is not following his conscience, the internal voice.
Now the voice of conscience seems to supply the ground for
Newman's argument for personal infallibility:

> Starting then with the being of a God, (which, as I have said, is as
> certain to me as the certainty of my own existence, though when I try
> to put the grounds of that certainty into logical shape I find a difficulty
> in doing so in mood and figure to my satisfaction,) I look out of myself
> into the world of men, and there I see a sight which fills me with
> unspeakable distress. The world seems simply to give the lie to that
> great truth, of which my whole being is so full; and the effect upon me

is, in consequence, as a matter of necessity, as confusing as if it denied that I am in existence myself. *If I looked into a mirror, and did not see my face,* I should have the sort of feeling which actually comes upon me, when I look into this living busy world, and see no reflexion of its Creator. . . . Were it not for this voice, speaking so clearly in my conscience and my heart, I should be an atheist, or a pantheist, or a polytheist when I looked into the world. I am speaking for myself only; and I am far from denying the real force of the arguments in proof of a God . . . but these do not warm me or enlighten me. . . . The sight of the world is nothing else than the prophet's scroll, full of 'lamentations, and mourning, and woe.' (p. 186 [italics mine])

Several obvious things can be said about this famous passage. It follows the familiar pattern of *apocarteresis;* it manifests all of the metaphysical oppositions which we have seen at work in the text so far; it dramatizes how Newman's distinction between good and bad writing (and with it each one of the other oppositions) takes itself apart even as he sets it up.

First, the apocarteretic pattern of dilemma and resolution. The dilemma is twofold. On the one hand, it consists of Newman's difficulty in putting the "grounds of that certainty of his own, and hence, of God's, existence into logical shape," of expressing the good writing of conscience in the bad writing of logic. On the other hand, the dilemma is one of faith, how to reconcile the "great truth" of that certainty with the "lie" given it by a world without God.

In the first case, the dilemma of conscience and logic, Newman resorts to a rhetoric of negation which allows him *not* to state the grounds of his certainty, his belief in conscience, not to contaminate it with logic, while at the same time implying it. He makes the implied positive statement antithetical by turning it inside out. Instead of "when I see myself I see God," we find "if I didn't see myself it would be like not seeing God." The antithetical statement carries the positive statement embedded within it. This "figure" seems to fulfill Newman's desire to affirm good writing by means of, but without contaminating it with, bad writing, "logical shape." In fact, the metaphor of the empty mirror succeeds in defusing logic altogether by using a vehicle which is a logical impossibility—the self contemplating its own death, Newman not seeing himself in the mirror.

Newman's "grounds" are alien to logic, and logic becomes illogical when it tries to contain them.

In the second case, the dilemma of the self's truth and the world's lie, Newman resolves the paradox of faith by turning from the bad writing of the world ("The sight of the world is . . . the prophet's *scroll*") to good writing, the voice of conscience—"Were it not for this voice . . . I should be an atheist . . . when I looked into the world." Within this turn from bad to good writing, or voice, therefore, is implied the more general turn from atheism and scepticism to faith and belief, and it is for this reason that Newman is so sceptical of logical proofs of God's existence—"these do not warm or enlighten me." Logic is also the instrument of scepticism, whereas conscience can only be the instrument of faith. Newman accepts a temporary loss of faith (the "feeling which actually comes upon me, when I . . . see no reflexion of the world's Creator") and of self ("as if it denied that I am in existence myself") in order to turn towards a regaining of faith and of self ("I am speaking for myself only"). He simulates a fall into bad writing in order to demonstrate the inadequacy of logic and the hopelessness of the world and to strengthen thereby his assertion of voice, of good writing. In this way he seems successfully to appropriate bad writing and make it a function of his affirmation of the superiority of good writing.

Secondly, the hierarchical positioning of good writing over bad writing. As I have suggested, this opposition contains within it all the other oppositions which uphold Newman's metaphysical theology. In order to elevate the interior, living self-presence of the self in consciousness ("the certainty of my own existence") which guarantees the "truth" of God's existence, and in order to privilege the voice of conscience as the vehicle of His Presence and the grounds for real assent, Newman must reject the "lie" of the external world as the sign of His Absence, disqualify the artificial mechanism of logic which leads only to notional inference, and suppress writing as the mode of consciousness-less, the carrier of death, the sign of non-self-presence—"If I looked into a mirror and did not see my face."

For the empty mirror is writing, the figure of figuration, the metaphor of metaphors, the scarecrow.

Thirdly, the taking apart of the opposition between good and bad writing. Metaphor is traditionally conceived as being a detour to truth,[20] and this is how Newman uses the mirror metaphor. The truth, which passes "outside itself" while remaining "inside itself"[21] in the metaphor of the mirror, is the fact that Newman is alive and conscious of himself as being alive. The presence that is re-presented is the self's self-presence. The implied understatement of the metaphor is: "I am alive." It has been suggested that at a point in a text where a metaphor "seems to suppress its implications," thus revealing "its self-transgression, its undecidability," the text deconstructs itself, dismantles the metaphysical presuppositions which govern it. Let us explore further what implications, if any, are suppressed by the metaphor of the empty mirror. How is it undecidable? We can begin by reading the metaphor "as such," for its own truth, rather than as a detour to truth. What it literally says is : "I am dead." The empty mirror is a dramatization of death. Yet it also doesn't say this. The "I" looking into the mirror is not dead. It looks and is offered the image (which is of course the absence of an image) of its own death, as if it were dead: "If I looked into a mirror and did not see my face." I am alive, but I see (that is, don't see) myself, as if I were dead. Read literally, the metaphor says both "I am dead" and "I am alive. Both are equally "true," and it is this undecidability which lends the force of ambiguity to Newman's argument. But it might also take apart his argument. For what the metaphor itself implies is that the two statements—"I am alive," "I am dead"—are contiguous with each other. In other words, the metaphor conceals a metonymy. The metaphor implies the statement "I am alive" by means of its substitute, "I am dead" ("If I were presented with the image of my own death"), but within the metaphor itself "I am alive" touches and is part of its opposite. It is a metonymy of its opposite. "I am alive" is such only in so much as it is also "I am dead," and vice versa. It implies its other; it is its difference and its deferment. Life here contains death as its difference and deferment; life is an economy of death.

Like Pater in *Marius the Epicurean*, Newman desires to overcome death, to appropriate expropriation. The logic of the sentence demands that we interpret it as asserting the livingness of the living man. He guarantees that the absence in the mirror is an absence, *his* absence. It is his property, and as such it reciprocally guarantees his self-possession. It implies knowledge through the lack of knowledge. Since his being alive is beyond question, we are supposed to be surprised by the image of death. Newman desires to make death signify life, to make the end of knowledge imply knowledge. But death is the unnameable, the insignificant, the unknowable, the expropriation which erodes all appropriation, even the appropriation of death. Newman can only use it in such a way that it retains the sovereignty of its lack of sovereignty. The logic of the sentence can as easily be reversed as left intact. In this way, we would be surprised that Newman is alive, since, from the lack of any image in the mirror, we would expect him to be dead. Assuming death, life becomes a logical impossibility.

Instead of a hierarchical opposition, the truth of the metaphor thus implies a relationship of complicity between opposites. Along with the hierarchical oppositions which Newman sets up by means of the metaphor in order to secure his defense, this truth of the metaphor is also part of the message of the text. Because they are interdependent, this message should prompt us to re-read all of Newman's metaphysical oppositions. Truth and falsity, meaning and words, the voice of conscience and the writing of logic, the real and the artificial, presence and absence, self and world, good writing and bad writing—not opposites in a hierarchy, but accomplices in an undecidable economy.

We can deconstruct Newman's privilege of the living voice of conscience over the writing of logic first by reversing his hierarchy and revealing a writing—the echo—already at work within the voice, a death already inhabiting the living, and secondly, by displacing the hierarchy into a new concept—the empty mirror—in which opposites are inter-implicating and no hierarchy is possible. But the mirror is also the traditional metaphor for autobiography, and we might say that the empty mirror dramatizes how all autobiography inevitably deconstructs its own presuppositions. Perhaps the most important of these is that there is a self to be known, that there is a subject which has undertaken to know itself as such—*auto*—and which, as a self-present presence—*bio*—, is the referent of the autobiographical text—*graph*. What the metaphor of the empty mirror implies, however, is that there is no self to be known "as such," that the desired self-present presence is perpetually deferred, that the text is not the sign of the self but what remains of it, irretrievably different the one from the other. But they might also be the "same," in that the self, which in its desire to capture and render itself as a presence, inevitably escapes, becomes absent, is therefore "itself" a "text," a structure of difference-deferment. In order to know itself at all, to constitute itself as an object for itself, the self must be absent from itself "outside itself, in itself." Its self-present presence can only occur in terms of its own absence from itself. It is this differentiating and deferring in the very act of autobiography which problematizes the self-identical self posited by traditional autobiography. This should lead us to reconsider the opposition text/self. The *Apologia* might be a metaphor for the self, but the self is itself a metaphor, an assumed identity where there is only a differential play. The mirror[22] is always empty(ing), becoming a structure of absence, even as it is filled with the image of the autobiographer's desire for presence.

The question of autobiography in the *Apologia*, whether it is autobiology or autography—the record of the self's becoming present to itself, or the interruption of that record which problematizes the notion of self-presence—is played out in the word "apologia" itself. *Apologus* means fable, parable, allegory—a history. It defines autobiography as that which traces a genetic development, a continuous history of a self. *Apologia* can be broken down into *apo*, meaning "away" or "off," and *logos*, "speech." The word implies, therefore, a speaking away of something. An apology makes something go away by means of words. It excuses and thereby removes guilt. Literally, it speaks it off. The work an apology performs is the elimination of something, one could even say, the death of something. In Newman's case, this "death work" is complicated by the fact that what he wishes to speak away is itself an image of death—the scarecrow—although his apology is for his life (*pro vita sua*). By tracing his own genetic development from his childhood sense of justification to his present joint consciousness of self-presence and of God's Presence, Newman seeks to guarantee life against death, the scarecrow, the empty mirror, and the "prophet's scroll" of the world. To speak away death for life (*pro vita*) by means of an assertion of one's own consciousness of being alive—in this sense, Newman's autobiography is autobiology. But, as we have seen, death obtrudes at the very moment Newman asserts life. Newman's assertion of self-presence can never be entirely autobiological, auto-affective. It must pass through something outside itself in order to be itself. Something external to it must become a sign for the interiority of the self. This is the mirror. Like a signature, it becomes something external which names the self. This autography, however, cannot help being as much a sign of death as of life. It marks the boundary of that process of death which surrounds and inhabits the self, constituting and defining it. Another name for that process is language. The mirror, as I have suggested, is an image of writing or language. It reflects the self, but it also produces the expropriation of subjectivity. Like the signature which appears to name the self, but instead names its name, thus inscribing the self in a linguistic play which is no longer its own property, the mirror is that whose reflection or giving back is also a taking away. In the autobiographical contract, language agrees to reflect the self's life, but at a price. It will also reveal the death which constitutes that life. Along with whatever "truths" the autobiographer may contract to reveal, he must also agree to be revealed as this "truth."

The life—*bio*—defined by autobiography is shown at the same time to be enclosed by death, writing, non-self-presence—*autography*. *Apologia*, in this sense, might have another meaning—*apo-logos*, away from the self, the speaking away of the self. We might say that this deconstruction of the category of the self is carried out in all autobiography. Like the bow of Heraclitus, it names the self's life, but at the same time it performs the work of death.

1.   Jacques Derrida, *La dissemination* (Paris, Minuit, 1972), p. 172.

2.   Jacques Derrida, *De la grammatologie* (Paris: Minuit, 1967), p. 29.

3.   John Henry Newman, *Apologia pro Vita Sua*, ed. David DeLaura (New York: Norton, 1968), p.6. All further references in the text will be to this edition.

4.   Harold L. Weatherby devotes an enlightening chapter to the relationship between Newman and Wordsworth in his *Cardinal Newman in His Age* (Nashville: Vanderbilt University Press, 1973).

5.   I am grateful to Prof. Geoffrey Hartman for bringing this to my attention.

6.   *The Anchor Bible: Job*, tr. Marvin H. Pope (New York, 1965), p. 10. All subsequent references in the text are to *The New Oxford Annotated Bible: Revised Standard Version*, ed. Herbert G. May, and Bruce M. Metzger (New York: Oxford University Press, 1973).

7.   One of the traditional ways of describing writing is to call it the clothing of speech, the outer garment of the internal speech/thought.

8.   John Henry Newman, *The Idea of a University* (New York: Holt, Rhinehart and Winston, 1960), p. 207. All further references in the text will be to this edition (hereafter cited as *Idea*).

9.   John Henry Newman, *Autobiographical Writings*, ed. Henry Tristram (New York: Sheed and Ward, 1955), p. 237.

10.   John Henry Cardinal Newman, *The Arians of the Fourth Century* (Westminster, 1968), p. 145. For an interesting discussion of the Economy, *see* Edward Said, *Joseph Conrad and the Fiction of Autobiography* (Cambridge, Mass.: Harvard University Press, 1966), p. 45.

11.   John Henry Cardinal Newman, *An Essay in Aid of a Grammar of Assent* (Westminster: Christian Classics, 1973), p. 91. All further references in the text will be to this edition (hereafter cited as *Gram*).

12.   For a description of the Platonic notion of writing as an aid to both memory and forgetfulness, *see* Derrida, "La pharmacie de Platon," in *La dissemination*.

13.   Francis Mary Flanagan (*Newman's Concept of Language*, Diss. The University of Iowa 1948) discusses the relationship between language and logic in Newman's system, as well as the place of his denigration of logic within his reaction to Whateley's *Elements of Logic*. For further discussion of the tension between logic and conscience in the *Grammar*, see Rev. Edmond Benard, *A Preface to Newman's Theology* (London: Herder, 1946) and Father Zeno, *John Henry Newman Our Way to Certitude* (Leiden: E. J. Brill, 1957), especially the section entitled "The Insufficiency of Logic" (p. 183).

14.   In light of the sub-title of the *Apologia*—"A History of My Religious Opinions"—it is significant that Newman had written in his history of the Arians that "To attempt comprehension of opinion . . . is to mistake arrangements of words, which have no existence except on paper, for habits which are realities" (p. 145).

15. John Henry Newman, *Lectures on the Doctrine of Justification* (Westminster: Christian Classics, 1966), p. 170. All further references in the text will be to this edition (hereafter cited as *Lect*).

16. *See* especially Adrian J. Boekraad and Henry Tristram, *The Argument from Conscience to the Existence of God according to J. H. Newman* (Louvain: Editions Nauwelaerts, 1961), p. 103; and Thomas Vargish, *Newman The Contemplation of Mind* (Oxford: Oxford University Press, 1970), p. 182. Vargish writes: "From a fact of which he has experience, his consciousness, he infers a fact which he does not directly experience, his existence. But if this essentially Cartesian argument is permitted, then we can infer the existence of God from the existence of conscience. 'Therefore the idea is not absurd that as from "sentio" I infer the existence of myself, so from "conscientiam habeo" I infer the existence of God . . .' (p. 183). In *The Philosophical Notebook* (New York: Humanities Press, 1970), Newman originally wrote "God" in place of "myself" (p. 78), but then changed it. This correction or slip could imply that, for Newman, the relationship between God's existence and the self's consciousness of its own existence is not as mediated by inference or analogy as Vargish seems to suggest. He is closer to what Newman has in mind when he writes later: ". . . the mind infers God from a recognition of its own nature, so that God and self are the two existences immediate to the intellect" (p. 183).

17. Jacques Derrida, "La differance," in *Marges de la philosophie* (Paris: Minuit, 1972), p. 18; tr. David B. Allison, "Difference," *Speech and Phenomena and Other Essays* (Evanston: Northwestern University Press, 1973), p. 148. Allison's unfortunate translation of "*économie*" as "systematic ordering" loses entirely the sense of exchange and of alternating expenditure and return contained in the French word.

18. Gayatri Chakravorty Spivak, "Translator's Preface," *Of Grammatology* (forthcoming from The Johns Hopkins University Press).

19. *See* Jonathan Robinson, "The *Apologia* and the *Grammar of Assent*," in *Newman's Apologia: A Classic Reconsidered*, ed. Vincent Blehl and Francis Connolly (New York: Harcourt, Brace and World, 1964), p. 145.

20. Spivak.

21. Spivak.

22. If we were to pursue the metaphor of the mirror throughout Newman's writings, we would of course turn to the *Idea* and the *Grammar*, but, most importantly perhaps, for its use in the *Apologia*, to a note of December 4, 1859 in *The Philosophical Notebook*: "Nay further—I may be puzzled *what* my present feeling is—just as you may look into a smeared & dustcovered mirror, and not be able to make out your features, & be aware you cannot . . . . Not indeed that consciousness can be wrong, but we may *fancy* that it reports, when really it reports nothing at all, and really does not act. As a mirror reflects rightly always, when it does reflect, & so far forth as it reflects—but sometimes does not reflect, or only partially" (p. 79). Newman speaks of a similar unconsciousness of consciousness, an absence inhabiting presence, in the *Grammar*: "The mind is a double mirror, in which reflexions of self within self multiply themselves till they are undistinguishable, and the first reflexion contains all the rest . . . what is more rare than self-knowledge? In proportion then to our ignorance of self, is our unconsciousness to those innumerable acts of assent, which we are incessantly making . . . And as we cannot see ourselves, so we cannot well see intellectual motives which are so intimately ours, and which spring up from the very constitution of our minds" (*Gram*, 138, 188, 195, 336). The constitution of the mind is external to the mind. Even when he describes the self's selfsameness. Newman does so in terms of an interiority which is even exterior to itself: "I am what I am, or I am nothing . . . and I am ever moving in a circle . . . . My only busi-

ness is to ascertain what I am . . . the laws under which I live . . . . My first disobedience is . . . to desire to change laws which are identical with myself" (*Gram*, 347). Adam's sin—"first disobedience"—of self-knowledge; to seek to know the laws of the self as something identical with the self is already to assert the self's non-identity with "itself," to break the laws, or to point out that the laws are always already broken. What Newman describes is the grammatology of the self, that its self-presence refers to itself as an absence. Even as the laws are identical with the self, they are different from it, and the self must seek to know them as something other. The self, therefore, is a trace structure whose presence is constituted by its own absence from itself. Perhaps this thought of Newman's prompted Jacques Lacan to compliment the book, however backhandedly ("Newman's *Grammar of Assent*—it's not without force, although forged for execrable ends—and I will perhaps have occasion to mention it again" (*Ecrits* [Paris: Seuil, 1966]), p. 862), and Thomas Vargish to remark on Newman's affinities with Freud (*Newman*, p. 58).

LINDA H. PETERSON

Audience and the Autobiographer's Art: An Approach to the *Autobiography* of Mrs. M. O. W. Oliphant

> Autobiographers write for different audiences. Lady Anne Fanshawe speaks familiarly to her son; Adolf Hitler singles out only his sympathizers as his audience; Edward Gibbon addresses the cultivated eighteenth-century community at large. The autobiographer's conception of his audience is obviously related to his guiding purpose in important ways.
> Barrett John Mandel, "The Autobiographer's Art"

> An autobiographer is really writing a story of two lives: his life as it appears to himself, from his own position, . . . and his life as it appears from outside in the minds of others; a view which tends to become in part his own view of himself also, since he is influenced by the opinion of those others.
> Stephen Spender, Preface to *World Within World*[1]

As Barrett Mandel and Stephen Spender remind us, an autobiographer writes for an audience, and an autobiographer's conception of his audience—as intimate or public, friendly or hostile, a single person or several diverse groups —inevitably influences him as he writes. As they further remind us, the *audience's* view of the *autobiographer* also influences him, affecting even what seems to be most private: the autobiographer's sense of who he is. With the exception of a few suggestive comments such as these, however, neither studies of autobiography in general nor studies of individual autobiographies have explored the relationship between audience and autobiographer.[2] Instead we have discussed autobiography only as a private act, as a process of self-discovery or a dialogue between a man's present self and his past selves, and have forgotten that it is also a public, audience-directed act. As an introduction to this problem, therefore, I suggest we consider the *Autobiography* of Mrs. M. O. W. Oliphant, a popular Victorian novelist, biographer, and critic, in terms of its audience and three aspects of autobiographical writing: the reasons for writing an autobiography; the version of the self presented in it;[3] and the rhetorical strategy employed to present that self.

An audience-centered approach is particularly appropriate for Mrs. Oliphant's *Autobiography*. In the first place, one of the work's primary concerns is the audience's view of the autobiographer—that is, the public's estimate of Mrs. Oliphant's achievement as a literary artist. To most Victorians Mrs. Oliphant was known as a prolific but decidedly second-rate writer. But by showing another side of her life, the *Autobiography* attempts to question if not the validity, at least the completeness of that view. Furthermore, because a change in audience occurred while the work was being written, Mrs. Oliphant was acutely aware of the audience problem and commented frequently upon it. According to both the editor's preface and the text of the *Autobiography*, Mrs. Oliphant had originally intended the narrative for her children, particularly for her younger and favorite son Cecco.[4] But before it was completed, both of her sons died: Cyril in November 1890, after what became Part I was completed; Cecco in October 1894, while Part II was being written. Thus when Mrs. Oliphant was approximately half finished with the work, its audience changed unexpectedly. As she ruefully noted, what had been intended for a loving, sympathetic audience, for a child "to read with tenderness, to hide some things, to cast perhaps an interpretation of love upon others, and to turn over all my papers with the consciousness of a full right to do so" (81), had to be redirected toward an impersonal and probably unsympathetic public interested only in being amused. As she also realized, changes were necessary—in purpose, in strategy, in the self to be presented publicly.

I

From Mrs. Oliphant's point of view, what changed most drastically when her audience changed was the reason for writing an autobiography. "How strange it is to me to write all this," she reflected after Cecco's death,

> with the effort of making light reading of it, and putting in anecdotes that will do to quote in the papers and make the book sell! . . . when I wrote it for my Cecco to read it was all very different, but now that I am doing it consciously for the public, with the aim (no evil aim) of leaving a little more money, I feel all this to be so vulgar, so common, so unnecessary, as if I were making pennyworths of myself. (75)

Apparently, Mrs. Oliphant had intended to write in the autobiographical tradition of Lord Herbert of Cherbury, whose *Life* she had discussed in a series on autobiography for *Blackwood's*. In this series she had characterized Lord Herbert's *Life* as a work designed for posterity, concerned less with his literary and philosophical accomplishments than with those more exciting aspects of his life likely to please his descendants:

> [S]ave a passing reference to "my Book," we hear nothing of any literary purpose until he has reached the last page of his delightful tale. . . . Perhaps he felt with the philosophy that is taught by years, that his "Posterity," fine gentlemen and patricians as he intended them to be, were likely to care far less about this achievement than about the duels and the noble figure their ancestor had made in the world.[5]

This is the sort of autobiography suited to Mrs. Oliphant's temperament. As she repeatedly insisted, she did not intend or desire to discuss her literary productions: "They are my work, which I like in the doing. . . . And when I have said that, I have said all that is in me to say" (5). And although she had no duels to report, she knew incidents in her life and in the history of the Oliphant family which would interest her son. The autobiography would be her last gift to him.

After Cecco died, however, she could no longer approach the work as a gift from mother to child; instead it became a commodity to be sold in the literary marketplace. Of course, this is Mrs. Oliphant's account of the effect that a change in audience had upon her reasons for writing in autobiography, and at best it is a partial explanation. As readers only slightly familiar with the *Autobiography* know, the work is also apologetic: it attempts to explain why Mrs. Oliphant, an industrious woman who wrote a great deal, never wrote a great novel.

In the opening pages, for example, Mrs. Oliphant calls herself a sort of Andrea del Sarto. Unlike George Eliot and George Sand, the women with whom she repeatedly compares herself just as Browning's Andrea compares himself with Rafael and Michelangelo, she had failed to produce first-rate novels and consequently had failed to make a name for herself. "No one even will mention me in the same breath with George Eliot," she realizes. "And that is just" (7). Yet in another sense she feels it is unjust, for like Browning's painter, she had been "given perhaps more than one Lucrezia to take care of":

> I have always had to think of other people, and to plan everything.
> . . . I have had a great deal of my own way, and have insisted upon
> getting what I wished, but only at the cost of infinite labour, and of
> carrying a whole little world with me whenever I moved. (6)

Now this sort of writing, as Mrs. Oliphant admitted, is casuistry, "altogether self-defence" (7). Furthermore, the incident which finally moved Mrs. Oliphant to write was also related to self-defense: "I have been tempted to begin writing by George Eliot's life—with that curious kind of self-compassion which one cannot get clear of. I wonder if I am a little envious of her" (4).

For our purposes, however, the interesting question is why Mrs. Oliphant chose to write the *Autobiography* for her son (for I think we can accept her statement that the work was originally meant for Cecco). After all, the public was responsible for Mrs. Oliphant's reputation, and she might just as easily have addressed *that* audience if she wished to counter its view of her. Again, the answer is suggested in the opening pages of the *Autobiography* and in the *Blackwood's* series.

When Mrs. Oliphant compares herself with George Eliot and George Sand in the opening pages, her essential concern is not literary reputation; the "praise and homage and honour" (8) which they achieved are not of utmost importance to her. What *is* of importance, however, is the love and affection that accompanies publicly acknowledged achievement such as theirs. Note that she says "I would not buy their fame . . . but I do feel very small, very obscure, beside them, rather a failure all round, *never securing any strong affection*, and . . . never impressing anybody" (8 [italics mine]). Here Mrs. Oliphant acknowledges what, according to Patricia Meyer Spacks, many another woman writer has discovered: that "publicly acknowledged achievement is a mode of power," that "accomplishment is . . . a means to love."[6] Having failed to secure the praise of the literary world, Mrs. Oliphant also failed to secure anyone's "strong affection." And what seems unfair is that she, who has spent her entire life providing for her family and sacrificing her best efforts as an artist to do so, should not receive in return the love she deserves. Thus, she addresses her autobiography to her favorite son, one who already cares for her and might, if he knew more, appreciate her even more. The task of the *Autobiography* is to secure love—not from the public but from a son who would read of her life as a mother and recognize her achievement in that role.

When writing her autobiography, then, was Mrs. Oliphant indifferent to public opinion? Was she unconcerned about justifying her life to a public as well as a private audience? Yes—and no. Her first audience seems to have been her son; her first desire, to secure his understanding and affection. At one point she even tells us that before Cecco's death, she had not expected her autobiographical fragments to be published:

> I used to feel that Cecco would use his discretion,—that most likely he would not print any of this at all, for he did not like publicity, and would have thought his mother's story of her life sacred. (65)

But although Mrs. Oliphant's first concern was not literary reputation, like all of us she was sensitive to public opinion, particularly when she felt that opinion unjust. If a public defense was to be made, however—whether as an autobiography or in some other form—I think she preferred that Cecco be responsible for it. We know from the passage just quoted that she looked upon Cecco as her editor, one who would "use discretion" in publishing an autobiography or writing a biography. And we know from her essay on the Duchess of Newcastle's autobiography that she was enchanted by public defenses made by loved ones: she reprinted a major portion of the Duke's defense of his wife and then remarked how "pleasant [it is] to see the old Duke roused out of his old age . . . to set lance in rest for the vindication of his lady and her honour."[7]

Here, then, we might speculate about another reason for addressing the *Autobiography* to her son. If her first purpose for writing prevailed and the *Autobiography* secured Cecco's love, then Cecco might in turn take the autobiographical fragments left to him and publish them along with his own testimony of his mother's life—which would make a far better apologia than the *Autobiography* alone. Of course, when Cecco died, the original intentions were abandoned. Mrs. Oliphant did not expect to win with one last piece of writing the admiration and affection of an audience which had read her work for fifty years and judged it inferior. But she did intend to continue explaining why that work was inferior, and that necessitated, she felt, a slightly different version of the self and different rhetorical techniques.

II

In one sense it is misleading to say that the version of the self presented in the *Autobiography* changes when the audience changes, for if anything remains constant, it is Mrs. Oliphant's sense of who and what she is: a woman, a mother. Nevertheless, upon returning to the *Autobiography* after Cecco's death, Mrs. Oliphant felt that certain changes were desirable. At the end of Part II, for example, she resolves that she will "try to change the tone of this record," that she will "try to remember more trivial things, the incidents that sometimes amuse me when I look back upon them" (64.65). Early in Part III she takes up the matter again, noting "how strange it is . . . to write all this, with the effort of making light reading of it, and putting in anecdotes that will do to quote in the papers and make the book sell" (75). As she understands it, the problem is accommodating a new audience. The *Autobiography* can either continue to discuss the personal concerns of a widow and mother, or it can concentrate instead on the more amusing incidents in the life of a well-known Victorian writer; Mrs. Oliphant can reveal her unseen agonies to the world, or she can display only that self which the public already knows—the pleasant, unassuming, rather commonplace woman novelist who associated with all the literary greats. At stake is the particular self which the *Autobiography* will present to its audience, and Mrs. Oliphant resolves to speak in her more cheerful public voice. She does not succeed entirely, but her attempt illuminates the relationship between the autobiographer's conception of his audience and his autobiography's presentation of the self.

"Motherhood," as Mrs. Oliphant's only biographer has said, "was her passion,"[8] and predictably, the concerns of motherhood dominate the first half of the *Autobiography*. The narrative begins with remembrances of her own mother who, beside the shadowy figure of her father and the less important figures of her brothers, stands as one of the few things Mrs. Oliphant can see distinctly as she looks back upon her early days: "My father is a very dim figure in all that phantasmagoria. . . . My mother was all in all" (11). Similarly, her mother's death and the births and deaths of her first children dominate her memories of early married life. Little is said of her husband Frank: the story of their courtship is omitted as "not a matter into which I can enter here" (28) and she avoids speaking of their relationship as husband and wife. Only Frank's illness occupies an important place in the first half of the *Autobiography*—but necessarily so, for at that point Mrs. Oliphant was forced to assume full responsibility for the support of her family.[9]

All in all, the first half of the *Autobiography* tells the

story of a mother who happened to be a writer too. Writing runs through everything, it is true: there is the classic example of her wedding day, on which the proofs for *Katie Stewart* arrived from *Blackwood's*. But just as in life "it was . . . subordinate to everything, to be pushed aside for any little necessity" (23), so in the first half of the *Autobiography* it is subordinate to the concerns of motherhood. Moreover, those incidents which she remembers with pleasure, those during which she felt most like her true self, were times when she was functioning as a mother, not as a professional writer. She remembers, for example, her introduction to literary society as disappointing, occasionally embarrassing. She had expected "everything that was superlative beautiful conversation, all about books and the finest subjects, great people whose notice would be an honour, poets and painters, and all the sympathy of congenial minds, and the feast of reason and the flow of the soul" (33-34), but she found none of these things. In contrast, the hours at home—especially those evenings when she sat with her needlework, her children above stairs, their father working below—are recalled with the "the sensation of that sweet calm and ease and peace" (45).

Since the *Autobiography* was originally intended for her children, its emphasis upon motherhood is appropriate. Yet midway through the work when Mrs. Oliphant resolves to shift its emphasis by speaking less of her trials as a wife and mother and more of her career as a writer, she finds it difficult to do so. Unwittingly, she keeps reverting to her concerns as a mother.

The first and most obvious sort of reversion occurs when Mrs. Oliphant forgets the literary matters she has been discussing and tells "baby stories" instead. As she recounts, for instance, the excitement over *Salem Chapel* and her beginning research on the biography of Edward Irving, she is misled into relating a story of one of Cecco's childhood illnesses. The reason she moves from a literary to a family matter is understandable enough: Cecco had recovered from a convulsion just before one of Jane Carlyle's visits; Mrs. Carlyle was visiting to discuss Edward Irving, her

former tutor; thus the incident is associated in Mrs. Oliphant's mind with the Irving biography. But it annoys
Mrs. Oliphant that she cannot speak of her work as a
writer:

> Here is a pretty thing. I should like if I could to write what people
> like about my books, being just then, as I have said, at my high
> tide, and instead of that all I have to say is a couple of baby stories.
> (86)

The role of the artist feels unnatural to her.

Despite her difficulty with the role, in Parts III and IV
she does include many incidents related to her literary life.
These are the sections of the *Autobiography* which show
her meeting the Carlyles and the Tennysons, working on
the biographies of Irving and Montalembert, dining with
Mrs. Duncan Stewart and the literary elite. But even as
she narrates these socio-professional anecdotes, another
sort of reversion occurs, again undermining her attempt to
play the artist. Here is the *Autobiography's* account of her
last meeting with Tennyson. First she describes the poet's
wife: "a shrunken old, old lady, laid upon a sofa from
which she never moved, the flood of life flowing past her
but never touching her" (137-38). Then she dates the incident: "It was after Lionel's death, and after my Cyril's
death" (138). Significantly, she remembers Mrs. Tennyson
as a mother who, like herself, had lost a son. Finally, she
tells of Lord Tennyson's delightful conversation and poetry
reading and gives thanks that her son "Cecco should see
him so" (138). In other words, Mrs. Oliphant interprets
the entire incident from a maternal rather than an artistic
point of view, and she dates it according to a maternal
time scheme—which, predictably, is the time scheme of the
Autobiography as a whole. Even when Mrs. Oliphant appears to fill the role of artist, she responds essentially
as a mother.

There are several explanations for Mrs. Oliphant's difficulty with the artist's role, one of them crucially related
to the issue of a woman's status in the Victorian literary
world. Q. D. Leavis has reminded us that women novelists

of the nineteenth century "could not claim or be granted professional status,"[10] and thus although Mrs. Oliphant was a popular novelist, a competent biographer, and a leading contributor to *Blackwood's* for nearly fifty years, she was not considered a professional by other literary people. Certainly Mrs. Oliphant knew this to be so: "Women," she once remarked, "must put up with the inevitable grievance of being classed as 'female writers,' just as Horace Walpole's 'royal and noble authors' must support the classification which seems to point them out as fine amateurs superior to, and scarcely worthy of, the full honours of the literary profession."[11] And in their treatment of her Tennyson and Carlyle implied the same: both, even when kind, turned her over to their wives. In other words, there was a basic uncertainty in the audience's view of Mrs. Oliphant, that "view in the minds of others," to return to Spender's comment, which becomes in turn part of the autobiographer's view of himself. If Mrs. Oliphant's contemporaries looked upon her primarily as a widow and a mother rather than as a professional writer, it is no wonder she had difficulty imagining and presenting herself autobiographically in the role of literary artist.

Then, too, there is the matter of fidelity to truth. Throughout her entire life Mrs. Oliphant had felt miscast in the role of artist: the *Autobiography* is filled with comments about her inability to "make an impression" in literary society and with anecdotes about unknown writers usurping her place as literary guest of honor. To present herself as an artist and suggest that the role was a natural one would falsify the truth of her life; it would violate the unspoken contract between the autobiographer and his audience. Finally, Mrs. Oliphant's maternal concerns seem simply to have been stronger than her artistic ones, and as she proceeded with the second half of her autobiography, I think she realized that her attempt to suppress those concerns was impossible and unnecessary. The real issue of the *Autobiography* was not to separate the artist from the mother but to define the relationship between the two. The *Autobiography's* unity depended upon that definition.

Whatever the specifics of Mrs. Oliphant's case, her autobiography demonstrates the problem which faces every
autobiographer, man or woman: the problem of reconcil-
ing his own sense of himself with his audience's conception of who he is. An autobiographer may simply choose
to deny that his audience's view has validity and proceed
to show instead what he considers to be his real self. Or
like Mrs. Oliphant, he may attempt to satisfy his audience's
expectations by showing more of the self it already recognizes. Either way he works with a tension between these
inner and outer views, and the artistic success of his autobiography depends upon his ability to make sense of both.

III

If even the autobiographer's view of himself is influenced by his audience, certainly his rhetorical strategy is
influenced by it also.[12] For by definition, rhetoric is an
audience-oriented art. In autobiography, its end is to persuade the audience that the autobiographer's presentation
of himself is truthful, and its strategies include elements
as major as structure and as minute as the individual word.
Since this is a rather large matter, we shall consider only
two aspects of the *Autobiography's* strategy: the structural
pattern of the work and the use of anecdotes.

As we have seen, one of the primary motives behind
the writing of the *Autobiography* was "self-defence" (7).
Although this defense was at first intended for a private
audience, the death of that audience did not lessen the
apologetic concern of the work. Quite the contrary, since
Mrs. Oliphant could no longer count upon a son to defend
her before the public, it became all the more important for
the *Autobiography* itself to present an effective apology
for her life. It must convince its readers to see her life as
she herself saw it—as that of a Victorian Andrea del Sarto,
a promising young artist whose family misfortunes had repeatedly forced him to compromise his artistic goals.

One of the ways the *Autobiography* convinces is through
structure, the shaping of the events of Mrs. Oliphant's life

into a pattern not inherent in the events themselves but discovered in (or imposed upon) those events as the auto-biographer looks back upon the course of his life. Now by themselves the events of Mrs. Oliphant's life are enough to elicit the sympathy of even the most hard-hearted reader. In the first years of her marriage she lost two of her infant children and her "dearest mother" (33); soon after, her husband was stricken with tuberculosis and died, leaving her with a debt of £1000 and three children to support; Maggie, her only daughter, died next; and then, just when she was achieving a measure of financial and literary suc-cess, her brother Frank declared bankruptcy and left her to support his family and to educate his son. Mrs. Oliphant met all these crises faithfully, supporting her brother's family, her nephew, and her own two sons by working at a furious pace. There was little reward for her faithfulness, however; for soon after the boys completed their educations, all three of them died—first her nephew Frank, then her sons Cyril and Cecco.

The *Autobiography* does not present these events hap-hazardly. Instead it connects Mrs. Oliphant's personal tragedies with her failures as an artist by shaping the events into what might be called a "del Sarto" pattern: early achievement and promise—family crisis—artistic com-promise. This pattern provides the structural framework for the work as a whole and for each of its four sections. Each begins on a note of hope but ends with personal tragedy and often artistic failure.

The opening pages of Part II, for example, tell of a period of relative happiness in both artistic and family matters. Mrs. Oliphant has recovered from the deaths of her mother and her two babies; she gives birth to a healthy son, be-comes immersed in decorating a new house, and produces several successful stories and novels. But prosperity is short-lived. Frank learns that he is fatally ill, and the Oli-phant family must leave for Italy. The *Autobiography* links this family tragedy with a period of artistic dearth:

> I have the clearest vision of him sitting close by the little stove in the corner of the room, wrapped up, with a rug upon his knees, and

saying nothing, while I sat near the window, trying with less success than ever before to write, and longing for a word, a cheerful
look, to disperse a little the heavy atmosphere of trouble. . . . I
had to go on working all the time, and not very successfully (53, 52).

In the early sections of the *Autobiography*, the pattern
of family crisis leading to artistic compromise is only partially operative. Mrs. Oliphant recovered from the catastrophe of Part II, just as she recovered from the deaths of
her mother and infant children recounted in Part I and
from the death of her daughter Maggie which concludes
Part III. These are temporary setbacks, overcome through
resolution and hard work. But in Part IV the pattern becomes incontrovertible. In terms of the *Autobiography's*
patterning of events, this was the turning point in Mrs.
Oliphant's career: her Carlingford series had been launched
and was creating quite a stir; the Irving and Montalembert
books had secured her reputation as a biographer; and a
steady flow of articles to *Blackwood's* gave her financial
security, if not wealth. Now, if ever, she would begin to
write great novels. Unfortunately, just at this moment her
brother Frank filed bankruptcy, and the support of his family, including the expensive education of his son, fell upon
her shoulders. As Mrs. Oliphant believed then and when
she wrote in 1895, the crisis demanded that an irreversible
decision be made: her family or her art. "I never did nor
could," she states,

hesitate for a moment as to what had to be done. It had to be done, and
that was enough, and there is no doubt that it was much more congenial to me to drive on and keep everything going, with a certain scorn
of increased work, and metaphorical toss of my head, as if it mattered!
than it ever would have been to labour with an artist's fervour and
concentration to produce a masterpiece. (125)

Each section repeats the basic structural pattern with
increasing insistence: achievement interrupted by a family
crisis resulting in a compromise of artistic goals and the
production of inferior work. Of course, another person looking independently at the events of Mrs. Oliphant's life might
not discover the same pattern. One critic of her work, in

fact, denies that family crises had any significant influence upon the quality of her work and considers the *Autobiography* "one of Mrs. Oliphant's better fictional efforts."[13] Structure is, therefore, strategy. Its task is not simply to organize the work but to present convincingly the auto-biographer's conception of himself and his life's pattern.

The incidents and anecdotes included within the overall structure are also part of the *Autobiography's* strategy. However, unlike the basic structural pattern which remains constant, apparently unaffected by the change in audience which occurs midway through the work, the incidents with-in the structure change markedly after Part II. Not only do they increase in number, giving texture to what Mrs. Oliphant called "the thread of my life" (65), but they differ in kind.

Some of these anecdotes are obviously intended to amuse: the witty repartee between Montalembert and Mrs. Oliphant about Carlyle, the sketch of old Father Prout and his aged lover, the description of the Norman-French *bonne*. Others are "literary" anecdotes included to satisfy readers curious about the private lives of literary figures: the stories of Tennyson and Carlyle mentioned earlier, of William E. Aytoun, of Leslie Stephen, and of the Blackwoods. "I am now going to try to remember more trivial things, the inci-dents that sometimes amuse me when I look back upon them," Mrs. Oliphant had decided after Cecco's death. But these incidents are designed to amuse her audience as well, to make the book sell, and to bring it good reviews.

There is another sort of anecdote included in Parts III and IV, however, which functions not merely as entertainment— stories of older, often lonely women such as Little Nelly, the Eton neighbor, and Mrs. Duncan Stewart. This material, I would suggest, betrays Mrs. Oliphant's great fear of being misunderstood or undervalued by outsiders—precisely the problem which motivates her to write an autobiography. Paradoxically, this material also provides a solution to that fear, for with it Mrs. Oliphant teaches her audience to look for the truth about others and to judge them with sympathy and compassion.

In each of these sketches Mrs. Oliphant contrasts the public view of the woman (incomplete, erroneous, unkind) with her own private view. Little Nelly, for example, had devoted her life to the care of her old mother and invalid brother. But because Nelly was not outwardly pleasing and because she often committed foolish blunders, public opinion was rather heartless: she was "general reputed a rather silly little woman" (115) and often made the butt of little mockeries. Mrs. Oliphant sees—and forces her audience to see—the private side of Nelly, the woman with "a heart of gold" who, after her family died, devoted herself "to take other burdens on her shoulders, and save other wounded creatures of God" (116). Similarly, the Eton neighbor, a "clever, witty, pretty" widow, had once made a silly social blunder—"some foolish rash attempt to secure a very brilliant marriage at home for [her] beautiful daughter" (117) —and had prejudiced society against her. Again, Mrs. Oliphant countered public opinion, knowing that "there are some people who never get any credit for what is good in them" (118). And Mrs. Duncan Stewart, an older woman well-known in London literary circles, had been made the subject of "a cruel sketch" in the *Saturday Review*. "Nothing could be easier," Mrs. Oliphant remarked, "than to travesty this sweet and bright old lady into a spectre of society, clinging on to the last to social dissipations, and incapable of being alone—and nothing more absolutely untrue" (134).

Each of these women resembles Mrs. Oliphant in some fundamental way: Nelly in her selfless devotion to family, the widow with her social blunders, Mrs. Stewart as an old woman in literary society. Each of these women was misinterpreted by the public. No doubt Mrs. Oliphant feared that the same sort of error would be made when public opinion pronounced its final judgment upon her life.

Both the editor's preface and the introductory section of the *Autobiography* make it clear that Mrs. Oliphant did not want an official biography to be written,[14] and her wish is understandable in light of her fear. As she well knew, at best a public biography would praise her as a courageous woman and an industrious writer of the second rank;[15] at worst it might misjudge her as the *Saturday Review* essayist had misjudged Mrs. Stewart. But neither would represent a true account of her life. As Mrs. Oliphant realized, the public view inevitably misses what can be seen only by one who has known his subject intimately and has studied him with sympathy and understanding. When Cecco died, the possibility for this sort of biography died with him, and the *Autobiography* was left to accomplish what it could. Victorian readers were likely to approach it with the official view of things, as the story of a second-rate female writer who had lived past her prime. But through structure the *Autobiography* could persuade its audience to read the tragic pattern in Mrs. Oliphant's life. Through anecdotes it could teach its audience to read that pattern sympathetically.

1.   Barrett John Mandel, "The Autobiographer's Art," *Journal of Aesthetics and Art Criticism*, 27 (1968), 221; and Stephen Spender, *World Within World* (New York: Harcourt, Brace, 1948), p. vi.

2.   Two noteworthy exceptions are Martin J. Svaglic's "Why Newman Wrote the *Apologia*" and Edward Kelly's "The Apologia and the Ultramontanes," both printed in *Newman's Apologia: A Classic Reconsidered*, ed. Vincent Ferrer Blehl, S. J. and Francis X. Connolly (New York: Harcourt, Brace, 1964). Svaglic and Kelly suggest that much of the content of the *Apologia* was intended not for Newman's Protestant accusers but for fellow Catholics, many of whom had doubts about his loyalty to Rome.

3.   Obviously, I have borrowed the phrase from John N. Morris' *Versions of the Self: Studies in English Autobiography from John Bunyan to John Stuart Mill* (New York: Basic Books, 1966) to refer to that particular aspect of the autobiographer's life which he chooses to present in his autobiography—whether his spiritual self (Bunyan in *Grace Abounding*), his artistic self (Wordsworth in *The Prelude*), his intellectual self (Mill in his *Autobiography*), or some other.

4.   See *The Autobiography and Letters of Mrs. M. O. W. Oliphant*, ed. Mrs. Harry Coghill (New York: Dodd, Mead, 1899), pp. ix, 65, 75. The *Autobiography* has recently been reprinted with an introduction by Q. D. Leavis (n. p.: Leicester University Press, 1974); pagination is the same in both the 1899 and modern reprint edition.

We might also note here that the *Autobiography* was published in four sections, presumably following MS divisions: Part I, dated 1st February 1885; Part II, dated January 18, 1891; Part III, dated December 30, 1894; and Part IV, dated 1894 but probably written in 1895 since III was begun late in 1894 and continued on January 22 of the next year.

5.   "Autobiographies: No. II.—Lord Herbert of Cherbury," *Blackwood's Edinburgh Magazine*, 129 (March 1881), 407. This series, which seems to have influenced Mrs. Oliphant's thinking on autobiographical approaches and form, also included essays on the autobiographies of Benvenuto Cellini, the Duchess of Newcastle, Edward Gibbon, Carlo Goldoni, Lucy Hutchinson and Alice Thornton, and Madame Roland.

6.   Patricia M. Spacks, *The Female Imagination* (New York: Alfred A. Knopf, 1975), p. 160.

7.   "Autobiographies: No. III.—Margaret, Duchess of Newcastle," *Blackwood's* 129 (May 1881), 638.

8.   Vineta and Robert A. Colby, *The Equivocal Virtue: Mrs. Oliphant and the Victorian Literary Market Place* (n.p.: Archon Books, 1966), p. 29.

9.   Significantly, at this point in the *Autobiography* Mrs. Oliphant tells of her affection for Albertinelli's painting of the Visitation: mothers comforting and encouraging one another.

10.   "Introduction," *The Autobiography and Letters of Mrs. M. O. W. Oliphant* (n. p.: Leicester University Press, 1974), p. 14.

11.   "Autobiographies: No. III.—Margaret, Duchess of Newcastle, *Blackwood's*, 129 (May 1881), 619.

12.   I am not speaking here of classical rhetoric, in which Mrs. Oliphant had no formal training, but of rhetoric simply as a means of persuading an audience.

13.   William Evans Mosier, "Mrs. Oliphant's Literary Criticism," Dissertation, Northwestern University 1967, p. 9.

14.   *See* the "Preface," p. ix and also pp. 7–8. The editor, Mrs. Coghill, who was also Mrs. Oliphant's niece, states that "one distinct injunction she laid upon us—no biography of her was to be written."

15.   Mrs. Oliphant was correct. The only biography of her published to date— the Colby's *The Equivocal Virtue*—takes precisely this view, the "equivocal virtue" being her industry.

SARAH C. FRERICHS

Elizabeth Missing Sewell:
Concealment and Revelation
In a Victorian Everywoman

Who was Elizabeth Missing Sewell (1815–1906) and for whom did she write her life story? The title page of the original edition of the *Autobiography*[1] identifies its author as "Elizabeth M. Sewell of Ashcliff, Bonchurch, Isle of Wight," and this identification in terms of location is significant: Except for two years of boarding school at Bath and occasional visits to Oxford, London, and the continent, Elizabeth Sewell spent her ninety-one years on the Isle of Wight; and for over sixty years of that long life span, she called Ashcliff, in the village of Bonchurch, home. She would no doubt wish to be remembered as Elizabeth Missing Sewell, author and educator, but "E. M. Sewell, Churchwoman," might also please this writer of High Church fiction, meditations, and textbooks, and founder of St. Boniface Diocesan School.

In the Preface to the original *Autobiography*, Elizabeth Sewell explains why and for whom she wrote:

> The following Autobiographical Sketch has been written in fulfilment of a promise made to my mother, and with the wish to place on record certain facts connected with the College founded by my brother William at Radley, which have been open to misrepresentation. I desire also to state here (what I find I have omitted in the Sketch) that my brother Henry was, in the course of years, able to pay off the liabilities of the Newport business. . . . The narrative is personal—because I have thought it well to say truly of myself and my writings what it is possible might some day unintentionally be said untruly.

175

Ostensibly, Elizabeth Sewell's *Autobiography*, which she modestly refers to as a "sketch," is prompted by family duty and—since it is printed for "private circulation"—is intended for a small audience of intimates. Yet theorists of the art of autobiography insist that all narrators of their own lives write out of vanity or egotism and with "an intent to obtain immortality."[2] Can this be true of the self-effacing Miss Sewell, who takes care to observe "how entirely the children [nine nieces and nephews] became the one interest of our lives—taking the place with me of any desire for literary society, or any craving for literary fame"?[3] To put the question differently, can an autobiographer be both self-effacing and vain? Leslie Stephen replies, yes, in his well-known *Cornhill* essay on "Autobiography," arguing from the self-evident premise that "human nature is in some sense a contradictory compound." He demonstrates the reader's problem in discovering the real man or woman behind the "shadow cast upon the coloured and distorted mists of memory," but holds that a perceptive reader can correct autobiographical distortions, because autobiographers always reveal more than they intend—possibly even more than they know of themselves.[4] In *The Female Imagination* Patricia Spacks convincingly argues that in women autobiographers the conflict between concealing and revealing, between self-denial and self-expression, is particularly marked. She finds this in every woman writer whom she discusses, from the Duchess of Newcastle to Betty MacDonald of *The Egg and I*. Furthermore, according to Spacks, "women . . . who have, despite their 'selflessness,' written about themselves, consistently reveal an anger which creates the energy of self-castigation to prevent undue self-exertion."[5] The conflict between concealment and revelation pointed out by Leslie Stephen, and discussed specifically in relation to women writers by Patricia Spacks, is particularly acute in women of the nineteenth century, and Elizabeth Missing Sewell's *Autobiography* and *Journal* have much to tell us about the problems of women—and women autobiographers—in the reign of Queen Victoria.

Elizabeth Sewell herself reveals some awareness of the mixed motives from which she writes. For example, after mentioning the promise to her mother to continue the family history begun by her parent and after instancing the ways in which family honor is to be vindicated, she allows that her narrative is personal "because I have thought it well to say truly of myself and my writings what it is possible might some day unintentionally be said untruly." It is clearly, then, not only the Sewell family reputations but her own professional one which is at stake. What is more, the dutiful daughter, sitting down within a fortnight of her mother's death to make good her commitment, progresses no further than the second paragraph when she acknowledges the inevitable shift from the "history of a family" to the "history of the person who writes." By way of apology she explains that "as nearly the youngest of twelve children, my recollections cannot go back very far to the childhood of others." Then blurring the line between singular and plural, she quickly heaps teleological assumption upon value judgment: "We have all as a family been singularly cared for, and, on looking back can trace the most clear working of God's Providence for our good, both as regards myself and others."[6]

What is really happening here? How far does Elizabeth Sewell's self-awareness go? Certainly she knows at the outset that her own life and work will be the focus of the narrative. In short, she knows what she is going to write, an autobiography, but she is less perceptive about for whom she is writing. She is not fully aware that she is writing both for herself and for an audience larger than her immediate friends and relatives. Certainly she is not aware that, like most other persons who write their own life story, she writes out of certain deep-seated psychological needs.

At least four somewhat overlapping needs suggest themselves in the case of Elizabeth Sewell: 1) the need to affirm her self-image as womanly, dutiful, and pious; 2) the need to deal with undesirable feelings such as anger and religious doubt; 3) the need to see life in teleological terms; and 4) the need to order her experience, working out an ac-

ceptable balance between private and professional life. The
last of these points takes us back to the first. The author's
urge to rationalize the fact of becoming a writer suggests
the need to assure herself that writing in no way interferes
with her primary roles as daughter, sister, aunt. One may ex-
trapolate from the narrative several assertions, which, para-
phrased and juxtaposed, make the following claims: I
began writing for a religious purpose. I sought my mother's
and brother's approval. I continued writing out of economic
necessity. I always put duty to family before desire for
fame. I took no pleasure in literary renown when it came.

Although these self-justifying statements are not untrue, they fail to tell the whole story, as the *Autobiography's*
account of how she became an author will illustrate. Her
first experience as an author came when she dramatized
the story of Ali Cogia in the *Arabian Nights* for a doll's
theater. The fifteen-year-old playwright's next effort was a
story of her own with a "moral purpose." Aside from two
abortive stories, one of them religious, the author attempted no more creative writing until she was in her
twenties possibly because, as she tells it, "I had all the
time a great dislike to authoresses, and once . . . [stated]
it as my opinion that women had no business to write."
Still, her enjoyment of Maria Edgeworth's stories made
her wonder whether she might not write some on that order
—a thought, she records, followed by "a painful consciousness of having been terribly conceited" *(Life,* p. 54).

Elizabeth Sewell decided to try her hand at religious
fiction when, browsing in a bookstore in Newport on the
Isle of Wight, she was attracted to a few copies of *Tracts
for the Times.* She had already become involved in district
work of the Anglican Church, and eager to know more of
"Church principles," Elizabeth found an enthusiastic mentor in her clergyman brother William, who was at that time
very much involved in the Oxford Movement.[7] Herself
committed to the ideals of the High Church, she saw that
the tracts written by Newman and others were unsuited to
the needs of the uneducated, while the existing ones supplied by the Christian Knowledge Society struck her as

"dull." Thus she felt the incentive to "try and write something more interesting." The results were her first published works: *Stories on the Lord's Prayer* (1840) and *Amy Herbert* (1844), the latter destined to become a best seller in England and America.[8]

The theme of these first two books was, in Miss Sewell's phrase, "the blessing bestowed on a Christian by Baptism." This doctrine, elsewhere styled "baptismal regeneration," was but one of the "Church principles" which, Elizabeth Sewell says, "harmonized with my feelings and were attractive to me" because they allowed for religious reserve and did not demand describing children as "quoting texts, and talking of their feelings in an unnatural way" as the children did in "Mrs. Sherwood's Tales" (*Life*, p. 58). Thus she had found her subject and her style. Not all difficulties were obviated, however, for she tells us candidly that *Amy Herbert* was put aside for a while because "working out anything like a plot seemed beyond me" (*Life*, p. 59).

The early fiction was what the author intended it to be— a needed contribution to Christian education—and such writing met her own needs as well. When she could take Church doctrine and shape it to the interests of the young, she both satisfied her own craving for the comforts of religion and gratified her tastes in its expression. Another factor of which she is but partially aware was her infatuation for her brother William, whom she "idolized" because he "captivated" her with his sermons, poetry, and conversation. It is remarkable that she can write, "I never loved anyone else in the same intense way. . . . But the feeling . . . brought suffering with it, very acute at times" (*Life*, p. 42). What she seems not to have recognized is the way in which the love for William, unrequited in its intensity, was sublimated into a drive to meet the young theologian on his own ground. She must have wanted to prove herself worthy of remarks less condescending than she reports. "You can't understand that," William had said, when he found her one day with Butler's *Analogy* in her hand (*Life*, p. 53). Was it, perhaps, unacknowledged anger at this verbal slap that drove her to write, despite the "shell of reserve" into which she shrank? In any case she sought William's permission before the manuscript of *Stories on the Lord's Prayer* was sent off to the *Cottager's Monthly Visitor.* Thus William Sewell became the editor for the works authored "by a Lady."

Not until 1852, when she published *The Experience of Life,* did "E. M. Sewell" appear on the title page of a novel, and in the same year she took management of financial affairs into her own hands, also making a decision to purchase Ashcliff in her own name. These three acts of independence together mark Elizabeth Sewell's attainment of emotional maturity, and her own words, "I have never repented it [the independent action]" (p. 140), carry a heavy emotional freight, for it is almost as though she had written, "The divorce of my affections from William has become final." What the autobiographer does not intend to reveal—perhaps does not know about herself—is the romantic, even sexual, coloration to her feeling for her brother. Incestuous feeling, suppressed in the *Autobiography,* comes out strongly in two of the novels—in the feeling of Edith for Edward in *Gertrude* (1845) and in the relationship between the heroine and her idealized older brother Roger in *Ursula* (1858). Particularly telling is Mrs. Kemp's rebuke to Ursula, "God made you and Roger brother and sister, not husband and wife," and her warning to Ursula not to "bestow upon Roger a wife's affection."[9]

In the section of the *Autobiography* which narrates her beginnings as an author, Elizabeth Sewell discusses two other family-related incentives to her literary career. First, her reading aloud *Amy Herbert* soothed her mother following Elizabeth's father's death on June 25, 1842, and second, her writing met an economic necessity created by his death. "Retrenchments" were necessary for the Sewell family when its members discovered the debts owed by the once-successful solicitor and overseer, for the children were determined not to enter bankruptcy. The psychological effect upon the conscientious Elizabeth, the next-oldest daughter, was incalculable. In her father's last days she had already felt the weight of "a new life of anxiety . . . of which I was to bear the burden for others as well as for myself" and by which "only God could keep me from being crushed" (*Life,* p. 69). In practical terms—and Elizabeth Sewell was eminently practical—accepting the burden meant using her first payment for *Amy Herbert* to pay a doctor's bill for Janetta, one of her two chronically ill sisters.

With the death of Henry Sewell's wife in 1844, followed by that of Robert's wife five years later, nine children fell to the care of Aunts Elizabeth and Ellen at Ashcliff. Comments throughout the *Autobiography* suggest that Elizabeth, at least, sought her own martyrdom—if such it was—to these children. In any case, faced with financial and familial pressures, Elizabeth Sewell responded in the only two ways open to a genteel, upper middle-class woman of the period: she taught school and wrote books. Of the two occupations, the latter seems to have been more congenial to her, though pupils write in glowing terms of her effectiveness as a teacher of history and religion.[10]

The image of herself as self-sacrificing mother figure appears conspicuously throughout the *Autobiography,* while she suppresses her roles as a literary and professional person. Sometimes the reader wonders which is cause and which is effect in the balancing of personal over against professional values. True, Elizabeth Sewell placed obligations before literary renown, but her natural reserve made the security of the family circle more attractive than "lionising" (a favorite term of hers) would have been. The *Autobiography* records the dislike for oral praise of her work; written praise was something else again. Elizabeth Sewell describes herself as "too shy and too conscious of my literary deficiencies" to cultivate the acquaintance of literary luminaries. How unfortunate, since Tennyson was a neighbor and Dickens visited from time to time on the Isle of Wight! At Oxford she attended dinner parties with Newman and Browning,[11] but these occasions were never repeated. When she "first had a name," Elizabeth Sewell tells us, a few persons asked for an introduction. Her own account provides us with insights into her character:

> Mrs. Sarah Austin called upon me one day, just before our early din-
> ner. She awed me greatly, as she led the conversation, whilst I said
> only what was absolutely necessary in reply; and when she took leave
> of me I felt as I had been reading a long article in the *Quarterly
> Review*, and rushed away to my early dinner, and the society of my
> sisters, with a feeling of intense relief. Sir Charles Trevelyan also
> called—but there again I was quite unprepared to meet him on literary
> ground, and felt all the time he was talking that he had simply come to
> look at me and see what I was like. It was a curiosity which I knew
> would find nothing to satisfy it, as my brother (the Warden of New
> College)[12] once said of me to a lady who made some inquiries about
> me, 'My sister Elizabeth is not remarkable in any way,' and I heartily
> endorsed the opinion. (*Life*, p. 96)

Unfortunately, such diffidence blocked one means of
sharpening and enlarging a mind already lively and, though
lacking formal education beyond the age of fifteen, well
stocked with ideas culled from wide reading. In her later
years she overcame her reticence to the extent of telling the
Vicar of Holy Trinity Church, Newport, that he "sometimes
strain[ed] the types of the Old Testament" (*Life*, p. 235),
and she was always ready to discuss her educational philosophy and practice, either in person or in print.[13]

The family, which remained the focus of Elizabeth
Sewell's personal life, also became the center of all her educational theory and practice. She believed, for example,
that girls' boarding schools and colleges should remain
small and be run like a family. So too the family is at the
center of all her fiction, for domestic realism is the category
to which all her best fiction may be assigned.

In nine out of the thirteen Sewell novels or—as she called
them—tales, the strong authority figure in the home is not a
parent but a mother substitute. Here again the *Autobiography* demonstrates Elizabeth Sewell's awareness of the
way in which her writing brings the vicarious satisfaction of
seeing herself as the Good Mother:

> That which principally touched myself in writing *Laneton Parsonage*
> was the affection of Lady Catherine Hyde for Alice, her adopted
> child. The interest of my life was at the time chiefly concentrated in
> Lucy's children. The feeling for them, which we all more or less
> shared, was not likely to be understood by the world generally, who
> knew nothing of their mother's charm, and the way in which they had
> been left to us almost as a legacy. By the outside world we were

naturally regarded simply as aunts, undertaking a duty which could not be avoided; and it was a real relief to me to be able to express through Lady Catherine's affection for Alice, the love which lay deep in my own heart, but which I did not venture to bring forward openly, lest it should be regarded as exaggerated. (*Life*, p. 98)

Once again the *Autobiography* lays bare the real-life equivalent to a fictional situation; that is, Lady Catherine's feeling for Alice recapitulates the author's feeling for Lucy's children. It suggests another dimension: devotion to the child reflects the intensity of the foster mother's feeling for the real mother. It ignores a third element: the author identifies herself with a *titled* lady. In *Margaret Percival* (1847) Elizabeth Sewell deals with "the fascination which the Countess Novera exercised over Margaret Percival" (*Life*, p. 100), later paralleled by Lady Emily's attraction for Sarah in *The Experience of Life* (1852). The mere inclusion of titled characters would not necessarily signify anything; the romance surrounding them does—a romance carried to absurd heights in the beautiful young consumptive heiress of *The Earl's Daughter* (1850). Real life prototypes include Lady Charlotte Copley, Lady Hampson, Lady Lansdowne, and Lady Jane Swinburne, mother of Algernon and a near neighbor as long as the Swinburnes remained on the Isle of Wight.

In *Home Life and After Life* (1867–68) Elizabeth Sewell was still working out the problems of a mother-figure—this time a widowed stepmother to two teen-age girls and mother to four young children. In these companion volumes she writes expressly to illustrate the ideas expounded in her didactic treatise, *Principles of Education* (1865).[14] Here, as with Lady Catherine of the earlier work, the author finds it difficult to give warmth and life to her mother-figure, the protagonist and narrator, Mrs. Anstruther. In the *Autobiography* Elizabeth Sewell attributes the problem of Mrs. Anstruther's stiffness to the changing taste of the day in which the didactic novel gave way to the sensation novel, and to the difficulty inherent in the first-person point of view:

The form I had chosen was a journal. To describe the look, manners, and tone of voice of the writer, Mrs. Anstruther, was, therefore, out of

the question. I put into her mouth the words which I felt I should have
uttered myself; I made her act as I thought it likely I should have acted
myself; I described her feelings from my own experience; and then,
when I presented her to the public my friends said, 'What a dreadful
caricature of yourself—we can't endure her.' I had given the features,
but not the expression; the form, and not the spirit of the words. It had
never struck me that it was necessary to say, what in fact, writing in
the first person, could not be said, 'Mrs. Anstruther's words were
severe, but her tone and manner were loving.' (p. 199)

Elizabeth Sewell must have realized Mrs. Anstruther's
limitations, if not her own, for she gave Mrs. Anstruther an
alter ego in Mrs. Bradshaw, her "rather sharp though
friendly critic" (*Life*, p. 200), whose merry irreverence for
anything solemn showed a side of the author's nature which
she either would not or could not reveal more directly.

Together the autobiographical writing and the fiction suggest that writing about herself, either directly or indirectly,
helped Elizabeth Sewell handle feelings which she could not
express so easily in day-to-day living. If the resulting portrait does not awaken warm responses in the reader, the
problem may be the same one that Patricia Spacks posits
for Johnson's friend, Mrs. Thrale: "The emotional cost of
constant submerged anger was diminished capacity for feeling" (Spacks, p. 201). Indeed Elizabeth Sewell must have
repressed considerable emotion—love, resentment, religious
doubt, all violent emotions—during her progress through
childhood and young womanhood. Allowing for some exag-
geration (bragging?) in her characterization of herself as
violent-tempered, self-willed, perverse, and too early a
gatherer of "the fruit of the Tree of Knowledge of Good and
Evil," one nevertheless senses that the self-control admired
by all who knew her was not easily come by, and one wonders at what cost it was attained.

We have already observed the results of suppressing her
love for her brother William. She also resented a father
whom she describes as "irritable and cold-mannered" and a
mother who, though of a warmer nature, was in the habit of
turning to her sister Anne, rather than to her daughters, for
companionship. This sister lived with the Sewells until her
death in 1837, but by then Elizabeth, who was twenty-two,

found her own "habits of independence" so firmly established that closeness with her mother was difficult to achieve.
It is typical of Elizabeth Sewell that she later reproached
herself for neglecting "the duty of endeavouring to fill up the
blank in her [the mother's] life." Thus the daughter made
what was basically a deficiency in her mother into grounds
for feelings of guilt.

Certainly, Elizabeth Sewell had been well schooled in
the casuistry of the overrefined conscience, for even in an
age known for its cruel and unusual punishment of school
children Belinda Crooke's educational system was notorious. Elizabeth and her sisters remained under this absolute
despot's tutelage from her fifth to her fourteenth year, first
as day pupils, then as boarders. The physical arrangements
at Miss Crooke's were "chilling and depress'ng" enough,
and Elizabeth Sewell's recollections of the room in which she
and her sisters lived once they became boarding pupils
read like something out of *Jane Eyre*. In this room the
floor was uncarpeted, two windows were blocked up, the
third out of bounds, and jugs held "rain water, in which
wonderful specimens of entomology disported themselves" (*Life*, p. 17).

More damaging than physical deprivation was Miss
Crooke's demerit system, which entailed the wearing of a
ram's horn or "brown paper ass's ears." Black and gold
tickets of merit, tea and sugar, gravy with the meat—these
were the promised rewards for distinction. The pupil with
a tender conscience, however, had little hope of gaining
Paradise because "the smallest deceit, the slightest equivo-
cation, was punished by a month's disgrace" during which
no tickets might be gained (*Life*, p. 13). Extra lessons were
assigned as a penalty for grammatical lapses such as "come
here" for "come hither." Since self-accusation was the rule,
Elizabeth once found herself "seventy lessons in arrears,"
and confession became so obsessive for her that Miss
Crooke grew alarmed enough to consult Mrs. Sewell.

Mrs. Sewell herself had meanwhile become the subject of
one of her daughter's "strange scrupulous fancies." After
reading of Jephtha's vow, twelve-year-old Elizabeth worried,

she confides to the reader, "whether I was not bound to kill
my mother, because I thought I had made a vow I would"
(p. 25). Lacking a confidante, she determined on self-cure
by deliberate repression of the unwelcome thoughts.

Her repression of such thoughts was so successful that
Elizabeth Sewell adapted it to dealing with religious doubts
as well. When skeptical thoughts assailed her around the
time of her confirmation in the Anglican Church, she dealt
with them by means of "a short, quick prayer, and an almost physical effort to turn away from the suggestions"
(*Life*, p. 38). Thus she "kept under" unacceptable thoughts,
but their effect remained like a healed wound which might
reopen at any time, and, in fact, not until middle life could
she "face these phantom doubts boldly."

In early adolescence, then, Elizabeth Sewell found herself
burdened with guilt and, worse still, a "dread of not being
forgiven"—a Cowper-like sense of doom which, twenty years
later, she was to refer to as her severest trial. She never
fully delineates the "spectre of evil" but does recall sitting in the drawing room at Camden Place,[15] "practicing
my music mechanically, whilst reasoning upon the proba-
bility of the Jewish miracles till I was nearly wild" (*Life*,
p. 39). It is no wonder that Elizabeth Sewell produced
heroines of whom Margaret Maison wrote: "Her female
characters have the tenderest consciences in all religious
fiction, their self-examinations are the most analytic, their
scruples the most minutely exacting . . . and it is into this
secret personal feminine world that she so successfully
penetrates."[16]

Instead of rebelling either against a Church whose teach-
ings filled her with such agonizing guilt and doubt, or
against a family and teachers so inadequate to meet her
emotional and intellectual needs, Elizabeth Sewell submitted to authority, finding comfort, according to an early
Journal entry (June 20, 1845),[17] in Newman's sermon on
"Obedience, the Remedy for Religious Perplexity." Repressing any unacceptable ideas or emotions, Miss Sewell
works out her conflicts in her writing—both in the fiction
and other works intended for wide circulation and in the

Autobiography and the *Private Journal* kept from 1845 to 1891.

The *Journal* reveals even more than the *Autobiography* the great effort it took to subdue emotional conflicts, presenting to herself and to the world the image of a calm, controlled woman of settled opinions. One of the stated purposes of the *Autobiography* in fact becomes the major preoccupation of the *Journal*: "to trace the most clear working of God's Providence for our good." The conception of divine Providence controlling the events of each human life in order to effect a predetermined purpose was of course widely held in the 1840's, when Elizabeth Sewell began to write. For her particular understanding of this belief, in philosophical terms, she draws on Bishop Butler's *The Analogy of Religion, Natural and Revealed, to the Constitution and Course of Nature* (1736). Like Newman, she lists Butler's *Analogy* among the major influences on her thinking, revealing her indebtedness both in the *Autobiography* (pp. 53–54), and in her *Principles of Education, Drawn from Nature and Revelation, and Applied to Female Education in the Upper Classes* (1865), which quotes Butler to the effect that "the government of the world is uniform, and one, and moral; that virtue shall finally have the advantage, and prevail over . . . wickedness, under the conduct of one supreme Governor."[18] Needing desperately to believe that her trials are part of God's plan to prepare her soul for Heaven, and that good will triumph over evil, she asserts that "the Sewell destiny . . . is to labour and struggle and hope against hope."[19] Toward the end of her active life, wishing to reassure herself that the labor has not been in vain, she writes on January 6, 1891: "If I could have foreseen at the beginning of life's struggle the peace which has been granted at its close I might have been a happier, but I should not have been a better woman" (*Life*, p. 207).

The *Journal* throughout illustrates Elizabeth's Sewell's understanding of what Calvin termed "the uses of adversity." Consider the entry for May 20, 1857. Elizabeth Sewell, age forty-two, writes as she often does on the anniversary of her mother's death. She begins with a quotation from the *Sermons* of Tauler, the German mystic, which likens God to a painter, concluding: "God takes a thousand times more pains with us than the artist with his picture, by many touches of sorrow, and by many colours of circumstance to bring man into the form which is highest and noblest in His sight" (*Journal*, p. 101). Half a page on, the metaphor changes from the strokes of a paint brush on canvas to a "heavy crushing mill" in which she has been placed by God. Then the paint brush imagery reappears, softening her closing lament for the lost opportunity to give herself to her mother as, she writes, "I never did, and never felt that I was bound to do, when she was living" (p. 102).

The next *Journal* entry less than three weeks later announces that she has "just finished Mrs. Gaskell's 'Life of Miss Brontë' "—a life which she finds "intensely, painfully interesting" because "a purer, more high-minded person it seems there could scarcely be, wonderfully gifted, and with a man's energy and power of will, and passionate impulse; and yet gentle and womanly in all her ways, so as to be infinitely touching" (*Life*, p. 160). The *Journal* then speculates whether Mrs. Gaskell was incapable, as a Unitarian, of understanding Charlotte Brontë's deeper religious feelings, or whether these feelings were actually inadequate to sustain Miss Brontë in sorrow. Buried within Elizabeth Sewell's reflections on Gaskell's *Life of Charlotte Brontë* lie several contradictions within the journal-keeper herself, which are of interest because they are typical of the Victorian Everywoman—a middle-class Christian, bright but indifferently educated and conforming at least outwardly to the expected patterns. For convenience they may be called: 1) the masculine-feminine (or aggressive-passive) paradox, 2) the subjective-objective (or inner-outer) paradox, and 3) the insular-universal (or narrow-broad) paradox. To examine these paradoxes, one at a time, will demonstrate the conflicts that Elizabeth Sewell seeks to resolve through the act of writing about herself.

The masculine-feminine paradox, viewed from Elizabeth Sewell's conventional mid-nineteenth century perspective, becomes the conflict between the aggressive, self-affirming side of her own nature and its passive, self-denying side. When Elizabeth Sewell lays stress on Charlotte Brontë's androgynous personality, she is describing an idealized Elizabeth Sewell—"high-minded," "gifted," "with a man's energy and power of will," yet "gentle and womanly." Five years before Elizabeth Sewell read the Gaskell biography she had already drawn her idealized self-portrait in Aunt Sarah Mortimer of her best-loved novel, *The Experience of Life*. Aunt Sarah, by precept and example, guides her namesake, young Sarah or Sally (surely Elizabeth's spiritual twin) from a "sickly, plain, and indifferently educated" girl intended to "live in the shade" into a serene, useful spinster. Aunt Sarah's advice balances femininity with strength: "Don't try to be a man when you are only a woman." But, "Don't be a burden upon any one." Marriage should never be a woman's goal, both Sarahs feel strongly—and here they are ahead of their time. From her own experience in the course of the novel Sally learns that "a single life need not be solitary and unblest."[20]

Creating Aunt Sarah was a congenial task. Not so congenial was the writing of a book like *Passing Thoughts on Religion* (1860), and in the *Journal*, Elizabeth Sewell tells why: "I don't like putting out so much of myself in so undisguised a form" (p. 140). Again the reticent, self-deprecating, "feminine" Elizabeth Sewell comes to the fore.

Opposed to this epitome of womanly reserve is the other Elizabeth Sewell—the confident critic who in her *Journal* of September 1846 accuses another woman author[21] of "too much womanish humility," boasting "I should never consider it an intrusion to go wherever men go" (*Life*, p. 131). Looking back on her childhood, she seems instinctively to identify with the masculine role in a number of cases, and then to retreat, back away. In a passage omitted from the posthumously published *Autobiography*, she describes holidays at the Hermitage, her godfather's country house, where the Sewell children were allowed to "run wild." She recalls experiencing "feelings of independence, and energy and romance, and what *in a man* [italics added] would be ambition."[22] What is implied here is of course that, while ambition is not appropriate to a girl, a girl nevertheless feels its equivalent. In fact, ambition by whatever name comes through so strongly in the *Journal* that the reader feels the lady doth protest too much. For example, after admiring Southey's contentment despite "pecuniary anxieties" in the entry for August 19, 1850, she notes the publication of her novel, *The Earl's Daughter* (a sort of *Love Story* without the romance), and then adds, "I get heaps of praise, and am lionised till I am heart-sick and headachy" (*Life*, p. 153). Seven years later, too much praise is evidently no longer a problem, for she records on the last day of 1857 a conversation in which Parker, the publisher, tells her that her day is past. From the Longman brothers, however, she receives sufficient encouragement to write four more novels, a variety of text books and meditations, and the *Principles of Education*, which saw reprinting until three years after her death.

Unable any longer to feel guilt for her popularity as an author, Elizabeth Sewell on May 20, 1881 can still apologize for being successful with the school at Ashcliff. "When others struggle," she writes, "I feel ashamed of having been so successful" (*Journal*, p. 297). This entry is neither a polite apology nor a bit of superficial humility. Rather, it arises out of two needs deep in the author's nature: the need to achieve—a masculine feeling, according to the Victorians—and the need to feel guilty about achieving—since achievement is considered unfeminine.

Within the professional arena Elizabeth Sewell is often in conflict between giving priority to her writing and devoting herself to teaching. At some points she seems to resent the time taken away from writing by the demands of the school at Ashcliff. Her *Journal* entry for August 14, 1855, however, refers wistfully to a plan she has been

formulating "for years" to establish a training school for
governesses in connection with Queen's College, London:
"If I were free and alone, I should certainly try something
of this kind" (*Life*, p. 155). But she is not free and alone,
having chosen to do what she had once resolved never to
do—"to be a useful aunt." Once again the "masculine" drive
toward solid professional achievement has been subordin-
ated to the proper female domestic role.

To keep a school in one's own home fits the womanly
image well enough. The Ashcliff pupils, who never num-
bered more than ten at any given time, called the sisters
"aunts" and, as Elizabeth Sewell wrote on May 27, 1863,
"They are so entirely one's own children—no others could
be like them" (*Journal*, p. 171). By the time she founded
St. Boniface School "for girls of the middle classes" in
1865, the Sewell nieces and nephews were fairly well
grown-up, and her role at St. Boniface was, in any case,
that of supervisor and occasional lecturer. Thus by 1865,
the masculine-feminine role conflict had found resolution.

Twenty years earlier there was already a plan under
discussion whereby Elizabeth Sewell might become the
head of "a Church School or College for girls." In recording this incident on July 20, 1845, she says that the following criterion was introduced: "to determine all things
by the *objective* rather than the *subjective*, not to ask
whether we are fitted to attempt a plan likely to do good,
but whether circumstances point it out as our duty" (*Journal*,
p. 5). These categories, subjective and objective, bring us
to the second pair of opposites which she sought to reconcile through her autobiographical writings. The *Autobiography* and the *Journal* display a preoccupation with balancing the inner and outer sides to her nature and a reliance
upon external authority to settle the claims of conflicting
feelings, or to point out a duty which might make her forget
the absence of feeling. From those early self-accusing days
at Miss Crooke's Elizabeth Sewell fled the casuistry of conscience and sought the comfort of duty. But duty could,
from our present-day perspective, involve its own casuistry

when it caused her to set aside questions like, "Am I capable of being the head of a school?" and "Would I like to be head of a school?" in favor of "Do family circumstances dictate that I should be doing something else?" Family seems often to have formed a blind spot in "Aunt Elizabeth's" perspective.

The line between subjective and objective is nowhere more difficult to draw than in the area of her personal religious experience. Like most of us Elizabeth Sewell claimed great objectivity in assessing the religion of other persons and prided herself on her ability to spot their subjective fallacies. When discussing Mrs. Gaskell's *Life of Charlotte Brontë*, for example, she wonders whether Mrs. Gaskell, as a Unitarian, might have "failed to bring out feelings which she could not understand" in Miss Brontë, the evangelical Christian—a chain of reasoning which obviously involves certain *a priori* assumptions about Unitarians. But, assuming that Mrs. Gaskell was accurate, Elizabeth Sewell notes a two-fold lack in the Brontë religious experience—her failure to realize "the constant presence of a Saviour" and "a singular absence of active daily sympathy with the poor" (*Journal*, p. 103). Laying aside any question of the adequacy of her diagnosis of Brontë's spiritual ills, the passage bespeaks Elizabeth Sewell's recognition of the inner and outer sides of religious experience. It also shows that she finds it hard to be objective in her own judgments where religion is concerned.

In the *Autobiography* and *Journal* one senses a failure ever to be satisfied with the balance between inner and outer in her own experience. First, there is the conviction, accompanied by a certain amount of frustration, that one's inner nature can never be fully known. On her forty-fifth birthday, February 19, 1860, Elizabeth Sewell writes in her *Journal*: "The 'tale' of one's life is very marvelous. . . . How untrue any biography—even an autobiography—of any human being must be! How much there is which can never be told except to God, but on which all that is really life has depended" (*Life*, p. 163). Her sensitive nature, as we have seen, recoils from probing too deeply into the feelings of another, and resists the efforts of others to pry out her secrets. She is more comfortable, we have noted, revealing her own thoughts and feelings indirectly through her fictional characters, and in the *Autobiography* she uses the figure of a cryptogram to explain the way in which the transference of feeling from her life to her fiction takes place. Writing of the terminal illness of a young girl, she admits: "The disposition of my much-loved pupil, Louise Cookson, is exactly portrayed in that of Cecil Anstruther [in *Home Life*]. It was a relief to me to describe my own feelings and experience under a feigned name, and with feigned incidents—to make the story, as it were, a cryptogram" (*Life*, p. 201).

Elizabeth Sewell probably would say of her own *Journal* what she has her narrator, Mrs. Anstruther, say of hers in *Journal of a Home Life*:

> This is not a journal of what people call spiritual experiences; I could never keep that. It always seems to me that my best feelings are like the lovely figure of a young girl I once heard of, as having been discovered in a cave in Greece. It had been buried for centuries, and whilst it lay hidden, and no eye but that of God could look upon it, it retained all its freshness and grace, but no sooner was it exposed to the outward air, and the curious gaze of man, than it crumbled to dust.[23]

If the "better feelings" cannot survive being brought to light, what of the worst? Again the attitude is cautious, possibly because of the early experiences at Miss Crooke's. Elizabeth Sewell warns that children's confessions are undesirable, and other confession runs the risk of a component of vanity, "especially with women" (*Life*, p. 130). Such vanity she herself unconsciously illustrates when she boasts of being a perverse child and a schoolgirl so knowledgeable in evil.

If one must be chary of confession to others, then self-examination becomes all important to the discipline of the soul, and Elizabeth Sewell formed the habit of self-examination early. At the Misses Aldridges' school in Bath, which she attended from thirteen to fifteen, she fled the "railway pace" by retreating to a small storage room where, standing up, she engaged in prayer and self-examination. As a young teacher and parish worker, she welcomed "*work for the Lord*" as an antidote to the "fidgety self-worrying state" in which she often found herself. As she grew older the balance between action and reflection was even harder to maintain. With the responsibilities of a large household, boarding pupils, and publisher's deadlines weighing upon her, she worried lest she had lost the knack for contemplative thought. In the same passage (May 20, 1857) in which she quotes from Tauler's *Sermons*, she refers to a suggestion of Archdeacon Manning that "it is good for us to put aside some one day, to be spent as though it were the last of one's life." She declares guiltily that she had "wished to do so with this day" but found herself begrudging "the hours taken away from my usual employments, and given to thought and devotion" (*Journal*, p. 101). Years later (1874) she confesses to yielding to the temptation to become "business-weighted." "The things I am interested in seem good, and are in a certain sense duties," she observes, "but the cares of this life check growth as much as pleasures" (*Journal*, p. 282).

What Elizabeth Sewell fears from time to time is that cares will crush the power of feeling altogether, leaving her with only the shell of an outer life covering a hollow core— the "great hole" or "diminished capacity" of which Patricia Spacks writes. At the age of thirty Elizabeth Sewell goes on a donkey-back expedition to a favorite haunt of her girlhood. Depressed at being unable to recapture what she had once felt there, she writes in her *Journal*: "My heart never bounds now, and all I can enjoy is the *memory* of a feeling" (*Life*, p. 128). This state of mind is not to last, however, for we read in the *Journal* entry for August 16, 1854: "As we get into middle life care crushes us down, until we think the very power of enjoyment is dead. But . . . it must be as immortal as the soul, and God teaches us this at times. . . .

This has been a changing, flickering morning, . . . and when the sun shone into my room, and the sky and the white clouds were seen above the trees, it seemed as if—take but away the daily burden of anxiety—even at nine-and-thirty the heart would spring up rejoicing as eagerly as at nineteen, and perhaps far more deeply and thankfully" (*Life*, p. 154).

According to Elizabeth Sewell, the world of feeling— whether religious awe or simple joy—is to be cherished and is never to be given short shrift, as when Miss Caroline Aldridge of the Bath School would remark at Sunday dinner, "We had a beautiful and instructive sermon today. I trust we shall all profit by it; . . . which will you have— beef or mutton?" (*Life*, pp. 32–33) On the other hand, the religious emotions are not to be played upon, as in the case of the Bishop of Oxford's appeal on behalf of the Society for the Propagation of the Gospel. The good bishop's sermon on the occasion was, according to the Sewell *Journal* for December 1864, "too strained to be really impressive." Here she observes, "One is perverse enough never to be affected by an evident attempt to touch the conscience or the heart" (*Life*, p. 171).

In her early years Elizabeth Sewell would never have presumed to criticize a bishop—at least not an Anglican bishop. In her later years she was no longer awed by authority to the point that she "supposed that every clergyman must be perfect, or formed exactly upon the Oxford model" (*Life*, p. 197). Conversely, she no longer presumed all Rationalists to be wicked, all non-Church people to be uncongenial, nor all feminists misguided. Yet she did not become consistently more tolerant. The disparity between the insular and the universal sides of her nature continued to the end of her life. The dilemma in which she found herself was essentially that of any person who hopes to remain both orthodox and tolerant. The problem, in her terms, was "how to harmonise condemnation with pity—to acknowledge the good of a search after Truth, to see the different views which may be taken of Truth, and still to hold fast Faith" (*Journal*, p. 181).

The need to hold fast her own faith while acknowledging
the sincerity of another's search and to test everything by
the moral aesthetic led Elizabeth Sewell to some interesting conclusions on literature and on life. The narrow-broad
paradox is at work in the *Journal* passage on Charlotte
Brontë. The sectarian Elizabeth Sewell deplores the apparent inadequacy of Miss Brontë's personal religion; the
sympathetic, nonsectarian Elizabeth Sewell adds: "But one
writes in ignorance. She was heartily, thoroughly good,
that I feel; and now, at last there is rest for her" (*Journal*,
p. 103). The heart divided between tolerance and intoler-
ance is particularly evident in her responses to foreign
literature. (She learned French in school then taught herself Spanish, German and Italian.) Goethe was beyond her
appreciation, but in Victor Hugo she could see the "saint"
as well as the "blasphemous revolutionary" (*Journal*, p.
174).

On August 14, 1854, Elizabeth Sewell comments in her
Journal on Ruskin's *Lectures on Architecture and Painting*.
In these she finds "wonderful thought" and "an intense
feeling for truth," but terms Ruskin's "exaggerated tirades
against Romanism" a disfigurement (*Life*, p. 153), unaware
evidently that the view of Catholicism she condemns in
Ruskin is also implied in her references to a processional
for the Virgin as "theatrical and frippery" (*Journal*, p. 115)
and her comparison of "Romish services" to the opera
(*Journal*, p. 122).

In her personal life Elizabeth Sewell grew from the
conviction that she could not breathe in "irreligious society"
(*Life*, p. 51) to the point of marvelling, in 1863, that she
and an American friend, identified only as "A.H.," had
"advanced far on the path of intimacy and sympathy,
though she stands outside the Church" (*Journal*, p. 176).
Nonetheless, politically and socially she remained conservative, and, like most of her contemporaries, she viewed
universal suffrage in France with alarm. Born into a Tory
household she seems never to have changed her ways,
believing that people should remain in "that station" of
life to which God has called them. In *Katharine Ashton*

(1854) she demonstrated that a young girl of the "commercial class" might be a lady in every true sense behind her father's shop counter, but argued that she must not try to rise above her own class. Education was for all classes and both sexes, but should take the form that would best serve any of the spheres "ordained by God."

On the question of woman suffrage Elizabeth Sewell's ambivalent views emerge from the barely fictionalized dialogues of a late work entitled *Note-Book of an Elderly Lady* (1881). Mrs. Blair, who seems to speak for Miss Sewell herself, concedes that "there is no valid argument to be brought forward against giving the suffrage to women" yet denies that "women's interests would be furthered by the possession of the so-called privilege."[24] As the dialogue continues between the moderate Mrs. Blair and the feminist Miss Brown, Elizabeth Sewell gives Miss Brown some telling arguments; she even unwittingly wins the reader's sympathies to the feminist side with Miss Brown's impatient, "Too slow! too slow!"

Through the impassioned arguments of Miss Brown, Elizabeth Sewell gives vent to the anger and doubt she must have experienced often in the grip of "the Victorian trap of selflessness"—a snare all but unavoidable to the upper middle-class woman of orthodox religion and conservative politics.[25] Through the moderate (as she perceives it) voice of Mrs. Blair, Elizabeth Sewell reaffirms the concerns discovered in the formally autobiographical writing. She justifies the self-image she has built by reminding younger women that their first duty is to be womanly. She expresses the felt guilt of her own sex by assigning a large measure of "women's wrongs" to their own "timidity and indolence." She reiterates her teleological assumptions by insisting on the reliability of the "moral sense implanted by God in the human race," that is, the male electorate. Finally she justifies her own professional activity by applauding Florence Nightingale for "claiming her work as that which naturally belonged to women."[26]

The dialogue, which is really between the two natures of Elizabeth Missing Sewell, ends with Mrs. Blair quoting

Wordsworth's lines on the perfect woman and noting, "So we ended our talk—neither of us convinced." The self-denying Elizabeth Sewell and the self-expressing Elizabeth Sewell continue their not altogether peaceful coexistence, and it is left to the reader to determine where concealment ends and revelation begins.

1. *Autobiography of Elizabeth M. Sewell*, printed for private circulation (Edinburgh: St. Giles, 1893). A second and larger edition followed in 1907. Edited by her niece, this posthumous edition adds brief essays by pupils and friends and interweaves selections from Miss Sewell's *Journal*, published originally in *Extracts from a Private Journal Kept from 1845 to 1891* by Elizabeth M. Sewell. These extracts were printed for private circulation, principally to her nephews and nieces and their children.

2. "Autobiographies," *North British Review* 51 (Jan., 1870), 208.

3. *The Autobiography of Elizabeth M. Sewell*, ed. Eleanor L. Sewell (London: Longmans, 1907), p. 84. This work is hereafter cited as *Life*. Quotations are from this edition unless otherwise noted.

4. *Cornhill Magazine* 43 (April, 1881), 410, 418, 422.

5. Patricia M. Spacks, *The Female Imagination* (New York: Knopf, 1975), p. 218.

6. *Autobiography* (1893), p. 9.

7. William Sewell (1804–1874), then a tutor at Exeter College, is best known as a writer and professor of moral philosophy at Oxford.

8. Longmans' 1858 edition of *Gertrude* boasts of 10,000 copies of *Amy Herbert* sold in England. At least an equal number had been circulated in America by June, 1845. See *Life*, p. 121.

9. Elizabeth M. Sewell, *Ursula* (New York: Appleton, 1858), II, 115.

10. See Mrs. Hugh Fraser, *A Diplomatist's Wife in Many Lands* (New York: Dodd, Mead, 1910), and C. M. Whitehead, *Recollections of Miss Elizabeth Sewell and Her Sisters*, (Ventnor, I. W.: Knight's Library, 1910). See also *Life*, pp. 209–242.

11. See *Life*, pp. 61–65, for her account of meeting most of the Oxford Movement leaders at dinner in 1840, and *Life*, pp. 182–184, for her record of her conversation with Browning in 1869.

12. James Edwards Sewell (1810–1903).

13. See E. M. Sewell's "The Reign of Pedantry in Girls' Schools," *The Nineteenth Century* 23 (Feb., 1883), 216–238, to which Dorothea Beale replied in "Girls' Schools Past and Present," *The Nineteenth Century* 23 (April, 1888), 541–554.

14. See *Life*, p. 198.

15. Camden Place, Bath, was the location of the Misses Aldridges' School, which Elizabeth and Ellen Sewell attended 1828–30.

16. *Search Your Soul, Eustace: A Survey of the Religious Novel in the Victorian Age* (London: Sheed and Ward, 1961), p. 43.

17. *Life*, p. 119. Where *Journal* entries are reprinted in the posthumous *Autobiography* (*Life*), they will be cited accordingly.

18. Quoted from Butler's *Analogy*, Part I, Chapter III, by E. M. Sewell in *Principles of Education* (New York: Appleton, 1866), p. 342.

19. *Extracts from a Private Journal kept from 1845 to 1891* (Edinburgh: St. Giles, 1891), p. 98. This work is hereafter cited as *Journal*.

20. *The Experience of Life* (London: Longmans, 1866), pp. 16, 30, 318, 341.

21. Cecilia F. Tilley in *Chollerton* (1846).

22. *Autobiography* (Edinburgh, 1893), p. 25.

23. *The Journal of a Home Life* (New York: Appleton, 1867), pp. 217–18.

24. *Note-Book of an Elderly Lady* (London: Walter Smith, 1881), p. 151.

25. Spacks, p. 285.

26. *Note-Book of an Elderly Lady*, pp. 156 57, 164, 174.

GEORGE BORNSTEIN

The Antinomial Structure of
John Butler Yeats's *Early Memories:*
Some Chapters of Autobiography

John Butler Yeats's *Early Memories: Some Chapters of Autobiography*[1] forms one of the most delightful neglected works of post-romantic literature. Son of an obscure Church of Ireland rector named William Butler Yeats and father of the famous poet who carried on his ancestor's name, John Butler Yeats[2] (1839–1922) was born in County Down, educated first at minor Victorian boarding schools and then at Trinity College, Dublin, and called to the bar in 1866 before deciding the next year to turn his talent for sketching into a career. He became a minor artist of the end of the century, dividing his time between disappointing assaults on the art worlds of London and Dublin before emigrating in 1907 to New York, where he died in 1922.[3] Artist, theorist, bohemian, and talker, he left behind paintings which include some famous portraits of Irish political and cultural leaders, a large number of sketches and illustrations, a volume of criticism, two already published volumes of letters (one selected by Ezra Pound), numerous fugitive pieces, and *Early Memories.* Prodded by his son and others, he had begun the autobiography toward the end of his life.[4] In it he recalls chiefly his formal and informal education from his father's first abortive efforts through the Trinity College years, with flashes of his later life in England and Ireland. Mixing sometimes wicked and sometimes generous character sketches with spirited speculation on art and society, the book seems at first a distillation of that splendid conversation at which John Butler Yeats excelled.[5]

Only gradually does the reader recognize the tight organization of the volume and the intimate connection of the philosophy it propounds with the personalities it projects. Its plan and contents find their closest analogue in the work of William Butler Yeats, who developed his own literary principles partly in conversation and correspondence with his father. Like his son, John Butler Yeats saw human experience in terms of paired opposites struggling against each other. *Early Memories* continually spins off antinomies: the social ones of Irish against English, medieval against modern, or civility against rudeness; the more personal ones of imagination against calculation, solitude against companionship, or cheerfulness against melancholy; and the doubly applicable ones of individual against social loyalty, inner against outer control, and pleasure against puritanism. These operate centripetally rather than centrifugally. Yeats based his master antinomy on the distinction between deep personality which expresses the true self and superficial character which reflects environment and may be marked by contentious opinion—a dichotomy his son also used.[6] He valued other pairs according to whether their terms tended to produce personality or only character. In general, Yeats stood for a traditional Irish world, one of medieval hierarchy in which social obligation supported art and imagination, and he saw the chief menace to his ideal in the modern industrial society which had already captured England, producing a mentality hostile to beauty and manners alike.

Such polarities inform the personal profiles which occupy so much of the work. John Butler Yeats does not introduce them on grounds of fame or innate interest, although those are sometimes present, nor on the score of their importance to his development, although many of them affected him in significant ways. He presents them because they illustrate one or more terms of his antinomies and so offer concrete examples of his general doctrines. This principle of selection explains the otherwise dispa-

rate mixture—chiefly his parents and their servant Sam
Matchett; his friend (and later brother-in-law) George
Pollexfen and uncle Robert Corbet; Dante Rossetti and
George Meredith; the mathematician Sir Andrew Hart
and his barrister son George Vaughan Hart; J. S. Mill, the
Home Rule leader Isaac Butt, and William Allingham's
brother Thomas.[7] Rossetti, for example, emerges as the
man of personality free from conformity and opinion, in
contrast to Meredith, whom Yeats saw as permeated with
upper middle-class convention. A similar didacticism informs the successive vignettes of small societies—his early
home, the two boarding schools, Trinity College, and the
households of his cousin "F.B." on Lough Dan, of Robert
Corbet at Sandymount Castle, of the surveyor John Yeats
at Monasterevan, and of the Pollexfens at Sligo.[8] Each
group functions as a microcosm fostering one or another
term of an antinomy. For instance, if Atholl Academy substituted outer for inner control, Sandymount Castle banished external restraint without begetting internal discipline. Of course, most autobiographies use their materials
illustratively. Yeats's differs by the nearly geometric
quality of its schema. Going back to the characters of
Theophrastus and inmates of Dante's *Comedy*, Yeats's
procedure most resembles that of his son's *Autobiographies* and *A Vision*, both of which use historical characters to dramatize theoretical polarities. We are not far off
if we read *Early Memories* the way we read the other two
works. Elsewhere John Butler Yeats, who had even more
trouble with artistic order than did William, showed notorious difficulty in finding a final form for his pictures. He
once abandoned a painting of the pond at Burnham
Beeches, begun in the spring, only when he found himself
painting snow on its banks the following winter, and he
never finished the self-portrait that occupied so many of
the years in New York.[9] But in *Early Memories* he found
an apt device for self-expression. The notion of antinomies
enabled him to deploy his perceptions serially yet still
within an ordering framework, a more modest version of
his son's vast designs.

Those formal procedures shape *Early Memories* into a distinctive prose portrait of the artist as a young man. Incidents appear not for their personal but for their representative value. The prolific antinomies permit him to analyze the artistic psyche, while each of the character studies illuminates an aspect of artistic personality and each of the social groups the kind of society in which an artist can flourish. The entire book centers on the creative personality: it begins with the question of why John Butler Yeats became an artist and ends with the reasons why his friend George Pollexfen failed to become "a writer of note and power" (99). The opening paragraphs provide an example. Yeats says that he became an artist because his father was "an Irish gentleman of the old school and not at all thrifty" (1) who provided his son plentifully with paper despite the high taxes on it. We soon learn, however, that to be an Irish gentleman of the old school implies more than prodigality with paper. It involves the whole range of romantic personality, social values, and admiration of civilized accomplishment appropriate to "delicious visionary hopefulness" (35) and "romantic imagination" (38). The combination made the senior Yeats an evangelical rector, teller of tall tales, and expert horseman; it made his son an artist.

If his early upbringing encouraged artistic temperament, John Butler Yeats's formal education did not, for it fostered the wrong terms of his antinomies. He renders his two boarding schools as typical Victorian horrors, making Miss Davenport's School near Liverpool embody a bleak and fearsome religiosity foreign to Yeats's evangelical yet easy-going household: "hell was the driving force" (6). Although founded on faith in the Bible, the school chastened all other youthful forms of the credulity which Yeats came to think necessary for the artist. This assault on "solitary fantasy" continued at Atholl Academy, a gloomy pile on the Isle of Man run by a hard-flogging Scotchman. That school's rigorous external dsicipline blocked the growth of internal control and abetted a "perfectly unconscious selfishness" (34). Its puritan devotion to law, fact, and implicit egotism collided with the emphasis on personality, imagination, and affection of his parents' home. "My history ever since has been the conflict between these two principles," he concluded. While vastly preferable to the two academies, even Trinity College failed to nourish the proper qualities. To Yeats the lack of beauty in its buildings and grounds signalled a mental severity hostile to art and emotion. Trinity College inspired "no love" and except for purely intellectual learning and mathematics had a "lean history" (68-69). All three schools thus illustrate negative rather than positive poles of his philosophy.

Private households offered John Butler Yeats the kind of development he missed in educational institutions. The homes of his relatives became his true schools. Three of them nourished his social sense, each in a different way. The country house and estate of his cousin F.B. contained "a sort of civility not to be found everywhere" (44). Its master, mistress, children, coachman, old butler and elderly French cook made a harmonious and cordial society. They seemed not modern but medieval and suggested a "golden age when no one was in a hurry and so had time to enjoy themselves, and for the sake of enjoyment to be courteous and witty and pleasant" (45). If Lough Dan showed the medieval social virtues, Sandymount Castle epitomized the "old-fashioned, eighteenth century gregarious worldliness" of its master, Yeats's uncle Robert Corbet (56). With its corps of gardeners, plentiful wildlife, attractive pond, and store of family keepsakes, Sandymount Castle, which he called his Capua, became a sort of Renaissance court to Yeats from 1857 to 1862. Fond of friends and relations, Robert Corbet believed in personal kindness but detested the sort of abstract theory and humanitarianism which Yeats was shortly to imbibe from John Stuart Mill (and so to propel himself beyond the Sandymount stage). Yet even Sandymount had a defect: it replaced the repressive regime of Atholl Academy with an opposite extreme of indulgence. "I did not think, I did not work, I had no ambition, I dreamed," he recalled. "As far as the demands of that sympathetic circle went, I satisfied everybody, and was well-behaved" (56). The household of County Surveyor John Yeats in the village of Monasterevan showed even more concern for social sensitivity: "these people lived for other people" (77). They created enormous happiness for themselves and others, yet the children grew up in a kind of innocence which ultimately deprived them of "mental power and effectiveness." Like all good teachers, these enclaves stimulated their pupil in a way that ultimately drove him beyond them.

Yeats took that step in 1862 at the end of his postgraduate year at Trinity, when he won a ten pound prize in Political Economy. He used the money to finance a trip to Sligo to visit his old school friend George Pollexfen. The Pollexfens were summering in the village of Rosses Point, five miles outside town. In their household he encountered an antithesis to his Dublin life which, unlike Miss Davenport's or Atholl Academy, seemed positive rather than negative. The new antimony posited two goods rather than a good and a bad:

> At Sligo, I was the social man where it was the individual man that counted. It is a curious fact that entering this sombre house of stern preoccupation with business I for the first time in my life felt myself to be a free man, and that I was invited by the example of everyone around me to be my very self, thereby receiving the most important lesson in my life (89).

He had previously subscribed to "the social principle" (87), which prescribed mutual allegiance and civilized enjoyment but slighted the strong passions of "the lower abysses of human nature" (88). In pursuing enjoyment rather than sincerity his friends had cut themselves off from true force. In contrast, the Pollexfens followed the principle of "self-loyalty" (87) which gave their personalities a nearly elemental power. True, they occasionally suffered from the malady of "self-exaggeration," but they more often attained a deep sincerity. If they took a long time to make up their minds, that was because they had so much mind to make up. To combine the social Yeatsian virtues

with the individual Pollexfen ones would produce
an artistic temperament of a high order: "Let any young
poet stay for a while among the puritans and practice all
the restraints of self-loyalty, and he will turn his sociable
activity and animated sympathy into something which
is much better, namely force" (91).

Looking back from old age on those social circles of
his youth, Yeats classified their members by antinomies relating to the production of forceful personality. Sometimes
he illustrated his terms asymmetrically, but usually he
divided minor characters into pairs. The muscular family
servant Sam Matchett kindled young Yeats's admiration
for physical activity, while the dour schoolmistress Miss
Betsy sought to suppress it: Sam lifted Rev. William Yeats
with the palm of his hand, while Betsy caned small boys for
tree-climbing. The autobiography holds up a series of foils
to Rev. William Yeats, who plays a central role: his wife
encouraged affections while he stimulated intellect; his
rector's bad temper momentarily condemned everything
from his horsemanship to evangelicalism; and Thomas Allingham embodied the danger of too much education in
contrast to Rev. William Yeats's sense of his own inadequate schooling. The charismatic mathematician and Vice-
Provost of Trinity, Sir Andrew Hart, imposed restraint on
others through his own gentle manners, in contrast to a
bumptious Belfast cousin of Yeats's who complained that
he could not get men to be civil to him. An account of a
lecture by John Stuart Mill improbably describes him as
"of all men the most winning" (57), in contrast to the aggressive dogmatism he inspired in young Yeats. Finally,
the scientist George Fitzgerald's ability to love the sinner
while deploring the sin counterpoints Carlyle's hatred of
the sinner, yet even Carlyle's fierce anger was preferable
to Froude's cold cruelty. These figures illustrate easily
graspable antinomies, and Yeats parades them past us
quickly, though, as we have already seen, he spends more
time on closer embodiments of his ideals like his father
and Robert Corbet.

The artist Dante Gabriel Rossetti, barrister George

Vaughan Hart, and political leader Isaac Butt all displayed the power of personality that became Yeats's standard: "A personality is a man brought into unity by a mood, not a static unity, (that is character) but alive and glowing like a star, all in harmony with himself" (29). When Yeats adds peaceful yet vigilant conscience and unified spiritual and sexual desires to the list, one can understand his exemplifying the concept in Rossetti only by remembering that he had never met him. Yeats belonged to a group of young painters "agog about Rossetti," whom they saw as a type of the pure artist—"a personality naked and unashamed" (27), indifferent to mere opinion and full of unself-conscious harmony. Admiring a painting of John Butler Yeats's at the Dudley, Rossetti sent three messengers (one of them his brother) to invite Yeats to call, but timidity about self and work prevented acceptance. Yeats later thought that meeting Rossetti would have transformed his own questioning intellect into an imaginative whole, but it would more likely have shattered the icon.

Yeats knew his other two heroes personally. George Vaughan Hart was a successful barrister and enthusiastic gardener with a fine sense of humor. Yeats deliberately selects an almost trivial incident to illustrate his behavior, a tremendous thunder-storm during which Hart joked with the family gathered in his drawing room at Howth Hill. In metamorphosing the energy of fear into merriment, Hart cleansed it in the way that beauty could cleanse sexual feeling or Shakespeare's language cleanse pity and terror. His "mirthfulness" (52) anticipates the gaiety of "Lapis Lazuli" in a minor mode. The formidable Isaac Butt, for whom Yeats may have clerked before giving up the legal profession, projected an even stronger personality. "In Butt's magnanimous mind and imagination were tides of feeling and of old memory" that could overcome even a bitter quarrel with Robert Corbet for the sake of helping young "Mr. Johnnie" (62). Whether changing from Tory to Nationalist M.P., bewitching a jury of simple people, helping a ragged farmer instead of titled magnates, posing as guide in Madame Tussaud's waxworks, or playing back-

gammon with old ladies, Butt showed the dynamic self-
unity and flair for dramatic gesture which impressed others
with his authenticity. At first uncertain of the source of
Butt's power, Yeats concluded that "in Butt himself was
such a fountain of naturalness and humanity that people
said 'This is the thing itself, compared to which our moral
codes are only the scaffolding' " (66). All three men have
their foils in the book—Rossetti in the conventional Meredith,
Hart in a terrified maiden aunt, and Butt in the more
congenial professor of moral philosophy Archer Butler.

Yeats broods most of all over the personality of his
estranged friend George Pollexfen. He interrupts his account of Atholl Academy with a lengthy meditation on
Pollexfen, whom he met there, and closes the book with
another long revery about him. Pollexfen, we come to
understand, completes Yeats's own antinomy. He embodies
those qualities which Yeats thought of as "puritan" and
opposite to his own—melancholy instead of cheerful, solitary instead of social, pessimistic rather than optimistic
about human nature, and believing man to be made for
law rather than law for man. Yeats particularly admired
his skilled horsemanship and freedom from opinion, which
suggested complementary harmonies. In one of those
surprising juxtapositions of world-famous figures with
relatively obscure Celts at which his son later excelled,
John Butler Yeats favorably contrasted Pollexfen to
Dostoevsky, and Tolstoi in old age. While Tolstoi "made
strange incursions into the world of opinion" and Dostoevsky "fell back on the Orthodox Greek Church," Pollexfen
remained "a man richly endowed with instincts as count-
less as the threads in a piece of embroidery, each with its
own intelligence as true as the instinct of a nesting bird,
and yet no opinions, no more than if he were a visitant
come from a distant star" (21–22). That quality particularly
attracted Yeats, who saw himself as a man enmeshed in
endless theory. Pollexfen, in short, seemed to have an
ideal personality for an artist. Yet he became only an accomplished astrologer.

By the closing portrait of Pollexfen we understand why.

Echoing portions of the earlier account, the final one focuses even more precisely on why he failed to "become a
writer of note and power" (99). For all his virtues, Pollexfen
represents only half an antinomy. If John Butler Yeats
found in Sligo the antithesis of his earlier, social education,
George Pollexfen needed to find in Dublin the antithesis of
his early individual one. Particularly, he needed to have
gone to Trinity College and gained entrance to the world
of "books and intellectual companionship" (99) which it
commanded. Instead, he buried himself in isolated commercial life in the west of Ireland. He could never cast
off that puritanism which would have freed him in combination with its opposite.

In analyzing George Pollexfen, Yeats obliquely criticizes
himself as well. If Pollexfen failed to become a writer,
Yeats failed to become a great artist. He saw himself as
spending his life in "this entangling web of grey theory"
(28). The liberating vision of self-loyalty in Sligo had come
too late, and while Pollexfen never got clear of puritanism,
John Butler Yeats never escaped from the social principle.
He theorized about forceful personality more than he attained it, just as his pictures often blurred their form. The
implied hero of *Early Memories* is William Butler Yeats.
The father described the result of his marriage to Susan
Pollexfen by the famous and beautiful antinomy of having
"given a tongue to the sea-cliffs" (20). He explained his
meaning later in the volume as part of a self-critique:

> Among my friends and in their type of civilization we made enjoy-
> ment of the first importance, and for that reason we were eager
> for art and poetry, which are all made for enjoyment. Yet it was
> bound to come to nothing, because we had not that deep sincerity,
> which is another name for what may be indifferently called human
> force or, better still, genius. Inarticulate as the sea cliffs were the
> Pollexfen heart and brain, lying buried under mountains of silence.
> They were released from bondage by contact with the joyous
> amiability of my family, and of my bringing up, and so all my four
> children are articulate, and yet with the Pollexfen force. (92)

The child who most impinged upon the book was Willie.
Early Memories implies that as son of a Yeats and a Pol-

lexfen, and favorite pupil of both the aging artist and the arcane astrologer, he was to achieve that personality "alive and glowing like a star" which the book idealizes. Playing that filial role was difficult, and the relation between father and son could be stormy as well as sympathetic. Yet *Early Memories* suggests how much the two Yeatses came to share—not only myriad ideas (like the authenticity of the folk imagination) or perceptions (like seeing Irish households as Renaissance courts) but also a common allegiance to the principle of personality in their special sense of the word. Most important of all, they believed in antinomies as both philosophic and formal pattern, and in his mature art William developed in true Pollexfen depth and Yeatsian articulation the central device which orders the life story of his father.

1. (Churchtown, Dundrum: Cuala Press, 1923). All quotations from *Early Memories* refer to this edition and are identified by the page number inside parentheses.

2. He also had a brother named William Butler Yeats, who emigrated to Brazil and became a rich stockbroker. Scholarly interest in John Butler Yeats started slowly but has increased recently. For general accounts *see* Joseph Hone, "Memoir of John Butler Yeats," in *J. B. Yeats: Letters to his Son W. B. Yeats and Others 1869–1922* (London: Faber and Faber Limited, 1944), pp. 23–46; A. Norman Jeffares, "John Butler Yeats, Anglo-Irishman," in *The Circus Animals: Essays on W. B. Yeats* (Stanford: Stanford University Press, 1960), pp. 117–146; and Douglas N. Archibald's brief *John Butler Yeats* (Lewisburg: Bucknell University Press, 1974) and the fine essay "Father and Son: John Butler and William Butler Yeats," *Massachusetts Review* 15 (1974), 481–501. William M. Murphy's massive *Prodigal Father: The Life of John Butler Yeats (1839–1922)* (Ithaca and London: Cornell University Press, 1978), which appeared while the present essay was in press, supersedes his earlier and valuable series of articles on John Butler Yeats and other ancestors of the poet: "Father and Son: the Early Education of William Butler Yeats," *Review of English Literature* 8 (1967): 75–96; " 'In Memory of Alfred Pollexfen': W. B. Yeats and the Theme of Family," *Irish University Review* 1 (1970) 30–47; "The Ancestry of William Butler Yeats," *Yeats Studies* 1 (1970, 1–19. Murphy has also written *The Yeats Family and the Pollexfens of Sligo* (Dublin: The Dolmen Press, 1971). I am additionally indebted to him for his careful scrutiny of the present essay. For an account of Yeats as portrait painter see James White, *John Butler Yeats and the Irish Renaissance* (Dublin: The Dolmen Press, 1972). Information on John Butler Yeats may be gleaned readily from accounts by and about celebrities he affected; the most important is the account by his son W. B. in *Reveries over Childhood and Youth.*

3. William M. Murphy's *Prodigal Father* establishes that Yeats arrived in New York between Christmas and New Year's Eve, 1907, rather than in 1908.

4. *Early Memories* should not be confused with the unpublished autobiographical material described by Murphy in "Father and Son," p. 78.

5. Perhaps because of that, the autobiography has served regularly as a source of information but has received little attention as a work of art in its own right. For example Hone, who draws on it for his "Memoir," says that "There are delightful things in this little book, but it is repetitive and unconstructed" (p. 40). I mean instead to discuss *Early Memories* as a literary work and to call particular attention to its structure.

6. Cf. *J. B. Yeats: Letters to his Son W. B. Yeats and Others 1869–1922*, p. 128: "My dear Willie—I think my last letter will show that we are quite of the same mind and that your splendid sentence 'character is the ash of personality' has my full assent."

7. The paradigmatic emphasis also helps explain the occasional discrepancy between Yeats's presentations in *Early Memories* and his statements elsewhere.

8. "F. B.," as Yeats calls him in the autobiography, is Fred Beatty, a distant cousin related to him through the Armstrongs. I am grateful to William Murphy for this identification.

9. For W. B. Yeats's account of the pond painting *see Autobiographies* (London: Macmillan, 1966), p. 28, and of the self-portrait *see* his preface to *Early Memories*.

PART THREE

Autobiography and Autobiographicality

AVROM FLEISHMAN

Personal Myth:
Three Victorian Autobiographers

"Although nobody," writes Malraux in his *Anti-Memoirs*,
"now believes that the object of the self-portrait, or even the
portrait, from the effigies of the Egyptian sculptors to the
Cubists, was simply to imitate nature, people still believe it
of literary portraiture."[1] As in the study of historical fiction,
much of the criticism of autobiography and autobiographical
fiction revolves around questions of fact: what is the correspondence of the text to a past state of affairs presumably
known to be the case on other evidence? An outstanding
book by Roy Pascal, *Design and Truth in Autobiography*,
takes a step beyond the correspondence discussion by
raising the question of coherence: the autobiographer gives
an order to the facts of his history, an order of his own
devising and therefore a reflection of the truth about himself more informative than the facts which he manipulates.
Although Pascal gives short shrift to the hermeneutic theories of Dilthey, he has shifted the discussion from the realm
of fact to that of *meaning*. What is the meaning of an
autobiography—in the sense that we ask for the meaning of
any other work of art?

Meaning is directional: it is intention, sense, a movement
towards implication. The meaning of a work of art is its
total form, a sequence of connections completed and
determinate. (I moot here the question of open form.) The
meaning of a life is similarly the sequence of connections
moving toward and completed by its end—closing it into
just that personal life. As Yeats put it, " 'Man can embody

215

truth but he cannot know it.' I must embody it in the completion of my life."[2]

Autobiography must tell the story of the life as it moves
toward its end, but this story is different from other stories
in being inherently incomplete. That is to say, quite simply,
the autobiographer writes the story of his life while he is yet
living, and therefore cannot tell the whole story. In the
logical sense, autobiography (the story of one's whole life) is
impossible, but autobiographers, not content with such
logic, write their life-stories anyway. They have recourse to
a subtle evasion of their embarrassment by adopting an
imaginative attitude toward their lives: they tell their story
as if it were already over—and many consciously write from
the standpoint of their death. Not only do they move in
two times, narrative past and dramatic present, and in
two linguistic forms, historical and discursive, but every
autobiographer tells his life as the tale of another being—
someone he creates as a fictive object in the creation of
his story. The double personality of the autobiographer is
not an accident of perception, in which the author, now
changed from his past self, sees himself as someone other
than he is (or was). In the necessary act of finishing his
story and tracing its subject to the end, the autobiographer
creates something that has not existed before. To this
entity, generated in the act of writing autobiography, I shall
give the name *self*, and thereby arrive at a definition of
autobiography: it is a literary form for the creation of selfhood.

There are a number of literary resources for developing
coherent accounts of the self, even in works written over
many years and with changing motives. One resource is to
choose a metaphor of the self and develop it in a narrative
or other sequence, which may be called a conversion of
metaphor into myth. As Frye has said: "The assumed
metaphors in their turn become the units of the myth or
constructive principle of the argument. While we read, we
are aware of a sequence of metaphorical identifications;
when we have finished, we are aware of an organizing

structural pattern or conceptualized myth."[3] This common phenomenon of metaphoric narration becoming myth has a special working in the case of autobiography, where what is narrated is a series of metaphors of the self (or of the course of its life). The completed sequence is a *personal myth*—or what Edwin Muir calls in his autobiography his "fable": "I should like to write that fable, but I cannot even live it. . . . One or two stages in it I can recognize: . . . they are not historical events; they are stages in the fable."[4]

A number of characteristic autobiographical works of the last century repeatedly revert to a particular scene of past events, or bring forward repeatedly a particular metaphor in the course of exposition. I propose to set out some of these recurrent images, but I wish to establish more than the esthetic unity or rhetorical effectiveness of these works. These reiterated images are not only formal but substantive; they not only bring unity to the work but also constitute the author's subject-matter, which in the case of autobiography is himself. In writing his autobiography, the author is *writing himself*, transposing himself into verbal form, and the discovery of appropriate terms in which to portray himself goes hand in hand with a discovery of his own nature. Since it is a moot question whether this nature is made or found—surely the two processes are reciprocal— I have used the term "self-creation" to designate the complex process by which recognizable individuals are formed out of metaphoric materials—in the case of autobiography, out of the language in which the remembered events of a life are set down.

What is the end-product of the formative process? It may be an arrangement of the writings, the deeds, the character-traits, the memory-sensations of a man's life. But there is always at least one end-product of the lives described in autobiographies: the autobiography itself. The autobiography is thus not only a discovery-mechanism by which the meaning of a life is found, but it is also the visible demonstration of that life—i.e., it is the symbolic equivalent or *icon* of self-creation.

* * *

The image that arises from John Stuart Mill's *Auto-biography* (1873) is that of a thoroughly transparent being, who is nonetheless opaque to himself. There is no room in Mill's intellectual system for inexpressible mysteries or obscure revelations, and there is little wavering in his objective estimation of himself. Bitterness appears and passion rises sometimes to a lyrical pitch, but Mill does not inquire more deeply into himself than he can know. It is all too easy for psychoanalysts to probe a man who tells us that the turning point in his mental crisis was the relief of tears when reading about a boy who vowed to take the place of his dead father for his family—and who tells us this without giving any sign of recognizing the Oedipal feelings about his own father which the scene brings to the surface. Mill's disturbed feelings may come into play but they hardly come to consciousness, and it is not surprising to find that this work—made famous by its *exposé* of an educational system which forced a boy to perform intellectual wonders at the expense of normal physical and social development—was written partly as a defense, though a critical one, of that very system.

Mill's rationalism has some room for myth, however, and the one he grasps to give shape to his own career is a synecdoche of the myth prevailing in his society. The myth holds that life *is* progress, in accordance with the liberal faith in human progress through educational enlightenment and utilitarian reform. He announces this part-whole relation of self and social progress in his statement of aims for the autobiography: "It has also seemed to me that in an age of transition in opinions, there may be somewhat both of interest and of benefit in noting the successive phases of any mind which was always pressing forward, equally ready to learn and to unlearn either from its own thoughts or from those of others."[5] There are few men who can claim so much for their own development and not meet with derision, but Mill is one of those men who so impress us with their honesty that we are willing to suspend our scepticism. When, however, we reach the final chapter, the

sense of progress rings hollow and we can catch the equivo-
cation in the prose: "From this time [1840, after meeting
his future wife], what is worth relating of my life will come
into a very small compass; for I have no further mental
changes to tell of, but only, as I hope, a continued mental
progress" (155). There follows a condensed chronicle of his
major publications, political enthusiasms (like women's liberation), and parliamentary career. It is progress, indeed,
which Mill describes during this period but it is also the
dullest part of the *Autobiography* and the part that Mill
seems to be setting down as a public service rather than as
self-expression. Even his other declared motive for writing—
to pay homage to others, especially his father and his wife—
is given short shrift during this stocktaking of achievements.
The developing mind of Mill may be found in this chronicle
of progress, but it is not the whole of Mill.

The famous nervous breakdown which forms the dramatic
center of the *Autobiography* is precisely a crisis in the
myth of progress, as well as in the young Mill's development. It is in terms of his attitudes toward social progress
that Mill describes the event:

> From the winter of 1821, when I first read Bentham, . . . I had
> what might truly be called an object in life; to be a reformer of
> the world. My conception of my own happiness was entirely identi-
> fied with this object. . . . I was accustomed to felicitate myself on
> the certainty of a happy life which I enjoyed, through placing my
> happiness in something durable and distant, in which some progress
> might be always making, while it could never be exhausted by
> complete attainment. . . .
> [It] occurred to me to put the question directly to myself: "Sup-
> pose that all your objects in life were realized; that all the changes
> in institutions and opinions which you are looking forward to, could
> be completely effected at this very instant: would this be a great
> joy and happiness to you?" And an irrepressible self-consciousness
> distinctly answered, "No!" At this my heart sank within me: the
> whole foundation on which my life was constructed fell down. All
> my happiness was to have been found in the continual pursuit of
> this end. The end had ceased to charm, and how could there ever
> again be any interest in the means? I seemed to have nothing left
> to live for. (93–94)

Lest there be any temptation to see these words as a
political recantation, it should be clear that Mill is not

saying that he renounced the goals of progress, nor even that he could not see others living happily in a perfected world. He conceives of happiness as movement (or as being *in* a movement) and progress is for him distinctly a felt state of change; any arrest of this motion, even by completion of the task, would be to arrest the excitement of transition which is, for him, the ambience of happiness. In a truly utilitarian way, Mill had strategically mapped out for himself a life of continual happiness by setting up a goal beyond his grasp; the sudden threat of realizing it and having "nothing left to live for" seemed to him not fulfillment but death.

What may be gained from such a negative discovery is a positive image of the self as process. The individual does not possess a given nature but is always moving beyond himself; the self is a progressive (but, presumably, possibly regressive) *activity,* always in course of formation. Such a view of the self as composed of interactions with others— as a continual shifting of roles or masks in response to life's situations—was later to be developed by the sociologist G. H. Mead; in Mead's theory of social behavior, which has gained wide favor in our time, the self is not what it is but what it does. Mill, however, did not generalize from his own experience to state a process-view of the self, perhaps because he recognized its dangerous implication (which Sartre was to face) that if the individual is always in the making, he is never fully formed—that the self is *nothing in itself.*

The danger of finding oneself nothing is particularly acute in a man formed by a powerful and clearly defined personality like James Mill. The disparity between the father's massive presence and the son's state, verging on nonexistence, is even more apparent in the early draft of the *Autobiography* than in its published form: "I was, as my father continually told me, like a person who had not the organs of sense: my eyes & ears seemed of no use to me, so little did I see or hear what was before me, & so little, even of what I did see or hear, did I observe & remember. My father was the extreme opposite in all these particulars: his senses & his mental faculties were always on the alert;

he carried decision & energy of character in his whole manner & into every action of life"[6] John Stuart bravely confesses that his personal deficiencies were his own fault
entirely, completely missing James' role in beating him
down. But much unconscious resentment shows up in his
numerous accounts of the father's failure to develop the
son's control of concrete objects and practical behavior.

The major progress in Mill's life may be described as a
shift from one authority-figure to another, from a demanding and angry father-god to a goddess of loving-kindness
and emotional enrichment. An ideal figure of life and fruitfulness replaces a patriarchal authority of law and order.
For if James Mill began as an insistent force for John
Stuart's mental progress, he emerges as a conservative
stumbling-block in the latter's efforts to make Benthamism
more humane and subtle in its progressive programme. The
transition in the *Autobiography* from James Mill's to Harriet Taylor's predominance represents the turning-point in
John Stuart Mill's formation as a self.

The shift also marks a change of stylistic mode in the
Autobiography, and simultaneously a change in Mill's
representation of himself. All these differences come down
to an emergence of a more-or-less conscious mythology:

> . . . she became to me a living type of the most admirable kind of
> human being. I had always wished for a friend whom I could admire
> wholly, without reservation & restriction, & I had now found one.
> To render this possible, it was necessary that the object of my admira-
> tion should be of a type very different from my own; should be a
> character preeminently of feeling, combined however as I had not
> in any other instance known it to be, with a vigorous & bold specu-
> lative intellect. Hers was not only all this but the perfection of a
> poet & artistic nature. . . . in any true classification of human
> beings such as I are only fit to be the subjects & ministers of such as
> her; & . . . the best thing I, in particular, could do for the world,
> would be to serve as a sort of prose interpreter of her poetry. . . .

Such frank personification of his highest humanistic ideals
has been almost universally derided, and Mill was conscious enough of the predictable reaction to suppress such
passages as the above and yet deliver almost equally high
encomiums. For Mill really *believed in* Harriet, and when

we put the case so we raise the question, what sort of belief is that? It is not, clearly, belief of the same kind as Mill obtains from his inductive-deductive method or any other technique in his *System of Logic*. Nor would it be fair to say that he was simply operating according to blind faith in his personal life, while eschewing all irrational forms of intellectual conviction. When he uses the term "living type" we can find in the phrase the natural supernaturalism of Wordsworth's "types and symbols of eternity," combined with a notion borrowed from the "religion of humanity" that a figure like Christ is a symbol representing the highest ideals of mankind. Harriet is such a symbol, not merely of Mill's own "best self," but of human perfectibility. Her perfection, beyond being a perfect type, is less important to Mill—as it should be to us—than her power as an inspirational mythos.

Harriet can symbolize Mill's higher self or ego-ideal because she is herself a process. She is not a moral absolute like the father, but a child like J. S. Mill, and in describing her life Mill has scope to enlarge upon his new-found sense of personal progress. Harriet becomes the deity not of achieved selfhood but of the power of the human spirit to develop its potentialities. She is the model of perfectibility, if not of perfection: "It is not to be supposed that she was, or that any one, at the age at which I first saw her, could be, all that she afterwards became. Least of all could this be true of her, with whom self-improvement, progress in the highest and in all senses, was a law of her nature. . . . In general spiritual characteristics, as well as in temperament and organisation, I have often compared her, as she was at this time, to Shelley: but in thought and intellect, Shelley, so far as his powers were developed in his short life, was but a child compared with what she ultimately became" (129–31). These claims are excessive, of course, but are saved from the ludicrous by Mill's awe at the capacity of man (and woman) to change and grow.[8] We need not wonder, then, that Mill concludes, "Her memory is to me a religion, and her approbation the standard by which, summing up as it does all worthiness, I endeavour to regulate my life" (170).

The *Autobiography* becomes an embodiment of Mill's self not by forming a unity corresponding to the sum of his parts, nor by generating symbols of the completed form of his identity, but in being consistently animated by the principle of change, transition, anticipation—by the informing principle, that is, of Mill's active life and philosophical thought. That the cost of maintaining this sense of self was payable in social insecurity, emotional instability, and physical awkwardness was only to be expected. Mill acknowledged this price—the price of trial-and-error in liberal individualism—in his ethical and social philosophy, and seems gradually to have accepted it for his own life. The political and cultural individuality celebrated in his classic essay "On Liberty" is accompanied by a tolerance of errors and inefficiencies in the individual's actions. On the one hand, Mill's systematic mind continued to map out and control larger and larger areas of difficulty in politics, economics, and logic, while on the other he was aware that the special mark of his thought was that it was "no system: only a conviction that the true system was something much more complex and many-sided than I had previously had any idea of" (113). This refusal of the finished and systematic in favor of the variable and unique came about not only through the shake-up of Mill's mental crisis and recovery through poetry and love but also with the help of his writing the *Autobiography* itself. In this sense his book is not only the visible image of his created self but the process through which he came to conceive and accept himself as a process.

* * *

Although the differences between autobiography and autobiographical fiction are sufficient to make the latter a special formal problem, I include Samuel Butler's *The Way of All Flesh* here as another outstanding example of a Victorian writer creating an image of himself in a more-or-less accurate account of his experience. The turns of plot in the novel depart far from the course of Butler's life, to be sure, but the portrayal of the central characters is close

to being an onslaught against actual persons, particularly
the Butler family. And the impulse to write the book clearly
derived from a need to establish the author's own identity,
for when he was at peace with his family he let it lie, but
took it up again after scenes of intense wrangling. *The
Way of All Flesh* may be seen not only as Butler's means of
mercilessly satirizing his family's religious hypocrisy and
crimes against himself as child, but also as his way of
objectifying the being that he struggled to make of himself against such odds.

Butler also had in mind an image of humanity and a
theory of the human species, something which is implied
by his generalizing title. As a number of studies have
shown, his series of books on the biological and social
implications of evolution was based on the Lamarckian
hypothesis of the heritability of acquired characteristics.
Though the theory had already been disavowed in biological science, it is none the weaker for that in Butler's
works, where it takes on a strong ethical and almost
theological force. Briefly, his theory ascribes much—and
indeed the most effective part—of our behavior to the unconscious and innate in mind and body, and it ascribes the
transmission of experience from generation to generation
not to a racial memory or other carrier of the data but to
the persistence of the organism itself. According to Butler,
the earlier generation does not experience, learn, and
modify its genetic material, transmitting this to the new
generation, after which it dies. Rather he believes that there
is a persistence of the being which learns from experience
and modifies herself, for it establishes itself in a new body,
thus dying in one form but continuing to live in the new.
Each of us is "*actually* the primordial cell which never
died nor dies, but has differentiated itself into the life of
the world, all living beings whatever being one with it, and
members one of another" (*Life and Habit*).[9]

It may readily be seen from this organic view of the
human species in what sense the hero's career is the way
of all flesh, since not only fathers and sons but all men
are literally one person—"one enormous individual ever in

process of change and self-fulfillment."[10] It may, however, take some effort to receive the full force of Butler's view that not merely the germ-plasm but the entire individual is continuous from generation to generation, so that the embryo is identical to the child, to the mature man, and to the embryo which he generates. This being is constantly changing, of course, as experience and volition modify it, but it is reproduced as a whole in the next generation. What we have here is not so much an intelligible genetic theory as a revived doctrine of the transmigration of the soul. When Butler comes to apply his thesis to his own case, he is sketching a rationale for his own identity and, by extension, for the immortality of the human soul and body.

The mystifications of this biological speculation go far to account for the large measure of mystery that is generated by *The Way of All Flesh*. Far from rendering a coolly rational satire even more perspicuous by scientific principles, as some commentators have tried to make them do, Butler's ideas help to explain the reader's almost inevitable impression that something strange indeed is being said—or rather, imaged—in the novel. The first hint of a mystery occurs in the portrait of the hero's great-grandfather, Old John Pontifex, who is celebrated as an eighteenth-century, pre-bourgeois craftsman of the yeoman tradition. The account of his death endows him with greater afflatus, however:

> The old man had a theory about sunsets and had had two steps built up against a wall in the kitchen garden on which he used to stand and watch the sun go down whenever it was clear. [The narrator's] father came on him in the afternoon, just as the sun was setting, and saw him with his arms resting on the top of the wall looking towards the sun over a field through which there was a path on which my father was. My father heard him say, 'Good bye sun, good bye sun' as the sun sank, and saw by his tone and manner that he was feeling very feeble. Before the next sunset he was gone.[11]

The scene remains merely touching until a point about midway in the novel when Ernest Pontifex, the hero, is wea-

rily leaving his public school, after a full series of mental
and moral castigations:

> There was a grey mist across the sun, so that the eye could bear its
> light, and Ernest . . . was looking right into the middle of the sun
> himself, as into the face of one he whom knew and was fond of. . . . Still
> looking into the eye of the sun and smiling dreamily, he thought how he
> had helped to burn his father in effigy, and his look grew merrier till at last
> he broke out into a laugh—exactly at this moment the light veil of cloud
> parted from the sun, and he was brought back to *terra firma* by the
> breaking forth of the sunshine. On this he became aware that he was being
> watched attentively by a fellow traveller opposite to him, an elderly
> gentleman with a large head and iron-grey hair.
> 'My young friend,' said he good-naturedly, 'you really must not
> carry on conversations with people in the sun, while you are in a pub-
> lic railway carriage.'
>   . . . The pair did not speak during the rest of the time they were
> in the carriage, but they eyed each other from time to time so that
> the face of each was impressed on the recollection of the other. (170–
> 71)

The effect of this passage is quite outside the major
movement of the plot and the explicit thrust of the satire.
It is only when Ernest is hauled up before a magistrate for
indecent advances to a fellow lodger that this note of the
otherworldly and freely imaginative is again sounded. For
the magistrate turns out to be the gentleman of the railway
carriage; he deals with Ernest in character—i.e., as a British
judge might be expected to act—by sentencing him to six
months' hard labor, but his reason for punishing him is the
remarkable one that Ernest doesn't have sense enough to
"distinguish between a respectable girl and a prostitute"
(238), i.e., that he is criminally naive. What is even more
provoking about this coincidence is that it leads in the next
chapter to a summary reversal of attitude to the hero by the
narrator: The Pontifexes' "case was hopeless; it would
be no use their even entering into their mothers' wombs
and being born again. They must not only be born again
but they must be born again each one of them of a new
father and of a new mother and of a different line of ancestry for many generations before their minds could become supple enough to learn anew . . . If a man is to en-

ter into the kingdom of heaven he must do so not only as a
little child but as a little embryo, or rather as a little zoösperm—and not only this but as one that has come of zoö-
sperms who have entered into the kingdom of heaven before him for many generations" (240–41). This gets as
close to biological fatalism as we can go, even in an age of
social Darwinism, for it cuts the ground from under every effort of the individual to repair the damage done
him by his parental endowment. But there is another side
to this remorseless logic.

The subtler implication of the argument is that Ernest
can look far back in his ancestry and find progenitors who
have *not* travelled down the road of the Pontifexes, that
there is an essential self or zoösperm at the outset of the
individual's career which is somehow—Butler does not tell us
how—recoverable. It is my contention that though Butler
does not give us an arguable theory of the recovery, he
shows us this essential self in the images of the novel.
Old John Pontifex is close to this originative seed and
bears the marks of it; he relates himself to it in his attention to—or worship of—the sun. The association of this
seminal source with the sun is nothing other than a late
appearance of an archetypal myth which many cultures
have fostered. It carries the notion that we are children of
the sun, that the sun is our father in heaven, and that
looking into the sun we see a person—"the face of one he
knew and was fond of," as Ernest discovers on the train.
Recovery of this progenitor is a recovery of oneself: it
brings us to laughter and a comic insight into our condition; it helps us to recognize the other men around us who
are true kin; and it may even bring on a rebuke for carrying on "conversations with people in the sun."

This is perhaps the most subversive doctrine in Butler's
outrageous repertoire: certain men are not simply better
but holier than others (quite different ones than British
Christian culture would lead one to expect); they are closer
to the sources of being and thereby more pure-bred incarnations of the human archetype. Butler's way of seizing
such truths has as little to do with Darwin and science as

it has to do with the Kingdom of Heaven and faith. The imagination behind such a world view would seem to be privy to a large fund of ancient myth and pagan learning, and Butler's own tastes ran to the classics (as can be seen in his remarkable study, *The Authoress of The Odyssey*). The hidden suggestion of the text is that Butler is in on the secret because he is a child of the sun himself. And that is ultimately what is given in this autobiographical fable: it is a projected image of Butler himself as a sublime man of wisdom.

To conclude that Butler's achievement in *The Way of All Flesh* is not so much an accurate record nor a fictive exposition of his life as it is a manifestation of himself as a man of wisdom is not to ascribe to him more than usual autobiographical egoism. He artfully erects not only a pathetically naive hero but a coldly sceptical narrator to control the reader's sympathies and avoid introducing himself directly into the tale. But the voices that echo in the novel are not only those of Butler's fledgling and mature selves but also that of his originating self or source. In an often-quoted passage, Butler allows Ernest's "more real" and "true self" to address his "reasoning and reflecting self" as a "prig," and to insist on its obedience—"for I, Ernest, am the God who made you" (116). This godly being is the eternal seed or source which Butler identifies with the sun, and by allowing it to speak in his novel he brings to expression a part of himself which he seems to regard as his most impressive and mysterious. It is almost an anticlimax when Butler makes the hero of his last fictional work, *Erewhon Revisited*, a revised version of his early, naive persona. The hero is taken in this never-never land to be a divine savior who appeared briefly and then ascended to his father in heaven—and Butler names this ironic final image of himself "the Sunchild."

*   *   *

George Gissing's *The Private Papers of Henry Ryecroft* is probably the least known of the autobiographical works we are considering. Although it is not fictional in the sense of having a consecutive narrative, it is a freely imaginative rendition of the author's state of mind in his declining years. On the one hand there is evidence that the work grew out of Gissing's own commonplace book, and it therefore has the status of a retrospective reflection; on the other side is Gissing's own testimony that "The thing is much more an aspiration than a memory."[12] In either case, the book is an impressive creation of a structure for Gissing's self, developing an elaborate metaphor to give an intelligible order to the string of meditational passages of which it is composed. Gissing's explanation in his preface that the need for an "arrangement" led him to divide his musings into "four chapters, named after the seasons"[13] makes them seem a matter of mere convenience, but it can be shown that the choice answers to the rhythms of Gissing's imagination. What the autobiographer here accomplishes is not so much to discover his own nature as allow it to live through its natural phases.

Jackson I. Cope has observed, in one of the few available studies commensurate with Gissing's learned mind,[14] a number of traditional *topoi* which should prepare us to recognize in the work a late appearance of the classical ideal of retirement. Gissing's persona inherits an annuity and, like the author, retires to a Devon cottage after a life of New Grub Street drudgery. The image of this universally desired condition is, of course, a widely varied and historically changing one, but it achieves a remarkable coherence when linked to a natural setting for the retirement. Pastoral, utopian, and horticultural traditions are deeply involved in the so-called "retirement myth," and all enter into Gissing's account. Another element frequently associated with the complex of *topoi* mentioned here is the seasonal cycle. The retired man summing up his life, the utopian gardener setting out his ideal realm, the pastoralist imagining himself back to the childhood of the race, all are attentive to the seasons. Pope claimed that his use of the seasonal tetrad was an innovation in the tradition of the pastoral, but modern scholarship has adduced an enormous body of learning and poetic imagery of the seasons—from which, e.g., Spenser had already drawn for his

(albeit monthly) calendar. Not all the traditional applica-
tions of the tetrad are made much of by Gissing, but one of
its chief parallels—to the four ages of man or stages of an individual life—is at the forefront of his work.

In setting out the course of Ryecroft's year, Gissing reveals that the themes and conventions of the *Ryecroft
Papers* are related to a traditional philosophic attitude
which upholds the norms of nature above mechanism, affirms common sense and moderation as pillars of a natural ethic, and proclaims a stoical acceptance of the course
of life with all its imperfections. The ideas are generally
traceable to the Stoic philosophers, and the *Ryecroft Pa-
papers* may have taken the form of a collection of meditative
passages in imitation of the writings of that school. Gissing
was a trained classicist and a lifelong devotee of late Roman culture particularly, to which several of his works, including his last novel, are devoted. At the heart of this literary taste are a number of attitudes to life which Gissing
shared with his Latin exemplars; his is the classical-conser-
vative mentality which includes a resigned pessimism, an
anti-democratic politics, an assertion of national and other
traditional virtues, and a scepticism of the so-called progressive trends in one's society—which does not preclude
a hearty contempt for many features of the status quo. All
these attitudes show up in the *Ryecroft Papers*, and supply
the book's range of opinions on a wide variety of subjects
—from deity to cooking, approximately.

The book opens in "Spring" (the title of the first section), and the first notes are those of the renewal of the old
man by fresh breezes and the revival of his memory of
youth: "Spring has restored to me something of the long-
forgotten vigour of youth; I walk without weariness; I sing
to myself like a boy, and the song is one I knew in boyhood" (27). The recovery of the force and the image of
youth is extended by memories of occasions in the course
of his later life when the impulse to return to innocence
and nature was expressed in flights to the countryside; "At
the end of March I escaped from my dim lodgings, and
before I had time to reflect on the details of my under-

taking, I found myself sitting in sunshine at a spot very near to where I now dwell. . . . That was one of the moments of my life when I have tasted exquisite joy. . . . Then first did I know myself for a sun-worshipper" (35). He is said to step into a "new life," but it is established that this is a fulfillment of his own youthful powers as they have "been developing unknown to me" (35). Yet the old man's synthetic reconstruction of his youthful sensibilities from several stages of life carries with it an awareness of youth's fated place in the cycle of life and death. Even the surge of vitality has its *memento mori*: "I enjoy with something of sadness remembering that this melodious silence is but the prelude of that deeper stillness which waits to enfold us all" (62); and again: "Walking in a favourite lane to-day, I found it covered with shed blossoms of the hawthorn. Creamy white, fragrant even in ruin, lay scattered the glory of the May. It told me that spring is over" (63).

The qualities of "Summer" are put forward in terms almost too stark for interpretation: "In this hot weather I like to walk at times amid the full glow of the sun . . . . there is a magnificence in the triumph of high summer which exalts one's mind" (74). Height, triumph, exaltation—these are the physical expressions of the fullness and maturity of the growing self. But even this moment of fulfillment is rendered equivocal, not only by an implicit knowledge of the whole cycle of life and death but also by the peculiarities of English weather: "July this year is clouded and windy, very cheerless even here in Devon. . . . Can I not have patience? Do I not know that some morning the east will open like a bursting bud into warmth and splendour. . . ?" (85) Instead of worrying about the end of summer, the Englishman waits for it fully to arrive; his time of enjoyment is not only transient but insufficiently achieved.

More certain than this prophecy, "Autumn" comes on. Its first appearance is not a physical but a metaphorically moral one: "Boy and man, I blundered into every ditch and bog which lay within sight of my way. Never did silly mortal reap such harvest of experience" (113). If the harvest is

bitter, the autumn develops its own special beauty: "Never,
I could fancy, did autumn clothe in such magnificence the
elms and beeches; never, I should think, did the leafage
on my walls blaze in such royal crimson" (133). The influence of the declining year on the declining man is to lead
him toward an acceptance of his failings and a grim satisfaction in his life, even though it is diminishing: "As I
walked to-day in the golden sunlight—this warm, still day on
the far verge of autumn—there suddenly came to me a
thought which checked my step and for the moment half
bewildered me. I said to myself: My life is over" (140-41).
In true stoic fashion, Ryecroft convinces himself that he
can be grateful that he has "suffered no intolerable wrong,"
and his dominant wish is to be attuned to the rhythm of
the seasons and thereby to the rhythm of his life: "To-
night the wind is loud, and rain dashes against my case-
ment; to-morrow I shall awake to a sky of winter" (144).

The effect of "Winter" is to stimulate the memory and
create a summing-up of the dark side of Ryecroft-Giss-
ing's life—one which counterbalances the gathering of
forces that had occurred in Spring: "In the middle years
of my life—those years that were the worst of all—I used to
dread the sound of a winter storm which woke me in the
night. . . . I lay thinking of the savage struggle of man
with man, and often saw before me no better fate than to
be trampled down into the mud of life. . . . But nowadays
I can lie and listen to a night-storm with no intolerable
thoughts; at worst, I fall into a compassionate sadness as
I remember those I loved and whom I shall see no more"
(160-61). The gathering of darker thoughts and dying impulses in a winter polarity is not, however, allowed to act
as a neat completion of the seasonal tetrad. The cycle begins anew with the quite natural corollary of the winter
mood: the anticipation of spring. This hope is not permitted to become sanguine in the aging man, and Gissing
deftly balances the hope of life and the fact of death: "All
through the morning the air was held in an ominous stillness. . . . I saw nothing but the broad, grey sky, a fea-
tureless expanse, cold melancholy. . . . A few minutes

more, and all was hidden with a descending veil of silent snow. It was a disappointment. Yesterday I half believed that the winter drew to its end; . . . I began to long for the days of light and warmth. My fancy wandered, leading me far and wide in a dream of summer England" (177). The dream of renewal and the chill touch of snow mingle in a complex winter stance.

At the close, Gissing expresses his balance of attitudes toward the cycle of life: "So, once more, the year has come full circle. . . . Now my life is rounded; it began with the natural irreflective happiness of childhood, it will close in the reasoned tranquillity of the mature mind" (182-83). But this sense of formal completion is accompanied by another trope that has all along been near to hand but not explicit in the *Ryecroft Papers:* the notion of one's life as a book, and the related notion of writing as the self-realization of a life: "How many a time after long labour on some piece of writing, brought at length to its conclusion, have I laid down the pen with a sigh of thankfulness; the work was full of faults, but I had wrought sincerely, had done what time and circumstance and my own nature permitted. Even so may it be with me in my last hour. May I look back on life as a long task duly completed—a piece of biography, faulty enough, but good as I could make it" (183). So Gissing completes his life itself—and he does so by the metaphor of living as the writing of a work of literature. How appropriate that he should specify in his metaphor of life not a book of any kind, but precisely a work of biography!

1. *Anti-Memoirs,* trans, Terence Kilmartin (New York: Holt, Rinehart and Winston, 1968; French, 1967), p. 5.

2. *The Letters of William Butler Yeats,* ed. Allan Wade (New York: Macmillan, 1955), p. 922.

3. *Anatomy of Criticism: Four Essays* (New York: Atheneum, 1968 [1957], p. 353.

4. *An Autobiography* (New York: Seabury Press, 1968 [1954]), p. 49.

5. *Autobiography of John Stuart Mill: Published from the Original Manuscript in the Columbia University Library,* preface by J. J. Coss (New York: Columbia University Press 1960 [1924]), p. 1; citations are hereafter made parenthetically.

6. *The Early Draft of John Stuart Mill's Autobiography*, ed. Jack Stillinger (Urbana: University of Illinois Press, 1961), p. 179; I have omitted editorial notations in the text. Compare the language used to describe a father "educated in the creed of Scotch presbyterianism": "he wound up by saying, that whatever I knew more than others, could not be ascribed to any merit in me, but to the very unusual advantage which had fallen to my lot, of having a father who was able to teach me . . . ; that it was no matter of praise to me, if I knew more than those who had not had a similar advantage, but the deepest disgrace to me if I did not" (*Autobiography*, p. 24). The language suggests the Mills' origins in the theology of merit and grace: "For by grace are ye saved . . . : Not of works, lest any man should boast" (Eph. 2:8–9).

7. *Early Draft*, pp. 198–99. In the curtailed version of this passage in the *Autobiography*, Mill speaks of himself as performing "the office in relation to her" of "an interpreter of original thinkers, and mediator between them and the public" (172)—but the language is still heavily laden with religious functions.

8. The debate on Harriet Taylor's nature and worth has occupied Mill studies disproportionately in recent years, yet shows little awareness that a distortion of vision (and of prose) may reveal significant truths about the distorting mind. One is anxious to vindicate neither Mill's knowledge of women nor Harriet's intelligence; one may know Mill from his reading of Harriet as myth, just as from his reading of the Romantic poets.

9. *The Shrewsbury Edition of the Works of Samuel Butler*, eds. H. F. Jones and A. T. Bartholomew (London: Jonathan Cape; New York: Dutton, 1923–25), IV, 70.

10. Claude T. Bissell, "A Study of *The Way of All Flesh*," in Herbert Davis *et al*, eds., *Nineteenth-Century Studies* (Ithaca, N.Y.: Cornell University Press, 1940), p. 285.

11. *Ernest Pontifex, or The Way of All Flesh*, ed. Daniel F. Howard (Boston: Houghton Mifflin, 1964 [1903]), p. 13; citations are hereafter made parenthetically.

12. From an unpublished letter (11 Feb. 1903), quoted in Jacob Korg, "The Main Source of The Ryecroft Papers," in Pierre Coustillas, ed., *Collected Articles on George Gissing* (New York and London: 1968), p. 173.

13. *The Private Papers of Henry Ryecroft* (New York: New American Library, 1961 [1903]), p. xxi; citations are hereafter made parenthetically.

14. "Definition as Structure in *The Ryecroft Papers*," in Coustillas, *op. cit.*, pp. 152–67.

LINDA H. PETERSON

Biblical Typology and the
Self-Portrait of the Poet
in Robert Browning

My title creates what to some will seem a most unlikely union. What has typology, an exegetical approach to the Old Testament, to do with nineteenth-century autobiography? And what has either typology or autobiography to do with Robert Browning's poetry—poetry which Browning repeatedly and emphatically insisted was "always dramatic in principle, and so many utterances of so many imaginary persons, not mine"?[1] Quite simply, I suggest that typology and typological habits of mind were an important influence on the structure of nineteenth-century autobiography and that this influence is evident in and helps illumine a series of Browning's autobiographical poems.

I. Biblical Typology and Autobiographical Structure

Since both the terms *autobiography* and *structure* are currently used in different, even contradictory ways and since the influence of typology on nineteenth-century literature has received little attention,[2] let me begin with definitions and explanations. In the strict sense of the term, Browning never wrote an autobiography. Late in life he composed the *Parleyings,* poems which include material relevant to his intellectual and artistic growth, but he did not write autobiography per se: a professedly truthful record of his life, composed as a single work and told from a consistent temporal point of view.[3] Nevertheless, some of his poems are autobiographical in that they describe his development

235

as an artist. In them Browning speaks as poet, discussing a particular aesthetic concern or recounting a crisis in his poetic career. In doing so, he draws upon traditional types to structure and thus interpret his experience.

In this essay, then, I limit my use of *structure* to autobiographical writing—specifically, to the shaping of the events of an autobiographer's life as a whole into a coherent pattern or to the relating of a limited number of events to a pattern. This pattern is not necessarily inherent in the events themselves, but is discovered in or imposed upon those events as the autobiographer looks back upon his life. The discovery of such a pattern is a primary task of the autobiographer: he must create order out of the chaotic events of his life. In his attempt to create order, of course, he must guard against falsifying the facts of his experience.[4] But if an autobiography is to be written at all, the autobiographer must discover or create an appropriate structure, and to do so, he may—and usually does—borrow structures from previous autobiography, from fiction, history, poetry, and other forms of discourse, altering them to suit his particular needs.

Many nineteenth-century autobiographers, I would suggest, derive their structures from biblical typology—either directly or indirectly, consciously or unconsciously, for a part of the work or for the whole. There are several reasons for this derivation. In the first place, typological exegesis encouraged men and women to view their lives as correlatives of Old Testament types. Strictly used, typology was an exegetical approach to the Bible which treated Old Testament persons, events, and things (*types*) as prefigurations of Christ or some aspect of his ministry (*antitypes*).[5] But in the eighteenth and nineteenth centuries these types were also applied to events in the history of the Church or to experiences in the life of the individual believer. For example, the great Victorian preacher Henry Melvill, minister of Camden Chapel, Camberwell, during Browning's youth and later Chaplain to Queen Victoria and Canon of St. Paul's, taught his parishoners that the history of Israel was "a figurative history, sketching, as in parable, much that befalls the Christian Church in general, and its members in particular"; it was, he added, a prophecy which would "find its accomplishment in the experiences of true disciples of Christ in every nation and age."[6] Similarly, John Wesley explained the temptations and wanderings of modern Christians as parallels to the wilderness state of the Israelites:

> After God had wrought a great deliverance for Israel, by bringing them out of the house of bondage, they did not immediately enter into the land which he had promised to their fathers; but "wandered out of the way in the wilderness," and were variously tempted and distressed. In like manner, after God has delivered them that fear him from the bondage of sin and Satan, . . . not many of them immediately enter into "the rest which remaineth for the people of God." The greater part of them wander . . . out of the good way into which he hath brought them. They come, as it were, into a "waste and howling desert," where they are variously tempted and tormented: and this, some . . . have termed, "A wilderness state."[7]

The classic example of this typological frame of mind is the popular eighteenth-century hymn "Guide me, O thou great Jehovah":

> Guide me, O thou great Jehovah,
> Pilgrim through this barren land;
> I am weak, but Thou art mighty;
> Hold me with Thy pow'rful hand:
> Bread of heaven, feed me till I want no more.
>
> Open, Lord, the crystal fountain,
> Whence the healing streams do flow;
> Let the fiery, cloudy pillar
> Lead me all my journey through.
> Strong Deliv'rer, be Thou still my Strength and Shield.
>
> When I tread the verge of Jordan,
> Bid my anxious fears subside:
> Death of death, and hell's Destruction,
> Land me safe on Canaan's side.
> Songs of praises, I will ever give to Thee.[8]

The history of the Israelites provides the structure for the personal history of the individual believer, and the significant events of the Exodus—the manna, the water from the rock, the pillars of cloud and fire, the crossing of Jordan, the entry into Canaan—become prefigurations of Christian experience. When men raised in Anglican churches or Dissenting chapels wrote formal autobiographies, then, it was natural to draw upon typological patterns.

There is another reason for the influence of typology upon English autobiography, secular as well as religious. The developmental autobiography,[9] the dominant mode of the nineteenth century, evolved from the spiritual autobiographies of the seventeenth and eighteenth, and these autobiographies had drawn explicitly upon typology for their structures.

Paul Delany has shown that at the beginning of the seventeenth century English autobiography had no prescribed form. Secular autobiographers imitated various fictional genres; religious autobiographers turned to the Bible for their models, especially to accounts of Old Testament leaders, the psalms of David, the Book of Job, and the Pauline conversion experience in Acts.[10] By the end of the seventeenth century, however, the form of spiritual autobiography had become fairly conventionalized, primarily through the influence of Bunyan's *Grace Abounding* and (among Quakers) Foxe's *Journals*. Following Bunyan, spiritual autobiographers built their narratives around a conversion experience. Generally, they began with an account of their sins and unrepentant ways, described a dramatic conversion, continued with a period of confusion or even backsliding, and ended on a note of spiritual felicity.[11] Where did Bunyan and his successors find this pattern?

It seems fairly obvious that their primary source was the Exodus account, traditionally a type of the Christian's experiences from this world to the next. The autobiographer's description of his unrepentant ways corresponds to the Egyptian bondage; the dramatic conversion, to the flight from Pharaoh and the crossing of the Red Sea; the period of confusion or backsliding, to the wilderness wandering; and the final peace, to the entry into Canaan.[12] In the preface to *Grace Abounding*, in fact, Bunyan draws upon the Exodus account to justify the writing of a personal narrative:

> Moses (Numb.33.1,2) writ of the Journeyings of the children of Israel, from Egypt to the Land of Canaan; and commanded also that they did remember their forty years travel in the wilderness. . . . Wherefore this have I endeavoured to do; and not onely so, but to publish it also; that, if God will, others may be put in remembrance of what he hath done for their Souls, by reading his work upon me.[13]

Implicit in this justification is a typological application of the Exodus. Bunyan views himself as a spiritual Israelite, and thus the overall structure of his autobiography takes on the pattern of a modern exodus.

The spiritual autobiographer also drew upon typology not only for the overall structure of his work but to illumine specific events within it. Bunyan uses types in this way in section 38 when he, yet an unrepentant sinner, meets some Christians in Bedford:

> And me thought they spake as if joy did make them speak: they spake with such pleasantness of Scripture language, and with such appearance of grace in all they said, that they were to me as if they had found a new world, as if they were people that dwelt alone, and were not to be reckoned among their Neighbours, Num. 23.9. At this I felt my own heart began to shake, as mistrusting my condition to be naught.[14]

Numbers 23:9 records the unwitting blessing of Balaam upon Israel, a blessing imposed upon him by God in place of an intended curse. Thus, by analogy, the unrepentant Bunyan found himself blessing Christians whom he might otherwise have scorned.

Now these two uses of typology in seventeenth-century autobiography influenced the form and content of nineteenth-century autobiography—both religious autobiography per se and the secularized "developmental" autobiography. In *Versions of the Self* John N. Morris has already demonstrated a general relationship between seventeenth-century spiritual autobiography and nineteenth-century developmental autobiography: "the experiences recorded in

nineteenth-century autobiography are . . . secular counterparts of the religious melancholy and conversions set
down in the autobiographies of earlier heroes of religion.
. . . '[S]elf' is the modern word for 'soul.' "[15] I am simply
suggesting two other aspects of that relationship: first,
that the habit of viewing one's life as a spiritual exodus
influenced the general *form* of many nineteenth-century
autobiographies so that both religious and secular works
tended to be organized around a dramatic conversion,
preceded by a period of bondage and succeeded (despite
the conversion) by a period of confusion or wandering; and
second, that the habit of drawing parallels between Old
Testament types and one's own life frequently influenced
the *content* of nineteenth-century spiritual autobiographies
and even some secular ones.

Carlyle's *Sartor Resartus*, the classic secularized spiritual
autobiography of the period, demonstrates both of these
influences. Consider, for example, the Editor's introduction to Teufelsdröckh's biography. He queries, "By what
singular stair-steps . . . and subterranean passages, and
sloughs of Despair, and steep Pisgah hills, has he reached
this wonderful prophetic Hebron . . . where he now
dwells?" and then warns us "that this Genesis of his can
properly be nothing but an Exodus."[16] In Book Second itself
Teufelsdröckh's experiences assume the structure of a
spiritual exodus. First, Teufelsdröckh leaves the "Egypt
of an Auscultatorship" where he "painfully toiled, baking
bricks without stubble"; then he wanders through a "slough
of Despair" and over "steep Pisgah hills" with "no Pillar
of Cloud by day, and no Pillar of Fire by night"; finally,
he reaches a "wonderful prophetic Hebron," but only after
he affirms that the "Universe is not dead and demonical,
a charnel-house with spectres; but god-like, and my
Father's."[17] Even the three central chapters of the biography
show the influence of Exodus typology—"The Everlasting
No" paralleling the rebellion against Pharaoh; "Centre of
Indifference," the wilderness wandering; and "The Everlasting Yea," the entry into Canaan. Of course, Teufelsdröckh's is an exodus after the disappearance of God, for

throughout his wanderings there is no sign of God's presence, no pillar of cloud by day or pillar of fire by night. But traditional types still provide the structure of the auto-biography.[18]

Types further contribute to our understanding of specific incidents within *Sartor Resartus*. Joseph Sigman's recent study of biblical allusions in *Sartor* notes, for example, that the description of Paris streets as "pavements as hot as Nebuchadnezzar's Furnace" depends upon a well-known type to make a moral judgment on the Enlightenment:

> Paris, the capital of the Enlightenment, is spiritually the Babylon in which the three young men were cast into the furnace because they would not "fall down and worship the golden image" (Dan. 3:10). The furnace, a general biblical image for captivity, torment, and testing, . . . is the cultural environment that rejects the prophets and believes only in the senses.[19]

Carlyle also makes Teufelsdröckh and his experiences into modern correlatives of other familiar types: Melchizedek, Moses, Isaiah, the Babylonian captivity, the ark of the covenant, and others. For our purposes, the significance is this: Carlyle, writing a new spiritual autobiography for nineteenth-century man, drew quite consciously upon a typological pattern for the structure of his work; he also drew upon other types to interpret specific incidents within that work. And one can find similar uses of typology in other major nineteenth-century autobiographies. Ruskin's *Praeterita* contains a series of failed Pisgah visions. In the *Apologia* Newman views himself as a "Moses in the desert" and an "Elijah excommunicated from the Temple." Even Mill's *Autobiography*, which makes no explicit use of types, derives its basic pattern of bondage-crisis-confusion-ultimate redemption from the Exodus.[20]

Browning tends to use typology in his autobiographical poems to interpret specific incidents within his life rather than to provide an overarching structure for it (although, as we shall see, he returns again and again to Moses, using every major event in that type's life). Generally, these types are not applied to explicitly spiritual crises; thus he does not use the exodus as a type of his own spiritual experience. The closest Browning comes to treating himself as an antitype of the Israelites is in *Christmas Eve*, a poem not literally autobiographical ("all the incidents are imaginary," Browning told W. G. Kingsland, "—save the lunar rainbow"[21]) but one which allegorically reconstructs a religious crisis in Browning's life.

The crisis was a common enough one in the Victorian era: which form of Christianity to embrace. As Browning considered the alternatives, the most important were Nonconformity, the way of his mother and wife; Roman Catholicism, the way of Newman; and German rationalism, the way of Strauss and his English followers. Browning chose the first and in the final section of *Christmas Eve* described his decision with a type:

> May truth shine out, stand ever before us!
> I put up pencil and join chorus
> To Hepzibah Tune, without further apology,
> The last five verses of the third section
> Of the seventeenth hymn of Whitfield's Collection.

Hepzibah was Isaiah's name for the nation of Israel, restored after the Babylonian captivity, but also, according to typological interpretation, restored finally and completely at the second coming of Christ. "Hepzibah Tune" in Whitfield's collection was probably the popular hymn, "Come we that Love the Lord," a song of saints "marching thro' Immanuel's Ground / To fairer Worlds on high."[22] Thus in *Christmas Eve* Browning makes himself a modern Israelite, returning after years of exile.

This particular type, however, raises more questions than it answers. From what sort of exile was Browning returning? No doubt, as DeVane suggests, from the religious waywardness of his youth and indifference of his manhood.[23] To what did he return? Probably not to the evangelicalism of his youth, but to the *form* of worship represented by the chapel, a worship without the elaborate trappings and restricting dogmas of Catholicism on the one hand or the skepticism of the German rationalists on the other. But one suspects that Browning deliberately chose a very commonplace type to avoid being specific.

In its application of typology to a personal religious crisis *Christmas Eve* is an anomaly. Usually, when Browning applies types autobiographically, it is to interpret his experiences as a poet. These interpretations cannot be found within a single poem; instead, throughout his career he used types to define his concept of the poet and to describe specific difficulties he encountered as an artist. In the remainder of this essay I want to look first at three relatively early pieces—the narrator's intrusion in Book III of *Sordello, Bells and Pomegranates,* and "Saul"—to see how Browning used types to find his poetic self. Then, I shall turn to four later poems—"One Word More," Book I of *The Ring and the Book,* the "Prologue" to *Asolando,* and "Pisgah Sights"—to see how Browning used types to interpret an artistic predicament or explain an aesthetic problem. What we shall see emerging is a series of autobiographical jottings, made with traditional Old Testament types.

II. Types and the Poet's Office

Browning first uses types autobiographically in *Sordello,* a poem about a gifted young man who fails to become either a mature, productive poet or an effective political leader. In one sense, as Browning's biographers and critics have frequently pointed out, the poem contains many autobiographical elements; it is, as Michael G. Yetman says, Browning's Portrait of the Artist as a Young Man.[24] But I am concerned here with a specific section of the poem in which Browning as narrator, musing "on a ruined palace-step / At Venice," speaks of his predicament as creator of *Sordello* and of the nature of the poet's office.

At the end of Book III, after 3,000 lines exploring the reasons for Sordello's failure as a poet, Browning imagines a dialogue between himself and his audience. The topic is the poet's task and the best way to carry out that task. Browning believes that the poet's responsibility is

to help suffering humanity and argues that in order to
help effectively, the poet must address the problem of
evil. For those poets who ignore this primary responsibility, versifying about inconsequential matters, he has
no patience:

> What, dullard? we and you in smothery chafe,
> Babes, baldheads, stumbled thus far into Zin
> The Horrid, getting neither out nor in,
> A hungry sun above us, sands that bung
> Our throats,—each dromedary lolls a tongue,
> Each camel churns a sick and frothy chap,
> And you, 'twixt tales of Potiphar's mishap,
> And sonnets on the earliest ass that spoke,
> —Remark, you wonder any one needs choke
> With founts about!

His audience is quick to point out, however, that Browning's performance in *Sordello* is not much to emulate:

> While awkwardly enough your Moses smites
> The rock, though he forego his Promised Land
> Thereby, have Satan claim his carcass, and
> Figure as Metaphysic Poet. . . .[25]

The lines allude to Numbers 20, the account of Moses
striking the rock at Meribah-Kadesh to provide water for
the drought-stricken and hence angry Israelites. (Zin was
the desert through which they travelled; the Numbers
account follows the narrative of Joseph's experiences in
Egypt [" 'twixt tales of Potiphar's mishap"] and precedes
the story of Balaam ["the earliest ass which spoke"];
Moses's punishment for striking the rock was exclusion
from Canaan.) On the simplest level, this biblical allusion
anticipates what Browning knew would be his audience's
reaction to *Sordello*: bewilderment, frustration, rebellion.
What the audience wants is water—that is, the story of
Sordello told in an intelligible manner. But this is not what
it gets. After the initial promise, "Who will, may hear
Sordelo's story," the narrator leads his readers through
some of the most difficult lines in English poetry, and still
they cannot understand Sordello's story or Browning's rea-

sons for telling it. Thus Browning expects his readers, like the Israelites, to murmur and complain.

The allusion to Moses striking the rock functions in a more complex way, however. The audience is not simply the Victorian reading public nor even the literary critics; more specifically it consists of Browning's poetic predecessors—those he mentions by name (Sidney, Shelley, Landor) and those he does not (Donne, Milton, the Romantics). The narrator is, in Harold Bloom's terminology, an *ephebe,* a young poet writing his first big poem, taking on the strong poets who precede him and who would prevent him from becoming, too, a strong poet.[26] Bloom would also call him a latecomer, a post-Miltonic poet struggling with the weight of the entire English poetic tradition.

At this point the typological interpretation of the Meribah-Kadesh incident can help us understand, as it helped Browning explain, his predicament as a latecomer. During the exodus Moses struck a rock twice to provide water for Israel: once early in the journey (Exodus 17: 1–7), once thirty-seven years later (Numbers 20: 1–13). It was on the second occasion that Moses incurred God's anger and was forbidden to enter the Promised Land. According to the Old Testament account, Moses was punished for unbelief:

> And the Lord spoke unto Moses and Aaron. Because ye believed me not, to sanctify me in the eyes of the children of Israel, therefore ye shall not bring this congregation into the land which I have given them. (Numbers 20:12)

Nineteenth-century typologists offered a fuller explanation for God's anger. As Henry Melvill explained in a sermon Browning may have heard, "It is generally allowed that this rock in Horeb was typical of Christ; and that the circumstances of the rock yielding no water, until smitten by the rod of Moses, represented the important truth, that the Mediator must receive the blows of the law, before He could be the source of salvation to a parched and perishing world."[27] By typological logic, then, since Christ needed to die only once, Moses needed to strike the rock only once. To strike twice was to spoil God's plan:

> Hence it would have been to violate the integrity and beauty of the
> type, that the rock should have been smitten again; it would have
> been to represent a necessity that Christ should be twice sacrificed,
> and thus to darken the whole Gospel scheme.[28]

But moved by the genuine need, frustrated by the complaints, and perhaps overconfident of his own abilities,
Moses struck twice.

Moses's dilemma is the dilemma of the latecomer: he
must repeat a task already undertaken, more or less successfully, at an earlier time. What is that task? As Browning believed, the poet must discover the source of and cure
for evil. Why, then, repeat the task—which, after all, had
been attempted by several major English poets and had
been accomplished brilliantly by Milton a century and a
half earlier? First, Browning repeats the task because the
needs of the people demand it; he cannot stand "on a
ruined palace step / At Venice" and observe "warped
souls and bodies" without responding to the need. But
Browning also repeats the task because the answers of his
poetic predecessors are not satisfactory for his generation.
Each poet, he goes on to explain, "constructs an engine"
which "Grows into shape by quarters and by halves." Just
when

> The scope of the whole engine's to be proved;
> We die: which means to say, the whole's removed,
> Dismounted wheel by wheel.

The next poet must

> set up anew elsewhere, begin
> A task indeed, but with a clearer clime
> Than the murk lodgment of our building-time.
> And then, I grant you, *it behoves forget*
> *How 'tis done.* [italics mine]

The final line pinpoints the predicament of every new poet.
The later poet may have "a clearer clime" than did his
predecessor, but—and here Browning outdoes Harold
Bloom—"it behoves forget." Remembering creates an anxiety of influence; forgetting helps the poet escape that

anxiety. Thus Browning does not begin his career optimistically, expecting to win acclaim or even great success. His Moses strikes the second time and expects to suffer for doing so.

Browning's choice of an Old Testament type to interpret his predicament as a young poet is only half the story, for (paradoxically) his choice also becomes an attempt to *escape* the anxiety of influence. To understand the strategy of this attempt we must ask why Browning chose *Moses* for the first type in his poetic autobiography.

Recent critics have recognized in *Sordello* Browning's attempt to escape the particular influence of Shelley. Michael Yetman, in fact, treats the poem as an exorcism of Shelley, an attempt "to dissociate himself most emphatically from that earlier poet whose work, because of its temporal priority over his own, appears to threaten or neutralize the originality of his achievement."[29] Browning performs this exorcism in several ways. To begin with, he simply tells Shelley to stay away in a sort of anti-invocation:

> stay—thou, spirit, come not near
> Now—not this time desert thy cloudy place
> To scare me, thus employed, with that pure face!

More importantly, as Yetman points out, Browning gives young Sordello some rather negative Shelleyan traits, "those vaguely idealist habits of mind" which are ultimately responsible for the young poet's downfall: his extreme solipsism, his ungovernable need for public acclaim, his unrealistic expectations about language, his political naiveté, his tempermental reluctance to accommodate himself to the notion of gradual change in human affairs rather than apocalyptic leaps forward, and his inability to translate mental growth into meaningful action.[30] I would add here that Browning's Moses provides another way of exorcising Shelley and of dissociating himself from his own earlier Shelleyan approach to poetry, for with Moses Browning suggests what the Shelleyan poet lacks.

In the first place, unlike the Shelleyan poet, Moses does

not look for truth within himself: his truth comes directly
from God. Browning's first heroes had all been Romantic
questers. The *Pauline* poet's method is self-confession and
self-discovery; Paracelsus insists that "Truth lies within
ourselves"; and young Sordello, too, remains "imprisoned
within the romantic ego,"[31] looking within the self for
answers and ignoring that "Power above [him] still / Which,
utterly incomprehensible, is out of rivalry." In contrast, the
narrator of *Sordello*—that is, the new Browning—links himself with Moses as a mediator, not a discoverer, of truth.
Like the Hebrew prophet, he is a *forth*teller of God's
message.

Second, unlike the Shelleyan poet, Moses defines his responsibility to his people in a specific, immediate way.
The *Pauline* poet was essentially an escapist; a "priest and
lover," he beckoned Pauline to "come with me, see how
I could build / A home for us, out of the world, in thought,"
much as the Keatsian devotee in "Ode to Psyche" vowed
to "build a fane / In some untrodden region of the mind."
Not completely an escapist, young Sordello intends to make
a positive impact on history, but ultimately fails. As Browning sees it, Sordello's failure (and Shelley's) stems from an
essential selfishness, a concern for others only as they relate
to his own achievement:[32]

> Sordello only cared to know
> About men as a means whereby he'd show
> Himself, and men had much or little worth
> According as they kept in or drew forth
> That self.

In contrast, the narrator sees the plight of a "sad dishevelled
ghost" and dedicates himself to her redemption:

> Warped souls and bodies! yet God spoke
> Of right-hand, foot and eye—selects our yoke,
> Sordello, as your poetship may find!
> So, sleep upon my shoulder, child, nor mind
> Their foolish talk; we'll manage reinstate
> Your old worth.

All this may be saying no more than that in *Sordello*
Browning first presented himself as a poet-prophet, a

common enough stance in the 1830s when young Victorian artists felt obliged to demonstrate their usefulness to society. If so, then Moses striking the rock was a particularly suitable type: Moses was the first prophet, a communicator of divine truth, and he was also the first poet, the author of the Song of Moses (Deut. 32). But I think Browning's use of Moses is significant in a third way, for with Moses Browning deliberately allies himself with two earlier Christian poets—Donne and Milton—and thereby attempts to bypass Shelley, his immediate predecessor.

Donne and Milton were two of Browning's acknowledged favorites, and he knew their poetry well enough to remember their important allusions to Moses, the poet.[33] In the *First Anniversary* Donne had cited Moses's example to defend his own use of poetry to record a serious historical event:

> Vouchsafe to call to minde that God did make
> A last, and lasting'st peece, a song. He spake
> To *Moses*, to deliver unto all,
> That song: because hee knew they would let fall,
> The Law, the Prophets, and the History,
> But keepe the song still in their memory:
> Such an opinion (in due measure) made
> Me this great Office boldly to invade.[34]

Milton, of course, alluded to Moses's song in the invocation to *Paradise Lost:*

> Sing Heav'nly Muse, that on the secret top
> Of *Oreb*, or of *Sinai*, didst inspire
> That Shepherd, who first taught the chosen Seed,
> In the Beginning how the Heav'ns and Earth
> Rose out of *Chaos*.[35]

In the *First Anniversary* and in *Paradise Lost* Donne and Milton present themselves in a public role as poet-prophets, and significantly, too, they address the problem of evil, the problem that haunts Browning in this passage of *Sordello*.

Using Moses as a correlative type, then, Browning both explains a personal predicament and attempts to solve it. The type identifies his fears as a young poet trying to

separate himself from his predecessors. It also helps him
make the separation by defining his sense of the poet's
role vis-à-vis God and vis-à-vis society.

In *Bells and Pomegranates*, the series published immediately after *Sordello*, Browning adds two other types to
clarify further his concept of the poet: the bells and
pomegranates of the high priest's robe and David, the Hebrew psalmist. The title of the series baffled many readers,
including Elizabeth Barrett. "Do tell me what you mean
precisely by your 'Bells and Pomegranates' title," she
wrote Browning. "I have always understood it to refer to
the Hebraic priestly garment—but Mr. Kenyon held against
me the other day that your reference was different, though
he had not the remotest idea how."[36] In the final number
of *Bells and Pomegranates*, therefore, Browning explained
the title:

> I only meant by that title to indicate an endeavour towards something
> like an alternation, or mixture, of music with discoursing, sound
> with sense, poetry with thought; which looks too ambitious, thus
> expressed, so the symbol was preferred. It is little to the purpose,
> that such is actually one of the most familiar of the many Rabbinical
> (and Patristic) acceptations of the phrase.[37]

Browning cites Rabbinical and Patristic authorities, but
typological interpretations of the bells and pomegranates
were common enough in nineteenth-century exegesis. As
Elizabeth Barrett realized, the two items were part of the
high priest's garments, sewn alternately on the hem of his
robe (Exod. 28:33–34). Since the high priest himself and
every aspect of his dress typified Christ, typologists gave
this sort of interpretation: the bells represent Christ's
voice or "the sweet sound of the gospel which is gone
into all the earth"; the pomegranates are emblems of
"those fruits of righteousness with which the preaching of
the gospel is attended."[38] Hence, "sound and sense," as
Browning explained, or "faith and good works." He might
also have said, "My poetry and the fruit it will bear,"
but that would have been too explicit a declaration that
the plays and poems of *Bells and Pomegranates*, unlike
Sordello, would make a positive impact on those who read
them.

Bells and Pomegranates obviously signals a priestly role for the poet. Eleanor Cook sees in the title a decision to abandon (at least temporarily) the prophetic mode of *Sordello*, which had met an overwhelmingly hostile reception, and turn to a style which the public might more readily accept.[39] It is unlikely, however, that Browning considered the priestly and prophetic roles as mutually exclusive. According to traditional teaching, the offices of priest and prophet were related. Patrick Fairbairn explained, for example,

> The office of the priesthood . . . necessarily involved somewhat of a prophetical or teaching character, and in after times, when those destined lights of Israel became themselves sources of darkness and corruption, prophets were raised up, and generally from among the priesthood, for the express purpose of correcting the evil, and supplying the information which the others had failed to impart.[40]

More likely, with *Bells and Pomegranates* Browning attempted to add the priestly role to the prophetic, thus clarifying another aspect of the poet's relationship to society. Such a practice would have been exegetically legitimate, for typologists frequently used several Old Testament types to explain a single antitype. It would also have been in character for Browning who, early in his career, decided to be an artist of many talents and under different pseudonyms write a series of poems, novels, operas, speeches, and so on.[41]

Bells and Pomegranates does, however, signal a different sort of poetry. The bells are not direct utterances of God's law but instead pleasant sounds which *remind* the listeners of God's law as the priest walks among them. This describes, it seems to me, the method of *Pippa Passes*, which was the first number of the series. As Pippa wanders through Asolo, her songs are heard by others. The point is not that her songs are to be taken as specific messages from God or that they are to be evaluated theologically, as some critics have done; rather, they remind the listener of some forgotten truth.[42] This approach also describes Browning's method in *Bells and Pomegranates* as a whole. The plays and the new dramatic monologues are not direct utterances, but "sweet sounds" which remind the reader of some truth he already knows and thus carry with them the promise of fruit.

In "Saul," originally published in the seventh number of *Bells and Pomegranates*, Browning adds a third Old Testament character with numerous typological associations to his poetic autobiography—David. As Ward Hellstrom pointed out several years ago, "Saul" itself is thoroughly typological. Not only are Saul and David types of Christ in their roles as king and God's anointed; in almost every stanza typological imagery serves to unify the poem and move it logically to David's final vision: "See the Christ stand!"[43] In addition to this fairly orthodox use of types, Browning uses David as a correlative type to explore his own responsibility as a poet and to explain the sort of poetry he, as a modern David, should write.

David was, after all, the chief Hebrew psalmist, and as such, he became a model for Christian poets and hymn-writers. Isaac Watts, for instance, invoked David's example to justify free translations of the psalms and original hymns:

> They [the psalms] ought to be translated in such a manner as we have reason to believe David would have composed them if he had lived in our day: And therefore his poems are given as a *pattern* to be imitated in our composures, rather than as the precise and invariable matter of our psalmody.[44]

Christopher Smart's "A Song to David," which Browning gave as his inspiration for "Saul," treats David as the supreme poet who in his psalms and in his person fore-shadowed Christ.[45] And Browning seems to have viewed David as the archetypal poet-seer; in *An Essay on Shelley* he compares a visionary passage of Shelley's poetry with "David's pregnant conclusions so long ago."[46] Most important, David's predicament in "Saul" defines the situation of the nineteenth-century poet, and it is this similarity of circumstance which makes David an appropriate type. Just as David must sing to assuage Saul's deep psychological and spiritual needs, so must the modern poet's song alleviate the burdens of his society. For David the psalmist and Browning the poet the question becomes, then, what sort of poetry has such power?

The first fifteen stanzas of "Saul" tell us what sort of poetry does *not* have this power. First, David plays the simple songs of nature and man in nature: "the tune all our sheep know," "the tune, for which quails on the corn-land will each leave his mate," "the help-tune of our reap-pers," "the glad chaunt / Of the marriage," and "the last song / When the dead man is praised on his journey." None of these songs can elicit more than a shudder from Saul. Next, David sings of the joys life has to offer Saul and of the fame which will last when life is over:

Is Saul dead? In the depth of the vale make his tomb—bid arise
A gray mountain of marble heaped four-square, till, built to the skies,
Let it mark where the great First King slumbers: whose fame would ye
    know?
Up above see the rock's naked face, where the record shall go
In great characters cut by the scribe,—Such was Saul, so he did;
With the sages directing the work, by the populace chid,—
For not half, they'll affirm, is comprised there!

But these songs, too, fail to heal Saul. Only after David's vision of God's love in Christ, revealed through his own love for Saul, can David understand what sort of poetry he must sing.

The poem never tells us explicitly what sort of poetry that is, for after stanza fifteen, David recounts his vision, not his song. But Browning implies two things: (1) The Wordsworthian poetry of nature and the Shelleyan internal quest are inadequate; the poet needs a help beyond nature and himself. Here we have returned to the final section of *Sordello* and to Browning's analysis of Sordello's failure:

Ah my Sordello, I this once befriend
And speak for you. Of a Power above you still
Which, utterly incomprehensible,
Is out of rivalry, which thus you can
Love, tho' unloving all conceived by man—
What need! And of . . .
    . . . a Power its representative
Who, being for authority the same,
Communication different, should claim
A course, the first chose but this last revealed—
This Human clear, as that Divine concealed—
What utter need!

David learns what Sordello, who remained trapped within himself, failed to learn: mere human knowledge and love are inadequate to heal; if the poet is to speak effectively, his power and his message must be divinely inspired. (2) Nevertheless, the poet communicates this divinely inspired message through physical, earthly things. Thomas J. Collins has pointed out that within the poem David (or rather Browning) translates this pattern of the earthly revealing the divine into an aesthetic theory. David uses "the world of material reality as 'the starting point and basis alike' of successful poetry" and in the final stanzas builds on the physical and human to achieve a spiritual vision.[47] David functions, then, as a type of Browning the poet. For Browning the aesthetic principle is the same—the human reveals the divine; the physical, the spiritual; the earthly, the heavenly. The only difference between David's poetry and the modern poet's is this: what David writes looks forward in time to Christ's life on earth (hence, the typological imagery in "Saul"); what Browning writes commemorates Christ's life and translates Christian truth into contemporary terms (hence, the use of correlative typology in poems such as *The Ring and the Book*).

III.   Types and the Poet: Later Additions

Prophet, priest, and psalmist helped Browning formulate his conception of the poet, a conception which remained more or less the same throughout his career. In several later poems, however, he returns to two prophetic types— Moses and Elisha—to reassess his view of the poet and to comment further on specific personal and aesthetic problems. I have labelled these later comments (1) repetition, (2) resuscitation, and (3) revision.

In "One Word More," the epilogue to *Men and Women*, Browning once again uses Moses and the account of water from the rock. This time his concern is not self-definition or aesthetic theory, but the personal price one pays for being a poet. Addressed "To E.B.B." and admittedly autobiographical, the poem uses the type to contrast "the man's joy" in painting a picture or writing a poem for his lover with "the artist's sorrow" in undertaking the same task for a public audience:

> Wherefore? Heaven's gift takes earth's abatement!
> He who smites the rock and spreads the water,
> Bidding drink and live a crowd beneath him,
> Even he, the minute makes immortal,
> Proves, perchance, but mortal in the minute,
> Desecrates, belike, the deed in doing.

George P. Landow has already explained the typological framework of the poem. In striking the rock, Moses participated in a figurative event, providing physical water for the Israelites and foreshadowing the spiritual water which Christ's death would make available to all mankind; thus, in effect secularizing the type, Browning suggests that the poet provides physical and spiritual sustenance for his audience.[48] Just as in *Sordello*, then, Browning uses the type to suggest the prophetic aspect of the poet's task.

But, again, as in *Sordello* Browning alludes to the second account of Moses striking the rock, and it is this account with its attendant typological tradition which enables him to explain a personal predicament:

> Even he, the minute makes immortal,
> Proves, perchance, but mortal in the minute,
> Desecrates, belike the deed in doing.
> While he smites, *how can he but remember,*
> *So he smote before,* in such a peril,
> When they stood and mocked—"Shall smiting help us?"
> When they drank and sneered—"A stroke is easy!"
> When they wiped their mouths and went their journey,
> Throwing him for thanks—"But drought was pleasant."
>
> [italics mine]

Moses desecrated the deed when he struck the rock a second time instead of speaking to it as God had commanded. How does Browning desecrate the deed? Obviously, by failing to write perfect poetry—the plight of every mortal who, like Browning, would "put the infinite within the finite."[49] But he also desecrates the deed by striking twice, by repeating an act attempted and accomplished earlier. In *Sordello*, as we have seen, this consciousness of repetition reflected the frustration of an ephebe: Browning feared repeating what his successors had already done successfully. In "One Word More," however, he seems concerned about repeating what he himself has already done:

> Thus old memories mar the actual triumph;
> Thus the doing savours of disrelish;
> Thus achievement lacks a gracious somewhat;
> O'er-importuned brows becloud the mandate,
> Carelessness or consciousness—the gesture.
> For he bears an ancient wrong about him,
> Sees and knows again those phalanxed faces,
> Hears, yet one time more, the 'customed prelude—
> "How should'st thou, of all men, smite, and save us?"

The emphasis is on the remembrance of a prior act.

What exactly did Browning feel he was repeating? If I have interpreted his use of types correctly, then the answer is plain enough: he was repeating what he had already attempted in *Sordello*. We have seen that with the completion of *Sordello* and the early numbers of *Bells and Pomegranates* Browning had worked out his conception of the poet as a servant of society, a communicator of divine truth, and a mediator between God and man. Thomas J. Collins' study of Browning's aesthetic theory additionally suggests that with *Sordello* the poet had solved the moral and aesthetic problems of *Pauline* (the danger of isolation, the lack of a central motivating goal tenaciously pursued, and the failure to accept poetic compromise) and had posited a moral-aesthetic synthesis which was to remain the basic principle of his thought throughout the rest of his career.[50] But in *Sordello* Browning had also attempted a new type of poetry complementary to this moral-aesthetic theory, and it was this new poetry which caused problems.

Book III of *Sordello* explains this new poetry as more than mere description or even description plus interpretation. Instead, it allows the reader to see with the eyes of the poet:

> The office of ourselves—nor blind nor dumb,
> And seeing somewhat of man's state,—has been

> For the worst of us, to say they so have seen;
> For the better, what it was they saw; the best
> Impart the gift of seeing to the rest.[51]

Book V defined it as "synthetic" poetry. Superseding the epic, in which the author *tells* the reader of moral good and evil, and the dramatic, in which the author manipulates characters to *show* good and evil, this new poetry draws the reader fully into the creative-interpretive process:

> Leave the mere rude
> Explicit details! 'tis but brother's speech
> We need, speech where an accent's change gives each
> The other's soul—no speech to understand
> By former audience: need were then to expand,
> Expatiate—hardly were we brothers! true—
> Nor I lament my small remove from you,
> Nor reconstruct what stands already. Ends
> Accomplished turn to means: my art intends
> New structure from the ancient.

Unfortunately, as everyone knows, the "brother speech" of *Sordello* was a disaster. Readers judged the poem "incomprehensible" and called its style "offensive and vicious." "What this poem may be," said the anonymous *Spectator* reviewer, "we are unable to say, for we *cannot* read it."[52] Thus Browning found himself caught in an embarrassing discrepancy between his theory of the poet as the communicator of truth and the actuality of *Sordello*—which no one could understand.

After the failure of *Sordello* Browning spent fifteen years re-working the practical application of his moral-aesthetic theory. *Men and Women* was the culmination of this process, for in this volume Browning actually does "impart the gift of seeing" and make the reader an integral part of the poem. But as the typological allusion in "One Word More" suggests, there was bitterness mixed with the achievement: "old memories mar the actual triumph." Surely, as he published *Men and Women,* Browning remembered the contemptuous reviews of *Sordello* and the disaster of his first attempt as poet-prophet. The

second use of Moses striking the rock is therefore ironically appropriate. It invokes the example of Moses, who
suffered personally for attempting to serve his people but
for serving inadequately, and it also explains the predicament of a poet who must repeat himself and pay the price
of repetition.

Resuscitation rather than repetition becomes Browning's concern in Book I of *The Ring and the Book*. In this
introductory monologue the poet speaks of his materials
and his method, and to explain the method, he turns to
Elisha and the miracle of the Shunammite's son. The mood
here is different from that in "One Word More." Whereas
Browning's use of Moses in that poem reflected the bitterness of artistic failure, Elisha in Book I serves for a
spirited defense of Browning's choice of subject: a forgotten Roman murder story which many readers might consider dead and irrelevant historical debris.

Browning argues otherwise. At first he compares himself to Faust: "I raise a ghost." But then, changing his
mind, he claims a higher authority for his method:

> Oh, Faust, why Faust? Was not Elisha once?—
> Who bade them lay his staff on a corpse-face.
> There was no voice, no hearing: he went in
> Therefore, and shut the door upon them twain,
> And prayed unto the Lord: and he went up
> And lay upon the corpse, dead on the couch,
> And put his mouth upon its mouth, his eyes
> Upon its eyes, his hands upon its hands,
> And stretched him on the flesh; the flesh waxed warm:
> And he returned, walked to and fro the house,
> And went up, stretched him on the flesh again,
> And the eyes opened. 'Tis a credible feat
> With the right man and way.

The raising of the Shunammite's son, to which the passage
refers, was commonly treated as a type of Christ's miracles
of resurrection—the raising of Lazarus and Jairus' daughter and the resurrection of his own body; some commentators also saw in it a foreshadowing of the final resurrection of the elect to eternal life.[53] Using these interpretations,

we can see the relevance of Elisha's miracle to Browning's technique. In his art the poet imitates (and commemorates) Christ by bringing what was dead to life. Browning, in fact, introduces this *imitatio Christi* theme earlier in Book I when he compares the poet's act of creation to God's creation of the world:

> I find first
> Writ down for very A B C of fact,
> "In the beginning God made heaven and earth;"
> From which, no matter with what lisp, I spell
> And speak you out a consequence—that man,
> Man,—as befits the made, the inferior thing,—
> Purposed, since made, to grow, not make in turn,
> Yet forced to try and make, else fail to grow,—
> Formed to rise, reach at, if not grasp and gain
> The good beyond him,—which attempt is growth,—
> Repeats God's process in man's due degree,
> Attaining man's proportionate result,—
> Creates, no, but resuscitates, perhaps.

The comparison with Elisha follows and is carefully chosen to illustrate Browning's aesthetic theory.

Elisha's resuscitation miracles had a second possible typological interpretation. According to Samuel Mather,

There might also be a *Spiritual Application* and Accommodation of them, as to the quickening of Mens *Souls,* the healing of the Diseases of the Soul, feeding them with the Bread of Life, pouring into empty Vessels, empty Souls, the Oyl of Gladness, the Joys and Graces of his Spirit.[54]

That is, the miracles signify a spiritual revitalization, a meeting of the soul's needs. This spiritual interpretation of the type explains, it seems to me, why Browning abandoned Faust as a symbol of the poet and chose Elisha instead. It was not simply, as Eleanor Cook says, that Browning frequently wavered between mage and prophet or even that Faust, who dealt in black magic, was ultimately damned for his art. Faust as artist was inadequate, for *The Ring and the Book* attempted more than the raising of a ghost. As the final monologue of the poet insists, Browning intended the poem to produce "a quickening of men's souls":

> Art may tell a truth
> Obliquely, do the thing shall breed the thought,
> Nor wrong the thought, missing the mediate word. . . .
> So write a book shall mean beyond the facts,
> Suffice the eye and save the soul beside.

Of all the prophetic types, Elisha best served Browning's need to explain his method and intention in *The Ring and the Book*. According to typological exegesis, Elisha's miracle represented a literal, historical fact which signified an ultimate, spiritual salvation.[55]

In two late poems, "Pisgah Sights" and the "Prologue" to *Asolando,* Browning returns to Moses as a type of the poet. Both poems are revisionary—they look back to an earlier time in his career when "Sinai-forehead's cloven brilliance" was his style, and with a certain irony, they smile at young Browning, the poet-prophet.

"Pisgah Sights," published in 1876, takes its title from the mountain upon which Moses viewed the Promised Land just before his death. The details of Moses's death were in themselves typological, prefiguring the death, resurrection, and ascension of Christ, but here Browning focuses on the prophet's vision of Canaan as a type of his own prophetic vision of earthly existence.

It is quite easy to mistake the poem for another (mediocre) example of Browning's "Sinai-forehead's cloven brilliance." Stanzas such as

> Over the ball of it,
>   Peering and prying.
> How I see all of it,
>   Life there, outlying!
> Roughness and smoothness,
>   Shine and defilement,
> Grace and uncouthness:
>   One reconcilement.

or

> "Which things must—*why* be?"
>   Vain our endeavor!
> So shall things aye be
>   As they were ever.

> "Such things should *so* be!"
>   Sage our desistence!
> Rough-smooth let globe be,
>   Mixed—man's existence!

seem to contain the sort of prophetic pronouncements that Browningites of the early twentieth century loved to quote admiringly. Even DeVane, whose notes on the poems are generally perceptive, sees only contentment and reconciliation in the poem and thus is misled to conclude that it is "a curious commentary upon some of the less genial poems of the *Pacchiarotto* volume."[57]

But Browning's ironies undercut (or at least seriously call into question) the pronouncements and his own role as prophet. First of all, the poem is a *Pisgah* vision, a vision granted to the speaker, as to Moses, only at his death when it can be of no worldly use to him:

> Honey yet gall of it!
>   There's the life lying,
> And I see all of it,
>   Only, I'm dying!

It becomes perhaps his punishment for those earlier "imperial fiats," just as Moses's punishment for striking the rock twice was exclusion from the Promised Land. Second, because it is given at death, the vision is of no use to mankind. Even if he could return to earth and proclaim it, the speaker says he would not:

> Could I but live again
>   Twice my life over
> Would I once strive again?

* * *

> Only a learner,
>   Quick one or slow one,
> Just a discerner,
>   I would teach no one.
> I am earth's native:
>   No rearranging it!
> *I* be creative,
>   Chopping and changing it?

The vision leads to a renunciation of the prophetic role and to a questioning of the value of a life spent "rearranging" things on earth. Finally, there is even a touch of bitterness reminiscent of "One Word More" in the lines,

> Those who, below me,
>   (Distance makes great so)
> Free to forego me,
>   Fancy you hate so!

Standing on Pisgah's heights, the poet-prohet remembers the negative reception he received during his lifetime and imagines the additional negative comments now that he stands above other men. Thus the poem looks back to earlier works—*Sordello, Men and Women, The Ring and the Book* —in which Browning had assumed the responsibilities of prophet. There through types he had shown himself striking the rock and dispensing the water of life. Here he shows us the prophet's reward—a Pisgah vision riddled with ironies. The reward scarcely seems just recompense for a life of service.

In *Asolando,* the final volume of Browning's poetry, the prophet makes his peace with his past, his audience, and himself. The "Prologue" returns to a familiar Mosaic type to contrast the poet's age with his youth and to reaffim his calling as a poet-prophet. Appropriately, Browning uses the first incident in Moses' prophetic career—the vision of the burning bush—as a correlative of his own calling:

> "The Poet's age is sad: for why?
>   In youth, the natural world could show
> No common object but his eye
>   At once involved with alien glow—
> His own soul's iris-bow["].

* * *

> How many a year, my Asolo,
>   Since—one step just from sea to land—
> I found you, loved yet feared you so—
>   For natural objects seemed to stand
> Palpably fire-clothed! No—

> No mastery of mine o'er these!
> > Terror with beauty, like the Bush
> Burning yet unconsumed. Bend knees,
> > Drop eyes to earthward! Language? Tush!
> Silence 'tis awe decrees.

When the poet returns to the scene of his calling, he finds that the bush has changed.

> And now? The lambent flame is—where?
> > Lost from the naked world: earth, sky,
> Hill, vale, tree, flower,—Italia's rare
> > O'er-running beauty crowds the eye—
> But flame? The Bush is bare.

Lest this absence of flame (the equivalent of Wordsworth's "glory passed away from the earth" in the *Intimations Ode*)[58] be mistaken for a revocation of his poetic calling, Browning quickly adds another aspect of the incident:

> > What then?
> > A Voice spake thence which straight unlinked
> > Fancy from fact . . .
>
> > . . . for the purged ear apprehends
> > Earth's import, not the eye late dazed.
> > The Voice said, "Call my works thy friends!
> > At Nature dost thou shrink amazed?
> > God is it who transcends."

Thus, at his death Browning both revises and reasserts his claim as prophet. The young poet who looked for spiritual meaning in every physical thing has become the mature poet who has learned the distinction between God and his creation.

The "Prologue" to *Asolando* completes Browning's poetic autobiography with a conscious repetition of Moses as type of Browning the poet. Browning had first visited Asolo in 1838 while writing *Sordello*. As we know from Book III, one result of that visit was his dedication to "suffering humanity," a dedication symbolized in his use of the prophet Moses. At the end of his life, Browning returned to

Asolo—literally, for he died there on December 12, 1889.
But he also returned poetically, once again using Moses as
a correlative type and reaffirming his claim as modern
prophet.

1.   From the advertisement on the second page of the original *Dramatic
Lyrics,* quoted in William Clyde DeVane's *A Browning Handbook,* 2nd ed.
(Englewood Cliffs, N.J.: Prentice-Hall, 1955), p. 104. For Browning's poetry
I have followed the text of *The Poetrical Works of Robert Browning,* 2 vols.
(London: Smith, Elder, 1897).

2.   The only introductory study of typology in nineteenth-century literature
is George P. Landow's "Moses Striking the Rock: Typological Symbolism in
Victorian Poetry," in *Literary Uses of Typology from the Late Middle Ages to
the Present,* ed. Earl Miner (Princeton: Princeton University Press, 1977), pp.
315–44.

3.   Wayne Shumaker's definition in *English Autobiography: Its Emergence,
Materials, and Forms* (Berkeley and Los Angeles: University of California
Press, 1954), p. 106.

4.   For a thorough introduction to the problem of telling the truth versus
creating a coherent form, see Roy Pascal, *Design and Truth in Autobiography*
(London: Routledge and Kegan Paul, 1960).

5.   The classic nineteenth-century study of typology is Patrick Fairbairn's
The Typology of Scripture, 4th ed. (1900; rpt. Grand Rapids: Baker Book House,
1975), esp. I, 42–85. Following Barbara K. Lewalski (*"Samson Agonistes* and
the 'Tragedy' of the Apocalypse," *PMLA* 85 [1970], 1050–62), I use the term
"correlative type" to indicate a latter-day fulfillment of a type.

6.   "Honey from the Rock," *Lectures on Practical Subjects* (New York:
Stanford and Swords, 1853), pp. 30–31. For a discussion of Browning's familiarity
with Melvill's preaching, *see* my "Browning's Chapel Attendance: Two Cor-
rections," *Studies in Browning and His Circle,* 4 (1976), 76–85.

7.   Sermon XLVI, "The Wilderness State," in *The Works of the Rev. John
Wesley,* 3rd ed. (New York: Carlton and Phillips, 1853), I, 408–09.

8.   This translation of William William's Welsh hymn, composed in 1745,
is taken from *The Hymnal of the Presbyterian Church in the United States of
America* (Philadelphia: Presbyterian Board of Christian Education, 1933), but
translations were included in most of the major eighteenth and nineteenth-
century collections of hymns.

9.   The term is Shumaker's, who applies it to autobiographical works which
focus on the continuous growth of the self, rather than on external events.

10.   *British Autobiography in the Seventeenth Century* (London: Routledge
and Kegan Paul, 1969), esp. ch. III, V, and VI. Delany does not consider the
influence of typology on autobiography.

11.   Cf. Roger Sharrock's outline of Bunyan's *Grace Abounding to the Chief
of Sinners* (Oxford: Clarendon Press, 1962), p. xxix:

(i) Early providential mercies and opportunities.
(ii) Unregenerate life: sin and resistance to the Gospel.
(iii) Conversion, often ushered in by an "awakening" sermon.
(iv) Calling; vocation to preach the Gospel.

12. The Pauline conversion story contributed, of course, many of the specific conventions of the conversion accounts—e.g., the "chiefest of sinners' " theme. The overall structure of the autobiography, however, seems to originate in the Exodus account.

13. Sharrock, p. 2, 11. 9–11, 15–17.

14. Sharrock, p. 15, 11. 1–7. *See* also U. Milo Kaufman's discussion in *The Pilgrim's Progress and the Tradition of Puritan Meditation* (New Haven: Yale University Press, 1966), pp. 25–60, for other types used in *Grace Abounding.*

15. *Versions of the Self: Studies in English Autobiography from John Bunyan to John Stuart Mill* (New York: Basic Books, 1966), pp. 5–6.

16. *Sartor Resartus: The Life and Opinions of Herr Teufelsdröckh,* ed. Charles Frederick Harrold (New York: Odyssey Press, 1937), pp. 76, 81.

17. Carlyle, pp. 131, 161, 188.

18. The structure of *Sartor Resartus* is a frequently disputed topic; *see* esp. G. B. Tennyson, *Sartor Called Resartus* (Princeton: Princeton University Press, 1965) and Walter L. Reed, "The Pattern of Conversion in *Sartor Resartus,*" *ELH,* 38 (1971), 411–23. Reed is correct in pointing out that *Sartor* does not use an Augustinian pattern of conversion, as Tennyson states; but Reed errs in suggesting that it reveals *no* Christian pattern of conversion, for it does employ a very traditional typological one.

19. "Adam-Kadmon, Nifl, Muspel, and the Biblical Symbolism of *Sartor Resartus,*" *ELH,* 41 (1974), 238. Sigman is not interested in typological allusions or patterns per se, but many of the biblical symbols he discusses are well-known types.

20. George P. Landow's introduction to this collection suggests this interpretation of Ruskin's *Praeterita;* for Newman, see the *Apologia Pro Vita Sua* (New York: Modern Library, 1950), p. 171. Mill is aware that his autobiography resembles conversion accounts; in "A Crisis in My Mental History" he describes his condition as "the state, I should think, in which converts to Methodism usually are, when smitten by their first 'conviction of sin.' " *Autobiography and Other Writings,* ed. Jack Stillinger (Boston: Houghton Mifflin, 1969), p. 81.

21. DeVane, p. 199.

22. George Whitfield, *A Collection of Hymns for Social Worship,* 7th ed. (London: William Strahan, 1758), sec. II, no. 17. Section III has only introits, benedictions, and so on.

23. DeVane, pp. 195–97.

24. "Exorcising Shelley Out of Browning: *Sordello* and the Problem of Poetic Identity," *Victorian Poetry,* 13 (1975), 79–98. *See* also DeVane, pp. 72–85; Betty Miller, *Robert Browning: A Portrait* (London: John Murray, 1952), pp. 23–28, 47–49; William Irvine and Park Honan, *The Book, the Ring, and the Poet* (London: Bodley Head, 1974), pp. 76–92; and Stewart Walker Holmes's comments on the "psychotherapeutic" effect of Sordello in "Browning's *Sordello* and Jung: Browning's *Sordello* in the Light of Jung's Theory of Types," *PMLA,* 56 (1941), 758–96.

25. Although critics have not noticed it, there is some disagreement over who speaks what lines in this passage. Thomas J. Collins gives this entire speech (III, 816–829) to Browning the narrator as an attack on poets "who indulge in triteness when mankind is racked with pain" (*Robert Browning's Moral-Aesthetic Theory, 1833–1855* [Lincoln: University of Nebraska Press, 1967], pp. 74–75); the "you," in other words, is the other poets. Eleanor Cook (*Browning's Lyrics: An Exploration* [Toronto: University of Toronto Press, 1974], pp. 46–47) and Lionel Stevenson ("The Key Poem of the Victorian Age," *Essays in American and English Literature*

Presented to Bruce Robert McElderry, Jr. [Athens: Ohio University Press, 1967], p. 287) simply read the passage as Browning's identification with Moses, ignoring the pronoun problem. The poem was published originally without quotation marks, leaving it to the reader to notice the shifts in dialogue (*see The Complete Works of Robert Browning*, ed. Roma A. King [Athens: Ohio University Press, 1970], II, 223–24). I read ll. 826–29 as an interruption from the audience and treat the rest of the passage as the narrator's.

26.   *See The Anxiety of Influence: A Theory of Poetry* (New York: Oxford University Press, 1973), *passim,* and also *A Map of Misreading* (New York: Oxford University Press, 1975) and *Poetry and Repression: Revisionism from Blake to Stevens* (New Haven: Yale University Press, 1976). Bloom does not treat *Sordello* or any of the other poems discussed in this section.

27.   *Sermons* (London: J. G. & F. Rivington, 1838), II, 163–64. This sermon is discussed at length by George P. Landow, *The Aesthetic and Critical Theories of John Ruskin* (Princeton: Princeton University Press, 1971), pp. 341–50.

28.   Melvill, II, 166.

29.   Yetman, p. 84. *See* also Daniel Stempel, "Browning's *Sordello:* The Art of the Makers-See," *PMLA,* 80 (1965), 554–61.

30.   Yetman, p. 83.

31.   Stempel's phrase, p. 561.

32.   Bloom would no doubt consider this an example of Browning's misreading of Shelley. After all, it was Shelley who had called poets "the unacknowledged legislators of the world," and it was Shelley's mantle which Browning claimed when he attempted, as Lionel Stevenson suggests in "The Key Poem of the Victorian Age" (p. 267), "to demonstrate that poetry . . . could apply its unique power to themes of contemporary life with such subtlety, vividness, compression, and emotional intensity that it was more than a match for prose."

33.   Unlike other Victorians, Browning knew Donne's poetry well, and his admiration for this seventeenth-century metaphysical became "notorious"; *see* A. J. Smith, ed., *John Donne: The Critical Heritage* (London: Routledge and Kegan Paul, 1975), pp. 347–50, and Joseph E. Duncan, "The Intellectual Kinship of John Donne and Robert Browning," *Studies in Philology,* 50 (1953), 81–100. Browning had read Milton's poetry thoroughly by the age of fourteen (Irvine and Honan, pp. 7, 15) and in his maturity kept a picture of Milton above his desk and a lock of Milton's hair under glass (James G. Nelson, *The Sublime Puritan: Milton and the Victorians* [Madison: University of Wisconsin Press, 1963], p. 4).

34.   Ll. 461–68. *The Poems of John Donne,* ed. Herbert J. Grierson (Oxford: Oxford University Press, 1912), I, 245.

35.   Ll. 6–10, *The Complete Poetry of John Milton,* ed. John T. Shawcross, rev. ed. (New York: Anchor Books, 1971), p. 251.

36.   Letter 132 (October 17, 1845) in *The Letters of Robert Browning and Elizabeth Barrett Barrett, 1845–1846,* ed. Elvan Kintner (Cambridge, Mass.: Belknap Press, 1969), I, 239.

37.   Quoted by DeVane, p. 89.

38.   This interpretation comes from William McEwen's popular *Grace and Truth,* 5th ed. (Edinburgh: Gavin Alston, 1777), p. 64. *See* also Thomas Scott's notes on Exod. 28:33–34 in *A Commentary on the Holy Bible* (Philadelphia: William S. and Alfred Martien, 1858); Samuel Mather, *The Figures or Types of the Old Testament,* ed. Mason I. Lowance (1705; facsimile rpt. New York: Johnson Reprint Corp., 1969), pp. 503–04; Patrick Fairbairn, *The Typology of Scripture* (1900: rpt. Grand Rapids: Baker Book House, 1975), II, 242; and Walter Lewis Wilson, *Wilson's Dictionary of Bible Types* (Grand Rapids: Wm. B. Eerdmans, 1957), s.v.

"bell" and "pomegranate." Judith Berlin-Lieberman's *Robert Browning and Hebraism* (Jerusalem: Azriel Printing, 1934), pp. 19–29, discusses the Rabbinical backgrounds.

39. Cook, pp. 69–70. For the critical reception of *Sordello, see* Boyd Litzinger and Donald Smalley, eds., *Browning: The Critical Heritage* (New York: Barnes and Noble, 1970), pp. 60–69.

40. Fairbairn, II, 236.

41. In the copy of *Pauline* given to John Forster, Browning wrote: "The following Poem was written in pursuance of a foolish plan which occupied me mightily for a time, and which had for its object the enabling me to assume & realize I know not how many different characters;—meanwhile the world was never to guess that 'Brown, Smith, Jones & Robinson' (as the spelling books have it) the respective authors of this poem, the other novel, such an opera, such a speech, etc. etc. were no other than one and the same individual." *See* DeVane, p. 41.

42. Thus, e.g., Sebald hears Pippa's song—

> The lark's on the wing;
> The snail's on the thorn;
> God's in his heaven—
> All's right with the world!

—remembers God's law, and judges himself and Ottima guilty of sin. The point is not that Pippa's song contains a profound truth, but that it reminds the listener of truth he already knows.

43. "Time and Type in Browning's *Saul*," *ELH*, 33 (1966), 370–89. The types Hellstrom discusses include David as shepherd and Anointed One, the brazen serpent, the tabernacle, the three-day darkness, and (of course) David and Saul as kings.

44. "A Short Essay toward the Improvement of Psalmody," *The Works of the Rev. Isaac Watts, D. D.* (Leeds: Edward Baines, [1800]), p. 9.

45. *See,* e.g., the last stanza.

> Glorious—more glorious is the crown
> Of Him, that brought salvation down
> By meakness, called thy Son;
> Thou at stupendous truth believed,
> And now the matchless deed's achieved.
> DETERMINED, DARED, and DONE.

and its gloss, "which is wrought up to this conclusion, that the best poet which ever lived was thought worthy of the highest honor which possibly can be conceived, as *the Saviour of the World was ascribed to his house, and called his son in the body.*" *Norton Anthology of English Literature,* ed. M. H. Abrams, et. al. (New York: W. W. Norton, 1974), I, 2404.

46. "An Essay on Shelley," *The Complete Poetic and Dramatic Works of Robert Browning* (Boston: Houghton Mifflin, 1895), p. 1013.

47. Collins, p. 122.

48. Landow, "Moses Striking the Rock," pp. 340–41. *See* also Eleanor Cook, p. 235, who recognizes the iconographical tradition behind the allusion and stresses the miraculous element in the creative process.

49. *The Works of John Ruskin,* ed. E. T. Cook and Alexander Wedderburn (London, 1909), XXXVI, 34.

50. Collins, p. 77.

51. Browning's aesthetic theories here anticipate those Ruskin presents in *The Stones of Venice* (1851–52) and *Modern Painters* III (1856); *see* Landow, *Aesthetic and Critical Theories of Ruskin,* pp. 370–99. Both men's theories exem-

plify the transference of evangelical ideas to art.

52. Litzinger and Smalley, pp. 60, 62, 64.

53. Mather, p. 113.

54. Mather, p. 113.

55. Paul F. Matthiessen's "Uproar in the Echo: The Existential Aesthetic of Browning's *The Ring and the Book*" (*Literary Monographs*, no. 3 [Madison: University of Wisconsin Press, 1970], pp. 178–79) adds a further twist to Browning's use of types in Book I. Mattheissen points out that early in the monologue, when Browning discovers the Old Yellow Book, a "chant made for midsummer nights [that] always came and went with June" is deliberately mentioned. This chant was the hymn "sung at the Vesper services on the Vigil of the Nativity of St. John the Baptist (June 23), and again on the day of the Feast itself (June 24), the only such important feast which occurs during the month of June." In the homilies recited on that feast day, John the Baptist's typological significance is stressed: "John was a figure of the Old Testament, and typified the law in himself; and therefore John foretold the Saviour, just as the law preceded grace." Later in the monologue Browning compares himself to Elisha, a type of Christ himself. Thus, concludes Matthiessen, "Browning imagines himself first (before creating the poem) as a herald of Christ and then as a type of Christ, fulfilling his own prophesy."

56. According to Deut. 34:6 God buried Moses's body, "but no man knows the place of his burial to this day." For typological interpretations, *see* Mather, p. 113.

57. The *Pacchiarotto* volume contains many harshly satiric poems, including an attack on the critic Alfred Austin, "Of Pacchiarotto, and How He Worked in Distemper."

58. For readings of the "Prologue" as Browning's *Intimations Ode*, *see* Harold Bloom, *Poetry and Repression*, pp. 195–96, and Clyde de L. Ryals, *Browning's Later Poetry* (Ithaca: Cornell University Press, 1975), pp. 228–30.

ROBERT L. PATTEN

Autobiography Into Autobiography: The Evolution of *David Copperfield*

Man lives forward and understands backward.

—Kierkegaard

I

The lasting element in thinking is the way. And ways of thinking hold within them that mysterious quality that we can walk
them forward and backward, and that indeed only the way
back will lead us forward.

—Heidegger

Throughout the eighteen-forties, Dickens tried to come to
terms with the past—with revolution, romanticism, pre-in-
dustrialism, his own life.[1] In June 1845 while staying in
Genoa he told Forster for the first time about his early
theatrical ambitions.[2] Seventeen months later he sent the
initial chapter of *Dombey and Son* III to Forster, explaining that Mrs. Pipchin's "establishment . . . is from the life,
and I was there—I don't suppose I was eight years old; but
I remember it all as well, and certainly understood it as
well, as I do now."[3] Mrs. Pipchin, née Roylance in the
number plans,[4] has been variously identified as the "reduced old lady, long known" to the family, who took the
twelve-year-old Dickens in while his father was incarcer-
ated in the Marshalsea, later accommodating the rest of
the family too,[5] and as "an old lodging-house keeper in an
English watering place" (probably Southsea) to which the
family travelled during the summer of 1814, when Dickens'
brother Alfred was born and died.[6] Neither of these events
squares with the notion that Dickens was "eight years old."

269

Nor is it at all clear, from other evidence, that Dickens "understood it," whatever "it" is, then, though it may be true that he "understood it [then] as well" as he did in 1846.

For Dickens hadn't come to any full understanding of his past and of its complex relation to his present. Some lessons seemed obvious: "We should be devilish sharp in what we do to children," he continued to Forster. However limited their perspective and comprehension, children know intuitively, feel acutely, and perceive selectively. Through his children and memories of his own past Dickens had been getting in touch with those responses for some time: "I thought of that passage in my small life, at Geneva," he added. "Shall I leave you my life in MS when I die? There are some things in it that would touch you very much, and that might go on the same shelf with the first volume of Holcroft's [*Memoirs*]."

Alan Horsman, in his "Introduction" to the Clarendon *Dombey*, concludes that "there is then a close relationship between the [autobiographical] fragment and *Dombey and Son*, in the time of gestation and composition as well as in part of the content, and, behind both of these, though whether as cause or consequence is uncertain, in the increasing adoption of the child's standpoint as the early part of the novel proceeds."[7] What Paul understands—which according to Dickens' testimony reflects what he himself understands of this composite past—is a product of the way Paul sees others, sees himself, and sees his possibilities. Mrs. Pipchin is an "ogress"—"a marvellous ill-favoured, ill-conditioned old lady, of a stooping figure, with a mottled face, like bad marble, a hook nose, and hard grey eye, that looked as if it might have been hammered at on an anvil without sustaining any injury"—and a "child-queller," whose secret for success as a child-manager "was, to give them everything that they didn't like, and nothing that they did."[8] In short, she takes her place in a Dickensian genealogy of life-denying mothers: she still wears black bombazine mourning as the relict of a husband who broke his heart, not in romance, but over an unsuccessful speculation "in pumping water out of the Peruvian Mines."[9] These non-nurturing parents go back in Dickens' fiction at least as far as Oliver's foster-mother, the ominously named Mrs. Mann.[10] Mrs. Pipchin's indoor garden provides a fair sample of her capacity to foster fertile, vital, pleasant life: the epitome of violent vegetation, it contains writhing hairy cactuses, creeping sticky-leaved vegetables, and spidery pot plants, "in which Mrs. Pipchin's dwelling was uncommonly prolific, though perhaps it challenged competition still more proudly, in the season, in point of earwigs."[11]

Paul, by contrast, is diminutive, wise beyond his years, physically impotent, but spiritually incorruptible. He confounds his father with a catechism on money, and Mrs. Pipchin with similar innocent questions. The result of the confrontation of knowing but dependent boy and ogress in her Castle is a kind of stand-off, a truce, a conversion of the potentially fatal opposition into complicit stasis; each develops a "grotesque attraction"[12] for the other, and they often sit staring at one another before the fire.

When Dickens saw the plate depicting this scene, on which he hoped Browne would expend "a little extra care,"[13] he blew up:

> I am really *distressed* by the illustration of Mrs. Pipchin and Paul. It is so frightfully and wildly wide of the mark. Good Heaven! in the commonest and most literal construction of the text, it is all wrong. She is described as an old lady, and Paul's "miniature armchair" is mentioned more than once. He ought to be sitting in a little armchair down in a corner of the fireplace, staring up at her. I can't say what pain and vexation it is to be so utterly misrepresented. I would cheerfully have given a hundred pounds to have kept this illustration out of the book. He never could have got that idea of Mrs. Pipchin if he had attended to the text. Indeed I think he does better without the text; for then the notion is made easy to him in short description, and he can't help taking it in.[14]

Yet the original design and the plate both seem quite compatible with the text: Mrs. Pipchin is hardly young, Paul is sitting in a kind of small high chair looking up at her, though the text insists only that he looks "at" her, the cactuses are faithfully and spikily present, and together with the cat the three familiars interact in Browne's graphic presentation exactly as they do in the text:

She would make him move his chair to her side of the fire, instead of sitting opposite; and there he would remain in a nook between Mrs. Pipchin and the fender, with all the light of his little face absorbed into her black bombazeen drapery, studying every line and wrinkle of her countenance, and peering at the hard grey eye, until Mrs. Pipchin was sometimes fain to shut it, on pretence of dozing. Mrs. Pipchin had an old black cat, who generally lay coiled upon the centre foot of the fender, purring egotistically, and winking at the fire until the contracted pupils of his eyes were like two notes of admiration. The good old lady might have been—not to record it disrespectfully—a witch, and Paul and the cat her two familiars, as they all sat by the fire together.[15]

A possible explanation for Dickens' exasperation lies in the difference in point of view.[16] Chapter VIII, "Paul's further progress, growth, and character," hovers between the child's perspective and the adult's, between Paul's selective vision and spiritual incorruptibility and the narrator's more comprehensive insight, pity, and precognition that the result of the child's parental deprivation will be an early death: "Naturally delicate, perhaps, he pined and wasted after the dismissal of his nurse, and, for a long time, seemed but to wait his opportunity of gliding through their hands, and seeking his lost mother."[17] Browne finds no way to imitate graphically this unresolved tension of perspectives: he offers instead a box stage set, the characters and props arranged according to instructions, all three poised in attitudes of brooding, the cat at the fire, Mrs. Pipchin inwardly on her own past, Paul on "every line and wrinkle of her countenance"; but there is no mediating artistic lens. Paul's consciousness is within the picture, the adult narrator's outside it.

That convergence of perspective between eight-year-old and adult which Dickens claimed for his episode inheres neither in the novel's point of view, divided between innocence and experience, nor in the plot or myth, which gift Paul with preternatural wisdom and insufficient vitality. How can the living thirty-four-year-old Dickens say he "understood" an experience metamorphosed fictionally into unbearable and unresolvable tensions? He lies, in the Romantic way of lying, by projecting as defense another version of the wounded artist who knows through deprivation too much to survive.

II

I know how all these things have worked together to make me what I am.

—Dickens

Theatrical avatars, inhabiting someone else's clothes and language, were one way of surviving—or even more, of becoming adequate, potent.[18] But the connections between self and avatar lie in the contingent similarity or analogy; they are, beyond the choice of roles, not under the actor's control. Creating the characters as author (Dickens in the process of composition frequently acted out the roles in a mirror: writer, actor, and critic at once)[19] puts more of the vital connection between life and art, self and other, in the hands of the creator. Yet at the end of *Dombey* Dickens opts for a past and dying world over the present and living one, and continues to image the choice as one between mutually exclusive and destructive opposites.[20] At roughly the same time (earlier if the "life in MS" was written by *Dombey* III, later if it was prompted by Forster's casual inquiry in "March or April of 1847"),[21] however, Dickens composed his autobiographical fragment concerning the blacking warehouse, which may be an account of the time immediately preceding the family's stay at Mrs. Roylance's during and after the Marshalsea incident.[22]

The basic difference between this fragment and the Pipchin episode is that it is written by a survivor. Whatever the facts, they must explain how it was possible to live, to endure this deprivation. In Dickens' version, the child is, if anything, more abandoned and powerless even than Paul. He is "so easily cast away"; "no one had compassion enough"; "no one made any sign." He is marooned in a "crazy, tumbledown old house . . . literally overrun with rats." Worse than Mrs. Pipchin's cactus, this environment is characterized by consuming decay. And the companions are not mistresses of a household with whom one can hold secret and equal communion, but the orphan Bob Fagin who is kind to him when he succumbs to "a bad attack of my old disorder," and Paul (Poll) Green. Kindness and sympathy in such a place take on threatening aspects by offering friendship and accommodation and help for unwillingly confessed weakness; hence Bob Fagin's reward: "I took the liberty of using his name, long afterwards, in *Oliver Twist.*" Though not all the charity can be rejected; hence Poll Sweedlepipe in *Martin Chuzzlewit.*[23]

Abandonment by others into this lower order of existence leads to abandonment by self of one's dreams for a hopeful future. "No words can express the secret agony of my soul as I sunk into this companionship; compared these every day associates with those of my happier childhood; and felt my early hopes of growing up to be a learned and distinguished man, crushed in my breast." To make this sense of loss even more piercing, his sister Fanny continued at the Royal Academy of Music, pursuing a course of study that seemed to promise fame and fortune, and certainly singled her out in the present as preferred. He felt utterly neglected and hopeless, experienced shame and misery, grief and humiliation, saw all joy passing by.

Moreover, all this is done *to* him, *by* others. The child is essentially powerless to affect his fate; he is the victim of his parents and circumstances that cast him away, sink him, crush him, cut him off from parents, family, hope. His powerlessness is so great, his resources are so scanty, that he discovers his inability even to portion out his wages to last through the week, squandering on stale pastry set out at half price on trays in the confectioners' shops the pennies that should have been saved for dinner. Despite his best efforts he seems to be slipping into the condition of another self-consuming decayed relict. Self-discipline and self-reliance cannot withstand the temptations of the city, and Charles is poised to enact once again the familiar declension from poverty to hunger, and hunger to crime, paradigmatically displayed in the life of Moll Flanders: "I know that, but for the mercy of God, I might easily have been, for any care that was taken of me, a little robber or a little vagabond."

What is missing from this account is any causal agent.[24] It was "an evil hour" that cast him away and crushed him; though "utterly neglected and hopeless," he does not accuse his parents of that neglect. He has no assistance: "No advice, no counsel, no encouragement, no consolation, no support, from any one that I can call to mind, so help me God." But nobody to blame, either. There is not in this fragment a denunciation of the "Right Reverends and Wrong Reverends of every order" who reduce Jo,[25] nor a portrayal of the inhumane efficiency of institutional charity that supervises Oliver,[26] nor an arctic Dombey, nor a fiendish Fagin. He is "so young and childish, and so little qualified—how could I be otherwise?—to undertake the whole charge of my own existence," that the world seems reversed: the child must act the man, self-sufficient, self-employed, ordering a-la-mode beef in the best dining room of Johnson's beef-house, or ale at a pub in Parliament Street (an incident afterwards transferred to David in *Copperfield*), drinking coffee and eating bread and butter from behind a glass that symbolically and talismanically reversed the world's language: MOOR-EEFFOC. "If I ever find myself . . . where there is such an inscription on glass, and read it backward on the wrong side MOOR-EEFFOC (as I often used to do then, in a dismal reverie), a shock goes through my blood."

For all its deprivations, the life had certain covert and hard-won advantages. If there is no author to one's existence, no causal agent, one can make oneself, as Dickens did, becoming extremely skilled at his task, forcing a stoic silence on the pain, establishing by his conduct and manners "a space" between the others and himself, and creating, even in these surroundings, the persona of "the young gentleman," in imitation of his father's oratorically projected gentility. There was another kind of skill he appropriated to himself from his father, that facility with words as instruments for creating a different, better reality than the blacking warehouse or the Marshalsea. When the boy visits the prison he hears Captain Porter read the text of John Dickens' petition for permission to drink the king's health on his birthday "as if the words were something real in his mouth, and delicious to taste," while in a corner he "made out my own little character and story for every man who put his name to the sheet of paper."

But such practical skill and fantasy do not themselves

create or cancel the real world, nor make entirely adequate the lot of the abandoned child. However much one may imagine oneself to be "a child of singular abilities, quick, eager, delicate, and soon hurt, bodily or mentally," the reality as otherwise is exposed the moment one performs the task of tying up blacking bottles in a window before the admiring street public. And so Dickens, out of his powerful need to be lovable and loved, imagines that his father came to the window, saw him there like a figure in a play, and quarrelled with his relative James Lamert by letter, Charles serving as intermediary. There is no confirmation that the quarrel was about the window: "It was about me. It may have had some backward reference, in part, for anything I know, to my employment at the window." Dickens' release threw him into a very ambivalent frame of mind, for he had to acknowledge the end both of abandonment and self-creation: "With a relief so strange that it was like oppression, I went home."

But the story does not end with the child acknowledging his dependency again, returning to the hearth and heart of his family, and magically transforming from premature adult to fostered child. For Mrs. Dickens tried to accommodate the quarrel, to reconcile her husband to Lamert, and to restore her son to his self-creating servitude. John Dickens opposed this eminently practical, if insensitive, move, urging instead that the boy be sent to school to acquire that language which was John's real medium of being, if we are to judge from the extant texts and Mr. Micawber. Elizabeth Dickens seems to be concerned about feeding her family; John, about feeding their ambitions. Significantly, Dickens' hunger required even more of John's remedy, by this time, than of Elizabeth's.

"I do not write resentfully or angrily: for I know how all these things have worked together to make me what I am: but I never afterwards forgot, I never shall forget, I never can forget, that my mother was warm for my being sent back." It is another lie, a necessary fiction. Mrs. Dickens visited the boy often during the interval; Mr. Dickens, but seldom. The whole incident lasted a few months; but

Dickens has "no idea how long it lasted; whether for a year, or much more, or less." He makes claims for a kind of understanding of the uses of the past, "how all these things have worked together to make me what I am," but he exhibits no such understanding, no such forgiveness. The refusal to forget his mother's "warmness" (interesting ambivalence in itself, signifying in context heat but in meaning coldness) sounds like an incantation or spell not to forget, testimony that he has not forgotten, will not and can not forget, the narrowness of his rescue from a condition with which he was unable to cope. Having gone through the experience of abandonment, having come face to face with his insufficiency, Dickens then erected, and still (1847) maintains, the willed fiction of an abandoning mother. By that fiction, maintained secretly as talisman ("no word of that part of my childhood . . . has passed my lips to any human being"), Charles, boy and man, can keep the rewards of that dearly bought knowledge: a kind of masculine independence involving self-sufficiency, skill in work, sympathy with the oppressed and abandoned, and creation through imagination and language. He also fixes for himself a way of thinking about women that makes them either undependable as sources of nurture and protection, or idealized as the source of all the adequacies which the child perceives himself to lack.

In *The Haunted Man* (1848) Dickens claims that he taught "that bad and good are inextricably linked in remembrance, and that you could not choose the enjoyment of recollecting only the good. To have all the best of it you must remember the worst also."[27] Forster goes farther, appending a moral that is at once psychologically acute and utterly inapplicable to Dickens himself: "The old proverb does not tell you to forget that you may forgive, but to forgive that you may forget. It is forgiveness of wrong, for forgetfulness of the evil that was in it; such as poor old Lear begged of Cordelia."[28] But Dickens can not and will not forget or forgive, because complexly the recollection and preservation of the wrong done to him are the secret sources of his being. Yet he really does not understand that connection. The autobiographical fragment is incomplete, truncated; it bears no connection to the future life of the child or the present life of the adult; it projects no *telos* out of suffering that converts misery into accomplishment, trauma into understanding. The survivor can not say, will not admit, why he has survived.

David Copperfield becomes a third version of the abandoned child, another try at connecting past to present and writing oneself into adequacy.

III

Do you care to know that I was a great writer at 8 years old or so—was an actor and a speaker from a baby—and worked many childish experiences and many young struggles, into Copperfield?
—Dickens

It would be the greatest mistake to imagine anything like a complete identity of the fictitious novelist with the real one, beyond the Hungerford scenes; or to suppose that the youth, who then received his first harsh schooling in life, came out of it as little harmed or hardened as David did.
—Forster

Once entertained, the psychic material of Dickens' past would not go away. "Penetrated with the grief and humiliation" of the Hungerford stairs blacking warehouse days, he could not shake their memory and power, and "even now, famous and caressed and happy"—three adjectives that pregnantly convey the contrast between past and present—"I often forget in my dreams that I have a dear wife and children; even that I am a man; and wander desolately back to that time of my life."[29] Every word of his confession reveals the destructive cost to the self of this nodal past: "penetrated," "forget . . . I have . . . wife and children," "forget . . . even that I am a man," "wander," "desolately": the net result is an image of un-manning, of stripping away the power and personal integrity of adulthood to reveal again the vulnerable, lonely, dependent, lost, and despairing child.

But—and it is a momentous but—Dickens the writer can deal at arm's length, or more accurately at word's length, with these contradictory images of self. He can retrace, seeking for further connection and integration, the path of his soul, traversing, as Hegel put it, the series of its own stages of embodiment, like stages appointed for it by its own nature. He had already done so, in a highly fictionalized and displaced account, with Scrooge;[30] he had moved closer to the past with Paul Dombey, closer still with the autobiographical fragment; and he had at least set up a therapeutic model in the moral of *The Haunted Man*.

Events conspired to help him further. The enormous financial success of *Dombey* permitted Dickens, for the first time in his career, to choose the timing and subject of his next serial. Immersed in this quest to comprehend how all things worked to make him what he was, he continued the search in the book that became, significantly enough, his "favourite child." And once again, as so often in Dickens' life, John Forster made a crucial suggestion. Why not try a first person point of view? Dickens had attempted it once before, with Master Humphrey's "Personal Adventures," and found the multiple confinements so restrictive that he abandoned the fiction at the end of the third chapter of *The Old Curiosity Shop* with the clumsiest artistic ruthlessness of his entire life.[31] Now Forster's idea offered a perfect way to deal with the ambivalences of Dickens' understanding and perspective. The autobiography of a fictional character permitted him to establish a *cordon sanitaire* between the "I" of David and the "I" of Dickens; and a novel of the personal history and experiences of a child growing up could incorporate both the child's perceptions and the adult's. The divisions of *Dombey* and the autobiographical fragment were at a stroke resolved.

"Deepest despondency, as usual, in commencing, besets me," Dickens told Forster as he wrestled with selecting a name for his new work.[32] Whereas ordinary novels can wait to be christened until they are born, serial publications are delivered piecemeal, name first so that an advertising campaign can commence; then the "general drift" so that the illustrator can design a wrapper; then some number plans so that the "general drift" is spaced out across the quite exact number of pages, lines, and words of the whole; then the opening chapters; and only two years or so later, some nineteen months after publication of the first installment, do the conclusion and the preface get written. Naming the unborn child thus becomes unusually difficult and important; to a large extent the entire subsequent text is generated in idea and language from the title.

The first versions promised a return to the humorous Dickens of *Pickwick,* though they were open to the "difficulty of being 'too comic, my boy.' " *Mag's Diversions* was glossed as "Being the personal history of / MR. THOMAS MAG THE YOUNGER, / Of Blunderstone House." Then Thomas became David, and "personal history" expanded to "Personal History, Adventures, Experience, and Observation." Suddenly, via nickname, Mag underwent a sex change, emerging almost unrecognized as Aunt Betsey: "Mr. David Copperfield the Younger and his great-aunt Margaret." That metamorphosis is replicated in the novel in David's repeated transformation into Betsey Trotwood Copperfield.

"You will see that [I have given up] *Mag* altogether, and refer exclusively to one name—that which I last sent you," Dickens wrote to Forster on 26 February 1849. That "one name" was David Copperfield, who as "the Younger" possesses in many ways the potential to grow into a duplicate of his unfortunate father, David Copperfield the Elder, whose accomplishments during his brief life are all too well expressed in the name of his abode, Blunderstone House, Lodge, or Rookery (without rooks, of course). The next set of six titles sent with this letter establishes a second, and equally important, fiction. Three of them explicitly denote the book as the record of a completed life, and the other three titles, by implication or Dickens' suggested modifications, seem to share that notion too. What sort of precedent existed for novels that end not with marriage and happy-ever-aftering, but with death? Newgate novels: the outgrowth of confession, the picaresque, eighteenth-century sensationalist broadside publications, and nineteenth-century concern (Godwin, Bulwer, Dickens) with the origin of evil.[33] The third of Dickens' new batch of provisional titles makes the association between the orphaned child and the condemned man plain: "*The Last Living Speech and Confession of David Copperfield, Junior,* of Blunderstone Lodge, who was never executed at the Old Bailey."

Dickens piles reversal on reversal. A comic Newgate novel becomes possible if the protagonist, like Oliver and unlike Fagin, is "never executed." The life forms a comic whole, in Northrop Frye's terms. The patterns are complete only at the moment of death, yet an autobiography cannot be composed in an instant—the understanding obtained, the events selected, their significance ascribed, and the just conclusions reached, during the death rattle.[34] Further, there is something odd about publishing a personal history, something about making the private public that implies dishonesty, deliberate shaping, even fraud. The pattern might be imposed on, not discovered in, the events. So the subtitles insist that the novel is "his personal history found among his papers," or "his personal history left as a legacy," or that "he never meant [the papers] to be published on any account."

The biggest reversal of all, one that accounts for these others, took place when Dickens settled on Copperfield: "I doubt whether I could, on the whole, get a better name." For, as Forster pointed out to a "much startled" auditor, David's initials are Dickens' in reverse. Upon learning this odd fact, Dickens "protested it was just in keeping with the fates and chances which were always befalling him. 'Why else,' he said, 'should I so obstinately have kept to that name when once it turned up?' " Why else, indeed. It was not any abstract fate or chance. David the Younger (as child) is the reverse of Dickens the writer as adult, and so is the experience of Dickens as child playing adult epitomized by the reverse letters MOOR-EEFFOC. Projection, compensation, displacement, splitting or doubling, reverse psychology —call it what you will,[35] the fact remains that Dickens found in these inversions, reversals, and splits into doubled characters, sexes, and perspectives, these reformulations of past experience that affect everything from the alphabet and language to the fiction of a completed life written from incompletion, an artistically and psychologically satisfying way of resolving tensions, of creating a new child that would incorporate the old one but convert defeat into victory.

David is not Dickens. Forster shrewdly anticipates much twentieth-century criticism on autobiographical transformation when he warns that it would be a mistake to suppose Dickens came out of his "first harsh schooling in life . . . as little harmed or hardened as David did." And he identifies the fundamental difference between the two, a difference inherent in the radical discontinuity between language and life: "The language of the fiction reflects only faintly the narrative of the actual fact."[36] Forster understands that the fiction is shaped by generic expectations and by the tradition, that the effort to communicate involves transmuting the individual and transient into the general and permanent through myth embedded in language and structure. He perceives *that*, and *how*, David Copperfield finds his place in his own, not Dickens', story:

> The character of the hero of the novel finds indeed his right place in the story he is supposed to tell, rather by unlikeness than by likeness to Dickens, even where intentional resemblance might seem to be prominent. Take autobiography as a design to show that any man's life may be as a mirror of existence to all men, and the individual career becomes altogether secondary to the variety of experiences received and rendered back in it.[37]

Forster's comment goes to the heart of another organizing principle that Dickens discovered in his naming of the novel. In the subtitles he expands "personal history" to include "Adventures, Experience, and Observation" for the wrapper design, but conflates the paired terms to "Personal History and Experience" for the text headings. As Forster observes, the "individual career" ("history") is "altogether secondary" to the "variety of experiences": the facts, in autobiography, less important than the way they are taken, the significance they are accorded.[38] Thus "Personal History and Experience" divides the narrative from the general stream of language and event through "personal," and further divides fact from feeling, event from signification, objective from subjective, external from internal. The adult who as child had experienced sequentially through time and simultaneously in any instant his history and his experience divides the two up in his retrospective fiction: such and such happened, such and such is the way I felt. That division allows events to be seen in at least four different lights: first, by the child David Copperfield the Younger, who organizes and interprets experience in terms of hopeful forward *telea,* fairy-tales about future becoming;[39] second (and infrequently), by the adult David Copperfield the Elder, who never outgrows his foolish and impractical hopes; third, by the adult David Copperfield the Younger, who after replicating his father's errors grows further, and by organizing and interpreting experience in a different way, by looking backward, discovers in Switzerland an emerging *telos* concealed in his past life that permits him to compose a fiction making his beginnings concurrent with his ends; and fourth, by Charles Dickens the author, whose understanding of his life and his work emerges in the writing.[40] The child and child-like man, innocent, imagine the future; the adult writers, experienced, interpret the past. The same event may be seen as having alternate significations: Emily's dream of becoming a lady; Steerforth asleep, lying with his head upon his arm; David/Doady's child bride.

By separating "History" from "Experience" Dickens obtains a double principle of selectivity, one that is both psychological and thematic. He can recount those passages in David's life (and his own) which explain the present of the writer, not merely supply an undifferentiated history. And these incidents will be not only selected but also narrated in terms of their significance as understood by the crossed rays of the child's intelligence and the narrator's. Hence the extraordinary interplay of tones, of precise focus and blur of feeling, of incidents followed by the haze of "Retrospect," and of the poignant tension between the child's hopes and adult knowledge.

IV

Victorian novels are about ends: whatever sense of direction or purpose can be salvaged from experience.

—*Alexander Welsh*

So far, so good. Dickens imaginatively resolved all the
subsidiary problems by the decision to write a first person
novel about the history and experience of someone else.
Yet the major problem remained, to be worked out in the
writing: how to understand his own past well enough to
connect the child-figure to the adult, David Copperfield the
Younger to David Copperfield the writer. Whether Dickens
consciously intended it to or not, *David Copperfield* dramatizes and enacts the writer's coming into adequacy
through writing. Not only does the character become an
adequate writer, but also he becomes a hero, if at all,
through the writing of his life.

But Dickens, possessing no sure conclusion at the beginning of his story, aware in his own life of no certain
telos connecting past to present, starts the novel with perhaps the most open beginning in all literature, the declara-
tive sentence least constitutive of self-creation in any first-
person work: "Whether I shall turn out to be the hero of
my own life, or whether that station will be held by anybody else, these pages must show."[41] At the beginning,
meaning is radically indeterminate.

It is so for many reasons. Because the personal history,
at the moment of birth, is unlived, only potential. But since
it is only a convention of the fiction that the life is yet to
be lived, it being narrated after all by the survivor, the
sentence takes on meaning at a deeper level. Beyond the
convention that the future is open is the fact that its significance
remains undetermined even after living. What does the experience of that history amount to? Is David the hero, or
someone else? Is he the master of his fate and captain of
his soul, or product of the forces that shape his being and
his options? Has he acted or been acted upon?

There is yet a third level of indeterminacy hiding behind
the other two. For the decision about David's place as hero
rests not with the narrator who identifies an emerging
telos, but with the book itself: "these pages must show."
Does heroism reside in the character acting, in the narrator evaluating, or in the book as art? Dickens seems to open
the door not only to Conrad's baffling question whether hero-

ism depends on the doer (stoic or warrior) or on the interpreter, but even further, to unanswerable, nearly imponderable, speculations. *David Copperfield* as text defines David Copperfield as hero heuristically, but in a mysterious and disappointing way it defines neither David Copperfield nor heroism. The questions and answers remain teasingly and obstinately posed between the covers of the book.

The hermeneutic character of literature[42] is not addressed directly, however, until the novel's conclusion, when Dickens closes David's story and life with the extinguishing of the writer's lamp, transferring light and life from the fiction of life ("realities . . . melting . . . like the shadows") to the reality of the Christian soul: "Oh Agnes, oh my soul, so may thy face be by me when I close my life indeed; so may I, when realities are melting from me like the shadows which I now dismiss, still find thee near me, pointing upward!" The more immediate problem to work out is the secondary level of David's fate, whether, and in what sense, he is a hero.

Every portent is ambiguous. He is born at midnight, poised between Friday's and Saturday's child, unlucky and privileged, with a caul to protect him from shipwreck which may be the universal lot of man; posthumous, virtually motherless, hastened into the world by a bad fairy godmother who would deny his sexuality and identity from the start; nursed by a mother-substitute also named Clara who is comic but socially ineffective; threatened by a virile hairy stepfather associated with a biting dog (no friendly crocodile), whose existence seems purposed to punish the child for seeking physical and spiritual nourishment from a true parent. The caul is put up for sale but not sold, then ten years later raffled to an old lady whose proudest boast was "that she never had been on the water in her life, except upon a bridge"; and it is a remarkable fact that she died at ninety-two in her bed, and was never drowned.

Fact and signification remain perplexingly dissociated, while the imagination longs to bring them into concord. The old lady attacks "the impiety of mariners and others, who had the presumption to go 'meandering' about the world," saying, no matter what objections were raised to her prejudice, "Let us have no meandering."[43] Yet most, David included, are not able to live without travelling, cannot avoid risking their lives in journeys. Travel across water has been the archetype of the soul's progress from Biblical times to Jung. The narrator of *David Copperfield* immediately (and persistently) connects the journey across water literally and spiritually through life to the journey through language: "Not to meander myself, at present, I will go back to my birth."

Life and language may be coterminous and congruent; indeed life in some senses may not exist without the language of its experiencing. Thus David's life is the product of his fiction as Charles' is of his, in ways that are almost too complex and redundant to discriminate. The writer learns to make his reality through language, and learns that language makes, constitutes, possibly *is* reality. He becomes adequate through fictions of his adequacy; he becomes his own self-creating father and son, defining heroism to suit his condition.

One thing novelist and novel do is to examine the inadequacy of the fairy-tale *telea* David projects as a child: virtually every one of the hopeful futures dreamed by the characters—David, Emily, Ham, Peggotty, Steerforth, Rosa, the Heeps, the Wickfields—proves in time illusory, vain. The uneducated children turn out to be blind, conceited, unprepared, undisciplined.[44] Yet exiled in Switzerland the writer David discovers in the disappointment of expectations, through Agnes' letters, an emergent *telos* that makes him what he is and the book what it is: "As the endurance of my childish days had done its part to make me what I was, so greater calamities would nerve me on, to be yet better than I was; and so, as they had taught me, would I teach others."[45] He resolves to resume his pen, and working patiently and hard he composes "a Story, with a purpose growing, not remotely, out of my experience."[46]

Insofar as that fiction is *David Copperfield*, it is important to note that the novel incorporates Dickens' autobiographical fragment, which is now ultimately perceived in the structure as one of many times when the fictional protagonist re-creates himself in isolation, "abandoned and despairing, make[s] another Beginning,"[47] and discovers in that re-creation a power that renews life in those moments when he is afflicted by "a hopeless consciousness of all that I had lost—love, friendship, interest; of all that had been shattered —my first trust, my first affection, the whole airy castle of my life; of all that remained—a ruined blank and waste, lying wide around me, unbroken, to the dark horizon."[48] By joining the autobiographical fragment to other fragments, Dickens establishes the radical continuity between devitalized child and surviving adult, failure and success, wish and fulfillment.

Finally, Dickens can confront apocalypse: Emily's ruin, Steerforth's and Ham's deaths, Dora's fatal incompetence, his own shipwrecked hope. Out of that confrontation he develops his thesis about identity, the alternate *telos*, and the novel. That he and David together connect their ends with their beginnings triumphantly testifies to Dickens' understanding, at last, how all these things have worked together. In his search, his journey, however, he is sustained by a faith (a "caul"), a belief that in essence he has never ceased to be a sponsored child, the son of God. It was "the mercy of God" that preserved Dickens from becoming a thief; and he shares with Paul Dombey that radical transvaluation of values which is the Christian's consolation. The various inadequate women, from Clara Copperfield to Dora, who seem to preside over David's fate, are eventually replaced by Agnes and the recognition that she has supplied the real and lasting protection and encouragement. And what she stands for, as we have seen, becomes an extra-literary confirmation of David's identity.[49]

Thus, in his own act of writing, David/Dickens himself creates the world of his desire and discovers for himself and us its design and meaning. He unfolds the hero from his indeterminacy, discloses the writer in the name. The self-creating fantasies of the child become the self-fulfilling fictions of the adult, who in remaking his own child not in his image becomes a type of the creator whose works never die.

1.   A common observation, it is made with unusual clarity and pertinence by Kathleen Tillotson in "The Middle Years from the *Carol* to *Copperfield*," *Dickens Memorial Lectures 1970*, supplement to the September 1970 *Dickensian*, pp. [5]–19.

2.   *Letters*, ed. Walter Dexter, 3 vols. (Bloomsbury: The Nonesuch Press, 1938), I, 680–81. Hereafter cited as Nonesuch *Letters*.

3.   John Forster, *The Life of Charles Dickens*, ed. J.W.T. Ley (New York: Doubleday, Doran and Company, [1928]), VI, ii, 479; hereafter cited as Forster by book, chapter, and page.

4.   *See* Appendix B of *Dombey and Son*, ed. Alan Horsman (Oxford: Clarendon Press, 1974), p. 837. All citations are to this text of the novel.

5.   Forster, I, ii, 27 and 33.

6.   *See* the conjectures of James T. Fields and William J. Carleton summarized by Horsman, p. xxv.

7.   *Ibid.*

8.   Chapter viii, p. 100.

9.   Chapter viii, p. 99.

10.   On Oliver's struggle to find nurturing parents, *see* my article on "Capitalism and Compassion in *Oliver Twist*," *Studies in the Novel*, 1 (1969), 207–21.

11.   Chapter viii, p. 101.

12.   Chapter viii, p. 104.

13.   Forster, VI, ii, 478. Both versions of this plate are reproduced in Horsman's recent Clarendon edition of *Dombey and Son* (*see* note 4 above).

14.   *Ibid.*

15.   Chapter viii, pp. 104–105.

16.   Cf. Horsman, p. xxv: "Dickens's disappointment . . . with [the illustration] . . . may show him thinking as much of the reality for himself as of the actual plate."

17.   Chapter viii, p. 91.

18.   Dickens to Bulwer Lytton, 5 January 1851: "Assumption [of roles] has charms for me—I hardly know for how many wild reasons—so delightful, that I feel a loss of, oh! I can't say what exquisite foolery, when I lose a chance of being someone in voice, etc. not at all like myself" (Nonesuch *Letters*, II, 262).

19.   Mamie Dickens, *My Father as I Recall Him* (New York: E.P. Dutton & Co., [n.d.] (published as *Charles Dickens by His Eldest Daughter* [Mary Dickens]), London: Cassell, 1885), pp. 47–49:

> During our life at Tavistock House [1851–60], I had a long and serious illness, with an almost equally long convalescence. During the latter, my father suggested that I should be carried every day into his study to remain with him, and, although I was fearful of disturbing him, he assured me that he desired to have me with him. On one of these mornings, I was lying on the sofa endeavouring to keep perfectly quiet, while my father wrote busily and rapidly at his desk, when he suddenly jumped from his chair and rushed to a mirror which hung near, and in which I could see the reflection of some extraordinary facial contortions which he was making. He returned rapidly to his desk, wrote furiously for a few moments, and then

went again to the mirror. The facial pantomime was resumed, and then turning toward, but evidently not seeing, me, he began talking rapidly in a low voice. Ceasing this soon, however, he returned once more to his desk, where he remained silently writing until luncheon time. It was a most curious experience for me, and one of which, I did not until later years, fully appreciate the purport. Then I knew that with his natural intensity he had thrown himself completely into the character that he was creating, and that for the time being he had not only lost sight of his surroundings, but had actually become in action, as in imagination, the creature of his pen.

20. Again an observation common to many critics and especially well put by Kathleen Tillotson, *"Dombey and Son," Novels of the Eighteen-Forties* (Oxford: Clarendon Press, 1954), pp. 157–201.

21. Forster, I, ii, 23.

22. The fragment is printed in Forster, I, ii, 24–35, from which the subsequent quotations are taken. After this essay was completed in the fall of 1975 I profited from the counsel of Professors Albert D. Hutter, Wesley A. Morris, and Branwen Bailey Pratt, and was able to read, but not incorporate, these excellent and complementary essays on Dickens and autobiography: Barbara Charlesworth Gelpi, "The Innocent I: Dickens' Influence on Victorian Autobiography," in *The Worlds of Victorian Fiction*, ed. Jerome H. Buckley (Cambridge, Mass.: Harvard University Press, 1975), pp. 57–71; Avrom Fleishman, "The Fictions of Autobiographical Fiction," *Genre*, 9 (Spring 1976), 73–86; Albert D. Hutter, "Psychoanalysis and Biography: Dickens' Experience at Warren's Blacking," *Hartford Studies in Literature*, 8 (1976), 23–37; Sylvia Manning, "Masking and Self-Revelation: Dickens's Three Autobiographies," *DSN*, 7 (September 1976), 69–75; and Branwen Bailey Pratt, "Dickens and Father: Notes on the Family Romance," *Hartford Studies in Literature*, 8 (1976), 4–22.

23. Note that the name Poll was applied to a barber whose prototype, as J.W. T. Ley points out, may have been "a very odd old barber out of Dean-street, Soho, who was never tired of reviewing the events of the last war, and especially of detecting Napoleon's mistakes, and rearranging his whole life for him on a plan of his own. The boy [Dickens] wrote a description of this old barber, but never had courage to show it" (Forster, I, i, 12 and *fn.* 28, p. 22).

24. K. J. Fielding says that while David Copperfield blames his stepfather, "Dickens blamed his parents" (*Charles Dickens: A Critical Introduction*, 2nd edn., rev. (Boston: Houghton Mifflin Co., 1964), p. 5. That may be true of his mother's attempt to return him to the factory, but the remarkable fact about the fragment is that even Dickens seems to recognize how un- (not ir-) responsible his parents were; when he remonstrated to his father about lodging in more congenial surroundings during this period, John Dickens "began to think that it was not quite right. I do believe he had never thought so before, or thought about it. It was the first remonstrance I had ever made about my lot, and perhaps it opened up a little more than I intended" (Forster, I, ii, 29). Eventually he moved to Mrs. Roylance's. However, Professors Pratt and Hutter wisely caution me that this statement may also be a defensive maneuver, possibly to defuse Dickens' more painful and deeper feelings that he was not so much neglected as actively *unloved* for some act (Oedipal replacement?) he secretly wished to commit, possibly because Dickens cannot, especially after the partial reconciliation with his father by 1846, bring himself overtly to damn John.

25. Charles Dickens, *Bleak House* (London: Oxford University Press, 1948, The New Oxford Illustrated Dickens), Chapter xlvii, p. 649.

26. *See* my discussion of institutionalized charity in "Capitalism and Compassion in *Oliver Twist*."

27. Forster, VI, iv, 508. A fuller discussion of *The Haunted Man* and the function of memory may be found in my essay " 'A Surprising Transformation':

Dickens and the Hearth," in U.C. Knoepflmacher and G. B. Tennyson, eds., *Nature and the Victorian Imagination* (Berkeley and Los Angeles: University of California Press, 1977), pp. 153-70.

28.   Forster, VI, iv, 509.

29.   Forster, I, ii, 26.

30.   Robert L. Patten, "Dickens Time and Again," *Dickens Studies Annual*, ed. Robert B. Partlow, Jr., Vol. 2 (Carbondale and Edwardsville: Southern Illinois University Press; London and Amsterdam: Feffer & Simons, Inc., 1972), 163-96.

31.   This draconian step caused him insuperable difficulties at the novel's conclusion, as I discuss in " 'The Story-Weaver at His Loom': Dickens and the Beginning of *The Old Curiosity Shop*," *Dickens the Craftsman: Strategies of Presentation*, ed. Robert B. Partlow, Jr. (Carbondale and Edwardsville: Southern Illinois University Press; London and Amsterdam: Feffer & Simons, Inc., 1970), pp. 44-64.

32.   Forster, VI, vi, 524; all subsequent quotations concerning Dickens' names for his novel come from this or the succeeding page.

33.   Cf. Keith Hollingsworth, *The Newgate Novel 1830-1847* (Detroit: Wayne State University Press, 1963), though it has been supplemented in various ways by succeeding articles on more specialized aspects of the topic.

34.   *See* the brilliant comments by J. Hillis Miller in "Three Problems of Fictional Form: First-Person Narration in *David Copperfield* and *Huckeberry Finn*," an English Institute essay printed in *Experience in the Novel*, ed. Roy Harvey Pearce (New York and London: Columbia University Press, 1968), pp. 21-48. Miller's remarks are fairly general and structuralist, drawing little from the novel itself and nothing from previous treatments of the autobiographical material; at the end of his discussion, he expands on the significance of Agnes, first treated in his earlier book on Dickens (*see fn.* 49 below). My remarks, therefore, are to some extent to be seen as an elaboration of Miller's, although they developed out of rather different initial impulses.

35.   And some of these terms have been used or implied in psychological discussions of the novel from Forster to Edgar Johnson, *Charles Dickens: His Tragedy and Triumph*, 2 vols. (New York: Simon and Schuster, 1952); Leonard F. Manheim, "The Personal History of *David Copperfield*," *American Imago*, 9 (1953), 21-43; and Mark Spilka, "*David Copperfield* as Psychological Fiction," *Critical Quarterly*, 1 (1959), 292-301. For more literary, less psychological explanations of Dickens' autobiographical transformations, *see* Philip Collins, " 'David Copperfield': 'A Very Complicated Interweaving of Truth and Fiction,' " *Essays and Studies* n.s. 23 (1970), 71-86.

36.   Forster, VI, vii, 553.

37.   Forster, VI, vii, 553-54.

38.   Cf. J. Hillis Miller's comments in this regard during his brief discussion of *David Copperfield* in *Charles Dickens: The World of His Novels* (Cambridge, Mass.: Harvard University Press, 1959), pp. 150-59.

39.   For an authoritative analysis of the novel's fairy tales, *see* Harry Stone, "Fairy Tales and Ogres: Dickens' Imagination and *David Copperfield*," *Criticism*, 6 (1964), 324-30.

40.   The reader will recognize my extensive debt to Frank Kermode, *The Sense of an Ending* (New York: Oxford University Press, 1967).

41.   *David Copperfield* (London: Oxford University Press, 1948, The New Oxford Illustrated Dickens), p. 1. All citations are to this text of the novel. Contrast *Moby Dick*'s opening: "Call me Ishmael."

42.   By hermeneutics I intend not only the traditional sense of acts of interpretation, but also the sense articulated by Heidegger in his late dialogue of "the bearing of message and tidings" ("A Dialogue on Language," (1953/54) in

On the Way to Language, trans. Peter D. Hertz (New York: Harper & Row, 1971), p. 29).

' 43. Chapter i, p. 2.

44. On the undisciplined heart *see* the classic essay by Gwendolyn B. Needham, "The Undisciplined Heart of David Copperfield," *NCF*, 9 (1954), 81–107.

45. Chapter lviii, p. 815.

46. Chapter lviii, p. 816.

47. Title of Chapter xv, the "another" referring to the title of Chapter i, "I am Born," and that of Chapter xi, "I begin Life on my own Account, and don't like it." David Copperfield boy and novel both contain an extraordinary number of false starts on the journey through life. Mr. Peggotty makes "The Beginning of a Long Journey" seeking Emily after her false start in Chapter xxxii, and the trip of all the Peggotty entourage to Australia is "The Beginning of a Longer Journey" (Chapter li). Both "Return" (Chapter lix) as a physical journey and "Retrospect" (Chapters xviii, xliii, liii, and lxiv) as an emotional one through feeling and memory complement and eventually complete these voyages.

48. Chapter lviii, p. 813.

49. Miller, *Charles Dickens: The World of His Novels*, p. 157.

FREDERICK KIRCHHOFF

Travel as Anti-Autobiography:
William Morris's *Icelandic Journals**

William Morris visited Iceland in the summers of 1871 and
1873, keeping a personal record of both expeditions. He
revised the journal of the first voyage in the spring of 1873,
but, not insignificantly, could never bring himself to publish it, and he finally gave the manuscript of the revised
journal to Georgiana Burne-Jones, one of the few people
with whom he seems to have felt free to discuss his private
life.[1] The fragmentary 1873 "Diary" was left unrevised, its
final entries being little more than jottings. Although I shall
take up the question of the relationship between these two
documents, this essay chiefly concerns itself with the carefully wrought 1871 *Journal.*

Morris' use of the journal format has particular interest
to anyone concerned with Victorian writings about the self,
since they reveal him writing what we may well term "anti-
autobiography." The *Icelandic Journals,* in other words,
show Morris attempting to present deeply personal experience in an impersonal, "objective" mode. This notion of
"anti-autobiography" is substantiated by the relationship
between the experience of Iceland, the written *Journals,*
and the larger contexts of Morris' private life and intellectual development. Specifically, the two expeditions to Iceland coincide with the crisis in Morris' marriage, the begin-

*   I wish to thank the National Endowment for the Humanities for making
possible the Summer Seminar in connection with which this essay was completed,
and U. C. Knoepflmacher, director of the Seminar, for his suggestions and encouragement. For some apt criticisms of the manuscript, I am also grateful to my
colleague George Dillon.

292

ning of his break with Rossetti, and the turning point in his evolution as a poet and citizen.[2] Whether seen as an escape from England or a kind of secular retreat, the trips were responses to this multiple crisis in his life, and the *Journals* are both a record of these responses and an attempt to perceive an order in them. They are thus autobiographical expressions comparable to the artistic presentations of similar crises central to so many nineteenth-century literary autobiographies. Where Morris' self-confrontation differs is that it takes the form of an "objective" response to the Icelandic landscape. His introspection is contained and thus controlled by the "short swallow flights" of his daily journal entries. The *Journals* are anti-autobiography because they provide Morris with this alternative to conventional autobiographical self-examination, and as such they remind us that there were Victorians averse to the prolonged self-consciousness, however artfully arranged, of literary autobiography.

Morris had been fascinated with the North at least since his years at Oxford, but his visit to the island was a direct response to the intense study of Icelandic literature he had begun under the tutelage of Magnússon in 1868.[3] Morris travelled North in search of a world in which history and poetry are integrated with a timeless landscape. Nor was he disappointed. In his Preface to Volume I of *The Saga Library* (1891), Morris was able to contrast "the greater part of Europe" where "all knowledge of their historical past has faded from the memory of the people, and the last vestiges of their pre-historical memories are rapidly disappearing," with his first-hand experience of Iceland, where "every homestead, one may almost say every field, has its well-remembered history, and no peasant, however poor his surroundings may be, is ignorant of the traditions of his country, or dull to them; so that a journey in Iceland to the traveller read in its ancient literature is a continual illusion, freely and eagerly offered, of the books which contain the intimate history of its ancient folk."[4]

Insofar as Iceland represents an earlier stage in European civilization, Morris' journey is a return in historical time.

But it is also a return to his own past analogous to the backwards thrust of classic autobiography. The dominant mood
of his journey is innocence. He is a young bachelor once
more, seeing the world with fresh eyes. And there is a complementary boyishness in his carryings-on. He tells how
when exploring the Faroes, "we drank unlimited milk, and
then turned back up the slopes, but lay down a little way off
the house, and ate and drank, thoroughly comfortable, and
enjoying the rolling about in the fresh grass prodigiously."[5]
"Horseplay" (p. 43), spasms of "inextinguishable laughter"
(pp. 76, 79, 88), and frank quarreling (pp. 102, 156) characterize the interplay between the travellers. Morris writes
about himself with a keen sense of comic self-parody,
creating an autobiographical persona that is notably
unheroic. He dramatizes his "cockney" ineptitude, which
precipitates, among other things, a memorable "series of
losses"—first of his tin pannikin (p. 33), then of one of his
slippers (p. 35), later of the haversack containing his journal
notes and spare pipe (p. 87), and, near the end of the expedition, of the oars of a boat he was supposed to have been row-
ing (p. 176).[6] On the other hand, the circumstances give him
an opportunity to prove his skill as a cook, and the *Journal*
balances his clumsiness in riding and climbing—because, as
an Icelandic priest frankly explained, "you know you are so
fat" (p. 161)—with a series of well-made stews.

But his journey is more than a pilgrimage to the "land of
the sagas" and more than a return to schoolboy innocence.
It is also an act of putting himself quite literally in a world
defined for him by its narrative art. Thus, the Icelandic *Journals* represent a stage of self-confrontation in his development as a poet. As a consequence, despite the number of
"official" justifications for the trip, Morris can never be altogether clear about his reasons for going to Iceland.
Accepting the uncertainty of his own gesture is essential to
the meaning of the journey: he must open himself to the
unexpected and even the undesired.

His poem "Iceland First Seen" (contemporary with the
Journals) makes this uncertainty *thematic:*

> Ah! what came we forth for to see
> that our hearts are so hot with desire?
> Is it enough for our rest,
> the sight of this desolate strand,
> And the mountain-waste voiceless as death
> but for winds that may sleep not nor tire?

The answer to this question is only to be found in the experience of Iceland itself. Morris suspects it may have something to do with "the treasures of old" beneath its soil and the "tale of the Northland of old" he associates with its barren landscape. But the voice of Iceland rejects these simple explanations:

> "Not for this nor for that was I wrought
> Amid waning of realms and of riches
> and death of things worshipped and sure,
> I abide here the spouse of a God,
> and I made and I make and endure."

This statement of faith, while not a very direct answer to the poet's initial question, enables him to respond with a finer sense of what it is that fascinates him with the Northern landscape:

> O Queen of the grief without knowledge,
> of the courage that may not avail,
> Of the longing that may not attain,
> of the love that shall never forget,
> More joy than the gladness of laughter
> thy voice hath amidst of its wail:
> More hope than of pleasure fulfilled
> amidst of thy blindness is set;
> More glorious than gaining of all
> thine unfaltering hand that shall fail:
> For what is the mark on thy brow
> but the brand that thy Brynhild doth bear?
> Lone once, and loved and undone
> by a love that no ages outwear.

The "mark" on Iceland's brow is reminiscent of Cain's. A pagan world, long resistant to Judeo-Christian "civilization," Iceland attracts Morris because the land itself is an outsider, like its own Brynhild, "Lone once, and loved and undone."

Iceland, in other words, has much in common with Morris himself in 1871. He, too, is a man temperamentally isolated from his fellows. He, too, has loved and been undone. He, too, believes himself bound to a heroic past whose vestiges are a few broken artifacts and a handful of all-but-forgotten tales. But Iceland endures isolation and failure, and as a consequence she can know herself "the spouse of a God"— Baldur, as the poem later explains, who will someday return, bearing "from the heart of the Sun/Peace and the healing of Pain." The Wanderers of *The Earthly Paradise* (the final volume of which Morris published in 1870) found in art an escapist amelioration of suffering. Iceland rejects this solution of the sixties by offering Morris an alternative in self-fulfillment through labor ("I made and I make and endure") and in stoic acceptance of pain. Significantly, Morris' first narrative poem after the 1871 expedition was *Love is Enough* (1873), in which Pharamond's refusal to abandon what he acknowledges a failed quest results in his spousal with the dream-maiden Azalais is a setting reminiscent of the Icelandic landscape. Like Iceland, Pharamond is rewarded for his endurance, in the face of apparent hopelessness, with a divine marriage.

But this bare formula of acceptance and reward oversimplifies the significance of Iceland to Morris. His *Icelandic Journals* record the actual experience of this suffering, literally in the hazards of travel, empathetically in his response to Iceland and its people. The *Journals* recapitulate the quest of the Wanderers, but with the initial recognition that Nature does not provide the geological setting for any "Earthly Paradises." Thus, Morris' expedition to Iceland revises the escapism of *The Earthly Paradise*: it confronts the self-pitying aesthetic of the sixties poem with the reality of an Earthly Purgatory. But it also confronts the poet himself. Insofar as Iceland embodies elements of his own personality and circumstances, the *Journals* record a quest for self-knowledge whose closest analogues are Romantic poems of autobiographical confrontation like

The Prelude, in which we are offered a collection of symbolic journeys, and *The Fall of Hyperion*, whose Moneta bears a strong resemblance to the "Iceland" of Morris' poem. The journey to Iceland is a gesture that forces, that demands self-confrontation, and his mood on setting forth betrays as much anxiety as expectation: "I felt as if I should have been glad of any accident that had kept me at home, yet now it would have seemed unbearable to sleep in London another night" (p. 1).

* * *

The artistic dimension to Morris' quest is explicit in the first journal entries. The countryside after York is "dull and undramatic," but as the train takes him farther north, "the country gets cleaner"—an adjective he applies again and again to Iceland itself—and at last, with the sight of Holy Island and the North Sea, the landscape becomes "poetical-looking" (p. 2). The valleys of Scotland, which he was seeing for the first time, have "a wonderfully poetical character about them; not a bit like one's idea of Scotland, but rather like one's imagination of what the backgrounds to the border ballads ought to be" (p. 3). Although modern Edinburgh "must have been an impressive and poetical place" at one time it is now "very doleful" because "the poetry is pretty much gone" (p. 3). This concern for the poetic or imaginative aspect of landscape disappears in the details of ship-boarding and seasickness, but returns once Morris reaches the Faroes, his "first sight of a really northern land," whose "wild strange hills and narrow sounds . . . had something, I don't know what, of poetic and attractive about them" (pp. 11-12). Viewed from a mountain ridge, the islands' central firth seemed "like nothing I had ever seen, but strangely like my old imaginations of places for sea-wanderers to come to" (p. 14). The whole place touches him with "the air of romanticism" (p. 14), and an isolated farm strikes him as "a most beautiful and poetical place" (p. 15).

But the "poetry" of the Faroes is qualified by another, equally significant response. His "first sight of a really northern land" confronts Morris with a Nature "not savage but mournfully empty and barren" (p. 11). Having called Kirkiuboe farm "a most beautiful and poetical place," he goes on to acknowledge it "more remote and melancholy than I can say, in spite of the flowers and grass and bright sun: it looked as if you might live for a hundred years before you would ever see ship sailing into the bay there; as if the old life of the saga-time had gone, and the modern life never reached the place" (p. 15). Thus the relationship between the northern landscape and its poetic past is essentially elegiac. Like Keats' Grecian Urn, the hills and firths of the Faroes maintain their continuity with the past at the cost of full life in the present. Morris' search for a world in which timeless nature is infused with a timeless human imagination leads him to confront a barren landscape, where Kirkiuboe farm stands fixed in a no man's land "between two worlds, one dead, the other powerless to be born."

But the significant dualism in Morris' vision of the North is not a function of history but of the natural world itself. Although the word "poetic" is never felt so strongly as in the first pages of the 1871 *Journal*, Morris' experience of the Faroes is the prototype of his experience of the North as a whole, for expectations of "poetic" beauty continually give way to a recognition of the profoundly alien nature of the landscape, which in turn gives way to the experience of a new, more chastened sense of the sublime. Morris' wonderful account of leaving the Faroes exemplifies this pattern:

> I turned to look ahead as the ship met the first of the swell in the open sea, and when I looked astern a very few minutes after, I could see nothing at all of the gates we had come out by, no slopes of grass, or valleys opening out from the shore; nothing but a terrible wall of rent and furrowed rocks, the little clouds still entangled here and there about the tops of them: here the wall would be rent from top to bottom and its two sides would yawn as if they would have fallen asunder, here it was buttressed with great masses of stone that had slipped from its top; there it ran up into all manner of causeless-looking spikes: there was no beach below the wall, no foam breaking at its feet. It was midnight now and everything was grey and colourless and shadowless, yet there was light enough in the clear air to see every cranny and nook of the rocks, and in the north-east now the grey sky began to get a little lighter with dawn. I stood near the stern and looked backward a long time till the coast, which had seemed a great

crescent when we came out of the sound, was now a long flat line, and so then I went to bed, with the sky brightening quickly (pp. 17–18).

Taken as personal history, this passage is simply a factual rendering of Morris' experience. But read as literary autobiography, the description is deeply suggestive. Morris turns to renew his pleasure in the embracing openness of the natural world—an enclosing space akin to that in Wordsworth's "Home at Grasmere"—only to discover the gate closed, no longer even recognizable as a gate, and the hospitable landscape transformed into an image of "causeless" material force precipitating "grey and colourless" ruin. But on closer scrutiny this "midnight" vision yields first to an almost preternatural clarity and then to the light of dawn itself. The perception that Nature is empty and fundamentally inhuman enables Morris to respond with detached, chastened pleasure to a beauty characterized by brightness without warmth.

Morris' experience of the Faroes is echoed in his day-by-day account of the Icelandic terrain, in which beauty is inseparable from desolation. From his first sight of the island, these elements are intermingled: "the sky darkened overhead, but there was a streak of blue sky over the land, and the sun was bright on the desolate-looking heap of strangely shaped mountains" (p. 20). But very often it is the desolation that predominates. Leaving Reykjavik his first day on the road, "Most strange and awful the country looked to me as we passed through, in spite of my anticipations: a doleful land at first with its great rubbish heaps of sand" (p. 28). The cliffs of Gooaland have "caves in them just like the hell-mouths in 13th century illuminations . . . one could see" the "spiky white waves" of the Gooalands-Jokul [Glacier] "against the blue sky as we came up to it: but ugh! what a horrid sight it was when we were close . . . its great blocks cleft into dismal caves, half blocked up with the sand and dirt it had ground up, and dribbling wretched white streams into the plain below: a cold wind blew over it in the midst of the hot day" (p. 53). The "Midfirth valley, the birth-place of Grettir . . . cleft by an *untidy* river and bounded by a long down-like hill, looks empty and dead

and hopeless" (p. 98). The adjectives that recur again and
again in his descriptions of the Icelandic landscape are "dės-
olate," "gloomy," "ugly," "melancholy," "dismal," "awful,"
"dreadful," and "horrible," and not infrequently he is "a
little downhearted with the savagery of the place" (p. 54;
cf. p. 113). In contrast with the surrounding desolation, even
spots of gentle beauty (for which his favorite adjectives are
"sweet" and "soft") can move him to melancholy. Thus a
wood by the Barnafóss "had a softness about it that saddened one amidst all the grisliness surrounding it, more than
the grimmest desert I had seen" (pp. 161–162).

But this "heart-sickness" can give way to profounder
feelings. The central episode of the 1871 journey is Morris'
crossing the interior "wilderness" (pp. 75–89) in which desolation is dominant. For Morris, the "wilderness" is not
merely defined by the absence of human habitations.
Rather it is a place in its own right. It has a "wall" and a
"gate" (like the Faroe Islands) that "impresses itself on my
memory as a peculiarly solemn place" (p. 75) and, once
passed through, "shuts us out from the rest of the world on
that side" (p. 76). This notion of the wilderness as a termi-
nus is significant. The "Waste of Long-Jokul . . . looks as
if it ended the world, green-white and gleaming in the
doubtful sun" (p. 76).[7] This is Morris' zero vision, a negative world in which even the light—like the warmth—of the
sun is "doubtful." And appropriately it is here, in the most
physically trying section of the expedition, that Morris has
what "I think . . . was the most horrible sight of mountains I had the whole journey long" (p. 77). But the passage
of this "dreadful waste" is a turning point in Morris' journal. Struggling against a stiff wind and a first-of-August
snowstorm, Morris pauses to drink at a stream and "felt a
thrill of pride as a traveller, and a strange sensation, as I
noted and cried out that it was running north" (pp. 87–88).
"About here, when all the others were getting to their worst,
I began to revive, which I am glad of, for I got an impression of a very wonderful country" (p. 88). He has been
morose and homesick, sunken in "dreaming of people at
home," half-asleep on his pony. But one kind of withdrawal

gives way to another. His spirits rise at the very time the rest of the party's have begun to fail. This sense of a separate self and his exhilarated response to the "wonderful country" are mutually sustaining elements of Morris' reflex from depression. Precisely because he is acutely aware of his separation from Nature he is able to look on it with a renewed gusto. Precisely his gusto restores his self-confidence.

His experience of the wilderness thus parallels the earlier Faroes episode, and two other passages, in which natural description gives way to introspection, confirm the importance of this pattern. The first is Morris' account of Thorsmark:

> I could see its whole dismal length now, crowned with overhanging glaciers from which the water dripped in numberless falls that seemed to go nowhere; I suppose they were a long way off, but the air was so clear they seemed so close that one felt it strange they should be noiseless: at right angles to this mountain was the still higher wall that closed the valley, which as aforesaid had never changed or opened out as such places generally do; below was the flat black plain space of the valley, and all about it every kind of distortion and disruption, and the labyrinth of the furious brimstone-laden Markfleet winding amidst it lay between us and anything like smoothness: surely it was what I "came out for to see," yet for the moment I felt cowed, and as if I should never get back again: yet with that came a feeling of exaltation too, and I seemed to understand how people under all disadvantages should find their imaginations kindle amid such scenes (p. 54).

Here, as in the Faroes passage, Morris' response is twofold. The landscape is "closed" and "noiseless." Its waterfalls "seemed to go nowhere." But he is not merely "cowed" by these negations. He is afraid he may be trapped in this hellish valley with its "brimstone-laden" river. Once again, a gate shuts, but this time he is left (imaginatively) inside. Yet having submitted to this fear, he is then able to experience the second phase of his response: "a feeling of exaltation" and a corollary awareness of the human imagination's ability to "kindle amid such scenes"—an image structurally comparable to the sunlight's brightening the "grey and colourless" rocks of the Faroes coastline. Putting himself literally at the mercy of a hostile Nature frees his imagination much in the same way Shelley's less physically perilous confrontation with Mont Blanc confirms the power of the poet's "human intellect." Moreover, just as Shelley's experience teaches him the philosophical materialism needed "to repeal large codes of fraud and woe," so, too, Morris will later in life declare that his "one lesson" from the "romantic desert" of Iceland was the knowledge "that the most grinding poverty is a trifling evil compared with the inequality of classes"[8]—that, in other words, submission to the "natural limits of human happiness" frees him to reject the limits ("codes of fraud and woe") artificially imposed on human beings by human beings themselves.

Nonetheless, the pattern of Morris' confrontation is more essentially Wordsworthian than Shelleyan. Morris's experience of Thorsmark is remarkably similar to the Simplon Pass episode in Book VI of *The Prelude* in which Wordsworth confronts what he "came out for to see" and finds it lacking. His expectations of yet greater heights give way to a "melancholy slackening" and then to a long descent through the "gloomy strait" of a "narrow chasm." But disappointment gives way to exaltation; the "narrow chasm," to images "of first, and last, and midst, and without end." Admittedly Wordsworth's blank verse is stronger stuff than Morris' comparatively prosaic "feeling of exaltation." But this underplaying is a function of the *Journal's* anti-autobiographical form, which restrains Morris' imagination in the very act of giving it voice. For both poets, the attempt to discover a natural correlative to private aspirations gives way to a recognition of the inadequacy of Nature. And for both, a succession of similar experiences seems to have been necessary before they could accept the subdued visions, respectively, of Grasmere and Kelmscott Manor. Wordsworth's "Home at Grasmere" and the description of Kelmscott Manor in the final chapters of *News from Nowhere* are similar idealizations of a rural setting, in which human society is integrated both internally and with the external natural world. Both are, literally, returns home. Morris' communism, of course, is an important difference, but both poets must undergo some kind of political revolution before they can fully participate in the post-revolutionary pastoral.

Morris' account of his visit to Laxdala expresses another version of this pattern, all the more significant on account of the specifically "poetic" associations of the landscape with Morris' "Lovers of Gudrun," based on the Laxdala Saga and published in the final volume of *The Earthly Paradise* in 1870. Morris here confronts, for the first time, the scene of one of his own poems, and if he is to experience a personal relationship with the landscape any place, we might expect it to be here. Characteristically, he withdraws from his companions, who busy themselves pitching the tent:

I spent my time alone in trying to regain my spirits which had suddenly fallen very low almost ever since we came into Laxdale.

Just think, though, what a mournful place this is—Iceland I mean—setting aside the pleasure of one's animal life there: the fresh air, the riding and rough life, and feeling of adventure—how every place and name marks the death of its short-lived eagerness and glory; and withal so little is the life changed in some ways: Olaf Peacock went about summer and winter after his live-stock, and saw to his haymaking and fishing just as this little peak-nosed parson does; setting aside the coffee and brandy, his victuals under his hall, "marked with famous stories," were just the same as the little parson in his ten-foot square parlour eats: I don't doubt the house stands on the old ground. But Lord! what littleness and helplessness has taken the place of the old passion and violence that had placed here once—and all is unforgotten; so that one has no power to pass it by unnoticed: yet that must be something of a reward for the old life of the land, and I don't think their life now is more unworthy than most people's elsewhere, and they are happy enough by seeming. Yet it is an awful place: set aside the hope that the unseen sea gives you here, and the strange threatening change of the blue spiky mountains beyond the firth, and the rest seems emptiness and nothing else: a piece of turf under your feet, and the sky overhead, that's all; whatever solace your life is to have here must come out of yourself or these old stories, not over hopeful themselves. Something of all this I thought; and besides our heads were now fairly turned homeward, and now and again a few times I felt homesick—I hope I may be forgiven. (p. 108)

The exaltation of Thorsmark gives way to tragic resignation, but the vacillations of the passage suggest the wavering of Morris' mind between this stoic acceptance of man's fate and a despairing rejection both of the heroic past and of the unheroic present. His hesitant "yet that must be something of a reward" comes close to admitting there may be none whatsoever.

The "reward," of course, must be Morris himself. Only a

poet capable of reliving the "old life" in the fullness of his imagination can guarantee its continuity. As a consequence, the passage moves from a consideration of the plight of the modern Icelanders to an ambiguous "your," which includes Morris without specifying him outright. His awareness of his own limitations as a "skald"[9] prevents him any firmer affirmation than this vague inclusiveness. Nevertheless, Morris' response to Laxdale turns on his ability to use the Icelander's relationship to his natural environment as a paradigm for his own confrontation with the "littleness and helplessness" that "has taken the place of the old passion and violence" both in his own life and in Western life in general, in which the only "hope" derives from an imaginative perception of "the unseen seas" and "the strange threatening change of the blue spiky mountains beyond the firth"—in which, in other words, the topographical distance of landscape takes the place, as in Wordsworth's poetry, of an older "heroic."

Just why Morris needs to be "forgiven" has several explanations. Perhaps he needs to be forgiven for his homesickness, for doubting the efficacy of the "old stories," or for his general mood of introspection which violates the "objectivity" of the *Journal's* narrative. Or, perhaps he needs to be forgiven for admitting a split between the imagination and its natural setting. (He has "gone for to see" a world in which landscape and legend are interfused; he discovers instead that legend is a crude, often ineffectual means of staving off the terrors of landscape.) Characteristically, the journal format enables him to offer these possibilities without tracing them to a solution. They are "a day's experience" that need not relate significantly to his experience of Iceland on the days before or after.

Given this form, the meaning of Iceland emerges by bits and pieces, in which conscious introspection is the exception rather than the rule. It is more often pure description that bears the burden of Morris' state of mind. The tragic awareness of human fate he verbalizes at Laxdale more often expresses itself in the subdued manner and distance of his factual accounts of the landscape:

. . . the mountains we look back on, toothed and jagged in an inde-
scribable but well-remembered manner, are very noble and solemn. As
we rode along the winding path here we saw a strange sight: a huge
eagle quite within gunshot of us, and not caring at all for that, flew
across and across our path, always followed by a raven that seemed
teazing and buffeting him: this was the first eagle I had ever seen free
and on the wing, and it was a glorious sight, no less; the curves of his
flight, as he swept close by us, with every pen of his wings clear
against the sky was something not to be forgotten. Out at sea too we
saw a brigantine pitching about in what I thought must be a rough sea
enough. The day has been much like yesterday throughout, and is getting clearer as it wears. (p. 119)

Once again Morris has passed a natural barrier—the mountains with their anthropomorphic "teeth"—rendered "noble
and solemn" by distance. His reward is the "free" flight of
the eagle, which becomes, in a special sense, an expression
of Morris' own freedom of perception. The experience is
"something not to be forgotten," but Morris sets it down
with Parnassian control. The eagle's curving flight echoes
his own "winding path"; its movement on air, the liberation
of the poet's consciousness able to shape his response to
"teazing and buffeting" into aesthetic form. But Morris is
able to record this "glorious sight" without forgetting that it
is the expression of another order, an order not his own. The
very intensity of his vision derives from its precision and
clarity—elements which depend on the detached, self-contained position of the observer, and it is this stark clarity of
perception which is Morris' lesson from Iceland. He partic-
ipates in the eagle's flight, "every pen of his wings clear
against the sky," without humanizing the eagle. He offers,
without forcing on us, the implicit allegory of the raven's
"teazing." He includes the (very necessary) detail of the
brigantine without apparent concern for the fate of its crew
in the heavy seas. There is not a trace of sentimentality in his
description. This self-discipline, akin to the stoicism of the
sagas, is his ultimate response to the desolation of the Icelandic landscape.

But self-discipline is also a means of responding to the
crisis in his emotional life. Underlying Morris' description
of the eagle is a renewed sureness in his own identity. It is

no accident that the *Journals* were a work Rossetti could
never bring himself to admire, for they are the work in
which Morris implicitly rejects Rossetti and much that he
stood for. Instead of reshaping his past as an autobiographical fable, Morris redefines his personality by undergoing a "literary" adventure. And the strategy works precisely because the adventure *is* "literary." What Morris
learns from Iceland is a new point of view, but he can only
be confident in this new point of view when he sees it in
writing. Thus, the purpose of his journey turns out to be his
being able to write the *Icelandic Journals*, a work that
places his personal failure in the larger context of the tragedy of humankind and enables Morris to treat himself as a
literary "object" without giving way to self-pity. Iceland
alone can accomplish the first, but only the strategy of a
written journal can bring about the second.

* * *

But what is normal in Iceland is dreamlike in England. As
Morris takes his way homeward, the *Journal* transforms Iceland from a stark presence into "the shadows of the rocks
dimly looming through the mist" (p. 182). The ship *Diana*
lands in Scotland, and Morris finds himself "before the
ticket-door" of the Edinburgh station "quite bewildered,
and not knowing what to ask for. Lord, how strange it
seemed at first! So into the train, thinking what a little way
it was from Edinburgh to London" (p. 185). Thorshaven in
the Faroes had first seemed to him "like a toy Dutch town
of my childhood" (p. 13n). Now, not unlike Lemuel Gulliver
on his return to England, "I thought the houses and horses
looked so disproportionately big for the landscape that it
all looked like a scene at a theatre" (p. 185).

But Morris' equivocal homecoming is not the end of the
episode. The 1871 *Journal* concludes with this note:
"WILLIAM MORRIS finished writing this journal (from
notes made in Iceland at the above dates) on the 30th June
1873, intending to sail from Granton for Iceland the second
time on July 10th of the aforesaid year 1873." Morris
found it necessary to give literary coherence to his first

journey before undertaking his second. If the second was an intentional repetition of the first, it seems to have been important for him to come to terms with the first (through its textual revision) before he could know what he wanted to repeat.

In one sense, the second journey is superfluous, and this is probably why Morris left off writing the 1873 "Diary" once he had discovered that he *could* write it. But the unpolished fragment confirms our interpretation of the 1871 *Journal* by its concentration on the very elements central to the meaning of the earlier experience. The 1871 journey with Magnússon, Charles Faulkner and W. H. Evans kept to the relatively populous West of the island whereas the 1873 journey, with Faulkner and two Icelandic guides, undertakes a considerably more formidable encounter with the central wilderness. The 1873 "Diary" emphasizes, even more than the 1871 *Journal*, the intimate relationship between the beauty and terror of the Icelandic landscape— "so barren and dreadful it looks and yet has a kind of beauty about it" (p. 203). But what had been a discovery in 1871 is an expectation in 1873, and so the "Diary" is able to dwell on the strength of mind and heart this recognition gives Morris. He is still subject to depression—all the more so, because the 1873 summer was unusually cold and wet—but he is aware of mastering it like an old Norseman. "I was somewhat depressed, I suppose by an ungenial ending of a fine day and a cold I have got on me. I concealed it however" (p. 191). "And now the rain set in again worse than ever but we shut up the tent and made ourselves snug and refused to be depressed" (p. 192). "A most lovely morning when I got up at eight, still depressed and homesick, which depression I had to throw off in getting breakfast, so that by then I was in the saddle. I was excited and in good frame for travelling; moreover, there was something eminently touching about the valley and its nearness to the waste that gave me that momentary insight into what the whole thing means that blesses us sometimes and is gone again" (p. 225).

In confirming the meaning of the first experience of Iceland, the 1873 journey must also confirm Morris' full kinship with Iceland. It is important for him that the road from Reykjavik has been "made more familiar to me by the one intense sight of it than many years might have made another place" (p. 188) and that in setting forth he can feel "happy and light-hearted and quite at home, to wit, as if there had been no break between the old journey and this" (p. 188). Morris must affirm to himself that his "wonder" at Iceland "had lost none of its freshness" (p. 202). So when the opportunity comes of "camping in a more remarkable place," he is set on camping instead "in the same place as I was in last time" (p. 203).

Morris seems to have distrusted the very strangeness of his first experience of the North. He needs to be sure it is not the novelty of the place but Iceland itself which has moved him and that it can "do it again." Despite everything, he must maintain continuity with the kinship he had felt with the Icelandic past and its poetry on the 1871 journey. On returning to Gunnar's howe he discovers: "It was the same melancholy sort of day as yesterday and all looked somewhat drearier than before, two years ago on a bright evening, and it was not till I got back from the howe and wandered by myself about the said site of Gunnar's hall and looked out thence over the great grey plain that I could answer to the echoes of the beautiful story—but then at all events I did not fail" (p. 207). The knowledge that he "did not fail" is Morris' justification for the 1873 journey. Our proof is the self-disciplined manner of the *Journals* themselves. The *Icelandic Journals* may be an anti-autobiography because Morris distrusted conventional modes of self-scrutiny, but they are also anti-autobiography because Iceland itself taught Morris a stoic reticence that forbids speaking overmuch about one's private emotional life. Instead of prolonged introspection, they offer us what turns out to be just as expressive, just as deeply personal: a sequence of the "spots of time" in which Morris had glimpses of what he names "that momentary insight into what the whole thing means that blesses us sometimes and is gone again."

1. The fact that so many journals of travel in Iceland were being published in late nineteenth-century England may also account for Morris's decision to leave his own journal in manuscript. The decade before his 1871 expedition saw: Sabine Baring-Gould, *Iceland: Its Scenes and Sagas* (London: Smith, Elder, 1863); J. W. Clark, "Journal of a Yacht Voyage to the Faroe Islands and Iceland," in *Vacation Tourists and Notes of Travel in 1860* (Cambridge and London: Macmillan, 1861); E. T. Holland, "A Tour in Iceland in the Summer of 1861," in *Peaks, Passes and Glaciers: Excursions by Members of the Alpine Club* (London: 1862), I, 3–128; Frederick Metcalfe, *The Oxonian in Iceland* (London: Longman, Green, Longman and Roberts, 1861); C. W. Paijkull, *A Summer in Iceland,* trans. M. R. Barnard (London: Chapman and Hall, 1868); C. W. Shepherd, *The North-West Peninsula of Iceland* (London: Longmans, Green, 1870); Andrew James Symington, *Pen and Pencil Sketches of Faroe and Iceland* (London: Longman, Green, Longman, and Roberts, 1862).

2. This significance of the journeys has been generally agreed on by critics. J. W. Mackail, his official biographer, argues that the "importance in Morris's life" of the 1871 expedition "can hardly be over-estimated" (*Life of William Morris* [London: Longmans, Green, 1901] p. 240). Paul Thompson believes "It helped him to find a new attitude towards life" (*The Work of William Morris* [New York: Viking Press, 1967], p. 28), and E. P. Thompson holds that the Icelandic experience was "a draught of courage and hope, which was the prelude for Morris' entry into active political life in the later 1870's (*William Morris; Romantic to Revolutionary* [London: Lawrence and Wishart], 1955, p. 224). B. Ifor Evans compares Morris's response to the Icelandic stories to Keats' response to the mythology of *Hyperion* (*William Morris and His Poetry* [London: George Harrap, 1925], p. 122), and Maud Bodkin extends this comparison by likening "Morris's visit to Iceland" to "that of Keats to the Scottish mountains" (*Archetypal Patterns in Poetry* [London: Oxford University Press, 1934], p. 120), a view which George Ford in turn expands into a larger parallel between the two poets, who "both . . . after their respective trips, turned from romance to epic" *(Keats and the Victorians* [1944; rpt. London: Archon 1962], p. 162). *See* also Blue Calhoun, *The Pastoral Vision of William Morris* (Athens: University of Georgia Press, 1975), pp. 179–183.

3. The early prose romances, begun in 1855, show the influence of his rudimentary knowledge of Norse legend. By this time in his life, Morris was an admirer of Carlyle and familiar with Carlyle's reading of Icelandic mythology in the first lecture in *On Heroes and Hero-Worship* (1840). For an account of Northern reference in Morris's early work, *see* Karl Litzenberg. "William Morris and Scandinavian Literature, *Scandinavian Studies and Notes,* 8 (1935), 93–105; also the same author's *Victorians and Vikings,* University of Michigan Contributions to Modern Philology, No. 3 (Ann Arbor: University of Michigan Press, 1947).

4. (London: Bernard Quaritch, 1891), p. vi.

5. *The Collected Works of William Morris,* ed. May Morris (1910–1915; rpt. New York: Russell and Russell, 1966), VIII, 16; hereafter cited in text.

6. There is, of course, a darker side to this comedy. Morris's minor ineptitudes remind us of the major ineptitude as a husband he may have been trying to forget.

7. The phrase "end of the world" recurs, slightly modified, in the title of the late romance *The Well at the World's End* (1892), in which drinking from a spring reached after passage (by way of a trial) through a very Icelandic landscape strengthens the life force of the hero and heroine. Similar mountain "walls" are associated with experiences of confrontation and transformation in the other

"W" romances—*The Wood beyond the World* (1894) and *The Water of the Wondrous Isles* (1895).

8.   *The Letters of William Morris,* ed. Philip Henderson (London: Longmans, Green, 1950), p. 187.

9.   Although he seems to have been delighted when an Icelander explained his falling off a horse by observing that "The skald is not quite used to riding" (p. 57).

MUTLU KONUK BLASING

The Story of the Stories:
Henry James's Prefaces
as Autobiography

The series of prefaces that Henry James wrote for the New York edition of his works has received scant critical attention, and the handful of critics who have paid any attention to the Prefaces have considered them mainly as literary criticism.[1] Yet to consider the Prefaces solely as criticism is not only to simplify them greatly but to ignore James's suggestion that they "represent, over a considerable course, the continuity of an artist's endeavour, the growth of his whole operative consciousness."[2] Taken together, then, the Prefaces may be seen as the autobiography of an artist—the "story" or "representation" of a career. Moreover, as James's revisions of his novels for the New York Edition suggest, the "continuity" of his career required him to "re-see" it. Since in James's case the life and the career were closely identified, we witness in the Prefaces the process by which James rewrote his life in writing the story of his career. For writing the life or career necessarily meant rewriting it; in other words, the Prefaces are autobiographical and thus necessarily fictional.

To begin with, autobiographical writing fictionalizes life by introducing order and establishing connections or relations between events. In autobiography, then, what was perhaps arbitrary becomes necessary, and in the Prefaces it is precisely the "necessity" of his career that James asserts over and over again. While James intended in the Prefaces partly to develop a critical vocabulary as a means of shaping future criticism of his work, and while he was no doubt

311

motivated by the pleasures of recollection, it was primarily necessity and relatedness that he wished to establish. Indeed, the Prefaces demonstrate the necessity of the form of the individual books, of the project of the New York Edition, of the evolution of James's career as a whole, and, finally and most triumphantly, of the "clumsy Life" surrounding his career. Although we can discuss various parts of James's career separately, his life and art are ultimately one. Since the Prefaces themselves partly establish the wholeness of James's career, our divisions must unfortunately be arbitrary, for "thanks to the intimate connexion of things," we have in the Prefaces not only "the story of one's hero" and "the story of one's story itself" (313) but the story of the teller himself.

Whereas criticism reveals art to be artifice, James betrays the special nature of his task in his attempt to prove the "naturalness" of his art. For James, the development of a book is natural and necessary because organic. For example, a book originates with a "seed," a "wind-blown" germ (43), or "a mere grain of subject-matter" (98), which is then "transplanted to richer soil" (122) in the artist's consciousness and, "transferred to the sunny south window-sill of one's fonder attention" (127), subsequently "sprouts," "blooms," and bears fruit according to its nature. Elsewhere the germ-seed imagery becomes less benign. The "germ" of a story is the vague suggestion "at touch of which the novelist's imagination winces as at the prick of some sharp point: its virtue is all in its needle-like quality" (119). Inoculated with "the virus of suggestion," the disease runs its course in the artist's consciousness. Accordingly, James describes the creative act in the image of a pearl growing in "the deep well of unconscious cerebration" (23) and in time floating up to the top "with a firm iridescent surface and a notable increase of weight" (23). Fearful of "all disgracefully" betraying "the seam" and showing the "mechanical and superficial" (83), he repeatedly resorts to such organic images in order to prove his novels wholes, in which everything "counts." In the Prefaces, then, James rediscovers the process of creation as organic and thereby imputes something of a historical necessity to the works.

What finally establishes their necessity, however, is James's point of view. His stance in the Prefaces is precisely the position of the author in autobiography. First, he is looking backward and recollecting; second, he is looking inward—that is, his attitude is one of self-consciousness. To begin with, the creation of a work is not presented as a recollected sequence of events but is recreated as a process. For example, in the Prefaces to *What Maisie Knew, The Wings of the Dove*, and *The Ambassadors*, in which James discusses the evolution of the works, he at times is not even speaking in the past tense. Especially in the Preface to *The Ambassadors*, he works backward from the climax and thus imparts a necessity to the novel's development. Thus, in showing us how a certain book would "logically flower" (143), James presents us with a process of discovery, which may or may not be a faithful reproduction of the book's growth. Indeed, James's mapping out of a book's development in terms of an almost logical necessity recalls Poe's "The Philosophy of Composition," for James also characterizes the process as "inductive" (314). As Poe observes, however, "It is only with the *dénouement* constantly in view that we can give a plot its indispensable air of consequence, or causation, by making the incidents . . . tend to the development of the intention."[3] Likewise, James is aware that a retrospective view proves necessity: "Again and yet again, as, from book to book, I proceed with my survey, I find no source of interest equal to this verification after the fact . . . of the scheme of consistency 'gone in' for" (318–319). By running time backward from the already formed novel, then, James demonstrates the necessity of the choices that he made in order to arrive at that particular novel. In this process, the sequence of events is reversed, the book shrinks back into its seed as in a movie played backwards, and, as James writes about *The Ambassadors,* "Nothing can exceed the closeness with which the whole fits again into its germ" (308).

Like the retrospective point of view, an attitude of self-consciousness also saves the artist from "the baseness of the *arbitrary* stroke, the touch without its reason" (89). According to Paul Valéry, what makes the novel inferior to poetry and therefore less than "art" is its arbitrary quality, which results precisely from its unconscious conventions.[4] Consciousness of the artistic conventions that one is using, then, would tend in itself to invest a work with artistic necessity. Consequently, if—like Poe in "The Philosophy of Composition" and James in the Prefaces—one becomes his own audience, the accidental and the arbitrary are thereby purged, for whatever is consciously chosen becomes necessary. Thus, whereas James's imagery imputes a natural growth to his works, his criticism in fact articulates the artifice of the novels.

Self-consciousness, together with James's temporal perspective, generates the controlling principles of his criticism. Consciousness, for example, makes for "composition," which is art: "A picture without composition slights its most precious chance for beauty, and is moreover not composed at all unless the painter knows *how* that principle of health and safety, working as an absolutely premeditated art, has prevailed" (84). If consciousness makes for composition, as discrimination and selection it also makes for economy. Life, James writes, "has no direct sense whatever for the subject and is capable, luckily for us, of nothing but splendid waste. Hence the opportunity for the sublime economy of art, which rescues, which saves, and hoards and 'banks,' investing and reinvesting these fruits of toil in wondrous useful 'works' and thus making up for us, desperate spendthrifts that we all naturally are, the most princely of incomes" (120). Economy and "the subtle secrets of that system" (120) preoccupy James in the Prefaces, for the necessity that he discovers in retrospect while proceeding from the book to its creation is, in fact, a perfect economy. Starting with the finished product, James ends up exactly with what he started, and he can easily meet what he calls "the challenge of economic representation": "To put all that is possible of one's idea into a form and compass that will contain and express it only by delicate adjustments and an exquisite chemistry, so that there will at the end be neither a drop of one's liquor left nor a hair's breadth of the rim of one's glass to spare—every artist will remember how often that sort of necessity has carried with it its particular inspiration" (87). Moreover, "the challenge of economic representation" demanded in turn that consciousness or intelligence become a compositional center, for such a central intelligence would enable James not only to "most economize" the "value" of a character (37–38) but to "save" the surrounding "lump of life" (120) by casting it in the light of the relations and necessities that consciousness or "appreciation" creates.

* * *

James's retrospective point of view in the Prefaces permits him to look at his career as a whole in much the same way that he approaches his novels. To begin with, James is writing from the perspective of mature accomplishment; knowing what he has become, he can interpret the stages of his career as necessary steps in the evolution of the author of *The Ambassadors* and *The Golden Bowl*. James consciously attempts to shape his career around his development of the technique of using the "intelligence" or consciousness of one character as a compositional center. He confesses, "I should even like to give myself the pleasure of retracing from one of my own productions to another the play of a like instinctive disposition, of catching in the fact, at one point after another, from 'Roderick Hudson' to 'The Golden Bowl,' that provision for interest which consists in placing advantageously, placing right in the middle of the light, the most polished of possible mirrors of the subject" (70). Thus Rowland Mallet of *Roderick Hudson* and a character like Christopher Newman of *The American*, who is too typical to be particular, inward, or conscious enough, become the forerunners of a Lambert Strether, who *is* "a mirror verily of miraculous silver" (70).

At times James seems aware of the extent to which his present viewpoint distorts the early books, and he excuses the discrepancy between his statements about the books and the books as they are by claiming that he lacked the art to work out his conceptions. At other times, however, he appears to be quite unaware of how thoroughly he is imposing a present pattern on the past; as a result, his revision of an early work like *The American* reveals a number of lapses in judgment and taste. Yet the patterns that one "discovers" in looking backward are only half imposed. Since a receding temporal perspective serves—like a receding spatial perspective—to subdue details and differences and to reveal instead the larger patterns and agreements, James was to a certain extent truly discovering the shape of his career. Moreover, perhaps even the "impositions" should be regarded as necessary distortions, for a defined point of view is needed in order to establish connections at all. Accordingly, the nature of the pattern that James discovers in retrospect reflects the present *value* of consciousness for him. Thus consciousness, which is also James's *method* in the admittedly "monstrous" task of writing the Prefaces (47), becomes the basis not only of his relationship to his heroes and heroines but of their relationship to each other.

By a final turn of the screw in the Preface to *The Golden Bowl*, James justifies the Prefaces themselves and the revisions that accompany them. Characteristically recoiling from the "arbitrary," James claims in this apology of an apology that his present perspective *necessitated* the revisions. He insists that he was not working according to some imposed and foreign "theory" but was simply reading and recording his reading. Thus his "deviations" from the original texts were highly "spontaneous"—"things not of choice, but of immediate and perfect necessity: necessity to the end of dealing with the quantities in question at all" (336). Consequently, if the past was to be reappropriated at all, and if his works were to mirror *his* consciousness, James had to revise his early books. Indeed, he admits that the two efforts—rereading and rewriting—"proved to be but one," and he argues that he did not rewrite but merely re-saw. Accordingly, James writes, "the 'revised' element in the present Edition is . . . these rigid conditions of re-perusal, registered; so many close notes, as who should say, on the particular vision of the matter itself that experience had at last made the only possible one" (339).

In James's view, then, the text was like a mirror—fluid

and unformed; if it was to be read at all, it would have to be read as a reflection of the present. This view approximates Wolfgang Iser's conception of the literary work as a virtual meeting-place of the author's text and the reader. According to Iser, the work changes between the first and subsequent readings, mainly because the patterns of memory and expectation are different in each reading.[5] In reading his works for the New York Edition, James was reading them with the knowledge, so to speak, of "how it all ended." This retrospective view necessitated, then, the "re-vision" not only of individual books but of the career as a whole, and in both cases James partly discovered and partly imposed the order in each. Accordingly, as Roland Barthes has proposed, a necessary part of the activity of reading is reducing the new and unfamiliar patterns that one encounters in the text to the patterns of more familiar experience that one brought to the reading.[6] In James's case, the relatively unfamiliar earlier work had to be reduced to the more familiar patterns of his later language, style, and form. And James describes the process of revision in similar terms: "It was, all sensibly, as if the clear matter being still there, even as a shining expanse of snow spread over a plain, my exploring tread, for application to it, had quite unlearned the old pace and found itself naturally falling into another, which might sometimes indeed more or less agree with the original tracks, but might most often, or very nearly, break the surface in other places" (336).

* * *

The Prefaces represent James's "re-vision" not only of his literary career but, more important, of his life. "Our noted behaviour at large," James remarks, "may show for ragged, because it perpetually escapes our control" (348). As autobiography, the Prefaces bring the life itself under artistic control, not in order to justify it but in order precisely to eliminate the need for justification. For James continues, "on all the ground to which the pretension of performance by a series of exquisite laws may apply there reigns one sovereign truth—which decrees that, as art is nothing if not exemplary, care nothing if not active, finish nothing if not consistent, the proved error is the base apologetic deed, the helpless regret is the barren commentary, and 'connexions' are employable for finer purposes than mere gaping contrition" (348). Since James sets out in part to give his life something of the "roundness," wholeness, and necessity of art, the life itself becomes in the Prefaces such a ground where these "exquisite laws" may apply. James redeems the life partly by seeing it in retrospect as the context for the creation of art and partly by imparting to it—through the self-consciousness of the Prefaces—the quality of art.

Since the attempt to equate life and art informs as much James's personal writing as the autobiographical writings of Thoreau and Whitman, we may approach the Prefaces as autobiography by using the terms of the novelist's art. To begin with, in the Preface to *Roderick Hudson* James writes that experience must organize some system of observation in order to take account of itself. In this project of self-observation or self-consciousness, "Everything counts, nothing is superfluous in such a survey; the explorer's notebook strikes me here as endlessly receptive" (3). Thus, if experience starts taking notes, so to speak, it acquires a center around which to gather itself. For James, the art of representation was a way in which experience shaped itself, "saved" itself, and made itself "count" simply by being conscious of itself. More important, art "saved" as well the individual life that went into its creation—"the accidents and incidents of its growth" (7). James writes: "This accordingly is what I mean by the contributive value—or put it simply as, to one's own sense, the beguiling charm—of the *accessory* facts in a given artistic case. This is why, as one looks back, the private history of any sincere work, however modest its pretensions, looms with its own completeness in the rich, ambiguous aesthetic air, and seems at once to borrow a dignity and to mark, so to say, a station" (3–4).

Moreover, the Prefaces themselves should be seen as experience taking note of itself, for in their self-consciousness as a "re-presentation" of the creative process, they make "everything count" and thereby rescue the "clumsy Life"

that surrounds the art. Since necessity is the saving principle
of art, all of the events that can be brought into a relation
with the creation of art are saved from contingency and
become necessary rather than arbitrary. Thus, whereas seen
as recollection the Prefaces demonstrate the necessity of
James's individual works and his entire career, seen as
self-consciousness they argue for the necessity of the
"accessory facts" or the history. From the retrospective and
self-conscious viewpoint of autobiography, then, life par-
takes of the quality of art, for the necessity that life achieves
in retrospect and in the light of consciousness is, in fact, the
economy that is the very life, according to James, of the art
of representation. Life comes to "count," therefore, when it
achieves economy—that is, when it becomes a unified, self-
sufficient whole. At this point, however, it becomes art, since
the principle of economy is—as we have seen—basic to
James's conception of his art: "There is life and life, and as
waste is only life sacrificed and thereby prevented from
'counting,' I delight in a deep-breathing economy and an
organic form" (84).

Accordingly, in the Prefaces the art not only makes the
life relevant but can be said, in fact, to *make* the life. James
looks back from the work and creates the life that must
have been there in order for him to create the work in the
first place. In the Preface to *The Tragic Muse*, for example,
James discusses the origins of his conception: "What I make
out from furthest back is that I must have had from still
further back, must in fact practically have always had, the
happy thought of some dramatic picture of the 'artist-
life'. . . . To 'do something about art' . . . must have
been for me early a good deal of a nursed intention"
(79). Just as the fact of a particular novel necessitates the
"accidents" of its growth, the existence of the novels taken
together shapes the life as a whole, for they *are* the connections and relations that give it continuity. "We are condemned," James writes, "whether we will or no, to abandon
and outlive, to forget and disown and hand over to desolation, many vital or social performances—if only because the
traces, records, connexions, the very memorials we would

fain preserve, are practically impossible to rescue for that purpose from the general mixture." Whereas acts become disconnected from their actor, however, works of art remain connected, for "Our relation to them is essentially traceable, and in that fact abides, we feel, the incomparable luxury of the artist." The "luxury" of the artist, then, is his freedom from his past: "It rests altogether with himself not to break with his values, not to 'give away' his importances. Not to *be* disconnected, for the tradition of behaviour, he has but to feel that he is not; by his lightest touch the whole chain of relation and responsibility is reconstituted. . . . All of which means for him conduct with a vengeance, since it is conduct minutely and publicly attested" (348). Since the Prefaces recollect and reconstitute the "whole chain of relation and responsibility" between the artist and his works, and since the works make "relevant" the accidents of their growth, the Prefaces "minutely and publicly" redeem not only the art but the life from time and accident.

* * *

Whereas in their self-observation and recollection the Prefaces more or less consciously discover connections, by virtue of their form they necessarily fictionalize the past, for James casts them not as criticism but as first-person narrative or, to use his words, as a "story of one's story." In the Preface to *Roderick Hudson,* James admits that "Really, universally, relations stop nowhere, and the exquisite problem of the artist is eternally but to draw, by a geometry of his own, the circle within which they shall happily *appear* to do so" (5). The "continuity of things," then, is never broken save in art or "re-presentation." Since narration itself establishes connections and the limits— arbitrary and artificial—of relatedness, the order, cohesion, or wholeness that the Prefaces give to James's career and that any autobiography gives to the career of its writer is, in the end, a literary creation. Moreover, the continuously present consciousness or personality that autobiography creates is likewise a function of narrative, for just as one must set down or narrate an event for it to assume shape and order, one must also *tell* his story in order for it to be *his*. Insofar as life is a different entity from the "mere fact consciousness," then, it is a creation of words or a story that we tell ourselves. Since the telling imposes too rigid orders of causality and development on the life, however, it distorts the life, yet without this distortion there would be no past, for it is precisely the telling that discovers a life as *related* and as *ours*. Thus, if a narrative structure is necessarily fictional, it is also basic to the conception of life in a given language, and for this reason we conceive of our lives in the image of fiction.

Representation or the telling of events necessarily fictionalizes life, because narratives have beginnings and ends. As Roquentin in Jean-Paul Sartre's *Nausea* laments, "Nothing happens while you live. The scenery changes, people come in and go out, that's all. There are no beginnings."[7] It is in narrative that things "happen," for narration establishes beginnings and ends and draws the arbitrary "circle" around events. When beginnings and ends are fixed, however, the flow of time is reversed. Events happen in one direction, Roquentin continues, but we relate them in the opposite direction: "the story is going on backwards: moments have stopped piling themselves happy-go-luckily one on top of the other, they are caught up by the end of the story which draws them on and each one of them in turn the previous moment."[8] The telling of any event, then, not only saves it from the unremitting, forward flow of time but sends it running back upstream, so to speak. Consequently, insofar as our conscious life is a process of talking to ourselves continuously, we are living double lives, and our conscious existence is, in its temporal structure, a fictional existence. In the story that we tell ourselves, then, time runs backward, even as biological and historical time goes forward.

Since from a retrospective viewpoint time runs backward, the course of events becomes necessary in the telling. Moreover, since all narration has a retrospective viewpoint, art itself becomes necessary only in the story that one tells of it, and without the "story of the story" the art is an arbitrary construct. Paul Valéry, who in his practice of self-observation resembles James, writes, "Perhaps it would be interesting, *just once,* to write a work which at each juncture would show the diversity of solutions that can present themselves to the mind and from which it *chooses* the unique sequel to be found in the text. To do this would be to substitute for the illusion of a unique scheme which imitates reality that of the *possible-at-each-moment,* which I think more truthful."[9] Thus Valéry acknowledges the essentially arbitrary nature of any poem; in his view, a poem represents only a momentary order, which is always in danger of disintegrating in the confusion of daily language. James likewise is aware of the arbitrary nature of art, for to state that, ideally, relations stop nowhere amounts to saying that they may stop anywhere one wishes. Since the Prefaces argue for the necessity of the art, however, we may conclude that events—life, art—become necessary only in retrospect and in narration, for it is only in narration that we have significant connections and relations. The double meaning of "relation," then, is telling, for the relation or narration of a life is not a search for relations between possibly disparate events, but is itself the relation or relatedness of the events. Narrative makes for connectedness not only because it is retrospective but because it reflects—if it is to remain readable—connections universal to a culture. According to Roland Barthes, the most convincing narrative sequence is "the most 'cultural' sequence where one immediately recognizes a host of previous reading and conversation patterns."[10] Thus the connections that narration establishes are necessarily public and, therefore, justified, for a personal or private narrative logic is as impossible as a private language.

Moreover, Barthes suggests that the "readability" of the classical narrative lies in its "irreversibility."[11] Indeed, "to relate" derives from *referre* or "to bring back," and in the narrating of a recollection we arrive at irreversibility, for the present or even the future of what is being narrated has already become a past for the narrator. It is this irreversibility, then, that constitutes the fatedness of autobiographical narrative: an end point that is already reached gives shape to the past. Precisely because the present end point shapes the past, however, the past remains free or reinterpretable and reusable, for it changes with each successive "present." This conception of the past as free within its fatedness approximates James's vision of the past as a place, in Georges Poulet's words, "where one can not only recapture oneself but where one can also recapture 'the possible development of one's own nature one mayn't have missed.' "[12] It is in these terms that Poulet reads Strether's adventure; transported from one continent to another, Strether "at the same time transports with him the possibility of another Strether 'buried for years in dark corners' which is going to 'sprout again under forty-eight hours of Paris.' "[13] Strether, then, is not living his present—the future of the choices that he made in the past—but a past possibility, or the future of a choice that he in fact did not make in the past. In refusing to tell Chad what to do, Strether is no longer the man he is but the man he might have been. Accordingly, James's going back in time to revise books that were written some thirty years earlier shows his past to be as fluid as Strether's.

Finally, it is due to the nature of memory itself that the past is fictionalized in the Prefaces in particular and autobiography in general. According to Edmund Husserl, recollection is also shaped by the present, for memory is "oriented" toward "the future of the recollected." Every act of memory, Husserl writes, "contains intentions of expectation whose fulfillment leads to the present." Thus, "as the recollective process advances, [its] . . . horizon is continually opened up anew and becomes richer and more vivid. In view of this, the horizon is filled with recollected events which are always new. Events which formerly were only foreshadowed are now quasi-present, seemingly in the mode of the embodied present."[14] Memory, then, cannot recapture primary perception, for as the future of the perception comes to open up, the past correspondingly expands. Consequently, distortions like consciously or unconsciously selective memory, polemical pleading, or, in

Daniel Aaron's phrase, "ancestor worship" of the "living relic" who is himself his own ancestor[15] are simply conscious or unconscious exaggerations of the basic distortion of narrative. Distortions of the so-called "content," therefore, merely reflect the formal patterns of retrospective narration.

Since autobiography is not only a retrospective but a self-conscious and self-referring mode, it is riddled as well with the distortions that style engenders. In autobiography in general and James in particular, the distant past—when checked against the biographer's data—is always more distorted than the recent past, not only because present choices of patterns and significances tend to color the past, but because the style of the writing more closely resembles the personality of the recent past. Thus James's mature style in the Prefaces changes his earlier work, and since style always determines the form of experience, there are technical as well as psychological reasons for selective memory. As a result, the changes that James's later style effects are necessary if not—when recorded in his revisions—always altogether happy, for it is precisely the present style that in fact makes the past James's. Indeed, James admits that in retrospect the works hardly seem to be his, because their " 'private' character . . . quite insists on dropping out" (4). He can revive his "relation" to his early works, however, by reappropriating them in his new style. Thus revision becomes, in James's words, an "*act* of re-appropriation" (336), and what he is doing in the Prefaces may be called criticism only if we use *his* definition: "To criticise is to appreciate, to appropriate, to take intellectual possession, to establish in fine a relation with the criticised thing and make it one's own" (155).

Moreover, the past becomes conceivable and real—that is, a part of the way in which one in fact perceives and experiences the world—through the imposition of the present style. By "re-collecting" events in one present style and form, then, autobiography makes of the life *one life*. An autobiography, therefore, is not a search for order but, once again, is itself the order of the life, because it is in written language. It is an order that relates the facts, because it is a narrative; accordingly, it is an order that makes the life one's own life, because it has the unity of style. Finally, it is an order that humanizes, for by speaking in the public and inherited language of literature, the individual in autobiography places his history in its social and cultural context.

* * *

In the Preface to *Roderick Hudson*, James writes of himself as the artist: "Addicted to 'stories' and inclined to retrospect, he fondly takes under this backward view, his whole unfolding, his process of production, for a thrilling tale, almost for a wondrous adventure, only asking himself at what stage of remembrance the mark of the relevant will begin to fail. He frankly proposes to take this mark everywhere for granted" (4). This passage introduces the recurrent imagery of adventure that James uses to describe his career. *He* is the hero of the tale that he now is telling, and he is able to "show" *his* "several actions beautifully become one" (88), for everything that he remembers is not only relevant but of a piece. Indeed, we can describe James's adventure in the Prefaces in the same terms that he applies to his creation of fictional characters, because the Prefaces record more than one adventure. In recounting the story of *The Ambassadors,* for example, James charts not only the unfolding of Strether's adventure but the progress of his own adventure —"the thrilling ups and downs, the intricate ins and outs of the compositional problem" (319). More important, however, the Preface itself represents the adventure of now telling how he came to tell Strether's story; as James writes, "it comes to me again and again, over this licentious record, that one's bag of adventures . . . has been only half-emptied by the mere telling of one's story" (313). Thus the "story of the story" remained to be told, not only for "the joy of living over, as a chapter of experience, the particular intellectual adventure" (29), but for the "confirmed infatuation of retrospect," which made even of the "usual difficulties" a

record for James to "fairly cherish," "as some adventurer
in another line may hug the sense of his inveterate habit
of just saving in time the neck he ever undiscourageably
risks" (85). In this adventure of recollection, then, each
book is a chapter, the career the "thrilling tale," and
James its self-made hero.[16]

In the Preface to *The Tragic Muse*, however, James explains that an artist cannot properly be a fictional hero.
The artist's "triumph," James claims, "is but the triumph
of what he produces," and "His romance is the romance he
himself projects" (96). Consequently, the "privilege of the
hero—that is of the martyr or of the interesting and appealing and comparatively floundering *person*—places him in
quite a different category, belongs to him only as to the artist deluded, diverted, frustrated or vanquished" (96–97).
Since in personal or autobiographical writing the artist
tells the story of his romance, however, he can become the
hero, for now we see the artist not with his back turned to
us "as he bends over his work," but facing us in a repetition
of his original relation to the text. We see the hero in action, as it were, for novels, James asserts, are acts of the
highest order: "to 'put' things is very exactly and respon-
sibly and interminably to do them. Our expression of them,
and the terms on which we understand that, belong as
nearly to our conduct and our life as every other feature of
our freedom" (347). Although these acts may be diverse,
disparate, and unconnected in time and place, there is always the presence of the hero to pull them together. Accordingly, James's consciousness is not only the form but
the organizing principle of the Prefaces, and everything
that it comprehends thereby becomes significant and relevant. Consciousness itself, then, is relation, for, as St.
Augustine remarks about *his* task of recollection, to find relations or "to collect" is the meaning of "to think" (*cog-
itare*).[17]

James, therefore, is a hero on the model of his characters, for it is self-consciousness that redeems the lives of
his characters from the vulgarity of the arbitrary and ac-

cidental, because self-consciousness amounts to choosing
one's fate. Indeed, James's heroes meet him halfway, for
they were patterned after the artist in the first place. For
example, Hyacinth Robinson's experience of London in
The Princess Casamassima reflects James's own experience of the city, and James portrays him "watching very
much as I had watched" (60). James's characters, then,
mirror their author. To begin with, it is their awareness
that "*makes* absolutely the intensity of their adventure"
(62), because their adventures—like James's—are inward.
Yet James's heroes and heroines are self-conscious in a
more conventional sense. Writing about a "type" in American literature, Mary McCarthy observes that such characters leave the United States and go to Europe in order to
impersonate figures in a novel.[18] She includes in this group
Isabel Archer, but her observation would apply to many of
James's characters, whose lives thus become doubly fictional. Finally, for James's protagonists as well as for
James, consciousness makes life "count," because it makes
for economy. James's calling his intelligent "centres"
"registers" and "reflectors" recalls the theme of economy.
Indeed, a character like Milly Theale is as expert in economy as any artist: life *is* wealth, and she must economize
on it. James's characters in general know the value of economy and deplore waste, and each is something of an artist
or a person "on whom nothing is lost."[19] Thus compression and composition, which save art from becoming "vulgar," also save life, for they make life as well as art necessary.

Moreover, self-consciousness, which is the mode of the
Prefaces, necessarily involves the projection of the self
as hero, for self-consciousness is awareness of oneself as a
particular person and, at the same time, as part of—even
representative of—a species. Accordingly, literary self-consciousness, which creates the sense of personality, also
projects the personality as a representative hero in the
same act. For example, if one says, "I think; therefore,
I am" or, in more Jamesian terms, "I am aware; therefore,
I am alive," one becomes conscious of oneself not only as

doing the particular act of thinking or being aware, but as belonging to a species which *is* by thinking or being aware. In this way self-consciousness becomes representative and "heroic." As consciousness, therefore, James is universal; his particularity lies only in his "relations" with his works. No less than Thoreau and Whitman, then, James wrote his autobiography "in colossal cipher, or into universality."

Self-consciousness not only makes the self a hero and its experience a related whole, but involves the same reversal of time that characterizes life as "re-presented" in literature. For the self-conscious self-observer, each event happens twice, for if one is self-conscious, what one says or does has already happened once in the consciousness. Consequently, the actual happening of the event is a "re-presentation" or repetition, and life comes to assume the quality of art. As Kierkegaard has written, one's "own consciousness raised to the second power is repetition."[20] And repetition, in turn, makes for art, for "the affair of the painter is not the immediate, it is the reflected field of life, and realm not of application, but of *appreciation*" (65). Furthermore, since representation or repetition makes for relations and thus constitutes the subject of the painter of life—"the related state, to each other, of certain figures and things" (5), we may well say of the poet or artist that, in Wallace Stevens' words, "The man-hero is not the exceptional monster, / But he that of repetition is most master." If repetition makes for relatedness or art, James's Prefaces, which represent his career, make the career itself a work of art. Consequently, the impulse for "inward mastery of the outward experience" that, in R. P. Blackmur's phrase, characterizes James's heroes and heroines[21] also informs not only the Prefaces but all autobiographical writing, for it is through self-consciousness, repetition, and representation that "clumsy Life" is mastered. We may say, then, that self-consciousness or awareness of life as lived is a repetition of the temporal process of living, and that autobiography represents this repetition. Self-consciousness, therefore, provides the continuity of life as a

temporal process, much as primary memory provides
the temporal continuity in reading a book. In the writing of
autobiography, however, this immediate or primary self-
consciousness is superseded by a secondary self-consciousness, which recollects the perceptions of primary self-
consciousness. Again, this relationship resembles the
difference between remembering chapter one of a book while
reading chapter two, and recollecting the entire book after finishing it.

* * *

In the Prefaces James resembles a god looking into a mirror and finding himself reflected in his creations, the "genesis" of which he is in the process of recounting. As he describes Strether and subsequently characterizes himself
(320, 335), he is both hero and historian, conscious and
retrospective. The image of a mirror, which James continually uses to describe the consciousness of his characters, reflects his position as well. Indeed, James would
make of himself a mirror in order to reflect and represent
all that he sees. In his insatiable desire to "do" everything
that he sees, the "common air" comes to him for him to
"taste" of " 'Subjects' and situations, character and history, the tragedy and comedy of life" (59), and as he stalks
the "tragedy and comedy of life," "Possible stories, pre-
sentable figures, rise from the thick jungle . . . , flutter-
ing up like startled game" (60). Thus James is as inclusive
as Whitman and shares, in Quentin Anderson's words,
Whitman's "imperial ego,"[22] because for James, too, the
world is full of "dumb, beautiful ministers" awaiting their
voices. Similarly, the image of a mirror appropriately describes James's understanding of his work, for in his view
the artist's task was not "original" creation but reflection,
representation, or repetition. Just as in *What Maisie Knew*
Maisie's consciousness transforms "appearances in themselves vulgar and empty enough" (147) into a semblance
of dignity by connecting them with universals, the artist's
consciousness reflects the surrounding life, which thereby
becomes interesting and acquires value. Passive and re-

ceptive, then, the mind is for James "a reflecting and col-
ouring medium" (67).

Accordingly, since the mind-as-mirror gains content
only in reflecting, the patterns of its discovery are inseparable from the patterns that it discovers. For example,
James writes of Maggie in *The Golden Bowl*, "the Princess
. . . in addition to feeling everything she has to, and to
playing her part just in that proportion, duplicates, as it
were, her value and becomes a compositional resource,
and of the finest order, as well as a value intrinsic" (329).
As consciousness, then, she provides James with his subject *and* his form. Likewise, in the Prefaces James's own
consciousness not only provides him—retrospectively—with
his subject but constitutes the form of his autobiographical writing. In his "irrepressible and insatiable," "extrav-
agant and immoral" interest in "the 'nature' of a mind"
(156), therefore, the mind became for James both his subject and his form, with the result that words became his
acts as well as the tools of his art.

Consequently, as readers or critics we face two difficulties. First, the autobiographer's tools of observation—his
language, structure, and style—affect the past life or the
"facts" that he observes. Second, in James's case the
"facts" and the instruments of observation are phenomena
of the same order, for the life that is recalled is not one of
acts but one of words. Thus it becomes meaningless to
question the "truth" of James's account, because testing
the truth of his observations would be like testing the accuracy of a yardstick with another yardstick. On top of all
this, our method of discussing the Prefaces is equally controlled by the language and verbal structures. Even more,
our very experience of James's Prefaces shares the point
of view that informed his experience, for as readers or
critics we also are retrospective and relate what we have
read in a limited number of distinct patterns, which we
partly impose and partly discover. Finally, whereas reading
is a function of primary consciousness, writing about a
work is an act of self-consciousness, which, one hopes, is
also an act of awareness.

1. *See*, for example, R. P. Blackmur's Introduction to the Prefaces in *The Art of the Novel* (New York: Scribner's, 1934). Leon Edel, in *Henry James: The Master, 1901-1916* (Philadelphia: Lippincott, 1972), also views the Prefaces mainly as criticism or, in James's words to William D. Howells, as "a sort of plea for Criticism, for Discrimination, for Appreciation on other than infantile lines" ("August 17, 1908," *The Letters of Henry James*, ed. Percy Lubbock [New York: Scribner's, 1920], II, 99). C. F. Burgess, on the other hand, reads the Prefaces for the insights that they provide into the creative process. *See* "The Seeds of Art: Henry James's *Donnée*," *Literature and Psychology*, 8 (1963), 67–73. Finally, although René Wellek takes issue with R. P. Blackmur's high praise of the Prefaces as criticism and finds them "disappointing" as criticism, he does not offer an alternative approach beyond noting that the Prefaces have "the almost unique distinction of being an author's extended commentary on his own work." *See A History of Modern Criticism 1750-1950: The Later Nineteenth Century* (New Haven: Yale University Press, 1965), p. 213.

2. Henry James, *The Art of the Novel*, ed. R. P. Blackmur (New York: Scribner's, 1934), p. 4. Hereafter page numbers will be given in the text.

3. In *Selected Writings of Edgar Allan Poe*, ed. Edward H. Davidson (Boston: Houghton-Mifflin, 1956), p. 453.

4. "Memoirs of a Poem," in *The Art of Poetry*, trans. Denise Folliot (New York: Vintage-Random, 1958), p. 103.

5. "The Reading Process: A Phenomenological Approach," *New Literary History*, 3 (1972), 279, 283–84.

6. Roland Barthes, "Action Sequences," in *Patterns of Literary Style*, ed. Joseph Strelka (University Park: Pennsylvania State University Press, 1971), p. 9.

7. *Nausea*, trans. Lloyd Alexander (Norfolk, Conn.: New Directions, 1959), p. 57.

8. Although this passage can be found in *Nausea*, pp. 57–58, here I am using the more lucid translation that is found in *The Philosophy of Jean-Paul Sartre*, ed. Robert D. Cumming (New York: Random, 1965), p. 59.

9. Valéry, p. 104.

10. Barthes, p. 11.

11. *Ibid.*, p. 14.

12. *Studies in Human Time*, trans. Elliott Coleman (Baltimore: The Johns Hopkins University Press, 1956), p. 353.

13. *Ibid.*, p. 354.

14. *The Phenomenology of Internal Time-Consciousness*, ed. Martin Heidegger; trans. James S. Churchill (Bloomington: Indiana University Press, 1964), p. 76.

15. "The Treachery of Recollection: The Inner and the Outer History," in *Essays on History and Literature*, ed. Robert H. Bremner (Columbus: Ohio State University Press, 1966), p. 10.

16. John Paterson, who has noted the images of adventure in James's writings in general, takes such imagery to mean that for James the inner life was as fraught with peril as any adventure of Tom Sawyer. See "The Language of 'Adventure' in Henry James," *American Literature*, 32 (1960), 291–301. More to our purpose, however, is a story like "The Jolly Corner," in which the imagery of danger and adventure is specifically associated with meeting the double, the journey into the past, and self-consciousness in general.

17. *Confessions*, trans. R. S. Pine-Coffin (Baltimore: Penguin, 1961), pp. 218–19.

18. "A Guide to Exiles, Expatriates, and Internal Emigres," *The New York Review of Books*, 18 (March 9, 1972), 6.

19. "The Art of Fiction," in *Partial Portraits* (London: Macmillan, 1919), p. 388.

20. Søren Kierkegaard, *Repetition: An Essay in Experimental Psychology*, trans. Walter Lowrie (New York: Harper, 1941), p. 135.

21. "In the Country of the Blue," in *The Question of Henry James*, ed. F. W. Dupee (New York: Holt, 1945), p. 194.

22. *The Imperial Self: An Essay in American Literary and Cultural History* (New York: Vintage-Random, 1971).

DAVID J. DeLAURA

The Allegory of Life:
The Autobiographical Impulse
in Victorian Prose

George Saintsbury, himself an advocate of something very
close to style-for-its-own-sake, once complained—amus-
ingly, and instructively—that the mid-nineteenth-century
polemicists had *meant* so intensely that they neglected their
styles.[1] And it is true: various kinds of prose experiment,
as well as some of the famous passages of "heightened"
prose, often seem to exist quite apart from both the more
plainly argumentative passages and from more pervasive
elements of purpose and meaning. It remains, in short,
very difficult to describe the *unity* of Victorian prose works.
Certainly, the familiar vehicle of the review-essay gave
scarcely a semblance of preexisting form and pattern of
the sort available to novelists and poets, and a great deal of
the most notable prose of the century—even whole books-
full—consists of "passages" and highly digressive "essays."
The unities I want to suggest here are "modal," manifestations of a unique meditative or reflective strain, in which
certain identifiable themes, attitudes, and concerns intersect with special stylistic qualities that are considered their
adequate embodiment, the whole bound together by a
continuous, or at least intermittent, readiness for self-exploration and self-manifestation and the manipulation of
one's own personal presence for highly diverse ends.[2]

I want to examine some of these modes of procedure,
these favored "situations" and ways of exploring "history,"
both one's own experience and (intimately connected with
it) the larger shifts and movements of the culture. The area

to be explored is somewhat "lower" than the world of explicit argument and ideas in conflict well discussed by
Basil Willey, Walter Houghton, and Raymond Williams.
My concern is more an extension of John Holloway's
approach; but brilliant as his discussion of local strategies
and devices is, the "content" he discovers in his sages is
strangely reductive, even simplistic, and in a quite literal
sense, inconsequential.[3] I want, in short, to specify so far
as I can how a simultaneous concern for style, for an implicit theory of mind, consciousness, and language, and
for the exploration of personality creates an inter-region
of its own, lying between the two more familiar kingdoms
of explicit "content" on the one side, and "style," "form,"
and device on the other. I am trying to suggest the unity of
Victorian prose in ways not so readily evident in the usual
"philosophical" groupings and counter-groupings; the
process allows us to discern some unexpected alignments
and continuities.

I am particularly concerned to account for the role in the
nineteenth century of nostalgia and personal memory,
those controlling emotions in so many of the heightened
passages in De Quincey, Carlyle, Newman, and Arnold.
We need an approach to this pervasive reminiscential
mood that does not confine itself to autobiography in any
formal sense. Wordsworth is a key figure for understanding
this backward-looking mood of the century. The "humble"
fact to which he (like George Eliot after him) submitted
himself turned out, again and again, to be the remembered
fact, autobiographical or quasi-autobiographical. And personal memory, again and again, was the re-experiencing
of the "something that is gone," those "Fallings from us,
vanishings," that in their turn led to more universal perceptions of the "still, sad music of humanity," the thoughts
that "lie too deep for tears." The elegiac, in the nineteenth
century as earlier, involves not only a look backward and
inward, but "up," to a more general or even transcendent
perspective on the human situation. It is precisely the *present application* of these "shadowy recollections," their
forward-looking and propulsive function, as well as the inference of "something far more deeply interfused," that

are increasingly called into question in the colder climate
of the latter half of the century.

For the most part, I think the Victorians inherited the
Wordsworthian mode, even while putting it to new uses.
Pater captures another, weaker, side of the cult of nostalgia,
in describing "the ennuyé": "More than Childe Harold,
more than Werther, more than Réné himself, Coleridge
. . . represents the inexhaustible discontent, languor, and
home-sickness, that endless regret, the chords of which
ring all through our modern literature."[4] After about 1825,
Byronic pageants of the bleeding heart and Shelleyan musical wails—despite some shreds attaching to the early Tennyson and Browning, and of course to the reviled Spasmodics—seemed embarrassing, and "subjectivity" itself was
the constant object of critical attack, starting with critics
as diverse as Peacock, Macaulay, and Carlyle, and culminating in the onslaught on the feeble Spasmodics in the
fifties.[5]

Still, a good deal of the somewhat diffuse emotionality
we associate with early- and mid-Victorian literature un-
questionably centers on, precisely, memory and its melancholy inventory of past experience and loss. Though the
theme of loss and the elegiac emotions is pervasive in the
Old Testament, and in both Greek and Roman literature,
it is especially the new Victorian experience, a newly intensified and reorganized set of emotions derived from a
sense of cultural crisis, which a great many people, following the lead of their literary betters, learned to regard
as their own "essential" and personal emotions. A kind of
Victorian specialty, melancholy is as intense and as intimate as it was in Coleridge, Byron, and Shelley, but at the
same time more consciously restrained; it is the Wordsworthian mood, though no doubt colored in stronger tones.
(The mood found its perfect musical embodiment in the
adagio movements of Elgar at the turn of the century and
later.) The elegiac lies very close to the heart of what was
considered essentially "poetic," in all the forms employed
by the Victorians; it became, finally, for reasons I think
worth exploring, a central defining element of the specifically "human."

But the nineteenth century explored the passion of the past, and expressed its own broken-heartedness and its barely controlled sobbing, at several levels of seriousness and with varying degrees of adequacy. We know its more popular and unpersuasive manifestations in the continual re-appearance of medieval ruins in the poetry and fiction of the century, even for un-"Gothic" purposes.[6] The merely picturesque use of ruined castles and abbeys is a fairly harmless if persistent aspect of that often overrated and all too "literary" phenomenon, nineteenth-century medievalism.[7] But *below* the level of, say, Scott's undemanding picturesqueness, there were low-lying swamps of lachrymosity and self-pity; *above* it, there was a more serious and permanently available range of attitudes expressive of the personal and cultural losses suffered in a time of widespread and rapid change. These are among the *kinds* of feeling, however adequately embodied, that surprise us so frequently in Victorian writing, when the author (in Walter Houghton's words) "is suddenly swept by a gust of personal emotion which he cannot check or master sufficiently to integrate it with his theme."[8] My own view is that such passages, especially in non-fictional prose, though abrupt and sometimes ill-managed, are often not nearly so out of keeping with an author's overt argumentative point as may at first appear. Such passages have a supplementary "purposive" value of their own; they become part of the more or less implicit campaign to change England's self-awareness, and instruments for fighting the battle with the Philistines by other methods.

*   *   *

The special Victorian version of backward-looking emotions, with a constant implicit reference to one's own experience, is in part to be explained by the very rapid growth in historical awareness during the second quarter of the century—that time of "transition" when again and again writers analyzed their historical moment under such titles as "The Spirit of the Age," "Characteristics," and "Signs of the Times." Kathleen Tillotson has spoken of "the drag of the past" in the novels of the period, the great divide coming in the thirties and symbolized in the transforma-

tion of the English countryside by the coming of the railway.[9] This sense that the chasm in one's own personal history coincides with the great and decisive watershed of
modern history is particularly strong in those born around
1820, a group who came to adulthood in the troubled forties—the generation of John Ruskin, George Eliot, A. H.
Clough, Matthew Arnold, and J. A. Froude.

The union of the universal and the personal, *without*
reference to the historical moment, is no doubt most common, though even this variant operates at different levels
of generalization. One thinks of the scene of the younger
George Osborne, in Chapter Sixty-One of *Vanity Fair,*
as he comes across the letters G. O. scratched on the glass
of his grandfather's house, and his mother's unspoken
thoughts of the past; here the universality of human loss
is totally implicit—though not without its strong effect. In
contrast, the great elaborateness of Philip Pirrip's revisit-
ings of the scenes of his youth in *Great Expectations,* as
part of his growing sense of the loss of youthful innocence,
suggests Dickens' conscious attempt to link Philip's experience to a more universal pattern of loss and gain, in the
tradition of the *Bildungsroman.* But here the latent, but
important, element is that third factor, the strong and continuous autobiographical pressure of Dickens' self-awareness and painful self-exposure in his anti-hero's progress.[10]
There is even an identifiable Victorian "situation," in which
a young person, often a girl, coming upon "the happy
Autumn-fields" and the beauty of a "Goldengrove un-
leaving," experiences not the Keatsian fullness of being
and momentary stasis, but shocked tears, the result of a
sudden inrush of the fact of mortality, including one's own,
followed sometimes by a religious reflection. For us the
chief examples are, perhaps, the revisiting of Helstone in
Chapter Forty-Six of Mrs. Gaskell's *North and South*
(1854), and Hopkins' "Spring and Fall" ("Margaret,
are you grieving?").[11] The tears that rise while "thinking
of the days that are no more" are Tennyson's "Tears, idle
tears," but for the Victorians, as I want to argue, they were
not idle at all.[12]

My examples of personal memory and the universal

meaning derived from it have so far been drawn from fiction and poetry. Granted, the background of industrial
strife adds an extra dimension to Mrs. Gaskell's and Disraeli's treatment of loss and memory. But nonfictional
prose is particularly well suited to the new "uses" of memory, because of its free interplay between the author's personal remembrance and intimate self-revelation, on the one
hand, and its virtually unlimited scope in exploring universal significance, on the other. It could then treat the
changes in nineteenth-century society and sensibility as a
"third" or inter-area, a fresh analogue, and in the process
help grasp the significance of the new, disturbing, and
characteristically "modern" experiences which all sensitive
readers were confusedly undergoing. This presentation
of one's own past, as part of a search for new meanings in
a deteriorating cultural situation, is perhaps the most
central binding activity of serious nineteenth-century literature. It is the great "task," a kind of implicitly shared
program for the century. This everywhere evident autobiographical pressure of the period, deriving most obviously from the example of Wordsworth, reaches a kind of
climax around mid-century—most obviously, in such works
as *In Memoriam*, the poetry of Arnold and Clough, the
fiction of Charlotte Brontë, Thackeray's *Pendennis*, Dickens' *David Copperfield* and *Great Expectations,* and
George Eliot's *The Mill on the Floss*. The prose writers also
played an essential, and unique, role in carrying out the
program—and it has an untold history of its own.[13]
Of course the free "interpretative" power of essayistic
prose is not always exercised, and some of the most famous
passages work best when memory bears its own meaning
without explication and explicit "higher" reference. Hazlitt, who is mostly remembered today for his mode of
"abrupt" opinionatedness, can I think be credited with
virtually inventing that mood of "lofty thought or mournful memory"[14] that is so central to the "high" passages of
Victorian prose at all periods. In treating the Lake Poets,
especially, Hazlitt's mixture of brokenhearted affection
and blame for the betrayal of youthful social and political

ideals offered a useful pattern for the interpenetration of
personal feeling and larger intellectual and social considerations. In fact, it seems likely that Matthew Arnold, from
a very early date, borrowed his double-edged mode of
treating Newman—as a man of the highest spiritual and
imaginative power, who had exercised a great attraction
over him in his youth, but who had almost perversely mis-
used his gifts—from Hazlitt's treatment of Coleridge.[15]

We forget that Carlyle, too, for all the "rugged" tone
and the exhortations to endeavor and endurance, is a great
master of pathos. *The French Revolution* modulates between scenes of rather helpless and inexplicable mob violence, and portrait after portrait of human folly and failure.
Against a Luther, or a Cromwell, or a Frederick, there is
a counterbalancing John Sterling. Even in *Heroes,* with
its praise of vehement self-exertion, when the theme most
closely touches Carlyle himself the tone darkens and the
texture softens. Of the two greatest poets, the "sorrow-
stricken" Dante is "most touching" to Carlyle, for his lone-
liness, his "silent pain," his "grief." Even the "complete
and self-sufficing" Shakespeare "had his sorrows," "suffered," and had his share of "the troubles of other men."
The "notablest of all [modern] Literary Men," Goethe, is
the merest wraith, partly no doubt because Carlyle had
come to suspect that the "victory" allegedly achieved in
Goethe's career was only dubiously of the sort that Carlyle could in fact endorse. Of the three Heroes as Men of
Letters presented, Rousseau in his "misery" is least adequate or sympathetic; but Carlyle virtually identifies himself with Johnson, who lived "in an element of diseased
sorrow," "stalking mournful as a stranger in this earth,"
and even more with his fellow-Scot Burns, "dying brokenhearted as a Gauger," "swallowing down his many sore
sufferings daily into silence," his life "a great tragic sincerity."[16] His *Reminiscences,* mostly written late in life,
with their tremulous evocations of his father and Jane and
Edward Irving, rehearse in sorrow the semi-autobiograph-
ical experiences rather burlesqued in *Sartor.* Carlyle only
asserted (as he did in *Sartor*) that Time is one of the "deep-

est of all illusory Appearances." Closer to his continuous
and almost passionate *experience* of Time is the remark
made the following year, on his father's death: "Strange
Time! Endless Time, or of which I see neither end nor
beginning! All rushes on; man follows man; his life is as
a Tale that has been told." He only *hoped,* "under Time
does there not lie Eternity?"[17]

De Quincey can perhaps be called Wordsworth's chief
imitator in the continuous use of personal experience,
recollected in tranquillity.[18] A very large proportion of
what remains readable in De Quincey is in fact not, as he
called it, "impassioned prose," but the mode of "deep,
melancholic reverie" with which he treats the things of
his own remembered past[19]—in the dream-visions of the
Confessions and *Suspiria,* and even more in the *Literary
Reminiscences* (especially those of the Lake Poets) and
the *Autobiographic Sketches.* The mode and treatment in
the latter (written between 1834 and 1854), with their
detailed evocation of childhood consciousness, would re-
pay comparison with not only the best "childhood" novels
of mid-century, but with Wordsworth before him (though
not the *Prelude,* published in 1850), and later, with Ruskin's "The Two Boyhoods" (in *Modern Painters* V) and
Praeterita, the opening chapters of Mill's *Autobiography*
and Newman's *Apologia,* Pater's "A Child in the House"
and the early chapters of *Marius*—and for that matter the
opening of Joyce's *Portrait of the Artist,* since Joyce certainly knew most of these authors well and even parodied
some of them in the Oxen of the Sun episode of *Ulysses,*
where among his numerous imitations of nineteenth-century prose he includes a Lamb-like passage on "young
Leopold," "precociously manly."[20] We have heard much
lately of children, parents, and orphans in Victorian fiction; the memory of childhood in nonfictional prose, though
it has complex relations with poetry and fiction, forms a
distinctive tradition of its own. Its central figure is a small
lonely boy in the receding distance, separated from his
creator—his later self—by impassable historical and cultural
barriers. The attention given the orphaned or "lost" child

figure in the nineteenth century[21]—usually a version of one's own lost childhood—becomes in prose another continually available mode of treating personal experience not only as a universal pattern of loss and gain, and apart from "doctrine," but as an analogue of the "losses" of modern culture. This search for one's own childhood carries its authenticity in its continually "exploratory" character; it is a specific and centrally adaptable variant of the nineteenth-century's search for an almost pre-lapsarian "wholeness" of personality and consciousness, also sought in classical culture (as in Schiller's discussion of "naive" poetry) or distant civilizations—in any event, before the "fall" and the ensuing dissociation of sensibility, whether that took place in fifth-century B. C. Athens, or Ruskin's fifteenth-century Venice, or the Scholar-Gipsy's seventeenth-century Oxfordshire.

But it is finally Newman and Arnold who most effectively combine "heightened" prose, personal reminiscence, and a larger historical and cultural pattern. I refer to both their inherent literary and emotional power and to their virtually unprecedented influence on later consciousness. Those passages in Newman's prose that were continually cited throughout the century—such as the ending of "The Parting of Friends," the "invitation" concluding *The Development of Christian Doctrine,* and the farewell to Oxford in the *Apologia*—exhibit a precisely calculated pathos and self-pity, all the more effective for being carefully restrained in rhythm and figure and refraining from the more obvious kinds of rhetorical elaboration. This restraint is especially evident in the farewell, at the end of Chapter IV of the *Apologia,* where Newman speaks of leaving Oxford "for good" in February 1846, and saying farewell to various friends, the last of whom was Dr. Ogle, who had been his tutor when Newman was an undergraduate:

> In him I took leave of my first College, Trinity, which was so dear to me, and which held on its foundation so many who had been kind to me both when I was a boy, and all through my Oxford life. Trinity had never been unkind to me. There used to be much snap-dragon growing on the walls opposite my freshman's rooms there, and

I had for years taken it as the emblem of my own perpetual residence even unto death in my University.

On the morning of the 23rd I left the Observatory. I have never
seen Oxford since, excepting its spires, as they are seen from the
railway.

But something much more intellectually ambitious is attempted in the great, almost symphonic climax of Chapter V. Newman ends his account of his life, much of it
written as he says in tears, by offering his book as "a memorial of affection and gratitude" to his brother priests of
the Oratory. Of these he finally singles out Ambrose St.
John, an Oxford convert, as "the link between my old
life and my new." Newman goes on:

> And in you I gather up and bear in memory those familiar affec-
> tionate companions and counsellors, who in Oxford were given to
> me, one after another, to be my daily solace and relief; and all those
> others, of great name and high example, who were my thorough
> friends, and showed me true attachment in times long past; and
> also those many younger men, whether I knew them or not, who
> have never been disloyal to me by word or deed; and of all these,
> thus various in their relations to me, those especially who have
> joined the Catholic Church.
>
> And I earnestly pray for this whole company, with a hope against
> hope, that all of us, who once were united, and so happy in our
> union, may even now be brought at length, by the power of the Di-
> vine Will, into One Fold and under One Shepherd.

Here, Newman's personal pain in surrendering his place
of power and influence at Oxford is more clearly caught
up in the more widespread personal, and even national,
calamity of the breaking-up of the Movement in which
Newman's defection was both cause and effect. Newman
is at once the pathetic victim driven out by his one-time
friends, and the strong man beckoning from the farther
shore, daring them on to a new and even more dangerous
"venture of faith." The tangled emotions *toward Newman*
which this excruciatingly painful situation brought to his
former hearers, and to those who looked on at a greater distance—whether those who followed him across the divide,
or those who remained in the High-Church party, or even
those who as a result drifted away from serious preoccupa-

tion with religion altogether—could include pain, sorrow, pity, love and something close to despair: all these Newman plainly intended. They also included, for some of the participants—and Newman could foretell these, without quite intending them—blame, reproach, repudiation, bitter incomprehension. It is, I think, the most complex, clearly identifiable "situation" of the nineteenth century, extending over many years and renewed periodically, for the largest number of participants.[22]

This carefully staged pathetic self-presentation, in which Newman's personal experience is made to symbolize perfectly the decisive break-up of the "old" culture and the instatement of a triumphant Philistinism and Liberalism, is of a piece with Newman's deepest views of man's perennial situation as a scene of loss and failure. Newman's "anthropology," his view of man's terrestrial condition— as well as one of the reasons for his insisting on the "classical" sources of consciousness—can best be grasped in his notable attempt to explain why medieval men viewed Vergil "as if a prophet or a magician": "his single words and phrases, his pathetic half lines, giving utterance, as the voice of Nature herself, to that pain and weariness, yet hope of better things, which is the experience of her children in every time."[23] This was in *The Grammar of Assent*, published in 1870; six years earlier, in the *Apologia*, an even grimmer vision of the "heart-piercing, reason-bewildering fact" of human history, without even that "hope of better things," had joined the handful of most impressive passages in all of Newman's writing.

> To consider the world in its length and breadth, its various history, the many races of man, their starts, their fortunes, their mutual alienation, their conflicts, and then their ways, habits, governments, forms of worship; their enterprises, their aimless courses, their random achievements and acquirements, the impotent conclusion of long-standing facts, the tokens so faint and broken of a superintending design, the blind evolution of what turn out to be great powers or truths, the progress of things, as if from unreasoning elements, not towards final causes, the greatness and littleness of man, his far-reaching aims, his short duration, the curtain hung over his futurity, the disappointments of life, the defeat of good, the

success of evil, physical pain, mental anguish, the prevalence and intensity of sin, the pervading idolatries, the corruptions, the dreary hopeless irreligion, that condition of the whole race, so fearfully yet exactly described in the Apostle's words, 'having no hope and without God in the world,'—all this is a vision to dizzy and appal, and inflicts upon the mind the sense of a profound mystery, which is absolutely beyond human solution.[24]

Whether the inference drawn by Newman from his Pascalian vision of the "incompleteness" of man and human history is valid—that is, that an infallible Church is the providential means to preserve religion in such a world, given up to such purposes—is of course another question. But the fact is that these various passages are all cut from the same cloth: the personal, the cultural, and the universal planes intersect—and all are caught up in a religious vision of the "meaning" of these various levels of experience. Even for those who broke with Newman, and in some cases with all religion, the images continued to reverberate.[25] Part of Newman's continuing power lies in his uncompromising willingness to fling a "dark" and melancholy view of human nature into the teeth of liberal optimism and progressivism, evident even in the easier forms of contemporary religion. Again, Newman's view of man's nature and history is both pre- and sub-theological in its universality, as well as exactly (and quite explicitly) calculated to arrest the new and growing popular consciousness of the day by making it aware of its own shallowness and complacency, as well as its unhistorical character.

Somewhere very central in Matthew Arnold's lifelong campaign to change the consciousness of his English contemporaries lay this multi-level structure of feelings and images presented by Newman; and Arnold, unsurprisingly, was not behindhand in seizing them and shaping them to his own purposes. What is most notable about the famous elevated passages in Arnold is, first, that they form a more or less coherent "myth" regarding Arnold's life, and second, and perhaps more startlingly, that they are the elaboration of, as well as the response to, the pattern established by Newman. Arnold's favored emotions in his most "personal" passages are not merely reminiscential in the general way some critics have noted; instead, they rehearse the experiences of a specially situated group of young men at Oxford in the 1840s, who had felt in various degrees the attraction of Newman, and who in his defection and the collapse of Tractarianism had been—as one of them put it— cast up as intellectual "wrecks . . . on every shore."[26] Many of them remained permanently unsettled, wandering between two worlds, the "impossible" old and the unspeakable new. Arnold in effect established a new mode in his early poetry for describing the intellectual, emotional, and spiritual situation of a generation of disciples and near-disciples of Newman. Especially in the troubled poetry of the 1852 volume, including the lightly veiled autobiography of "Empedocles on Etna" itself, as well as in "Dover Beach," "The Scholar-Gipsy," "Stanzas from the Grande Chartreuse," and the major poems of the sixties, Arnold again counted the personal costs of honestly facing the new dislocation. More than in Wordsworth, and at least as much as in Byron, he takes as his ostensible subject an elaborate body of historical and literary criticism, but constantly implies that its meaning is inseparable from the special experiences of a small "band" of uniquely placed and specially alert participants—himself and a very few "children of the second birth." Arnold explains (in his first Obermann poem) that *his* generation was born too late to share in "Wordsworth's sweet calm, or Goethe's wide/ And luminous view," but that of course they were deeply affected by the still powerful "voices" of that generation during the 1840s; implicitly, and just as importantly, those born too late even to witness the upheaval of the foundations in that decade are perforce cut off from full contact with those sources of deepest poetic and spiritual power, now defunct. (It was *literally* true, as he says of Wordsworth, in "Memorial Verses" in 1850, that "The last poetic voice is dumb.")

In effect, Arnold created a powerful myth of a "lost" generation, a myth explored at least as coherently as the individual traumas of that even more cataclysmic decade, the 1790s, and perhaps not so distant from that perennial "lost" mood of the 1920s, caught by Hemingway and Fitzgerald. So successful was Arnold, throughout his career, in embodying this myth of generational loss that the description of his wandering and in-between state became a continually renewable experience (with whatever force of logic) for a host of readers thereafter: sorrow over the "end" of the old world and a bitter distrust of the new, combined with a restrained self-pity and a certain unwillingness to put one's hand firmly to the work of the world —all of these became a permanent "structure" of consciousness for literarily-oriented people. Uncounted readers who have never seen Oxford, and have only the most general impression of the scope of Newman's career and of the issues of the 1840s, regularly feel the "Matthew Arnold" emotions, and have continued to use them to explain their own experience.

Arnold's exploration of his own situation in the poetry, in close proximity to the deeper stratum of contemporary problems, was continued in the prose, but in a somewhat more hopeful vein, and with a shift in the balance of forces. For where in the poetry the center had been the *personal experience* of cultural crisis, now both the framework and the explicit content tended to be the intellectual or spiritual problem itself, "objectively" viewed, and the more personal voice is heard only in momentary, though not ineffective, glances dramatically "lighting up" the intellectual battleground. When this cooler intellectual balance of the prose is shaken and more private passions are glimpsed, the sudden surge of emotion, and sometimes pain, brings the realization that the speaker is indeed the same specially privileged and uniquely placed participant more steadily observable in the poetry.[27] Perhaps the most extraordinary glimpse of this sort occurs at the end of "Pagan and Medieval Religious Sentiment" (1863), where medieval Christianity, up to this point the winner in an apparent struggle with late-pagan religion, is suddenly put aside in favor of the "balance" of Sophocles and his century. But the elevated religious tone of the illustra-

tion from Sophocles is followed by a jolting descent into a
final fling, of questionable taste but startlingly personal:
"Let St. Francis,—nay, or Luther either,—beat that!"[28]

The continual revisiting, and revaluation, of Arnold's
own youthful experience is clear enough in the famous
passages—such as those on Oxford and Newman, George
Sand, the four "voices" heard in the forties, and the virtually autobiographical salute to Falkland.[29] It is important to note that the emotions of these personal passages—
loss, regret, separation, alienation—are in effect supplemented by the melancholy and the strong pathos of the con-
troversial touchstones that stud Arnold's prose from the
time of the Homer lectures in the 1860s, culminating in
"The Study of Poetry" in 1880. The secular touchstones
stress, as one critic puts it, "the grimness and darkness of
the human adventure," centering in loss, pain, grief,
death, and the transience of both glory and happiness.[30]
The touchstones thus "fill in" the landscape of Arnold's
writings and become more universal variants of his most
private emotions. Arnold's "Homeric" insistence that "in
our life here above ground we have, properly speaking,
to enact Hell"[31] is not, I think, very far from Newman's
reading of man's life, in the passage on the Vergilian
"pain and weariness," and more especially in the "appalling" panorama of human life, in the *Apologia*, as a
"profound mystery," the scene of an "aboriginal calamity" and Newman dwells, precisely, on states of alienation, disappointment, defeat, pain, and anguish.

Still, Arnold's standpoint is *not*, after all, that of Newman, and in the difference lies a crucial divergence of
tone and a contrast in artistry. For although Arnold can
freely "share" in Newman's own pathos and associate himself with the Tractarians and other Oxford causes ("we in
Oxford," "our attachment to . . . beaten causes"),[32] there
is a persistent irony, a deep-running doubleness of effect,
in some of the most intensely felt passages. The apparent
paean to Oxford as the "home of lost causes," in the Preface of 1865, written obviously in the afterglow of the
Apologia, is a jangle of doubtfully juxtaposed tones.

Beautiful and venerable herself, Oxford calls us to perfection and beauty—but as is not uncommon in Arnold, beauty
(like "poetry") is distressingly connected with *illusion*:
the moonlit adorable queen is a figure of "romance" and
"dream" and "enchantment," a worthwhile ideal no doubt,
but "unravaged" precisely because not in the *real* world
where Philistines have to be engaged frontally, and because in a disabling sense the "home of lost causes, and
forsaken beliefs, and unpopular names, and impossible loy-
alties" (*CPW*, III, 290). The ambiguity of the word "impossible" in the mouth of this "son" of Oxford becomes
very much clearer in Arnold's companion portrait of Newman in 1883. Even the perceptive Lewis Gates found in
the opening a "half-restrained pulsation in the rhythm, an
emotional throb that at times almost produces an effect
of metre." He finds in the rest of the essay "Arnold's usual
colloquial, self-consciously wary tone."[33] But Saintsbury
is far closer to the point when he notes: "In the words
about Newman, one seems to recognize very much more
than meets the ear—an explanation of much in the Arnold-
ian gospel, on something like the principle of soured
love."[34]

There are of course marked differences between the
two parts of the essay, and Gates is correct about the high-
pitched tone of the opening. But he entirely misses the
complexity and calculation of effect, and finally the pained
rejection, in the portrait of Newman. The language is very
close to that of the 1865 Preface, and as double-edged. Newman appeals to the "imagination" by "his genius and style";
his is the "charm" of a "spiritual apparition, gliding in the
dim afternoon light"; his words were "a religious music,—
subtle, sweet, mournful." We are not surprised when Arnold explicitly refers back to the words of 1865 and finds in
Newman those "last enchantments of the Middle Age."
There is, I think a half-hint that Newman *staged* his "haunting" mysterious presence; there is an even clearer hint that
this "apparition" and figure of "enchantment" is unreal
and somehow unsound; above all, *before* he presents this
skillfully managed portrait, Arnold could not be more expli-

cit in stating the ground of his reservation: "he has adopted, for the doubts and difficulties which beset men's minds today, a solution which, to speak frankly, is impossible" (*CPW*, X, 165–66). There is, then, an evident element of blame and reproach, and something like heartbroken personal sorrow, in Arnold's dealings with Newman and Oxford, as well as a certain need to put both in their place. Both are among the vital sources of his own most central values, and what he meant by a full and complex humanity: but they had forfeited their right to leadership by neglecting "criticism," "knowledge," "light."

The central cleavage in Arnold's own career lies exposed here: imagination, beauty, emotion, poetry, charm, history, and a full humanity, on the one side, and Arnold's deep and painful commitment not to blink the implications of modern naturalism, on the other. Again, it is a question of one's placement in time, and of having lived through the moment of crisis in the forties: the blankness and "unpoetrylessness" of Arnold's position and that of all who share his views is poignantly evident in the easily overlooked words, "No such voices as those which we heard in our youth at Oxford are sounding there now"—or, he implies, anywhere else! The generation of "Our fathers," "the former men"—Newman, Carlyle, Goethe, Emerson, Wordsworth—is not a repeatable phenomenon for each succeeding generation; at best, they are a receding "source," to be revisited and drawn upon by those who can in fading imagination relive the "in-between" experience of Arnold's own generation. And they, the "fathers," are partly to blame for "our" plight.[35] The result, I think, is that Arnold never quite got over the fear, expressed by the age of thirty, that he was "three parts iced over"; the need for a "second birth" that he preached to Clough[36] meant for himself something like a revival to a half-life, a tentative and somewhat fragile Lazarus-like existence.

If there is a single key passage in which Arnold expresses his mature, and more positive, sense of his relationship to his Oxford past and the possibilities of the future, it occurs in *Culture and Anarchy*, where he describes

rather vaguely a "new power" in politics, which rejects
the values of middle-class liberalism:

> And who will estimate how much the currents of feeling created
> by Dr. Newman's movement, the keen desire for beauty and sweet-
> ness which it nourished, the deep aversion it manifested to the hard-
> ness and vulgarity of middle-class liberalism, the strong light it
> turned on the hideous and grotesque illusions of middle-class Pro-
> testantism,—who will estimate how much all these contributed to
> swell the tide of secret dissatisfaction which has mined the ground
> under the self-confident liberalism of the last thirty years, and has
> prepared the way for its sudden collapse and supersession? It is in
> this manner that the sentiment of Oxford for beauty and sweetness
> conquers, and in this manner long may it continue to conquer!
> (*CPW,* V, 107).

This is, in effect, a kind of allegory of Arnold's own career.
He is the newly anointed figure, who, relying on Newman's "Oxford" virtues of beauty and sweetness, will continue the work of undermining liberal complacency. It is
Arnold's "secret"—and unverifiable—program; as his critics
promptly and stingingly complained, since these are intellectual and spiritual attitudes, they somehow exempt him from
the task of social amelioration of the usual humdrum and
tedious sort. He is the ultimate tightrope-walker, and the
stealer of divine fire: the man who barely escaped with
his life from the "thrilling summons" of Newman (in "The
Voice") also took with him the divine sources of inward-
ness and high spiritual percipience, guarded by the older
"priest" figure. Again, he—Arnold—is specially placed, by
history and temperament, to save the world, if it will listen; he has unique control over the necessary secret he has
managed to carry over into the new era. Taken as a whole,
Arnold's writings form a kind of complex *Bildungsroman,*
or even a quest-romance, in which the son (of Thomas
Arnold and Newman) who is the apparent failure, succeeds to a position of leadership, by carrying on more
adequately the program which the "fathers" were unable to carry to completion.

The strongly autobiographical flavor of much of the
Victorian prose I have been discussing provides an implicit
but effective unity, linking apparently diverse modes and

tones of expression. Whole careers in Victorian prose can be legitimately read as being as intensely and continuously "autobiographical" as the career of any novelist or poet. A number of writers—De Quincey, Carlyle, Newman, Ruskin, Arnold, and even Pater—spend their lives defining and redefining their own vocations, shaping and reshaping their past experience for present purposes, while ostensibly talking about something else: society, literature, or religion. Most importantly, Victorian "argumentative" prose uses memory as a medium of indirect persuasion, authenticating its more explicit views in a body of palpable and not easily refuted experience. I have dwelt at length here on Newman and Arnold because of the extraordinary complexity of their positions, and because Arnold's conception of his own career is so continuously, if ironically, intertwined with Newman's strategies of self-presentation, and because both men have remained vital forces even into our own time—their vitality being proved by the periodic need felt by many to "expose" or resist their claims on us. Moreover, their most famous personal and emotive passages, when examined closely, reveal— sometimes more exactly than their explicit argumentation —an "inner structure" of feeling and attitude that is the organizing pattern of their entire careers.

1. "Modern English Prose" (1876) and "English Prose Style" (1885), in *The Collected Essays and Papers of George Saintsbury, 1875–1920* (London: J. M. Dent, 1923), III, 63 64, 104 106. On Saintsbury and late-century "stylism," *see* Travis R. Merritt, "Taste, Opinion and Theory in the Rise of Victorian Prose Stylism," in *The Art of Victorian Prose,* ed. George Levine and William Madden (New York: Oxford University Press, 1968), pp. 3–38, and my "Newman and the Victorian Cult of Style," *Victorian Newsletter*, 51 (1977), 6–10.

2. I have tried to define a similar use of "ideas" in a highly personal context, in poetry around 1850, in "The Poetry of Thought," in *The Mind and Art of Victorian England,* ed. Josef L. Altholz (Minneapolis: University of Minnesota Press, 1976), pp. 35–57, 179–84.

3. I am referring especially to Chapter 1 of *The Victorian Sage* (1953). One of the best critiques occurred in A. Dwight Culler, "Method in the Study of Victorian Prose," *Victorian Newsletter*, 9 (1956), pp. 1–4.

4. *Appreciations* (Library Edition; London: Macmillan, 1910), p. 104. Gerald L. Bruns, "The Formal Nature of Victorian Thinking," *PMLA,* 90 (October 1975), 904–918, has written well of the ways in which "the transcendental imagin-

ation of the Romantics" gives way to the more "historical" mentality of the Victorians, a world of "movement, process, and transformation." But in my judgment he underplays the persisting "transcendental reference" in Victorian thought, or at least the uneasy possibility of such a reference. That is, where the monistic impulse of Romantic "natural supernaturalism" tends to compress and perhaps confuse the two realms, many of the Victorians tend to oscillate more sharply between a higher (and often more "Christian") transcendentalism, however fading, and a "lower" realm of mere physical and historical process. This last alternative is particularly evident in the "dead" world of Matthew Arnold's nature poetry.

5. I have written on this early-Victorian critical climate in "The Future of Poetry: A Background for Carlyle and Arnold" in *Carlyle and His Contemporaries: Essays in Honor of Charles Richard Sanders,* ed. John Clubbe (Durham, N.C.: Duke University Press, 1976), pp. 148–80. On attitudes toward the Spasmodics, *see* Mark A. Weinstein, *William Edmonstoune Aytoun and the Spasmodic Controversy,* Yale Studies in English, Vol., 165 (New Haven & London: Yale University Press, 1968), and my "Robert Browning the Spasmodic," *Studies in Browning and His Circle,* 2 (Spring 1974), 55–60.

6. A conspicuous case, for overt polemical purposes, occurs in the highly colored Bk. 1, Ch. V, of Disraeli's *Sybil* (1845). The hero of J. A. Froude's *The Nemesis of Faith* (1849) sentimentalizes freely about ruins and the sound of church-bells.

7. Alice Chandler, *A Dream of Order: The Medieval Ideal in Nineteenth-Century English Literature* (Lincoln: University of Nebraska Press, 1971), surveys the field, but not in my opinion with the penetration the material deserves.

8. Walter E. Houghton, "The Rhetoric of T. H. Huxley," *University of Toronto Quarterly,* 18 (January 1949), 166. The whole passage is worth reading, though Houghton does not confine himself to the specifically melancholic and nostalgic.

9. Kathleen Tillotson, *Novels of the Eighteen-Forties* (London: Oxford University Press, 1956), pp. 91–115.

10. The elaborateness of Dickens' use of repetition and contrast to suggest personal growth is well explored in J. H. Hagan, "Structural Patterns in Dickens' *Great Expectations,*" *ELH,* 21 (March 1954), 54–66. The relation to the tradition is suggested in Chapter II of Jerome Buckley's *Season of Youth: The Bildungsroman from Dickens to Golding* (Cambridge, Mass.: Harvard University Press, 1974).

11. In "Hopkins and Mrs. Gaskell: Margaret, Are You Grieving?" *Victorian Poetry,* 14 (Winter 1976), 34–45, I argue that something similar also happens in Bk. V, Ch. IV, and Bk. VI, Ch., XI, of *Sybil.* For other Victorian parallels, *see* Grover Smith, "A Source for Hopkins' 'Spring and Fall' in *The Mill on the Floss?*" *English Language Notes,* 1 (September 1963), 43–46; and William H. Shurr, "Sylvester Judd and G. M. Hopkins' Margaret," *Victorian Poetry,* 11 (Winter 1973), 337–39.

12. On the specifically *youthful* quality of the experience in "Tears, Idle Tears," *see* the evidence gathered in *The Poems of Tennyson,* ed. Christopher Ricks (London: Longmans, 1969), p. 785.

13. I am aware of course that all seriously creative work derives from and expresses the writer's inner self. But while fully acknowledging the intensity with which nostalgia and personal memory were exploited in fiction and poetry, I am attempting here to define the special ways in which essayistic prose undertook this self-expressive task by seizing the opportunities presented by the confluence of the newly self-aware medium and the special cultural moment. John R. Reed's wide-ranging and stimulating chapter on Memory in *Victorian*

Conventions (Athens, Ohio: Ohio University Press, 1975), at one point (p. 415) suggests "a connection between the fashioned nostalgia for the past, the wistful hope for an altered future, and the esthetic self-consciousness of the writers of the late nineteenth century in England"—but his approach is different from mine.

14. The words are C. T. Winchester's in *A Group of English Essayists of the Early Nineteenth Century* (New York: Macmillan, 1910), p. 56.

15. For Hazlitt's influence on Arnold's early poem, "The Voice," *see* my "Arnold and Hazlitt," *English Language Notes,* 9 (June 1972), 277–83; the phrase within dashes is borrowed from that article.

16. I have discussed the intensely autobiographical character of these portraits, in "Ishmael as Prophet: *Heroes and Hero-Worship* and the Self-Expressive Basis of Carlyle's Art," *Texas Studies in Literature and Language,* 11 (Spring 1969), 705–32.

17. *Sartor Resartus,* ed. Charles Frederick Harrold (New York: Odyssey Press, 1937), p. 260, *Reminiscences,* ed. Charles Eliot Norton (London: J. M. Dent, 1932), p. 33. And *see* William Minto, *A Manual of English Prose Literature, Biographical and Critical,* 2nd ed. (Edinburgh & London: William Blackwood, 1872): Carlyle's "most characteristic pathos is his subdued sorrow at the irresistible progress of time."

18. The tie with Wordsworth is well explored in Oliver Elton, *A Survey of English Literature, 1780–1830* (London: Edward Arnold, 1912), II, 312.

19. The phrase is Leslie Stephen's in "De Quincey," *Hours in a Library* (London: Smith, Elder, 1892), I, 241. Minto, p. 66, had spoken of "impassioned autobiography"; but as Stephen points out (p. 246), De Quincey's "melancholy is too dreamy to deserve the name of passion."

20. The best treatment of Joyce's parodies of "all the English prose styles" is now J. S. Atherton's, in *James Joyce's "Ulysses": Critical Essays,* ed. Clive Hart and David Hayman (Berkeley: University of California Press, 1974), pp. 313–39.

21. An excellent recent treatment is Nina Auerbach's "Incarnations of the Orphan," *ELH,* 42 (Fall 1975), 395–419.

22. The two citations are from *Apologia Pro Vita Sua,* ed. Martin J. Svaglic, Oxford English Texts (Oxford: Clarendon Press, 1967), pp. 213, 252–53. I have singled out one aspect of Newman's "aural image," in " 'O Unforgotten Voice': The Memory of Newman in the Nineteenth Century," *Sources for Reinterpretation: The Use of Nineteenth-Century Literary Documents: Essays in Honor of C. L. Cline* (Austin: Dept. of English and Humanities Research Center, The University of Texas at Austin, 1975), pp. 23–55.

23. *An Essay in Aid of a Grammar of Assent,* ed. Charles Frederick Harrold (New York: Longmans, 1947), p. 60.

24. *Apologia,* p. 217.

25. As John Duke Lord Coleridge, one of Newman's most fervent Anglican admirers, put it, "the outward interest in the teaching [of Newman at Oxford] was but one symptom of the deep and abiding influence which Cardinal Newman exercised then, and exercises now, over the thoughts and lives of many men who perhaps never saw him, who certainly never heard him. . . . It happened in a hundred instances . . . that men who have been unable to follow the Cardinal to his dogmatic conclusions have been penetrated and animated by his religious principles, and have lived their lives and striven to do their duty because of those principles which he was God's instrument to teach them." In William Knight, *Principal Shairp and His Friends* (London: John Murray, 1888), pp. 414–15.

26. Goldwin Smith, *Lectures on Modern History* (Oxford & London: J. H. and Jas. Parker, 1861), p. 34.

27. Two others who have seen "virtual" autobiography in Arnold's prose are A. Dwight Culler, " 'No Arnold Could Ever Write a Novel,' " *Victorian Newsletter,* No. 29 (Spring 1966), pp. 1–5; and Alan Roper, *Arnold's Poetic Landscapes* (Baltimore: Johns Hopkins Press, 1969), pp. 249–56.

28. *The Complete Prose Works of Matthew Arnold,* ed. R. H. Super (Ann Arbor: University of Michigan Press, 1960-), III, 231. Hereafter cited as *CPW.*

29. The autobiographical significance of the Falkland essay is illuminatingly explained in John P. Farrell, "Matthew Arnold's Tragic Vision," *PMLA,* 85 (January 1970), 107–17.

30. *See* the summary by John Shepard Eells, in *The Touchstones of Matthew Arnold* (New Haven: College and University Press, 1955): "the abiding pathos of young death; the manifold sorrow of man; the pathetic vicissitudes of man; the inward petrifaction caused by grief too deep for tears; the pain of living; the grandeur and majesty of a noble personality brought to ruin by a tragic flaw; the sense of the loss of something beloved." On the role of the touchstones in Arnold's evolving literary and religious thinking, see my "Arnold and Literary Criticism: Critical Ideas," in *Matthew Arnold; Writers and Their Background,* ed. Kenneth and Miriam Allott (London: Bell, 1975), pp. 118–48.

31. He is citing Goethe; *see CPW,* I, 102, 108, 149.

32. I have tried to explain the extreme complexity of this asserted identification in Chapter III of my *Hebrew and Hellene in Victorian England: Newman, Arnold, and Pater* (Austin: University of Texas Press, 1969).

33. Lewis E. Gates, *Three Studies in Literature* (New York: Macmillan, 1899), pp. 187–88.

34. George Saintsbury, *Matthew Arnold* (Edinburgh & London: William Blackwood, 1899), p. 199. The sentence concludes: "which accounts for still more in the careers of his contemporaries, Mr. Pattison and Mr. Froude."

35. This is the explicitly autobiographical drama of "Stanzas from the Grande Chartreuse," where not only the Romantics (Byron, Shelley, Senancour) are rejected as useless to our struggle, but the "rigorous teachers" and "masters of the mind," who can neither give him "ease" nor relieve him of "restlessness" and "pain."

36. *The Letters of Matthew Arnold to Arthur Hugh Clough,* ed. Howard Foster Lowry (London & New York: Oxford University Press, 1932), pp. 128, 109–10.

Index